GREEK FILM NOIR

Traditions in World Cinema

General Editors
Linda Badley (Middle Tennessee State University)
R. Barton Palmer (Clemson University)

Founding Editor
Steven Jay Schneider (New York University)

Titles in the series include:

Traditions in World Cinema
by Linda Badley, R. Barton Palmer and Steven Jay Schneider (eds)

Japanese Horror Cinema
by Jay McRoy (ed.)

New Punk Cinema
by Nicholas Rombes (ed.)

African Filmmaking
by Roy Armes

Palestinian Cinema
by Nurith Gertz and George Khleifi

Czech and Slovak Cinema
by Peter Hames

The New Neapolitan Cinema
by Alex Marlow-Mann

American Smart Cinema
by Claire Perkins

The International Film Musical
by Corey Creekmur and Linda Mokdad (eds)

Italian Neorealist Cinema
by Torunn Haaland

Magic Realist Cinema in East Central Europe
by Aga Skrodzka

Italian Post-Neorealist Cinema
by Luca Barattoni

Spanish Horror Film
by Antonio Lázaro-Reboll

Post-beur Cinema
by Will Higbee

New Taiwanese Cinema in Focus
by Flannery Wilson

International Noir
by Homer B. Pettey and R. Barton Palmer (eds)

Films on Ice
by Scott MacKenzie and Anna Westerståhl Stenport (eds)

Nordic Genre Film
by Tommy Gustafsson and Pietari Kääpä (eds)

Contemporary Japanese Cinema Since Hana-Bi
by Adam Bingham

Chinese Martial Arts Cinema (2nd edition)
by Stephen Teo

Slow Cinema
by Tiago de Luca and Nuno Barradas Jorge

Expressionism in Cinema
by Olaf Brill and Gary D. Rhodes (eds)

French Language Road Cinema: Borders, Diasporas, Migration and 'New Europe'
by Michael Gott

Transnational Film Remakes
by Iain Robert Smith and Constantine Verevis

Coming of Age in New Zealand
by Alistair Fox

New Transnationalisms in Contemporary Latin American Cinemas
by Dolores Tierney

Celluloid Singapore: Cinema, Performance and the National
by Edna Lim

Short Films from a Small Nation: Danish Informational Cinema 1935–1965
by C. Claire Thomson

B-Movie Gothic: International Perspectives
by Justin D. Edwards and Johan Höglund (eds)

Francophone Belgian Cinema: Filmmaking in Wallonia since 2001
by Jamie Steele

The New Romanian Cinema
by Christina Stojanova (ed.) with the participation of Dana Duma

French Blockbusters: Cultural Politics of a Transnational Cinema
by Charlie Michael

Nordic Film Cultures and Cinemas of Elsewhere
by Anna Westerståhl Stenport and Arne Lunde (eds)

New Realism: Contemporary British Cinema
by David Forrest

Contemporary Balkan Cinema: Transnational Exchanges and Global Circuits
by Lydia Papadimitriou and Ana Grgić (eds)

Images of Apartheid: Filmmaking on the Fringe in the Old South Africa
by Calum Waddell

Greek Film Noir
by Anna Poupou, Nikitas Fessas and Maria Chalkou (eds)

www.edinburghuniversitypress.com/series/TIWC

GREEK FILM NOIR

Edited by Anna Poupou, Nikitas Fessas
and Maria Chalkou

EDINBURGH
University Press

Edinburgh University Press is one of the leading university presses in the UK. We publish academic books and journals in our selected subject areas across the humanities and social sciences, combining cutting-edge scholarship with high editorial and production values to produce academic works of lasting importance. For more information visit our website: edinburghuniversitypress.com

© editorial matter and organisation, Anna Poupou, Nikitas Fessas and Maria Chalkou, 2022
© the chapters their several authors, 2022

Edinburgh University Press Ltd
The Tun – Holyrood Road
12(2f) Jackson's Entry
Edinburgh EH8 8PJ

First published in hardback by Edinburgh University Press 2022

Typeset in 10/12.5 pt Sabon
by IDSUK (DataConnection) Ltd, and
printed and bound by CPI Group (UK) Ltd,
Croydon, CR0 4YY

A CIP record for this book is available from the British Library

ISBN 978 1 4744 5899 3 (hardback)
ISBN 978 1 4744 5900 6 (paperback)
ISBN 978 1 4744 5901 3 (webready PDF)
ISBN 978 1 4744 5902 0 (epub)

The right of Anna Poupou, Nikitas Fessas and Maria Chalkou to be identified as the editors of this work has been asserted in accordance with the Copyright, Designs and Patents Act 1988, and the Copyright and Related Rights Regulations 2003 (SI No. 2498).

CONTENTS

List of Figures — vii
Acknowledgements — x
Contributors — xii
Traditions in World Cinema — xvii

Foreword — xix
Andrew Spicer

Introduction — 1
Anna Poupou, Nikitas Fessas and Maria Chalkou

PART I PARTNERS IN CRIME: RECEPTIONS, AFFINITIES, HYBRIDITIES

1. There Will Be Ogres: The Interstitial Aesthetics of Film Noir in the Early Films of Nikos Koundouros — 27
   Vrasidas Karalis

2. Of Mice, Men and Greek Film Noir: *The Little Mouse* — 46
   Maria A. Stassinopoulou

3. Historical Coincidence or Generic Cross-Pollination? *The Angry Hills* and the Birth of Film Noir in Greece — 62
   Yannis Tzioumakis

4. Noir Backstage: Yannis Maris from Page to Screen — 81
   Thanassis Agathos

5. Dark Cinema, Dark Sounds: Mimis Plessas and the Integration of Jazz into Greek Film Noir — 103
   Nick Poulakis

6	Fatal Absences and Female Gazes: Alternative Femininities in Greek Film Noir and the Psychological Thriller *Anna Poupou*	121
7	Bums and Dark Alleys: Constructing Queerness in a Mid-1960s Greek Noir *Nikitas Fessas*	139

PART II POLITICAL ASPECTS AND TRANSNATIONAL DYNAMICS OF THE GREEK NEO-NOIR

8	A Dark Intrigue of Murder: *Kierion* and *Reconstruction*, or Film Noir as Politics *Maria Chalkou*	163
9	Neo-Noir and 'Becoming-Murderer' in Tonia Marketaki's *John the Violent* *Ioulia Mermigka*	182
10	The Unbearable Queerness of *Singapore Sling*: Towards a Queer Ethics and Politics of Irony *Marios Psaras*	199
11	Hong Kong and Athens: Contested Spaces of the Global and the Local in the Neo-Noir of John Woo and Alexis Alexiou *Yun-hua Chen*	216
12	Darker Worlds Come in Small Packages: Neo-Noir Sensibility in Greek Cypriot Short Films *Costas Constandinides*	232
13	Greek Sleuths and Tough Cops: Noir Masculinities in Television Crime Shows (1992–2020) *Georgia Aitaki and Spyridon Chairetis*	247
14	Mediterranean Film Noir: Twilight Falls on *mare nostrum* *Dennis Broe*	263

Appendix: Greek Films and Television Series/Shows Featuring Dominant Noir or Neo-Noir Tropes   279
Nikitas Fessas

Index   291

FIGURES

I.1 Front cover of the weekly pulp magazine *Maska* (*Mask*) from its fourth period of circulation (1963–74) under the direction of Jimmy Corinis. The issue features the adventures of fictional detective Lemmy Caution, created by Peter Cheney. Undated issue, c.1963–64. Courtesy of Jimmy Corinis.   5
I.2 Photo from the shooting of the television show *38th Precinct*, directed by Jimmy Corinis (1972–73), the first police drama series to use real locations. Courtesy of Jimmy Corinis.   8
I.3 A page from Kyriakos Athanasiadis and Nikolas Kourtis, *Berlin: Protos Thanatos* (2020). Courtesy of Jemma Press.   11
I.4 Greek noir *avant la lettre*: Yannis Tsarouchis, *Neon Café (Night)* (1965–66), oil on canvas, 127 x 180 cm. Courtesy of National Gallery–Alexandros Soutsos Museum. Photographed by Stavros Psiroukis.   13
1.1 Chasing the gangsters, in the last scenes of *The Magic City*. Greek Film Archive collection. Courtesy of Sotiria Matziri.   32
1.2 Thomas the 'Ogre' (Dinos Iliopoulos) with Carmen (Maria Lekaki). Greek Film Archive collection. Courtesy of Sotiria Matziri.   39
2.1 Director Dinos Dimopoulos gives instructions to the actors Dinos Iliopoulos and Margarita Papageorgiou, during the shooting of *Joe the Terrible*. Greek Film Archive collection.   50

FIGURES

2.2	The two burglars open a safe using an oxyacetylene cutter in the opening scene of *The Little Mouse*. Greek Film Archive collection.	55
3.1	The lead character Morrison (Robert Mitchum), filmed in noir's trademark chiaroscuro, escapes his chasers, but only momentarily. Digital still from *The Angry Hills*.	72
3.2	A particularly 'Greek' picture in a noir film. Digital still from *The Angry Hills*.	74
4.1	Poster for *Murder in Kolonaki*. Greek Film Archive collection.	83
4.2	Inspector Bekas (Titos Vandis) leading the murder investigation, assisted by journalist Makris (Alekos Alexandrakis). Digital still from *Murder Backstage*.	94
5.1	A jazz band playing diegetic music, while a dancer performs a striptease act. Digital still from *Murder Backstage*.	109
5.2	Chalkia's confession scene: psychologically intense non-diegetic music, mixed with realistic sounds of police sirens. Digital still from *Murder Backstage*.	112
6.1	Actress Maro Kontou, who specialised in the type of the 'luxurious woman' in Greek noirs, with Inspector Bekas (Titos Vandis). Digital still from *Murder Backstage*.	131
6.2	Photo from the film shooting at the Bourdji Castle island in Nafplion. From Yannis Maris's archive. Courtesy of Angelos Tsirimokos.	134
7.1 & 7.2	Cruising: some of the original images that accompanied the *Athinaia* article in 1965; the low-key lighting/photography, the framing, camera angle, as well as the particular choice of settings contribute to a strikingly noir visual aesthetic.	147
7.3	Neon lights, disreputable backstreets: the construction of a queer noir Athens, both alluring and dangerous.	148
8.1	Vagenas (Anestis Vlahos) is tortured by the police. Digital still from *Kierion*.	167
9.1	John (Manolis Logiadis) and an officer (Minas Chatzisavvas) at the police station. Still from *John the Violent*. Greek Film Archive collection.	184
9.2	At the police station during the investigation. Still from *John the Violent*. Greek Film Archive collection.	190
10.1	Mother (Michelle Valley) and Daughter (Meredyth Herold) plotting over the unconscious body of the Detective (Panos Thanassoulis). Digital still from *Singapore Sling*.	202
10.2	The Detective and Daughter. Digital still from *Singapore Sling*.	208
11.1	The final scene on the roof of a deserted building in the centre of Athens. Stelios (Stelios Mainas) shooting his enemies. Digital still from *Wednesday 04:45*.	220

12.1 Digital still from *The Midnight Shift*. 234
13.1 The director of *Vice Squad*, Manousos Manousakis, on set. 250
13.2 From left to right: the criminologist Lainis (Pygmalion Dadakaridis) and officers Barasopoulos (Manos Vakousis) and Sklavis (Petros Lagoutis) investigating a crime. Still from the TV show *Eteros ego*. 256
14.1 The owner of the strip club announces to Agnieszka (Nikol Drizi) that she will be fired because of the recession, while a TV programme in the background comments on austerity measures. Digital still from *Wednesday 04:45*. 271
14.2 Stratos (Vangelis Mourikis), just before his first murder. Digital still from *Stratos*. 274

ACKNOWLEDGEMENTS

The editors would like to express their gratitude to Robert Hensley-King for graciously offering his tireless help in smoothing out parts of the text and suggesting helpful solutions on numerous occasions. He might have worked in the shadows, but he definitely deserves part of the spotlight.

We would also like to thank renowned scholar Professor Frank Krutnik for his encouragement while the project was still a vague idea, and for recommending a 'home' for it; Angelos Tsirimokos for warmly welcoming us to his famous father's house and granting us the privilege of accessing Yannis Maris's archive; legendary director Erricos Andreou for his priceless testimony, as well as his son Erricos for his vital assistance; Greek pulp 'pope' Jimmy Corinis for permission to use photos from his personal archive; the director of the Greek Film Archive, Professor Maria Komninos, for her generous permission to use photos and promotional material from the rich collection of the institution, as well as the archivist, Katerina Georgiou, for her valuable help in choosing the most appropriate images; Marie Louise Nikolaidis for her encouragement and for the two photos from Nikos Nikolaidis's personal archive; Sotiria Matziri for her kind permission to use material from Nikos Koundouros's films; Papandreou AE and Antonis Karatzopoulos for their permission to use stills from the films; Efi Papazahariou and the Greek Film Center for helping us trace the films' rights holders; veteran director, author and genre expert Dimitris Panayiotatos for his help and generosity; prolific director Manousos Manousakis and his wife, producer and writer Maria Manousaki, for courteously providing us with photos from their personal archive; the National Gallery's director, Marina Lambraki-Plaka, for granting us permission to reproduce here an iconic work by Yannis Tsarouchis, and Stavros Psiroukis for providing us with crisp copies of the painting; Jemma Press and Lefteris Stavrianos for allowing us to include published visual material; director and researcher Leonidas Papadopoulos for his support and help in locating archival sources; noir author and connoisseur extraordinaire Vangelis Dimitroglou for sharing his knowledge and spreading his passion for the genre; and Professor Andrew Spicer for trusting us with his foreword, and thus legitimising this collective effort with his undoubted authority.

We are also grateful to EUP's Senior Commissioning Editor for Film Studies, Gillian Leslie, for believing in this project from the beginning, and for her constant encouragement, patience and support throughout the ensuing long process, to Sam Johnson, Andrew Kirk, Fiona Conn, Caitlin Murphy and all the production team of EUP, as well to the series editors R. Barton Palmer and Linda Badley.

We are indebted to every person who helped in any way so that this volume saw the light of day; and, of course, to all the important contributors of various backgrounds and expertise who trusted us with original contributions. We are grateful to them for their hard work and admirable commitment. This book is the fruit of collaboration between many different people, whose common goal is the advancement and expansion of the field of Greek film studies while sharing an interest in, and a love for, Greek cinema, including its dark films.

CONTRIBUTORS

Thanassis Agathos is an Associate Professor of Modern Greek Literature in the Faculty of Philology of the National and Kapodistrian University of Athens. His research interests include modern Greek literature of the nineteenth and twentieth centuries, the relationship between literature and cinema, and the work of Nikos Kazantzakis and Vassilis Vassilikos. He is the author of five books: *From the Life and Days of Alexis Zorbas to Zorba the Greek* (2007), *The Era of the Novel* (2014), *The Cinematographic Aspect of Gregorios Xenopoulos* (2016), *Nikos Kazantzakis in the Cinema* (2017) and *Angelos Terzakis and the Cinema* (2020).

Georgia Aitaki is Senior Lecturer in Media and Communication Studies at Karlstad University, Sweden. Her doctoral dissertation, 'The Private Life of a Nation in Crisis: A Study on the Politics in/of Greek Television Fiction' (University of Gothenburg, 2018), addresses the role of television fiction in representing and shaping moments of heightened societal tension. Her current research focuses on critical approaches to television and popular culture and, specifically, on questions of inclusion/exclusion, with an empirical focus on Greek, Swedish and US media. Her work has appeared in journals such as *Media, Culture and Society*, *Social Semiotics*, *Screen*, *VIEW: Journal of European Television History & Culture* and in a number of anthologies.

Dennis Broe is an expert on 1940s Hollywood cinema, the crime film, and the art and culture of the Cold War. He is the author of *Film Noir, American*

Workers and Postwar Hollywood (2009), *Class, Crime and International Film Noir: Globalizing America's Dark Art* (2014) and *Cold War Expressionism: Perverting the Politics of Perception/Bombast, Blacklists and Blockades in the Postwar Art World* (2021). He is the author of two noir novels: *Left of Eden* (2020), about the Hollywood blacklist, and *A Hello to Arms* (2021), about the post-war build-up of the weapons industry. His is also the author of *Diary of a Digital Plague Year: Corona Culture, Serial TV and the Rise of the Streaming Services* (2021), *Birth of the Binge: Serial TV and the End of Leisure* (2019) and *Maverick or How the West Was Lost* (2015). His television criticism appears at Bro on the Global Television Beat.

Spyridon Chairetis holds a DPhil/PhD in media and cultural studies from the University of Oxford. He has published on Greek LGBTQI+ cinema and television, genre studies and auto-ethnography. His monograph titled *Greek Television Comedy: Popular Texts, Queer Readings* (Palgrave Macmillan) is forthcoming. His research interests revolve around media and sexuality studies, television fiction, gender anthropology and the relationship between media, culture and society. He is currently teaching television and media studies at Fårö Creative Learning in Athens, Greece.

Maria Chalkou is the principal editor of *Filmicon: Journal of Greek Film Studies*. She holds a PhD in film theory and history (University of Glasgow), sponsored by the Greek State Scholarships Foundation, and an MA in film and art theory (University of Kent). She is currently a post-doctoral researcher at Panteion University (CIVIL – Censorship in Visual Arts and Film, supported by ELIDEK) while teaching film history, film theory and documentary in the Department of Audio and Visual Arts of Ionian University. She has published on Greek cinema, film censorship, film criticism and cinematic representations of the past.

Yun-hua Chen is an independent film scholar, critic and curator. She holds a PhD in film studies from the University of St Andrews (Scotland) and writes academic articles and film reviews in English, Chinese and German. Her articles can be found in *Directory of World Cinema*, *Journal of Chinese Cinemas*, *Film International*, *Cinephilia* and several edited volumes. Her monograph *Mosaic Space and Mosaic Auteurs: Alejandro González Iñárritu, Atom Egoyan, Hou Hsiao-hsien, Michael Haneke*, funded by Geschwister Boehringer Ingelheim Stiftung, was published by Neofelis Verlag in Berlin in 2017. She has worked as the festival director of *dokumentART*, an annual film festival in Neubrandenburg (Germany), and as a Fipresci jury member at EMAF and DOK Leipzig.

Costas Constandinides is a Lecturer in Audiovisual Media in the Department of Social and Political Sciences at the University of Cyprus. He was previously a faculty member in the Department of Communications at the University of Nicosia. He is the author of *From Film Adaptation to Post-celluloid Adaptation* (2010) and co-editor of *Cypriot Cinemas: Memory, Conflict and Identity in the Margins of Europe* (2014). He is a member of the European Film Academy.

Nikitas Fessas holds a PhD in political and social sciences: communication sciences (focused on film) from Ghent University, Belgium. He has published numerous cultural criticism essays in both Greek and English-language media, as well as academic articles on Greek film noir in peer-reviewed journals. He has worked as a film reviewer for several years. Slavoj Žižek mentions him in his book *Less than Nothing: Hegel and the Shadow of Dialectical Materialism*.

Vrasidas Karalis holds the Chair of Sir Nicholas Laurantos in Modern Greek and Byzantine Studies at the University of Sydney. He has translated Patrick White's *Voss* and *The Vivisector*. He is the editor of *Modern Greek Studies (Australia and New Zealand)*. His main publications in English include *A History of Greek Cinema* (Continuum, 2012), *Realism in Greek Cinema* (I.B. Tauris, 2017), *Recollections of Mr Manoly Lascaris* (Brandl and Schlesinger, 2007), *The Demons of Athens* (Brandl and Schlesinger, 2013), *Reflections on Presence* (Re.Press, 2016) and *The Cinematic Language of Theo Angelopoulos* (Berghahn, 2021). He has also edited the collections *Cornelios Castoriadis and the Project of Radical Democracy* (2013), *Martin Heidegger and the Aesthetics of Being* (2008) and *Power, Justice and Judgement in Hannah Arendt* (2012). He is currently working on the Australian filmmaker George Miller.

Ioulia Mermigka studied media arts at the University of Plymouth (UK) and holds a PhD in cultural and cinema studies from the National and Kapodistrian University of Athens. She is currently a freelance researcher, lecturer at the University of Athens and an external collaborator of the Greek Film Archive. She has created experimental films and transmedia performances and her interests revolve around the intersections of grassroots politics, philosophy and aesthetics.

Nick Poulakis, PhD, serves as a staff member at the Ethnomusicology and Cultural Anthropology Laboratory in the Department of Music Studies of the National and Kapodistrian University of Athens, where he teaches film music, ethnographic cinema and applied ethnomusicology. He is also an adjunct instructor in the Modern Greek Culture Programme of the Hellenic Open University. He has been involved in various research projects and has written several articles and book chapters on ethnomusicological films, video life-stories of migrants, anthropology of film and TV music, media education and audiovisual literacy. His books *Musicology and Cinema: Critical Approaches to the Music* *of Modern Greek Films* and *Music from Optical Theater and Silent Cinema* have been recently published in Greek by Orpheus.

Anna Poupou teaches film history and theory in the Department of Digital Arts and Cinema of the National and Kapodistrian University of Athens. She holds a PhD in film studies from the University Sorbonne Nouvelle-Paris 3. She is co-editor of three volumes – *City and Cinema: Theoretical and Methodological Approaches* (Nisos, 2011), *Athens: World Film Locations* (Intellect, 2014) and *The Lost Highway of Greek Cinema 1960–1990* (Nefeli, 2019) – and author of two academic ebooks. She has worked as a programmer at the Greek Film Archive and she is a member of the research team *Film noir in Greece: Reception, assimilation and imitation of a US film genre, from the post-war period until today* (NKUA). Her research interests focus on the history of Greek cinema, film and history, urban spaces and cinema, and film noir.

Marios Psaras is a filmmaker and film scholar. He was born in Cyprus and lives in London. He holds a PhD in film studies from Queen Mary University of London. He has taught film theory at King's College London and Greenwich University and lectured across Europe. He has published on contemporary Greek, European and world queer cinema, including the monograph *The Queer Greek Weird Wave* (Palgrave Macmillan, 2016). He is artistic director of Cyprus Short Film Day (London) and a member of the Hellenic Film Academy. Before moving to London, he worked professionally in radio and TV production in Cyprus, as well as in the theatre. He has produced and directed four short films and two short documentaries, including the award-winning *The Call* (2020). As of 2018, he works as Cultural Counsellor at the Cyprus High Commission in London, curating and producing various interdisciplinary art and cultural projects in collaboration with major British and international academic and cultural institutions.

Andrew Spicer is Professor of Cultural Production at the University of the West of England (Bristol). He has published extensively on film noir including *Film Noir* (2002), *The Historical Dictionary of Film Noir* (2010) and the co-edited collections *European Film Noir* (2007) and *A Companion to Film Noir* (2013). He has also written about media production including the co-edited collections *Beyond the Bottom Line: The Producer in Film and Television Studies* (2014) and *Building Successful and Sustainable Film and Television Businesses: A Cross-National Perspective* (2017). He is currently developing a project exploring the politics of regional production, and a study of natural history filmmaking in Bristol, *The Green Hollywood*. His monograph *Sean Connery: Acting, Stardom and National Identity* is forthcoming from Manchester University Press.

CONTRIBUTORS

Maria A. Stassinopoulou is Professor of Modern Greek Studies at the University of Vienna. She has published widely on Greek social and cultural history from the eighteenth to the twentieth century. She is the author of *Weltgeschichte im Denken eines griechischen Aufklärers* (1992) and co-editor, among other volumes, of *Across the Danube: Southeastern Europeans and Their Traveling Identities (17th–19th ce.)* (2017). Her habilitation thesis 'Reality Bites' (2001) discusses Greek film in the context of Cold War Greece, in particular the 1950s and 1960s. In her articles on cinema, she focuses on the historical context of Greek film production and the narratives of historicity in Greek cinema in the second half of the twentieth century.

Yannis Tzioumakis is Reader in Film and Media Industries at the University of Liverpool. He is the author of five books, most recently *Acting Indie: Industry, Aesthetics, and Performance* (co-authored with Cynthia Baron, Palgrave, 2020), and is co-editor of six collections of essays, most recently *United Artists* (Routledge, 2020). He is currently finishing *Rock Around the Clock: Exploitation, Rock 'n' Roll and the Origins of Youth Culture* (co-authored with Siân Lincoln) and co-editing *Indie TV: Industry, Aesthetics and Medium Specificity*, before embarking on the monograph *When Hollywood Came to Greece, 1957–1967*, all for Routledge. He also co-edits the Routledge Hollywood Centenary and the Cinema and Youth Cultures book series.

TRADITIONS IN WORLD CINEMA

General editors: **Linda Badley and R. Barton Palmer**
Founding editor: **Steven Jay Schneider**

Traditions in World Cinema is a series of textbooks and monographs devoted to the analysis of currently popular and previously underexamined or undervalued film movements from around the globe. Also intended for general interest readers, the textbooks in this series offer undergraduate- and graduate-level film students accessible and comprehensive introductions to diverse traditions in world cinema. The monographs open up for advanced academic study more specialised groups of films, including those that require theoretically-oriented approaches. Both textbooks and monographs provide thorough examinations of the industrial, cultural, and socio-historical conditions of production and reception.

The flagship textbook for the series includes chapters by noted scholars on traditions of acknowledged importance (the French New Wave, German Expressionism), recent and emergent traditions (New Iranian, post-Cinema Novo), and those whose rightful claim to recognition has yet to be established (the Israeli persecution film, global found footage cinema). Other volumes concentrate on individual national, regional or global cinema traditions. As the introductory chapter to each volume makes clear, the films under discussion form a coherent group on the basis of substantive and relatively transparent, if not always obvious, commonalities. These commonalities may be formal, stylistic or thematic, and the groupings may, although they need not, be popularly identified as genres, cycles or movements (Japanese horror, Chinese martial arts cinema, Italian Neorealism). Indeed, in cases in which a group of films is not already commonly identified as a tradition, one purpose of the volume is to establish its claim to importance and make it visible (East Central European Magical Realist cinema, Palestinian cinema).

Textbooks and monographs include:

- An introduction that clarifies the rationale for the grouping of films under examination
- A concise history of the regional, national, or transnational cinema in question
- A summary of previous published work on the tradition
- Contextual analysis of industrial, cultural and socio-historical conditions of production and reception
- Textual analysis of specific and notable films, with clear and judicious application of relevant film theoretical approaches
- Bibliograph(ies)/filmograph(ies)

Monographs may additionally include:

- Discussion of the dynamics of cross-cultural exchange in light of current research and thinking about cultural imperialism and globalisation, as well as issues of regional/national cinema or political/aesthetic movements (such as new waves, postmodernism, or identity politics)
- Interview(s) with key filmmakers working within the tradition.

FOREWORD

Andrew Spicer

Film noir has always been a mutating, elusive, even fugitive category, at once a central body of films from American cinema that includes *Double Indemnity* (dir. Wilder, 1944), *Out of the Past* (dir. Tourneur, 1947), *Kiss Me Deadly* (dir. Aldrich, 1955) and *Touch of Evil* (dir. Welles, 1958), and a shaping discourse that constantly redefines the meaning of those films and the mode of filmmaking of which they form part. Film noir can be quite tightly defined and periodised, or understood as a much more diffuse phenomenon that stretches across different art forms (encompassing advertising, comics, graphic novels, short stories and novels, painting, photography, radio drama, television and music), different periods and different countries. If we abandon attempts to define (and thereby delimit) its essential characteristics and accept noir as a mode of attention, a sensibility, a particular approach to understanding the world, then I think we are open to understanding the full range of its seductive appeal and its pervasiveness.

When the label film noir first emerged – conventionally attributed to Nino Frank in an article published in *L'Écran français* in August 1946 – it served to designate a group of American crime films that had both an arresting visual style and a sombre, bleak view of American life. During the six-year absence of American films during the Occupation, it seemed to French critics that American cinema had come of age, and was capable of engaging with 'difficult' subjects: sexuality, corruption, betrayal, trauma, psychological breakdown – a raft of social, political and historical problems that had rarely found their way into films in the pre-war period. Of course, as always, it was a case of which films were given attention rather than an objective categorisation (the films discussed were not the ones that were most popular at the box office) but that attention served to identify films noirs as a critical, oppositional mode of filmmaking, films that were 'autopsies' of society, to invoke the term used by director Mike Hodges to describe his British neo-noir *Get Carter* (1971).

That founding moment confined how film noir was understood as a seemingly uniquely American form of cinema for the next forty years. Raymond Borde and Étienne Chaumeton's *Panorama du film noir américain* (1955) delineated 'a group of nationally identifiable films' whose common features of style, subject matter and 'atmosphere' gave them 'an inimitable quality' ([1955] 2002: 1), and dismissed other European claimants. When the term was finally taken up in Anglo-American discourse in Paul Schrader's seminal 'Notes on Film Noir' (1972), he argued that these films were a subset of the American gangster film whose development had been delayed by the war. Alain Silver and Elizabeth Ward in their edited collection *Film Noir* (1980) gave the authority of a 'canon' of some 300 films to establish 'an indigenous American form [. . .] a self-contained reflection of American cultural preoccupations [. . .] a unique example of a wholly American film style' (1980: 1). When the term 'neo-noir' emerged in the 1990s to describe films after the 'classic' period (1940–58) that were made in conscious acknowledgement of those earlier films, it simply extended the number of American films that could be included. Recognition of film noir's European antecedents – Weimar *Strassenfilm*, French Poetic Realism – and the importance of displaced European talent (Fritz Lang, Otto Preminger or Robert Siodmak) was corralled into 'influences', an index of the hegemony of Hollywood cinema that still persists.

Counter-arguments appeared sporadically, partly spurred by the obvious flaws in an argument conducted though assertion rather than ratiocination, and by an increasing body of scholarship that explored the distinctiveness of various national cinemas, elucidating their cultural traditions and characteristic preoccupations, and in the process uncovering or exhuming rich and complex bodies of film. The best of this scholarship – such as Pierre Sorlin's *European Cinemas, European Societies, 1939–1990* (1991), or Thomas Elsaesser's *Weimar Cinema and After: Germany's Historical Imaginary* (2000) – was driven by the determination to understand both the singularity of specific European cinemas and their complex and uneven relationship with global Hollywood. Thus the impulse to 'discover' European films noirs was informed by the recognition that, looked at in a wider historical purview, film noir had been, from its inception, a transnational phenomenon, and that filmmakers working in individual national cinemas were, unsurprisingly, knowledgeable about and influenced by American films. In their introduction to 'European precursors of film noir', which appeared in the spring 1996 issue of *Iris*, Janice

Morgan and Dudley Andrew argued that film noir was characterised by its 'cross-cultural' exchanges.

If Europe was one locus for the 'discovery' of non-American films noirs, Asian cinema became another rich terrain. Scholars have identified a 'Bombay noir', and others in China, Hong Kong, Japan, Singapore and South Korea. As in Europe, these films noirs are strongly influenced by indigenous cultural traditions, histories, social and political events and subjects, but also display an equally all-pervading relationship with Hollywood. In their overview, *Film Noir: Hard-Boiled Modernity and the Cultures of Globalization* (2010), Jennifer Fay and Justus Nieland make the case for the presence of film noir in Latin American cinema, including Mexico, and it is relatively straightforward to make the case for its presence in Australasian cinema. Fay and Nieland argue that film noir is the product of the uneven development of modernity as a global force and of the failure of capitalism to deliver social justice. Thus the various films noirs that exist are local manifestations of a transnational cultural phenomenon that exhibits a complex process of adaptation and assimilation, one that attains an energy and coherence in certain locations at particular moments, as Dennis Broe's illuminating *Class, Crime and International Film Noir: Globalizing America's Dark Art* (2014) makes abundantly clear.

When I put together the collection *European Film Noir* in 2006–07 – which attempted to document and analyse film noir and neo-noir in five European cinemas (France, Germany, Italy, Spain and the United Kingdom) – I was acutely conscious that this was, in all probability, only a fraction of the phenomenon and that other European films noirs were waiting to be discovered and defined. The emergence of Scandinavian film noir (Scandi noir/Nordic noir) is the obvious instance, stretching across Denmark, Finland, Iceland, Norway and Sweden. Crime fiction – such as Henning Mankell's Wallander series – provided, as in America, the platform, but Nordic noir's international recognition came through the success of 'high end' television series such as Denmark's *Forbrydelsen/The Killing* (DR1, 2007–12), which ran for 40 episodes over three seasons, or the Danish-Swedish co-production *Bron/Broen/The Bridge* (SVT1/DR1, 2011–18) – 38 episodes over four seasons. Their production values, intricate plots and complex characterisations made these television series arguably some of the most interesting and important manifestations of film noir in recent times – and led to a host of imitators – thus displacing film's cultural centrality, or at least rivalling it.

The present volume expands the corpus of European film noir further into Greek cinema. The contributors to this collection reveal the essential 'Greekness' of these noirs, their ability to deal with specific national crises, traditions, influences and cultural milieux, but also the interactions between the global and the local in which particular instances are dramatised as examples of wider phenomena. The chapters show how the core characteristics of film noir are played out in a national context, an oppositional form of filmmaking that often has to work by subterfuge, 'masked' narratives or allegory, in order to defeat censorship, but one determined to confront and explore challenging or even taboo subject matter, be it psychological, social, political or historical. Contributors locate the characteristic noir liminality that James Naremore identified in *More than Night: Film Noir in its Contexts* ([1998] 2008), films that occupy a shifting space somewhere between mainstream and arthouse. They discuss the rich visual complexity of these noirs, their aural sophistication and the various ways in which they manifest noir's concern with gender politics. *Femmes fatales* appear in Greek noir, but weak, inadequate or ineffective men perhaps somewhat less frequently – especially in the classical period – another example of a local inflection of a transnational mode. The noir sensibility in Greece ranges across different cultural forms – including films, television programmes, radio plays and podcasts – and also short films, a mode of production that has yet to receive sustained and systematic attention. As the editors' introduction argues, what emerges is an 'alternative history of Greek cinema', a 'darker Greece' than was permissible in conventional genres, a history that was late to start – it could only begin in the 1950s when Athens developed into a modern metropolis – intermittent and often tangential to the main developments, but nevertheless important to discuss, in its revelations of class tensions and various forms of social unease. As a low-cost mode of filmmaking, film noir provides a route for intelligent and ambitious creative talent to make its mark, even if its box-office appeal is never assured.

Noir retains its dynamism as a mode of production and of research inquiry, and I'm sure that other films noirs will be located and analysed by energetic and industrious academic exegesis. My hope is that those 'emergent' noirs will receive the same detailed and rigorous scrutiny as Greek film noir does in this excellent collection, which makes an important contribution to noir scholarship.

REFERENCES

Borde, Raymond, and Chaumeton, Étienne ([1955] 2002), *A Panorama of American Film Noir: 1941–1953*, San Francisco: City Lights.

Broe, Dennis (2014), *Class, Crime and International Film Noir: Globalizing America's Dark Art*, London: Palgrave Macmillan.

Elsaesser, Thomas (2000), *Weimar Cinema and After: Germany's Historical Imaginary*, Abingdon: Routledge.

Fay, Jennifer, and Nieland, Justus (2010), *Film Noir: Hard-Boiled Modernity and the Cultures of Globalization*, Abingdon: Routledge.

Frank, Nino (1946), 'Un nouveau genre "policier": l'aventure criminelle', *L'Écran français*, 61, pp. 8–9, 14.

Morgan, Janice, and Andrew, J. Dudley (eds) (1996), 'European Precursors of Film Noir', *Iris*, 21, pp. 3–4.

Naremore, James ([1998] 2008), *More than Night: Film Noir in its Contexts*, Berkeley, CA: University of California Press.
Schrader, Paul (1972), 'Notes on Film Noir', *Film Comment*, 8, pp. 8–13.
Silver, Alain, and Ward, Elizabeth (eds) (1980), *Film Noir: An Encyclopaedic Reference to the American Style*, New York: Overlook Press.
Sorlin, Pierre (1991), *European Cinemas, European Societies, 1939–1990*, Abingdon: Routledge.
Spicer, Andrew (ed.) (2007), *European Film Noir*, Manchester: Manchester University Press.

INTRODUCTION

Anna Poupou, Nikitas Fessas and Maria Chalkou

Transnational discussions on the subject of Greek cinema in the first quarter of the twenty-first century typically revolve around the 'Weird Wave', the awkward and bizarre cinema that is considered a product of the ten-year financial and political crisis that began in 2008, and that interrogates urgent biopolitical issues that emerged even before the Covid-19 pandemic (Papanikolaou 2021). This new visibility of Greek films, attributed to Yorgos Lanthimos and his fellow filmmakers, gave film scholarship the chance not only to discuss contemporary Greek cinema, but to revisit its history and put on a global map films and filmmakers that deserve to be known by a wider cinephile community. Only a decade ago, the majority of English-language academic literature on Greek cinema focused almost exclusively on the patriarchal figure of Theo Angelopoulos; we feel that now is the right moment to rewrite a transnational history of Greek cinema in a more inclusive way, relating cinema to critical strands of contemporary cultural theory, addressing issues that have remained obscure, and questioning certainties, cinematic myths and national stereotypes.

Why deal with the Greek version of the film noir? During this last decade, and in the midst of social turmoil in the country, many filmmakers turned to crime films and hybrid forms of the neo-noir, using as their backdrop the financial, political and migrant crisis, and expressing a critical view on neoliberalism, nationalism or gender discrimination. The Greek film *To thavma tis thalassas ton Sargasson/The Miracle of the Sargasso Sea* (dir. Tzoumerkas, 2019), which premiered at the 69th Berlinale, features as its protagonist a disgraced, alcoholic, no-nonsense, female local police chief who, while uncovering a monstrous conspiracy, bonds with an abused young woman, and together they wreak revenge against patriarchy. The film was reviewed as a neo-noir (Mitsis 2019), while its premise is considered a norm in different national contexts (from ITV's *Prime Suspect*, 1991, to *Destroyer*, dir. Kusama, 2018). However, by the standards of Greek genre cinema, and compared to the first attempts at Greek noir, we have come a long way. We have also, seemingly, moved on from fruitless debates about whether a Greek film noir category exists. Or have we?

Crime literature with plots firmly anchored in the environment of the Greek crisis, or set in the recent past just before it – such as Petros Markaris's novels – were the first Greek noir narratives that met with significant international recognition. This trend in cinema also boosted televisual fiction, true crime shows and other web-oriented narratives (true crime podcasts, noir theatrical radio plays, etc.) which flourished in the period between the two crises, the post-2009 one and the Covid-19 pandemic, something that led to an increased interest in the older forms of crime fiction. As a matter of fact, very few things have been written about crime film genres in Greece. Most of the historical accounts of Greek cinema neglect this genre (Mitropoulou [1980] 2005; Soldatos 1999), concluding that crime films in Greece never thrived for reasons of audience preference and film industry particularities, or that the few examples were just poor and unsuccessful imitations of American movies (Valoukos and Spiliopoulos 1985). The reasons for the critical denial of the labelling of the Greek film noir, as well as our approach to the term 'noir' and issues of genre in this volume, will be thoroughly addressed in the third part of this introduction.

Nevertheless, if we look at Greek film history from a different point of view, we can see several emblematic films that – by today's standards – epitomise the features of film noir, such as O *drakos*/*The Ogre of Athens* (dir. Koundouros, 1956) or *Efialtis*/*Nightmare* (dir. Andreou, 1961); others revitalise noir structures in a radical way such as *Anaparastasi*/*Reconstruction* (1970) by Angelopoulos or *Ioannis o viaios*/*John the Violent* (1973) by Tonia Marketaki. Therefore, the aim of this book is not only to search for less explored and neglected specimens that form a national paradigm of film noir, but also to recognise that some of the films that are considered masterpieces of Greek cinema bear a noir signature, which was acknowledged either too late or not at all. While exploring these films, we discover the multitude of international influences that have been embedded into a national film production from its early steps. By focusing on examples that until recently were conceived of as 'mere imitations of Hollywood', we shed light on the processes of integration, assimilation, hybridity and acculturation that made film noir an international phenomenon (Pettey and Palmer 2014; Spicer 2007). The films and filmmakers presented in this volume form an alternative history of Greek cinema, one that avoids the escapist stereotypes of an idyllic tourist destination, does not need to resort to ancient Greek culture as a point of reference (although the ghost of Oedipus inevitably haunts many of these films), distances itself from the dominant folkloric or self-exoticising representations of the country, and turns away from pictorialist approaches to the Greek landscape and light (cf. Petsini 2016: 267–9). The films in this volume investigate a darker Greece, hidden in the shadows that become sharper when contrasted with the burning sun; these filmmakers turn to the bloodiest periods of recent history, their crimes and traumas, while unearthing the family archive of gender troubles, home-made violence, kinship, patriarchy and repression; within structures of strict control, totalitarianism and censorship, the films in this volume use the noir cryptic codes to speak about the impermissible and thus become daring expressions of a – sometimes unaccomplished and unattained – modernity.

Greek Film Noir: A Possible Periodisation

Greece developed a systematic film production only in the late 1920s. However, the technological complexities resulting from the advent of sound, the financial crisis, and the fascist dictatorship of Metaxas created obstacles that delayed a normal development of the film industry. This happened only after the end of the Second World War and the Civil War (1944–49) that followed. After the liberation of Greece, as in other European countries occupied by the Nazis, previously forbidden Hollywood films flooded the Greek screens. Thus emblematic film noirs arrived in Athens during the 1945–46 film season – for example, *They Drive by Night* (dir. Walsh, 1940) was screened on 5 November 1945 and *Laura* (dir. Preminger, 1944) on 25 March 1946 – and for the next decade they would constitute one of the most popular film genres. In the following years the country was under the diplomatic, political and financial patronage of the US through the Marshall Plan, and this meant that Hollywood cinema represented the great majority of films screened. During the film season 1947–48, in the midst of the bloodiest moments of the Civil War, no less than 78 crime thrillers (61 from the USA, 12 from the UK, three from France, one from Greece and Germany) were screened in Athens. As the label 'noir' would be widely used much later, these films were identified as 'gangster films', 'police dramas', 'melodramas', and less often as 'detective films' or 'thrillers'. However, their influence was not directly reflected in native productions, as the film industry remained underdeveloped. The first attempts by Greek filmmakers to experiment with noir features were the crime melodramas *Prosopa lismonimena/Forgotten Faces* (dir. Tzavelas, 1946) and *Hamenoi angeloi/Fallen Angels* (dir. Tsiforos, 1948), but these efforts were not soon repeated.

In the early 1950s Greek films achieved a peak of popularity; this boosted a more systematic production and a studio system centred on the major company Finos Film, as well as smaller producers (Karalis 2012; Mitropoulou [1980] 2005; Papadimitriou 2006; Athanasatou 2001). In political terms, the early 1950s marked the end of the Civil War and the advent of a conservative and traditionalist government, while public life was forged around the notion of nationalism (*ethinokofrosyni* – meaning 'the correct' national mentality), accompanied by strong anti-communism, 'family values', strict ideological control and repression in order to exclude or rehabilitate a large part of the population that had been radicalised in the previous period through their participation in the Resistance forces and the Communist Party. In this authoritarian climate that left no room for social critique through cinema, popular Greek films were made for 'the entire family', while light comedies and melodramas became the dominant genres. During this period there were a few attempts at crime films, such as the police adventure *To Pontikaki/The Little Mouse* (dir. Tsiforos, 1954), and a satire of gangster films titled *Tzo o tromeros/Joe the Terrible* (dir. Dimopoulos, 1955) that are testimonies to an early French influence on crime films. In *The Ogre of Athens*, one of the most influential Greek art films of the 1950s, Koundouros used noir iconography to present a sinister image of post Civil War Athens, under constant surveillance and police control, and a hero in search of identity – his social, gender and class identities – in the marginal spaces of the capital. Despite the fact that during this early phase there were only scattered examples of thrillers and crime films that would later be labelled as 'films noirs', the growth of pulp fiction was noteworthy: magazines specialising in crime fiction reappeared after the end of the war, while newspapers regularly included serialised crime stories (Figure I.1). The most prolific crime novelist of the time was the journalist Yannis Maris, whose novels would be transferred to the screen in the following years. This early period came to an end in 1958 with the film *O anthropos tou trenou/The Man on the Train* (dir. Dimopoulos, 1958), a psychological thriller penned by Maris that revisited the traumas of the Occupation and the Resistance while, at the same time, illustrating the impasses and dilemmas in the era of post-war economic growth that Greece was about to enter.

The year 1958 marked a turning point in film production: new, well-equipped studios were built (such as Studio Alpha), and annual production started to rise significantly, as Greek films became extremely popular with native audiences. New sub-genres appeared, such as the teenage movie, the youth delinquency drama and the film musical, which addressed the hipper, younger, baby boomer audiences of the 1960s (Delveroudi 2004; Papadimitriou 2006; Poupou 2007). At the end of the decade the presence of Hollywood and international runaway productions in Greece pushed the film industry towards a transnational context; importantly, Robert Aldrich shot the noir *The Angry Hills* (1959) in Greece, and Jules Dassin was settled in Athens. At the same time the work of Greek auteurs, such as Michael Cacoyannis, Nikos Koundouros and, a few years later, Takis Kanellopoulos, gained international critical acclaim. 1958 was also marked by a political shift as, for the first time since the war, the

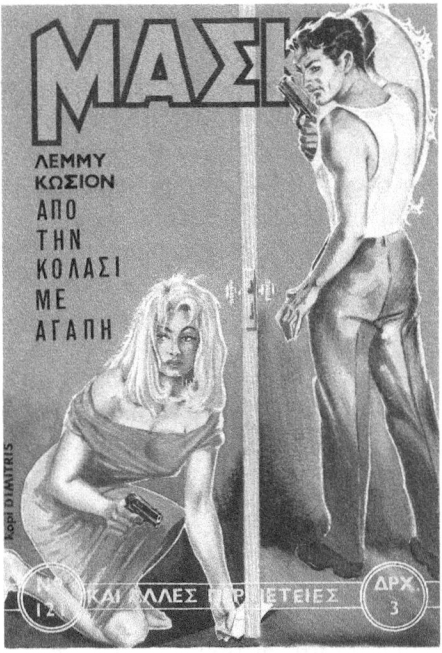

Figure I.1 Front cover of the weekly pulp magazine *Maska* (*Mask*) from its fourth period of circulation (1963–74) under the direction of Jimmy Corinis. The issue features the adventures of fictional detective Lemmy Caution, created by Peter Cheney. Undated issue, c.1963–64. Courtesy of Jimmy Corinis.

left-wing party EDA became the official opposition. This meant a relatively more inclusive public sphere, and the opening of debate on the painful events of the 1940s. From 1958 onwards, topics centred on war traumas, losses, crime and treason of the past can be found at the core of many genre films, triggering the plot of crime cinematic narratives.

The end of the 1950s is also considered the high point of the reconstruction of the Greek capital and the advent of the architectural modernism that transformed the Athenian cityscape: new dense modern districts, such as Pangrati, Kypseli, Kolonaki and Exarcheia, would accommodate the new rising stratum of the middle class, while the city received migrants from the impoverished peripheries to form an urbanised working class. As Maris describes in his crime novels, which are rich in social observation, newcomers arrived with high expectations in Athens, which became a symbol of modernity, affluence and anonymity, a place where one could invent a new identity and gain social mobility. It is exactly at this moment that the most dynamic cycle of Greek noir appeared with films such as *Eglima sto Kolonaki*/*Murder in Kolonaki* (dir. Aliferis, 1959), *Eglima sta paraskinia/Murder Backstage* (dir. Katsouridis, 1960) *Nightmare*, et al. One reason, among others, for the belatedness of the establishment of film noir in Greece is the fact that only in the late 1950s did the capital become a complex modern metropolis, which is one of the major prerequisites for the development of noir fiction (Poupou 2021). During this process of rapid reconstruction, Athens was represented as a cityscape that could express the urban, social and gender anxieties of the present, a certain fear of the future, and a hidden nostalgia for lost urban forms of the past (cf. Dimendberg 2004). Images of fast cars on the newly constructed highways, modernist lofts, scenes in fashionable nightclubs, theatres, cinemas and hotels, surveillance scenes and chases in the dense, modernist city centre contrasted with the marginal spaces on the periphery of Athens, hidden areas in the city centre that retained their vernacular architecture, the dangerous docks of Piraeus and lumpen remote suburbs that form the centripetal geography of the Athenian film noir. A tension between a superficial image of prosperity, a drive towards modernity and, at the same time, harsh social reality, as well as an effort to conceal the traumas of the recent past can be found at the heart of these films. Moreover, if gender relations and sexual identities became a constant site of negotiation in Greek films noirs (Hadjikyriacou 2013; Fessas 2019), expressing perhaps the most obvious transformation attributed to modernity, social, class and ideological tensions are also visible in their dynamics. The cynical acceptance of modernity by most Athenian films noirs and their tendency to abstain from picturesque or moralistic representations – as seen in melodramas – of working-class people and the spaces they inhabit can be considered as major features that distinguish film noir from the other genres of the time.

From 1959 and throughout the 1960s, the heyday of Greek cinema, to the fall of the dictatorship (1974) and the decline of the Greek commercial film, the Athenian noir cycle appeared fully developed, with more than sixty films being produced. A possible explanation for the industry's hesitation to invest in crime-related films in the 1940s and 1950s and their relative flourishing in the 1960s is that, according to the Decree-law 1108/1942, films with crime content were automatically characterised as 'inappropriate for the underage'. This meant that the market potential of crime movies was limited by definition, and producers were reluctant to take financial risks in a transitional period when the domestic industry was seeking to establish itself and struggling for commercial viability. Greek movies of the time addressed primarily family audiences and their producers were desperate to get screening permission from the censorship committees as 'suitable for the general public', often accepting extensive cuts. It was only in the late 1950s and especially in the 1960s, when the film audience was dramatically expanded and diversified, that established producers as well as ambitious newcomers began to experiment with crime narratives and bold subject matter. The spectacular expansion of the domestic market and the emergence of specialised target audiences allowed, on the one hand, filmmakers to include morally ambivalent and drifting characters as protagonists, violence and adult material; on the other, many 'immoral' films such as *To remali tis Fokionos Negri/ The Bum of Fokionos Negri* (dir. Karagiannis, 1965) attained popularity while being advertised and distributed as 'strictly for adults'. This process reflected also the marked liberalisation of the public sphere and the relative relaxation of censorship in the 1960s, especially after the rise to power of the centrist government of Georgios Papandreou in 1963, which permitted the treatment of previously unexplored and suppressed content (Chalkou 2008: 100–65).

Thus in the 1960s many filmmakers working within the studio system saw crime films and films noirs as a challenge: Dinos Katsouridis, Maria Plyta, Dinos Dimopoulos, Nikos Foskolos, Grigoris Grigoriou, Stavros Tsiolis and many others tested their skills in noir narratives, some of them with striking results. Moreover, independent filmmakers saw the genre as an opportunity to enter the film industry, such as young Erricos Andreou with *Nightmare*, while commercial filmmakers with intellectual ambitions used it as a vehicle to reintroduce themselves to audiences, such as Socrates Kapsaskis with his independent noir *O zestos minas Avgoustos/The Hot Month of August* (1966). Even if these works rarely entered the top five at the box office, most of them enjoyed a fair popularity and some met with spectacular success, such as, for example, *Pyretos stin asfalto/The Asphalt Fever* (dir. Dimopoulos, 1967) which sold 487,000 tickets and ranked fifth at the Greek box office (Dermentzopoulos 2021: 472–7).

The military coup of the Colonels in April 1967 put an untimely stop to the drive of Greek society towards modernity, throwing Greece back into repression, extreme nationalism, parochialism and the ideological triptych of 'nation, religion, family', while the country remained under the cultural influence of the US. Greek cinema at the time faced huge challenges, such as strict censorship and the advent of television broadcasting, which after 1969 brought about a dramatic decline in movie attendance (Sotiropoulou 1995: 37; Karalis 2012: 129; Hadjikyriacou 2013: 71–2). Whereas the annual output in the 1960s reached a peak with over a hundred films, in 1974 the numbers collapsed to 42 films, putting an end to the Greek studio system (Sotiropoulou 1995: 38; Hadjikyriacou 2013: 66, 108). Nevertheless, during the junta, noirish social dramas, police stories and spy adventures continued to be produced, while the producers also turned to televisual crime fiction (Figure I.2). At the time, in terms of ideology, crime and noir narratives appeared increasingly polarised: on the one hand, commercial films became more morally oriented, often expressing anxieties about corruption, modernity and the collapse of the traditional Greek family (*Panikos/Panic*, dir. Tsiolis, 1969); on the other, they became a platform for independent filmmakers to articulate alternative or oppositional voices (*Listeia stin Athina/Robbery in Athens*, dir. Serdaris, 1969). Importantly, the period was marked by the rise of New Greek Cinema, a politicised, auteur-driven and

Figure I.2 Photo from the shooting of the television show *38th Precinct*, directed by Jimmy Corinis (1972–73), the first police drama series to use real locations. Courtesy of Jimmy Corinis.

modernist film movement that reinvigorated Greek cinema. After a hiatus in the early years of the junta, the urge for experimentation, radicalism and the adoption of international avant-garde or modernist trends that permeated all artistic fields in the pre-dictatorship 1960s recovered. In this context, and influenced by the French New Wave's infatuation with film noir, young New Greek Cinema filmmakers such as Angelopoulos and Marketaki, like Dimos Theos a few years earlier, while positioning themselves against the studio system and commercial cinema, reused the conventions of film noir in their debut feature films in order to construct a new version of political film.

After the fall of the dictatorship in 1974, and especially in the late 1970s, 'film noir', as a label and as a reconsideration of Hollywood's crime thrillers of the 1940s, began to attract critical attention and to acquire a cult status, while in Greek cinephilic culture, the term 'noir' was broadly used to describe a wide range of international films (Bakoyiannopoulos 1976: 7; Poupou 2020). At the same time and continuously until the 1990s arthouse filmmakers entered into a creative dialogue with noir features, combining elements from US and French classical noirs as well as from modernist European crime films, proposing new, 'guilt-free' hybridities between the sci-fi film and the *giallo* or the horror film.

Films by Nikos Nikolaidis, Nikos Panayotopoulos, Frieda Liappa and Nikos Zervos crystallise this turn towards the postmodernist phase of the Greek film noir, including more than thirty feature films and almost forty crime TV serials and shows. During the 1990s versions of playful retro-noir films attempted to portray a full array of social, national and gender anxieties in a period of intense transformation for post-socialist Greek society after the collapse of the USSR and the change in Athenian demographics due to immigration. Realist police dramas in film and televisual fiction presented dark images of the Athenian underworld that appeared in stark contrast to the media discourse of the time, which focused on the glamorous surface of Greek society during the years of preparation for the 2004 Olympic Games (Nikolaidou 2012; Kassaveti and Papoulis 2019).

In the years of the crisis, and in line with the new visibility of the Weird Wave, Greek filmmakers experimented with the generic conventions of the neo-noir. The crime films of Economides (*Machairovgaltis/Knifer*, 2010; *Mikro Psari/Stratos*, 2014; *I balada tis trypias kardias/Ballad for a Pierced Heart*, 2020) combine the auteur's distinctive style with a wide range of influences from Melville to the Coen brothers and Tarantino, while remaining within the paradigm of arthouse cinema (Poupou 2018; 2020). Between the strict use of generic conventions and hybrid explorations of the crime film, various versions of Greek noir have emerged: the subtle homage, and even self-homage (see Nikolaidis's oeuvre); the vulgar parody (*Halvai 5-0*, dir. Kampitis, 2020); the post-classical, nostalgic noir (*Big Hit*, dir. Zonaras, 2012); the financial crisis neo-noir (*Oi aisthimaties/The Sentimentalists*, dir. Triantafyllidis, 2014; *Tetarti 04:45/Wednesday 04:45*, dir. Alexiou, 2015), the latter employing classical codes and tropes, but giving them a more explicitly political twist; and Greek television appropriations of Nordic noir (Fessas 2021). The noir mode and mood can also be found in the investigation crime film *Eteros ego/Other Me* (dir. Tsafoulias, 2016) and in the social drama thriller *O ehthros mou/The Enemy Within* (dir. Tsemberopoulos, 2013). Moreover, weird and surrealist thrillers such as *The Waiter* (dir. Krikris, 2019), dark neo-noirs in a Lynchean vein such as *The Miracle of the Sargasso Sea*, or quirky depictions of the petty crime milieu in *Prostimo/Amercement* (dir. Bogris, 2020) are signs of a serious growth in noir diversities. How do we then define the Greek film noir?

Towards a Pragmatic Approach to Greek Noir

A 2020 entry on the blog *Noirsville* reads the Greek melodrama *Ta kokkina fanaria/The Red Lanterns* (dir. Georgiadis, 1963) as a noir.[1] The blogger explains his choice by referring to 'the darker side of human dramas' in the European continent, the bold topics, the working-class characters, the disreputable *milieu* of marginalised have-nots, tragedy and style; he goes on to support his view with textual evidence, including posters and screenshots.

Less flexible, purist approaches to Greek cinema and (noir) genre would disagree with such a reading against the grain, forgetting that, like its American and European predecessors, Greek film noir is a label constructed and employed *post facto*, and has an *a posteriori* validity (cf. Bordwell, Staiger and Thompson [1985] 2005: 78; Krutnik 1991: 17, 28; Cowie 1993: 121; Naremore [1998] 2008: 10; Conard 2006: 11).[2] Unsurprisingly, (mostly) early critics, reviewers and scholars back in the day referred to Greek films today described as noirs using various, sometimes related, generic terms: mystery film, *astynomiko*[3] (cop, crime or detective movie), (melo)drama, thriller. Other times they talked about comedies or adventure films, prioritising non-noir elements in the same films. Koundouros's *The Ogre of Athens* (see Karalis's chapter in this volume), today regarded by many as Greece's greatest noir, was originally promoted as 'social satire' (Soldatos 2004: 267).

In any case, despite more recent works (Dermentzoglou 2005; 2007)[4] that manifestly campaign for the definite existence of a Greek noir category, there has been significant resistance, or even denialism, on the part of Greek criticism and academia. At the root of this lie structuralist preconceptions and textualist 'prejudices' (cf. Klinger 1994: xiii, xviii); crudely put, if there is no *femme fatale*, with a certain iconography, performing a specific narrative function, or if the film is shot in a conventional way (for example, with no Dutch angles), featuring mainstream Greek cinema aesthetics, it cannot possibly be considered a noir (cf. Copjec 1993: xi).

Especially early or earlier critics and academics have insisted on the auteur factor (see Kartalou 2005: 64–6, 76, 86), or on national specificity, neglecting noir's firmly established cosmopolitanism and transnationalism (Spicer 2007; Spicer and Hanson 2013; Fay and Nieland 2010). Such approaches are unproductive in various ways. As Kartalou (2000: 105) has also noted in a non-noir context, they obstruct any serious discussion of neglected cultural artefacts, while perpetuating obsolete, elitist distinctions between high- and low-brow culture. Furthermore, they overlook or undermine the usefulness of genre as a research tool (Kartalou 2005; Grant 2003: xvi). By staunchly guarding borders (Altman 1999: 6, 205) and acting as cultural gatekeepers (Neale 2000b: 216), they miss various, exciting cases of genre hybridism.[5] In their non-pragmatism, they miss interactions between texts and contexts; therefore, they fail to use noir/genre to interpret sociocultural changes in Greece (Fotiou and Fessas 2017), but also subtle shifts in the non-linear evolution of Greek cinema over the last seventy years.

How did (neo-)noir become part of the Greek cultural vocabulary? This can be partly attributed to latter-day specialised publications such as *CLM* (*Crimes and Letters*) and *Polar* addressing noir in literature, film and other media, as well as Greek stage plays and graphic novels that have been promoted and received as noirs (Figure I.3).[6] But what about the unacknowledged but tangible influence of (neo-)noir in/on other media and snubbed areas of 'mainstream'

Figure I.3 Contemporary Genettian paratextual, epitextual, extratextual, intertextual and contextual material constitutes an interpretative discursive matrix through which older Greek filmic texts can be retrospectively read from a noir-saturated cultural vantage point. A page from Kyriakos Athanasiadis and Nikolas Kourtis, *Berlin: Protos Thanatos* (2020). Courtesy of Jemma Press.

Greek culture? See, for instance, the 1999 music video for pop star Giorgos Mazonakis's song 'Ena Keno' [A Void], directed by the later celebrated 'Weird' auteur Babis Makridis, and photographed by Lanthimos's collaborator Thimios Bakatakis. With its current cultural, transmediatic omnipresence, noir melts the boundaries between 'arthouse' and 'commercial'.

Other discussions, including the quest for the first Greek noir, are often plagued by essentialism (cf. Klinger 1994: xv–xvii; Spicer 2007: 2; Naremore [1998] 2008: 6), and typically ignore the institutional power and the historical position of the reviewer or the scholar in the game of genre (cf. Altman 1999: 9, 28; Naremore [1998] 2008: 11; Dix 2008: 174). Unsurprisingly, in an arteriosclerotic context, imagined (online) communities (Benedict Anderson's term) of Greek noir aficionados and bloggers and the industry-unauthorised 'lateral communication' (Altman 1999: 164, 198) between them are ignored as regards their role in the process described by Altman as 'regenrification'. With Oedipal themes being a notable subject of noir scholarship, as well as a criterion of genericity, is calling the myth of Oedipus 'noir' an anachronism?[7] And what exactly is involved in Ioakim Milonas explicitly shooting Oedipus's myth à la *Sin City* (see Costas Constandinides's chapter in this volume)?

In any case, the issue of how and why Greek film noir came to be when it did can be approached in two main ways. On the one hand, the historicist approach emphasises the turbulent social conditions, including mass migration and immigration, intensive urbanisation accompanied by loneliness, alienation, disenchantment, displacement and crime;[8] the political and economic backdrop (stark inequalities, unemployment); and the cultural climate in post-WWII and post-Civil War Greece, prominently featuring imported ways of life, the buzzing capital being filled with fast cars and modern apartments, fashionable alcoholic beverages, cigarette smoke, litres of platinum hair-dye, nightclubs and seductive (strip-)dancing. Furthermore, one must include the changes in film production, with small Greek studios that lacked stars and budgets opting to specialise in genre.[9]

On the other hand, there is the psychoanalytically informed approach (for example, Doane 1991: 2–3), which, however, does not exclude, for instance, the historical anchoring of male anxieties to socio-economic developments and cultural specificities (cf. Bergstrom 1993: 113; Hanson 2007: xv), including the newly gained financial and sexual empowerment of Greek women (taking a *fatale* form on the big screen) at the time, the seismic permutations of gender hierarchies and the wobbling patriarchy under Greek modernity and modernisation's – delayed – momentum.[10]

The modernity (and modernism) of Greek film noir of the 1950s and the 1960s can be read as the dark obverse of the 'idyllic' image of peaceful orderliness (Prevelakis 1990: 36; Gallant 2001: 214), as well as the utopian vision of unbridled prosperity, consumerism, upward social mobility,[11] Western modes of entertainment and looser sexual morals negotiated in Greek comedies of the same period.[12] One should also include in this process of modernisation the (belated) popularisation of psychoanalytic ideas and themes in Greece (Atzina 2004: 257; Fessas 2020: 283) – psychoanalysis being a key component of noir since its inception (Krutnik 1991: ch. 4; Naremore [1998] 2008: 40). The high-brow version of Greek modernism should not be excluded from this narrative: the pulp stories of Yannis Maris, Nikos Foskolos and Jimmy Corinis could be read alongside, for example, Giorgos Seferis's modernist poetry, and definitely next to Yannis Tsarouchis's distinctively noir *Neon Café (Night)* (1965–66) (Figure I.4).[13]

Greek film noir's more immediate and obvious predecessors include Greek pulp literature (see the semi-clandestine circulation of extremely popular magazines such as *Maska*, *Nyhterida* and *Mystirio*),[14] Maris's serialised stories and, later on, his novels, but also radio crime shows (Apostolidis 2012), the most memorable being Nikos Foskolos's *Astynomikes istories/Crime Stories*. An approach to genre that takes into account paratexts (cf. Kääpä 2020: 118; Stougaard-Nielsen 2020), contexts[15] or even 'transcontexts'[16] should also note

Figure I.4 Greek noir *avant la lettre*: Yannis Tsarouchis, *Neon Café (Night)* (1965–66), oil on canvas, 127 x 180 cm. Courtesy of National Gallery–Alexandros Soutsos Museum. Photographed by Stavros Psiroukis. The faceless human figures (including a solitary one in the foreground) are overshadowed by the architectural structure, enveloped in the mysterious Athenian night.

factors such as the cover art for recent reprints of Maris's works that can be instantly recognised as noir, while varying significantly from that of the older editions of the same works.

What, then, makes a Greek film a noir, but also what makes a noir a Greek film? Can we employ the term 'noir', not as a straitjacket, but more inclusively and democratically, without compromising its precision (Krutnik 1991: 16), conceptual accuracy (Dix 2008: 170) and uniqueness? In this volume, generically related but not identical terms – crime or detective film, film noir – crop up, and might appear to be used interchangeably. We are aware of the differences between cycles (for example, the noir police procedural, the gothic noir, etc.), as well as the different nuanced meanings of terms such as *policier* and 'hard-boiled'. Nevertheless, we believe that, especially at this nascent stage of Greek noir scholarship, it is more useful and productive to study the different forms the Greek crime film took under the unifying stylistic and thematic umbrella of 'noir', rather than remaining on a microscopic level of differences (cf. Dix 2008: 184-5).

From Yannis Economides to Nikos Zervos, from auteurism (including the celebrated totem of Theo Angelopoulos) to cult and gritty B-movies, and from animation and short film to web series, widely and wildly diverse Greek and Greek-Cypriot films and TV series, including European co-productions, are today labelled as noirs, or as having noir elements. The question, then, is not so much 'Is there such thing as a Greek noir?', or even 'What does it look like?', but rather 'Why is it important to study it?' What meanings can be ascribed to its continuous relevance, paradoxically combined, in the Greek context, with meagre performances at the box office?

Furthermore, late capitalism/neoliberalism and its discontents have prompted a new series of European/international noirs: films such as *Money* (dir. Babluani, 2017) and *In the Fade* (dir. Akin, 2017), political (neo-)noirs that take place around the Mediterranean basin during the 'Arab Spring' turmoil, others against a bleak background of a further impoverished (lumpen) proletarian suburbia, immigration and the renewed phenomenon of neo-fascism and racism, alongside Greek neo-noirs that tackle many of these issues simultaneously. Some filmmakers explicitly vilify IMF bureaucrats (Fotiou and Fessas 2017), while others employ the tropes of the psychological thriller to explore transcultural gender identities (*Pari*, dir. Etemadi, 2020). As various chapters in this book will show in more detail, we believe that we can delineate a hermeneutic framework of Mediterranean, European and American noir synergies. In the context of the European South, next to marginal(ised) artistic voices coming from post-colonial national cinemas and exemplary cases of what Spivak has called the subaltern speaking (the Georgian-French Babluani, Swedish-Egyptian Saleh, German-Turkish Akin, Greek-Cypriot Economides and Greek-Iranian Etemadi all embody diasporic, hybrid identities), the study of Greek film noir is directly linked to how Greeks see themselves as part of an increasingly dystopian landscape, and how they negotiate issues of identity and (self-)representation. As contributors in this volume will argue, Greek film noir thrived, at least artistically, both during periods of financial crisis, as well as (superficial) prosperity. It is noir's particular malleability, polysemy and openness to allegorical readings that render it perpetually adaptable to our ever-changing times.

The Structure of this Book

This volume is divided into two parts: the first presents the background, processes and agents that led to the creation of the noir genre in the Greek context during the 1950s and the 1960s. The chapters examine the features and particularities of the Greek films noirs, propose close readings of gender and sexual representations, and explore the contribution of music and literature to the formation of the genre. The second part focuses on the mutations of the Greek neo-noir from the 1970s to the present day, while highlighting its political and transnational aspects.

The first chapter by Vrasidas Karalis traces the noir elements in the early work of Nikos Koundouros and discusses *The Ogre of Athens* (1956) as a noir. Koundouros's film is considered one of the most important art films of the 1950s and has remained a major source of inspiration for the younger generations of auteurs. Maria Stassinopoulou focuses on *The Little Mouse* (1953), a film promoted as 'the first Greek police drama', and explains the reasons for the belated development of film noir in Greece. Analysing the film's latent political discourse, Stassinopoulou relates crime narratives and the representation of the police authorities to issues of youth delinquency and rehabilitation during the post-Civil War period. Yannis Tzioumakis discusses *The Angry Hills* (1959), a noir spy adventure shot in Greece by the prolific film noir experts Robert Aldrich and screenwriter A. I. Bezzerides; the author presents the efforts of the Greek film industry to host major international 'runaway' productions and illustrates its fertile encounter with Hollywood players, practices and craftsmanship.

In the fourth chapter Thanassis Agathos presents the founder of Greek crime fiction, Yannis Maris, examining the polyvalent work of the journalist, editor-in-chief, public persona, pulp fiction writer and avid cinephile, who penned several scripts for crime films and TV series from 1958 to the 1970s. Agathos's chapter features a close reading of the most famous film to come out of Maris's work, *Murder Backstage* (1960), which introduced to cinema the iconic Greek police detective, Officer Bekas.[17] Nick Poulakis presents another crucial contributor to Greek noir of the 1960s, the jazz composer Mimis Plessas, whose music was one of the most recognisable features of the Greek noir soundscape. Poulakis performs an original, close reading of the audiovisual dimensions of *Murder Backstage*. In the sixth chapter, Anna Poupou writes about the absence of the *femme fatale* figure and studies alternative femininities in Greek film noir through a reading of the noir psychological thriller *The Man on the Train* (1958), again based on a novel and script by Maris. Similarly within the field of noir representations of gender and sexualities, Nikitas Fessas explores one of the most provocative erotic B-movies of the 1960s, *The Bum of Fokionos Negri* (1965). The author focuses on the construction of the Greek noir queer through a discursive Foucauldian-Lacanian framework, reading the film alongside a journalistic article of the same year.

The second part of the volume opens with a chapter by Maria Chalkou, who presents two iconic films that marked the emergence of New Greek Cinema: *Kierion* (1967–74) and *Reconstruction* (1970). Although these two films constitute key moments in the history of modernist cinema in Greece, their relation to noir conventions has never been discussed thoroughly. Drawing on the theoretical writings of Deuleze, Ioulia Mermigka analyses *John the Violent* (1973), one of the most controversial films made during the junta, and probably the only Greek neo-noir directed by a woman, Tonia Marketaki. Mermigka reads John's process of 'becoming-murderer' as intersected with issues such as police repression, the media fascination with sex crime and moral panics, as well as the juridical regimes of truth and judgement on crime and madness. Marios Psaras utilises an eclectic arsenal that mixes queer theory, psychoanalytic feminism and ethical philosophy to analyse postmodernist strategies employed in *Singapore Sling* (1990). While describing an unforgettable appropriation of noir aesthetics, the author digs out a mythical *bête noire*: director Nikos Nikolaidis's abject (non-)representational politics, and an 'unsafe' mode that turns the spotlight on the way the spectator is implicated in mainstream cinema's fetishistic treatment of images of sex, violence and suffering.

Yun-hua Chen reads Alexis Alexiou's *Wednesday 04:45* (2015) alongside John Woo's *A Better Tomorrow* (1986), drawing parallels between their different contexts: financial crisis Athens and post-handover Hong Kong. Alexiou has admitted that Woo was a major influence on him, and Chen uses this case study to delineate the transnational connections of neo-noir. She focuses on the dialectics between global and local, the universal or the generic and the specific, through the representation of bleak transitory spaces and 'non-places' reflecting metropolises in socio-economic and cultural turmoil, as well as through the notion of 'elsewhere'. Costas Constandinides' chapter examines the use of noir elements in four Greek-Cypriot fictional shorts produced during the last decade. He argues that their sinister themes and dark aesthetics challenge 'the cinema of the Cyprus Problem' and other 'official', stereotypical and idyllic visual narratives of Cypriot society and landscape. Georgia Aitaki and Spyridon Chairetis look at the construction of noir masculinities through the figure of the detective in three iconic Greek crime TV shows from the last three decades: *Tmima ithon/Vice Squad* (ANT1, 1992–95), *Oi istories tou astynomou Beka/The Stories of Officer Bekas* (ALPHA, 2006–08) and *Eteros ego: Hamenes psyches/The Other Me: Lost Souls* (COSMOTE, 2019–20). Opting for an approach that utilises textual, intertextual and extratextual elements, the authors follow the evolution of this character type in his various embodiments, analysing the performances as well as the actors' star images, which carry various connotations. Dennis Broe puts Greek (neo-)noir on the European, Mediterranean and international maps, offering a class-oriented historical perspective and retrospective, a valuable unifying narrative that includes various seminal instances of a vibrant style that is read here as a reaction to, and a critique of, various forms of capitalist exploitation, institutional repression and sociopolitical corruption. In the Appendix, Nikitas Fessas proposes a corpus spanning eight decades, which consists of celebrated as well as lesser-known Greek films and TV series that invite noir readings.

Acknowledgements

A version of the subsection entitled 'Towards a Pragmatic Approach to Greek Noir' (updated and adapted here by the author) is part of Nikitas Fessas's doctoral thesis (2019). In collaboration with Maria Chalkou, the subsection entitled 'Greek Film Noir: A Possible Periodisation' was developed and documented in the framework of the research project 'Film Noir in Greece: Reception, Assimilation and Imitation of a US Film Genre, from the Post-war Period until Today', which was financed by the Operational Programme Human Resources Development, Education and Lifelong Learning, P.A. 2014–20 (European Structural and Investment Funds of the European Union). Members of the research team were Leonidas Papadopoulos, Anna Poupou and Eva Stefani (National and Kapodistrian University of Athens).

Notes

1. The subheading actually classifies it within an even more specific and specialised sub-category of noir: 'Christmas noirs'.
2. For a Lacanian meta-critique, see Tyrer (2016).
3. See, for example, Stavrakas (1967); Kambanellis (1969); Mitropoulou ([1980] 2005: 118, quoted in Kartalou 2005: 61–2, 65).
4. See also Panayiotatos's documentary *Xenes se xeni hora: 50 ellinikes tainies mystiriou kai fantasias/Strangers in a Strange Land: 50 Greek Mystery and Fantasy Movies* (2009).
5. Cf. Staiger (1997); Neale (2000a; 2000b: 45, 65, 199, 201). In the Appendix at the end of this volume such issues are (at least partially) circumvented, as the list includes films and TV series featuring dominant (neo-)noir tropes.
6. In 2012 the stage adaptation of Maris's 1954 novel *Eglima sta paraskinia* [Murder Backstage] was promoted as a 'noir play' (Culturenow 2012). The recent wave

of Greek noir graphic novels includes Derveniotis's *Yesternow* (2017) and *Shark Nation* (2018), and *Berlin: Protos Thanatos/Berlin: First Death*, by Athanasiadis and Kourtis (2020).
7. Billy Wilder famously quipped: 'But certainly I would also think Oedipus is a play *noir*, right?' (Porfirio 2002: 103).
8. In Greece in the 1960s, 'individual interpersonal violence was [. . .] delegitimized [. . .] violence [. . .] becomes structural, faceless, big city, urban lifestyle-violence [. . .] against which [allegedly] only family relations can act protectively' (Avdela 2006: 238). This also happens to be an accurate description of the noir world, with the crucial addition that not even the family realm is safe in noir (cf. Harvey 1978).
9. For the account in this paragraph, see Kouvertaris and Dobratz (1987: 20); Gallant (2001: 188, 195); Delveroudi (2000: 165–70; 2002: 61–70); Athanasatou (2001); Milonaki (2004); Makrinioti (2006: 211–12); Kosma (2007b); Karalis (2012: 30, 63, 67, 82, 105–6, 108, 129); Hadjikyriacou (2013: 26, 44, 49–50, 62, n. 139, 76, 87, 91, 107, 126, 168, 173, 201, 242, 254).
10. See Delveroudi (2000; 2002; 2004); Makrinioti (2006); Kosma (2007a); Hadjikyriacou (2013: 28, 40–1, 195, 219–20, 262, 264); Fessas and Kosma (2017: 84–5, 90–1).
11. See Athanasatou (2001: 103); Close (2002: xiv, 59, 68); Milonaki (2004: 180–98, 294–6); Makrinioti (2006).
12. Delveroudi (2000: 172–3; 2002; 2004); Kosma (2007a; 2007b); Hadjikyriacou (2013: 147, n. 96).
13. Cf. Slavoj Žižek's relevant comments (Žižek 1991: 48–9; Van Hulle 2007: 325). Apostolidis (2012: 52) has argued that the 'pope' of Greek pulp/crime fiction of the time, Yannis Maris, was directly influenced by the modernist novel, in works such as *I exafanisi tou John Avlakioti* [The Disappearance of John Avlakiotis]. Naremore has talked about modernism and film noir ([1998] 2008: ch. 2), and has noted the relation between the institutionalisation of modern art, the popularisation of psychoanalytic ideas and film noir ([1998] 2008: 319, n. 16). See also Luhr (2012: 5).
14. See Angelakos (1984); Corinis (2010); Kouzeli (2012); Filippou (2018: 40–7, 51–62).
15. For the importance of careful contextualisation in relation to film(s) noir, see Palmer (2006: 189–90).
16. For Bateson (1972: 272–3), the transcontextual involves '[e]xogenous experience [that] may be framed in the context of dreams, and internal thought [that] may be projected into the contexts of the external world' (quoted by Silver 2006: 224).
17. In Maris's novels, the rank of Bekas is 'Officer' (*astynomos*), chief of the Third Police Department of Athens. However, in recent translations of his novels in English he is referred to as 'Inspector'.

References

Altman, Rick (1999), *Film/Genre*, London: BFI.
Angelakos, Christos (1984), 'Poios thymatai ti Maska' [Who Remembers 'Mask'], *Diavazo*, 86, pp. 10–11.

Apostolidis, Andreas (2012), *O kosmos tou Yanni Mari* [Yannis Maris's World], Athens: Agra.
Athanasatou, Yanna (2001), *Ellinikos kinimatografos (1950–1967): Laiki mnimi kai ideologia* [Greek Cinema (1950–1967): Popular Memory and Ideology], Athens: Finatec.
Athanasiadis, Kyriakos, and Kourtis, Nikolas (2020), *Berlin: Protos Thanatos* [Berlin: First Death], Piraeus: Jemma.
Atzina, Lena (2004), *I makra eisagogi tis psychanalysis stin Ellada* [The Long Introduction of Psychoanalysis in Greece], Athens: Exantas.
Avdela, Efi (2006), *Dia logous timis: Via, synaisthimata kai axies sti metemfyliaki Ellada* [For Reasons of Honour: Violence, Emotions and Values in Post-Civil War Greece], Athens: Nefeli.
Bakoyiannopoulos, Yannis (1976), 'Kritiki kinimatografou: Godard kai film noir se apolyto adiexodo' [Film Review: Godard and Film Noir at a Dead End], *Kathimerini*, 17 February, p. 7.
Bateson, Gregory (1972), *Steps to an Ecology of Mind*, New York: Ballantine.
Bergstrom, Janet (1993), 'The Mystery of *The Blue Gardenia*', in Joan Copjec (ed.), *Shades of Noir*, London: Verso, pp. 97–120.
Bordwell, David, Staiger, Janet, and Thompson, Kristin ([1985] 2005), *The Classical Hollywood Cinema: Film Style and Mode of Production to 1960*, London: Routledge.
Chalkou, Maria (2008), 'Towards the Creation of "Quality" Greek National Cinema in the 1960s', PhD dissertation, University of Glasgow.
Cigarjoe (2020), 'The Red Lanterns (1963) aka (Ta Kokkina Fanaria) Greek Noir', 6 January, <https://noirsville.blogspot.com/2020/01/the-red-lanterns-1963-aka-ta-kokkina.html?zx=ea2f458d88b94514> (last accessed 1 August 2021).
Close, David H. (2002), *Greece Since 1945: Politics, Economy and Society*, Abingdon: Routledge.
Conard, Mark T. (2006), *The Philosophy of Film Noir*, Lexington, KY: University Press of Kentucky.
Copjec, Joan (ed.) (1993), *Shades of Noir*, London: Verso.
Corinis, Jimmy (2010), 'Pulp Magazines – Stin epohi tis Maskas' [Pulp Magazines – In the Age of Mask], *Arta Press*, 53, <https://archive.artapress.gr/articles/608/> (last accessed 7 August 2021).
Cowie, Elizabeth (1993), 'Film Noir and Women', in Joan Copjec (ed.), *Shades of Noir*, London: Verso, pp. 121–65.
Culturenow (2012), 'Eglima sta paraskinia, tou Yanni Mari' [*Murder Backstage* by Yannis Maris], *Culturenow.gr*, 7 November, <https://www.culturenow.gr/egklima-sta-paraskinia-tou-gianni-mari/> (last accessed 7 August 2021).
Delveroudi, Eliza-Anna (2000), 'Ellinikos kinimatografos 1955–1965: Koinonikes allages tis metapolemikis epohis stin othoni' [Greek Cinema 1955–1965: Post-War Social Changes on Screen], in *1949–1967: I ekriktiki eikosaetia* [1949–1967: Twenty Explosive Years], Athens: Etaireia Spoudon Neoellinikou Politismou kai Yenikis Paideias, pp. 163–76.
Delveroudi, Eliza-Anna (2002), 'O thisavros tou makariti: I komodia, 1950–1970' [Dead Man's Treasure: The Comedy, 1950–1970], *Optikoakoustiki Koultoura*, 1:1, pp. 53–77.

Delveroudi, Eliza-Anna (2004), *Oi neoi stis komodies tou ellinikou kinimatografou: 1948–1974* [Young People in the Comedies of Greek Cinema: 1948–1974], Athens: National Hellenic Research Foundation.

Dermentzoglou, Alexis (2005), *To petagma tou anaptira: Sygritiki matia sto evropaiko kai sto amerikaniko noir* [The Throwing of the Lighter: A Comparative Look at European and American Noir], Thessaloniki: Erodios.

Dermentzoglou, Alexis (ed.) (2007), *In a Dark Passage: Film Noir in Greek Cinema*, Thessaloniki: Erodios.

Dermentzopoulos, Christos (2021), 'Tainies gia oli tin elliniki oikogeneia. O laikos kinimatografos stin Ellada (1950–1975)' [*Films for all the Greek Family*. Popular Cinema in Greece (1950–1975)], in Dermentzopoulos Christos and Yannis Papatheodorou (eds), *Synithismenoi anthropoi* [Common People], Patra: Opportuna, pp. 433–79.

Derveniotis, Spyros (2017), *Yesternow*, Athens: Haramada.

Derveniotis, Spyros (2018), *Shark Nation*, Athens: Haramada.

Dimendberg, Edward (2004), *Film Noir and the Spaces of Modernity*, Cambridge, MA: Harvard University Press.

Dix, Andrew (2008), *Beginning Film Studies*, Manchester: Manchester University Press.

Doane, Mary A. (1991), *Femmes Fatales: Feminism, Film Theory, Psychoanalysis*, New York: Routledge.

Fay, Jennifer, and Nieland, Justus (2010), *Film Noir: Hard-Boiled Modernity and the Cultures of Globalization*, Abingdon: Routledge.

Fessas, Nikitas (2019), 'Athens by Night: Representations of Gendered Sexualities in Greek Film Noir of the 1950s and the 1960s', PhD dissertation, University of Ghent.

Fessas, Nikitas (2020), 'Representations of Disability in 1960s Greek Film Noirs: *The Secret of the Red Mantle* and *The Fear*', *Journal of Literary & Cultural Disability Studies*, 14:3, pp. 281–99.

Fessas, Nikitas (2021), Review, '*Nordic Noir, Adaptation, Appropriation* by Linda Badley, Andrew Nestingen, and Jaakko Seppälä (eds)', *Critical Studies in Television*, 16:4, pp. 468–70.

Fessas, Nikitas, and Kosma, Yvonne (2017), 'The Crisis of Gender Identity in the Greek Film Noir: Sexuality, Paranoia and the Unconscious in *Efialtis/Nightmare* (1961) and *O Ergenis/The Bachelor* (1997)', *Filmicon: Journal of Greek Film Studies*, 4, pp. 83–109.

Filippou, Filippos (2018), *Istoria tis ellinikis astynomikis logotehnias: O Yannis Maris kai oi alloi* [History of Greek Crime Literature: Yannis Maris and the Others], Athens: Patakis.

Fotiou, Mikela, and Fessas, Nikitas (2017), 'Greek Neo-Noir: Reflecting a Narrative of Crisis', *Filmicon: Journal of Greek Film Studies*, 4, pp. 110–37.

Gallant, Thomas (2001), *Modern Greece: Brief Histories*, London: Arnold.

Grant, Barry Keith (2003), 'Introduction', in Barry Keith Grant (ed.), *Film Genre Reader III*, Austin, TX: University of Texas Press, pp. xv–xx.

Hadjikyriacou, Achilleas (2013), *Masculinity and Gender in Greek Cinema: 1949–1967*, New York: Bloomsbury.

Hanson, Helen (2007), *Hollywood Heroines: Women in Film Noir and the Female Gothic Film*, London: I.B. Tauris.

Harvey, Sylvia (1978), 'Woman's Place: The Absent Family of Film Noir', in E. Ann Kaplan (ed.), *Women in Film Noir*, London: BFI, pp. 22–34.

Kääpä, Pietari (2020), '"Why Don't We Do Television Like That in the UK?": Promotional and Paratextual Strategies in the Transnational Branding of Nordic Noir', in Linda Badley, Andrew Nestingen and Jaakko Seppälä (eds), *Nordic Noir, Adaptation, Appropriation*, Basingstoke: Palgrave Macmillan, pp. 113–33.

Kambanellis, Iakovos (1969), 'Skepseis kai diapistoseis' [Thoughts and Remarks], *Synchronos Kinimatografos*, 2, pp. 8–10.

Karalis, Vrasidas (2012), *A History of Greek Cinema*, New York: Continuum.

Kartalou, Athena (2000), 'Gender, Professional, and Class Identities in *Miss Director* and *Modern Cinderella*', *Journal of Modern Greek Studies*, 18:1, pp. 105–18.

Kartalou, Athena (2005), 'To anekpliroto eidos: Oi tainies koinonikis katangelias tis Finos Film' [The Uncompleted Genre: Finos Films' Films of Social Denouncement], PhD dissertation, Panteion University.

Kassaveti, Ursula-Helen, and Papoulis, Athanasios (2019), 'Outside of Society: The Representation of Athenian Outcasts in *Tmima Iton/Vice Squad*', *Filmicon: Journal of Greek Film Studies*, 6, pp. 40–68.

Klinger, Barbara (1994), *Melodrama and Meaning: History, Culture, and the Films of Douglas Sirk*, Bloomington, IN: Indiana University Press.

Kosma, Yvonne-Alexia (2007a), 'Eikones gia to fylo mesa apo ton elliniko kinimatografo sti dekaetia tou'60: Fylo kai sexualikotita sto eidos tis aisthimatikis comedi (1959–1967)' [Images of Gender in Greek Cinema of the 1960s: Gender and Sexuality in the Romantic Comedy Genre (1959–1967)], PhD dissertation, National and Kapodistrian University of Athens.

Kosma, Yvonne-Alexia (2007b), 'Representations of Gender in Narrative Film: Images of Femininity in Greek Romantic Comedies of the 1960s and Adapting the Hollywood Ideal', *The International Journal of Interdisciplinary Social Sciences: Annual Review*, 2:3, pp. 213–18.

Kouvertaris, Yorgos A., and Dobratz, Betty A. (1987), *A Profile of Modern Greece: In Search of Identity*, Oxford: Clarendon Press.

Kouzeli, Lambrini (2012), '"I Maska" ehei ti diki tis istoria' ['The Mask' Has its own History], *To Vima*, 29 July, <https://www.tovima.gr/2012/07/29/books-ideas/i-maska-exei-ti-diki-tis-istoria/> (last accessed 7 August 2021).

Krutnik, Frank (1991), *In a Lonely Street: Film Noir, Genre, Masculinity*, London: Routledge.

Luhr, William (2012), *Film Noir*, Malden, MA: Wiley-Blackwell.

Makrinioti, Dimitra (2006), 'Morfes diaheirisis tis paidikis ilikias stis tainies tis periodou 1950–1968' [Forms of Representation of Childhood in Films of the Period 1950–1968], in Vaso Theodorou, Maria Moumoulidou and Anastasia Oikonomidou (eds), *"Piase me, An Boreis. . .": I paidiki ilikia kai oi anaparastaseis tis ston synchrono elliniko kinimatografo* ['Catch Me if You Can . . .': Representations of Childhood in Contemporary Greek Cinema], Athens: Aigokeros, pp. 200–29.

Maris, Yannis (2008), *I Exafanisi tou Tzon Avlakioti* [The Disappearance of John Avlakiotis], Athens: Atlantis.

Milonaki, Angeliki (2004), 'Anaparastaseis tou astikou horou ston elliniko dimofili kinimatografo (1950–1970)' [Representations of the Urban Space in Greek Popular Cinema (1950–1970)], PhD dissertation, Aristotle University of Thessaloniki.

Mitropoulou, Aglaia ([1980] 2005), *Ellinikos kinimatografos* [Greek Cinema], Athens, Papazissis.

Mitsis, Christos (2019), 'To thavma tis thalassas ton Sargasson' [The Miracle of the Sargasso Sea], *Athinorama*, 21 November, <https://www.athinorama.gr/cinema/article/to_thauma_tis_thalassas_ton_sargasson-2538680.html> (last accessed 8 August 2021).

Naremore, James ([1998] 2008), *More Than Night: Film Noir in its Contexts*, Berkeley, CA: University of California Press.

Neale, Steve (2000a), 'Questions of Genre', in Robert Stam and Toby Miller (eds), *Film and Theory: An Anthology*, Malden, MA: Blackwell, pp. 157–78.

Neale, Steve (2000b), *Genre and Hollywood*, Abingdon: Routledge.

Nikolaidou, Afroditi (2012), 'Oi tainies polis tou ellinikou kinimatografou' [The City Films of Greek Cinema (1994–2004)], PhD dissertation, Panteion University.

Palmer, R. Barton (2006), 'Moral Man in the Dark City: Film Noir, the Postwar Religious Revival, and *The Accused*', in Mark T. Conard (ed.), *The Philosophy of Film Noir*, Lexington, KY: University Press of Kentucky, pp. 187–206.

Papadimitriou, Lydia (2006), *The Greek Film Musical: A Critical and Cultural History*, Jefferson, NC: McFarland.

Papanikolaou, Dimitris (2021), *Greek Weird Wave: A Cinema of Biopolitics*, Edinburgh: Edinburgh University Press.

Petsini, Penelope (2016), 'Logokritikoi michanismoi stin kataskevi "emvlimatikon morfon" tis ellinikis fotografias' [Censorship Mechanisms in the Creation of 'Emblematic Forms' of Greek Photography], in Penelope Petsini and Christopoulos Dimitris (eds), *I logokrisia stin Ellada* [Censorship in Greece], Athens: Rosa-Luxemburg-Stiftung, pp. 266–75.

Pettey, Homer B., and Palmer, Barton R. (2014), *International Noir*, Edinburgh: Edinburgh University Press.

Porfirio, Robert (2002), 'Billy Wilder', in Robert Porfirio, Alain Silver and James Ursini (eds), *Film Noir Reader 3: Interviews with Filmmakers of the Classic Noir Period*, New York: Limelight.

Poupou, Anna (2007), 'Représenter la reconstruction: Le paysage urbain dans les films grecs de la période 1950–1974', PhD dissertation, Sorbonne Nouvelle-Paris III.

Poupou, Anna (2018), 'Social Space, Architecture and the Crisis. Neo-noir Aesthetics in Contemporary Greek Cinema', in Filipa Rosário and Iván Villarmea Álvarez (eds), *New Approaches to Cinematic Space*, Abingdon: Routledge, pp. 27–41.

Poupou, Anna (2020), 'The Greek Version of Film Noir: Dark Narratives and Political Allegories in Periods of Crisis', in Vassilios Sabatakakis (ed.), *The Greek World in Periods of Crisis and Recovery, 1204–2018*, Athens: European Society of Modern Greek Studies, pp. 29–52.

Poupou, Anna (2021), 'Synitheis ypoptoi, asynithistoi horoi. I kinimagrafiki geografia tou ellinikou thriller' [Usual Suspects, Unusual Spaces. The Film Geography of the Greek Thriller], in Christos Dermentzopoulos and Yannis Papatheodorou (eds), *Synithismenoi anthropoi* [Common People], Patra: Opportuna, pp. 481–508.

Prevelakis, George (1990), 'Center–Periphery and the Urban Crisis of Athens', *Ekistics*, 57:340–1, pp. 35–43.

Silver, Alain (2006), 'Ride the Pink Horse: Money, Mischance, Murder, and the Monads of Film Noir', in Mark T. Conard (ed.), *The Philosophy of Film Noir*, Lexington, KY: University Press of Kentucky, pp. 223–37.

Soldatos, Yannis (1999), *Istoria tou ellinikou kinimatografou* [History of Greek Cinema], vol. 1, Athens: Aigokeros.

Soldatos, Yannis (2004), *Istoria tou ellinikou kinimatografou: Documenta 1900–1970* [History of Greek Cinema, Documents 1900–1970], vol. 4, Athens: Aigokeros.

Sotiropoulou, Chrysanthe (1995), *I diaspora ston elliniko kinimatografo – Epidraseis kai epiroes sti thematologiki exelixi ton tainion tis periodou 1945-1986* [The Diaspora in Greek Cinema – Effects and Influences on the Thematic Development of the Films of the Period 1945-1986], Athens: Themelio.

Spicer, Andrew (ed.) (2007), *European Film Noir*, Manchester: Manchester University Press.

Spicer, Andrew, and Hanson, Helen (eds) (2013), *A Companion to Film Noir*, Chichester: Wiley-Blackwell.

Staiger, Janet (1997), 'Hybrid or Inbred: The Purity Hypothesis and Hollywood Genre History', *Film Criticism*, 22:1, pp. 5–20.

Stassinopoulou, Maria A. (2000), 'Reality Bites: A Feature Film History of Greece 1950-1963', unpublished habilitation thesis, University of Vienna.

Stavrakas, Dimitris (1967), 'Poreia kai Prooptikes tou ellinikou kinimatografou' [Course and Prospects of Greek Cinema], *Ellinikos Kinimatografos*, 3–4, pp. 5–12.

Stougaard-Nielsen, Jakob (2020), 'Revisiting the Crime Scene: Intermedial Translation, Adaptation, and Novelization of The Killing', in Linda Badley, Andrew Nestingen and Jaakko Seppälä (eds), *Nordic Noir, Adaptation, Appropriation*, Basingstoke: Palgrave Macmillan, pp. 89–111.

Tyrer, Ben (2016), *Out of the Past: Lacan and Film Noir*, Basingstoke: Palgrave Macmillan.

Valoukos, Stathis, and Spiliopoulos, Vasilis (1985), *To Film Noir* [Film Noir], Athens: Nea Synora – A. A. Livanis.

Van Hulle, Dirk (2007), 'Modernism, Consciousness, Poetics of Process', in Astradur Eysteinsson and Vivian Liska (eds), *Modernism: A Comparative History of Literatures in European Languages*, vol. 1, Amsterdam: John Benjamins, pp. 321–37.

Žižek, Slavoj (1991), *Looking Awry: An Introduction to Jacques Lacan through Popular Culture*, Cambridge, MA: MIT Press.

PART I

PARTNERS IN CRIME: RECEPTIONS, AFFINITIES, HYBRIDITIES

1. THERE WILL BE OGRES: THE INTERSTITIAL AESTHETICS OF FILM NOIR IN THE EARLY FILMS OF NIKOS KOUNDOUROS

Vrasidas Karalis

CONDITIONS FOR THE RECEPTION OF A STYLE

Given the rather indeterminate nature and vague definition of film noir as a genre by scholars, even in its native country of the United States, there is always a question about which elements of its visual grammar, or parts of its thematic lines, or *mise en scène*, could have been adopted by a peripheral and, at that time, still unorganised film industry like that of Greece in the 1950s. Furthermore, film noir was not a genre whose theoretical or critical principles were formed or addressed in the concrete manner that we find in movements such as German Expressionism and Soviet montage cinematography before the Second World War, or Italian neorealism afterwards. It was a diffuse visual style, an emotional atmosphere more than a generic form, which eventually was transformed into an existential mood, defined by emotions generated in an unfriendly, alienated and horizonless urban world, a world of moral ambiguities in which everything was beyond human control. As Thomas Schatz (1981: 113) pointed out, film noir 'documented the growing disillusionment with certain traditional American values in the face of complex and often contradictory social, political, scientific and economic developments'.

Such an atmosphere of disillusionment, bordering on deep pessimism and, occasionally, nihilism, can be detected in the work of many popular directors since the beginning of cinema, reflecting or indeed *refracting* the various sociopolitical vicissitudes and aesthetic concerns of the post-war era. It also suggested the deep existential traumas, social panics, as well as psychological conflicts that dominated the visual imaginary, explored through the most advanced form of technological modernity, the cinema. In a way, it expressed cinematic versions of the 'problematic hero', whose emergence in the beginning of modernity defined the literary genre of the novel as experiencing 'transcendental homelessness' in an era of 'absolute sinfulness' (Lukács [1920] 1971: 18, 41). Such a homeless, indeed centreless, character without redemption in a sinful world is also the main thematic reference of most films noirs at least during the peak moment of the early 1950s.

The movies we call noir today were also veritable by-products of the film industry and its distribution system, in its promotional practice of selling blocks of films which was related to the structural need of the big studios to develop and test the emerging stars of the industry (see Kerr [1979] 1996; Maltby [1995] 2003). It therefore presupposed a high level of organisation, promotion and distribution networks which were central structural and operational characteristics of the studio era (Kerr [1979] 1996: 112–17), as well as an implied distinction between high and popular art, which we cannot find in the foundational and infrastructural presuppositions of Greek cinema.

In its cultural aspect, it foregrounded the dark subtexts that emerged under the optimistic façade of reconstruction that dominated the post-war cinematic imaginary in the United States, and that would resurface potently at the end of the next decade, when the genre turned its attention to the gradual transformation of the American dream into an authoritarian nightmare. However, James Naremore (1998: 2) sees the genre as 'one of the dominant intellectual categories of the late twentieth century, operating across the entire cultural arena of art, popular memory, and criticism'. From another point of view, we cannot really tell if the category is a projection from today's expectations on to the past, fabricated, as Mark Bould (2005: 23) claimed, through 'a congelation of narratives about certain films told by different discursive agents at specific historical junctures'; or whether it was consciously practised, or viewers were asking for it, in the intellectual horizon of the post-war era. In any case, film noir exhibited 'the state of tension created in the spectators by the disappearance of their psychological bearings. The vocation of film noir has been to create a specific sense of malaise' (Borde and Chaumeton [1955] 2002: 13). Such malaise was the central organising mythos of its structural poetics.

Moreover, film noir is about urban spaces and the tense psychodynamics of the sprawling cityscapes that emerged after the trauma of the war. They take place in trauma-scapes, when any existential balance is lost after an irregular presence appears, usually a *femme fatale* or someone from the past, who ruptures the continuity and the cohesion between the inner world of repression and the outer reality of oppression. At the same time, their *mise en scène* sets out a chain of events that indicates the cost of psychological adjustment to the new dominant social forces, which is always beyond and above the endurance of individuals. The collapsing individual, especially the masculine subject, stands at the heart of a transition towards a reconstructed reality in which there is no place for him. The lighting, the downbeat monochrome tones, the low camera angles, the stark contrasts between light and darkness indicate a new relationship with space, both physical and psychological. It is a *negative space*, expressionistically manipulated and distorted, which expels people from it by altering its balance, symmetry and proportion. In a way, it is the romantic imaginary in its cinematic version, presenting the nightmarish and absurd world that we see in Goya's *Capricios* or Piranesi's *Labyrinths*, translated into the realm of cultural or individual fantasies in which the irrational and the comically irrational converge and symbiotically coexist.

Consequently, the answer to the question whether, and to what extent, Greek directors could relate to the most popular genre of the period is rather self-evident. Many Greek but also global directors, as for example Akira Kurosawa in *Nora inu/Stray Dog* (1949), had already discovered *indirectly* elements of the film noir visual language: through German Expressionism, Soviet cinema and Italian neo-realism. Historically, film noir's stylistic forms originated from such movements. Fritz Lang's presence in Hollywood made the connection with pre-war German film production visible and active, and translated the representational codes of Expressionism into the more naturalistic and narrative-focused Hollywood films of the studio era. But also in France, elements of the 'dark style' can be detected in Jean Renoir's *Les Bas-Fonds/The Lower Depths* (1936), Julien Duvivier's *Pépé le Moko* (1937), Marcel Carné's *Le Quai des brumes/Port of Shadows* (1938) and *Le Jour se lève/Daybreak* (1939).

The noir style was the outcome of an accumulative reinscription of certain visual schemata through successive transcultural readaptations. Probably the prototype of the film noir aesthetic can be found in Boris Ingster's *Stranger on the Third Floor* (1940), which is considered the first 'true film noir of the classic period (1940–1959)' (Biesen 2005: 22), as suggested by many scholars. Nicholas Musuraca's camerawork in this film paved the way for more ambitious camera experiments by Gregg Toland (*Citizen Kane*, dir. Welles, 1941), Arthur Edeson (*The Maltese Falcon*, dir. Huston, 1941), John Alton (*He Walked by Night*, dir. Werker, 1948) and Max Greene (*Night and the City*, dir. Dassin, 1950) and, indirectly, for the cinematography of Greek camera stylists such as Jason Novak, Aristeidis Karydis-Fuchs and Kostas Theodoridis, whose camerawork defined the development of post-war cinema in Greece until the arrival of Walter Lassaly in Athens in 1955.

The style appeared in Greek cinema when radical changes *vis-à-vis* the production lines of the period were taking place. After the end of the Second World War, Greek cinema was becoming, for the first time, organised around studios, such as Finos Films, Anzervos and Spentzos Films, which wanted to monopolise the few venues and the distribution companies for local films, in their fierce competition with, mostly American, imported movies. The emergence of independent small producers, but also the proliferation of cinematic venues in the early 1950s, took place gradually during the expansive industrialisation and urbanisation of Athens. Furthermore, the screening of international art films from the United States, Britain, France, Italy and the Soviet Union indicated that the local film industry was gradually consolidating itself. In this process, the urgent quest for new directors, cinematographers, actors but, most importantly, successful films in popular styles started to gain momentum, and led to the explosive creativity of the 1950s and 1960s, the Golden Age of Greek cinema.

At this historical juncture, Greek cinema is inextricably connected with the work and career of Nikos Koundouros (1926–2017). From his first to his last film, Koundouros articulated, elaborated and renegotiated a visual language that provoked and challenged popular codes of representation and their ideological underpinnings. Almost all his films stood apart as unique visual testimonies to the gradual expansion of the field of visuality, in opposition to the optical regimes that became dominant in the Greek cinematic tradition and defined its various genres and narrative structures. Koundouros's dialogue with many genres and regimes of seeing, and especially with noir, is, however, of specific importance, because it indicates some of the most salient undercurrents in the field of visuality as established in the country during the Golden Age of Greek cinema. These undercurrents gradually led to the formation of a local version of the noir genre, starting with Dinos Dimopoulos's *O anthropos tou trenou/The Man on the Train* (1958), and developing into its later reincarnation with the neo-noir of Nikos Nikolaidis's films, as Mikela Fotiou and Nikitas Fessas have argued (2017).

The departure, within a wider movement of cinematic redefinition after the introduction of montage as a central cinematic practice, started around the end of the 1940s, when we can clearly detect new regimes of visual representation being explored after the gradual destructuration of the melodramas and costume period pieces that dominated the early decades. Definitely, the turning point came with Grigoris Grigoriou's *Pikro psomi/Bitter Bread* (1951), although his *O kokkinos vrahos/Red Cliff* (1949) can also be credited for stylistic innovations. Before Grigoriou, the unexpected visual experiments with light, space and narrative temporality found in the films of Yorgos Tzavellas must be mentioned. His early films, especially *Heirokrotimata/Applause* (1944) and *Prosopa lismonimena/Forgotten Faces* (1946), bear obvious traces of two major innovations: first the extensive use of montage and, second, the pervasive impact of continuity editing (Karalis 2017: 60). Other directors such as Stelios Tatasopoulos, Alekos Sakellarios and the first Greek woman director, Maria Plyta, employed analogous devices in the attempt to create a cinematic idiom based on the visual practices of local pictorial traditions and regimes of seeing.

The fusion of so many diverse, and somehow incommensurable, aesthetics became the springboard for one of the most important directors of the period, Michael Cacoyannis. They can also be found creatively reimagined in Koundouros's work, especially in his early films, representing his permanent contribution to the cinematic visuality of the nascent Greek film industry in the 1950s. Hence, the visual language and cinematic imaginary of Koundouros were made possible through the confluence of a number of technological, structural and stylistic innovations introduced between 1945 and 1955 in Greek cinema.

Furthermore, as I have argued elsewhere, Koundouros liked working with duologies, as Theo Angelopoulos later worked with trilogies. His first two films, *Magiki polis*/*The Magic City* (1954) and *O drakos*/*The Ogre of Athens* (1956), constitute a formal and thematic unity and employ similar stylistic devices, although the second film presents a more accomplished and amplified expression of certain forms found in the first (Karalis 2017: 121). Koundouros's later films explored differing representational codes, tending progressively towards more symbolic, cryptic and ultimately hermetic narrative and visual structures. His early films, especially *The Ogre of Athens*, however, strike an admirable balance between the symbolic and the pragmatic synthesising of various visual traditions, while infusing them with the traumatic spatiality of the Greek capital Athens, as it had emerged after the ravages caused by the German Occupation and the Greek Civil War.

In order to situate his images within the urban space of Athens and its underground histories, Koundouros managed empirically, and without any film studies background, to compile a cinematic style that made use of all previous achievements, and to establish a tradition of what he would later call 'pure cinema' (Soldatos 2007: 52). As he himself testifies, his early films are spaces of synthesising complexities: they bring together the stylistic innovations and the thematic storylines that had already started to become dominant in Greek cinema through a visual language that incorporated forms and styles from world cinema without the narrative dislocations and baroque inflations of his later films.

We can detect the presence of film noir codes in Koundouros's first films as being part of the prevailing *zeitgeist* of the period, especially with low-budget productions outside the mainstream distribution networks. The production company for his first films, the Athenian Cinematic Company, was also an informal cooperation of friends, with funding coming from personal sources, and in no way connected with mainstream producers or even the Greek state, which, at that period, was extremely reluctant to assist the industry. Undoubtedly, film noir visual devices can be found in different degrees in Koundouros's later films, despite the gradual opening-up in his spatial visuality to large rural landscapes with *Oi paranomoi*/*The Outlaws* (1958) and *To potami*/*The River* (1960) by the end of the decade.

His first two films are, indeed, extremely fertile in the way they employ the visual stratagems of low-budget films, which at that time were the norm in the rather spasmodic production system of the country. As visual spaces, they represent the convergent *topoi* of incongruous visual potentialities and the ultimate *habitus* of conflicting ideologies that can seemingly be found at the heart of all films noirs of the period, although we cannot really claim that they are films noirs in their cinematic language. His main cinematographer in his first two films, Kostas Theodoridis, contributed to their ultimate aesthetic unity and differentiation, with his marked preference for German Expressionism and Soviet montage (Figure 1.1).

Koundouros was himself imprisoned on the Greek island of Makronisos, where he met some of the central protagonists of his first film. The choice of actors such as Manos Katrakis, Thanassis Vengos and others was equally eloquent: they were all political prisoners, released after years of 're-education', struggling to find refuge and a haven in the anonymity of the densely populated Athenian suburbs. Even the presence of these individuals on the screen had itself an implied meaning of resistance and opposition, in the same way that many cinematographers symbolised resistance to McCarthyism in Hollywood

Figure 1.1 Chasing the gangsters, in the last scenes of *The Magic City*. Greek Film Archive collection. Courtesy of Sotiria Matziri.

during the same period. Such an atmosphere of fear and insecurity, dominating the early scenes of *The Ogre*, was exacerbated by the rapid and violent modernisation of Greek society, especially in the urban spaces of the capital city, where old buildings were being demolished and their residents were being evicted in order for modern blocks of flats to be built.

Koundouros's early films stand in stark contrast to the optimism of such violent modernisation, immersing their audiences in the shanty suburbs of refugees, the nightclubs of the marginalised and those left out of the capitalist growth, while struggling to find an oppositional anti-language to depict the dark subtexts of such modernisation and capitalist development. Moreover, his first films stand as emblematic monuments to the construction of a new cinematic language, focused on low-key lighting, dynamic shifts of perspective, fluid *chiaroscuro* contrast, anti-naturalistic settings, with the intention of altering and sometimes antagonising the lucid, sharp and crisp contours of Michael Cacoyannis's settings in *Stella* (1955), for example. In this process, Koundouros had to employ some of the most salient elements of the noir style, in order to expose the terrifying ambiguities of modernisation. His early films stand in an antagonistic and yet constructive dialogue with both American film aesthetics and Cacoyannis's films, establishing a generic hybridity that was to dominate mainstream Greek cinema until Theo Angelopoulos's *Anaparastasi/Reconstruction* (1970) recalibrated its temporality.

Nikos Koundouros's Film Noir as the Genre of Interstitial Visuality

In late 1952 Nikos Koundouros was released from the island of Makronisos, where he had been imprisoned since 1949 for his political views. As he stressed, since his early period, fear was the feeling that marked him, and it remained with him throughout his life. '*The Magic City*', he said later, 'is the movie of innocence. We felt innocent, while the guilty were on the opposite side' (Koundouros 1998). Despite its artistic innocence, which can also be seen in its continuity gaps and its rather melodramatic ending, the film is permeated by alarming and occasionally threatening signs that cannot be deciphered immediately. The underground and illegal world of smugglers and pimps delineates indirectly the precarious position and realities of the characters: they have to survive by any means possible in a world whose civil society exists only through oppressive public servants and police officers. The central *mise en scène* is obviously based on Italian neorealism. In his review, Marios Ploritis pointed out the film's reference to Vittorio de Sicca's *Miracolo a Milano/Miracle in Milan* (1951), especially the shantytowns depicted in both films as the background for their prospective neorealist fables (Soldatos 2001: 144). The similarities with neorealism, however, end there.

The Magic City is based on a real shantytown, which was built in an impromptu way to shelter refugees from Asia Minor after the 1922 Catastrophe. Koundouros was fascinated by the geometry of misery and abjection, the innate need of the refugees to impose order and balance on the chaotic materials of their life as pariahs. The camera insists on the built structures, the collapsing window panes, the non-existent streets, the dirt and the disorder of the open spaces, foregrounding something that dominated Koundouros's early films: the documentary impulse, the propensity of his camera to record, document and testify regarding a specific historical encounter or event, what Stuart Franklin (2016: 9), returning to the expression coined by the father of modern English documentary John Grierson, calls 'the creative treatment of actuality'.

The most important *actuality* that we see in this film, and which leads to its connection with film noir, is the violent transition from the organic community of pre-industrial neighbourhoods towards the new capitalist economy of growth, development and control. The noir element appears in the film only when a violent clash between the law and the underworld takes place. The gangsters and criminals function as markers of a larger dramatic subtext of opposition and reaction to the new social order. Koundouros's love for the lumpenproletariat makes him disregard the fact that they are devoid of class consciousness and revolutionary potential. Marios Ploritis emphasises the tense and bleak atmosphere of the film, but also the fact that 'here neorealism is grafted with recollections from cinematic anthologies and a number of *clichés* (especially from the style of American gangster films) that debase its truth' (Soldatos 2001: 144). Ploritis points out the hybrid form of Koundouros's first film, and its attempt to fuse neorealism and American cinema through incongruous stylistic devices and visual semantics employed to depict the fluid and transitional character of the actual realities.

Witnessing the transformation of the Athenian urban space, Koundouros struggles to construct a visual idiom to depict the fast pace of the emerging social order, and its destructive consequences for everyday life as it was known to him and others before the deleterious wars of the previous decade. The urban landscapes of his film are spaces of loss and absence, indeed of expulsion and sacrifice. The elegiac character of the narration and of the opening scenes also testifies to the lost spaces of a community struggling to stay together through the instruments of modernisation: the truck used by the main character is the ultimate proof of his illusory and precarious empowerment, as he must pay back the loan he took out to buy it, and his whole life depends on this.[1] The chase scenes at the dockyards, and within the large sewage pipes, photographed through wide-angle lens, create an atmosphere of urgency and danger that we see in quintessential noir films such as Elia Kazan's *Panic in the Streets* (1950) or Jules Dassin's *Night and the City* (1950), with an interesting reference, especially through employing the vehicle of modernised labour, to Henri-Georges Clouzot's *Le Salaire de la peur/The Wages of Fear* (1953).

The interchange between these compositional forms does not always work, mostly because the script by Margarita Lymberaki is too literary, and the dialogue, with its theatricality, fails to capture the unembellished raw idioms of the lumpenproletariat, even in the most 'underground' scenes. Against this, Theodoridis's camera plunges in and out of the shantytown of refugees and the dreamlike world of the social outcasts with their escapism. The images, together with the multi-tonal and polychromatic music by Manos Hatzidakis, frame a world of greyness and fluid indeterminate mentality that is still, however, rather outside the dangerous criminal atmosphere of authentic noirness.

The film ends 'innocently', with the optimistic triumph of the old order. All the neighbours contribute so that the truck is paid for and the young man can continue working. Under the eyes of the state representative who is simply 'doing his duty', the community comes together to offer their last resistance against the commodification of work and the depersonalisation of the individual. Films such as *O methistakas/The Drunkard* (1950) or *I kalpiki lira/The Counterfeit Coin* (1955) by Tzavellas, released during the same period, explored precisely the major social transformation that was happening, which was changing human relations, communitarian values and social hierarchies. The triumphant depiction of solidarity and support makes this film a docu-fiction in the *caméra-stylo* tradition, recording the final stand of the social ties and practices of traditional societies against large-scale modern industrial cultures, the resistance of *Gemeinschaft* confronting *Gesellschaft*, to use Ferdinand Tonnies's famous distinction.

The transition was not easy or smooth and, despite the comic aspects of the transformation of villagers into urban bourgeois, the subtext was one of profound anxiety and alienation. The violent abolition of self-sufficient, almost closed neighbourhoods of the pre-capitalist economy, which functioned as isolated enclaves consisting of populations from the same rural area or, as in this case, of Asia Minor refugees, led to a radical and sometimes violent cultural or, indeed, existential confrontation. The government was always 'suspicious, threatening, never allowing us a quiet moment', as Koundouros (2016: 35) states in his memoirs. Later he elaborated:

> I can state that my relation with this ridiculous state, the Greek one I mean, which since its establishment never ceased being a state hostile to its citizens, was, since my birth, very bad. I never got along well with power, and power never got along well with me. I never liked it, and it never liked me. (Soldatos 2007: 42)

Excessive individualism leading to despair, which dominated American noir films, is something from which Koundouros tried to shy away, at least in his first film, which culminates in a manifestation of empowering communitarian solidarity and mutual aid.

But if in *The Magic City* Koundouros still had some optimism about the resistance and endurance of communitarian values, his next film showed that he had no illusions about the actual reality around him, nor about the outcome of the conflict. *The Ogre* is probably one of the most enigmatic and mystifying films of Greek cinema, containing *in nuce* Koundouros's thematic norms, aesthetic principles, sound designs and visual cues. Recently, Peter Bradshaw (2011) called it 'a dark, satirical noir masterpiece', and asked for a fresh reinterpretation of its significance. When the film came out, in an era of political polarisation and social conflict, both left and right condemned it as 'the apotheosis of bouzouki, of the underworld, of thieves, of incomprehensibility', as the left-wing newspaper *I Avgi* wrote (Soldatos 2001: 151). The newspapers of the right also denounced it:

> We don't know what to bemoan first? The moronic stupidities of the smugglers? The pitiable and miserable chorus of drug addicts? The ridiculing of the Gospel? The horrible depiction and vilification of the police? Or the horrible and filthy suburbs of Athens and Piraeus, where this wretched product was filmed? (Soldatos 2001: 151)

The financial success of the film was extremely limited, but its legacy remained strong and resurfaced with certain noir films of later periods, such as Vangelis Serdaris's *Listeia stin Athina/Robbery in Athens* (1969) and, most notably, in the noir-ish stylistics of Tonia Marketaki's political thriller *Ioannis o Viaios/ John the Violent* (1973). After 1974 *The Ogre*'s canonisation became accepted by every critic and historian, and it is now considered by many as the best film ever produced in the country, even higher than Theo Angelopoulos's *O thiasos/ The Travelling Players* (1975). Angelopoulos himself praised the film in rather lukewarm terms as based on urban 'folklore' (Fainaru 2001: 71), although he recognised that he 'felt it very close to his own vision' (Mposkoitis 2020).

Indeed, there is something uniquely incommunicable, and probably unrepeatable, in the film itself. Koundouros believed that it led to the demise of his own cinematic imaginary, creating something that even he was unable to emulate or surpass. He wrote:

> When it was released in 1956, it was attacked by newspapers, critics, and audiences who left the theatre swearing and cursing for having wasted their money. It took ten years for it to be vindicated. When a bold cinema owner screened it around the end of the military junta (1974), and the audience identified with it. But meanwhile I had collapsed, I had no strength to fight back and defend *The Ogre*. *I abandoned this expressionist style and genre,*

> which Greek viewers rejected, as they were addicted to American cinema. Instead of saying 'the audience is wrong', I said 'Koundouros was in error'.
> (Koundouros 2016: 48, emphasis added)

Koundouros's statement is extremely pertinent in order to explore and interpret the complicated noirness of his dark masterpiece. In the first attempt to map the trajectory of the genre in Greece, Panos Kokkalenios (2007: 19) noted that 'in Koundouros's film *The Ogre* the noir influence is more tangible. The subject matter is very close to that of true noir film, despite the fact that the film includes many other genres, all with their corresponding references.' In the same publication, Alexis Dermentzoglou (2007: 13) unequivocally states that 'Nikos Koundouros's *The Ogre*, a great film, meets every noir criterion, including aesthetics'. Kokkalenios is right when he stresses the amalgam of styles and genres that we find in the structure of the film. It is a gangster film, plus political thriller, plus dark comedy, plus social satire, plus parodic tragedy (Voutsadaki 2006: 41); to these we must add other subtexts and underlying references to the criminal underworld, the rise of the police state, and the climate of political persecution, which make the film also a documentary about the social realities of the 1950s in Greece. The film is also in an implied dialogue with the existing discourse on the visual representation of such 'anti-social phenomena' in Greek cinema, and we do not have to see its noirness as simply an 'influence', or even a homage, to dominant genres of the period. Aglaia Mitropoulou also points out the presence of the aesthetics of shadow theatre and Charlie Chaplin in *The Ogre* (2006: 188), which indicates that Koundouros was also exploring the two-dimensional visuality of folk art based on the iconographic patterns of Byzantine painting.[2]

Furthermore, *The Ogre* begins through the framing of the poster of *The Magic City*, making a subtle inter-filmic reference to the continuity between the two films. The story of the film is both complex and simple and was written by Iakovos Kambanellis. There is a basic plot around the life of a shy and clumsy individual. The story begins *in medias res* and in an atmosphere of tension and fear, intensified through the expressionist manipulation of the sense of space that dominates the film from the initial credits. A bank clerk called Thomas bears an uncanny resemblance to the leader of the Athenian underworld, nicknamed 'the dragon' (whom we only see fleetingly in the film through newspaper photographs). Thomas is essentially forced by the gaze of others to abandon his dull quotidian life and experience the persecution that momentarily transforms him into the exact opposite of his own self. He reluctantly becomes the leader of the criminal gang, who project on to him their own psychosexual ambiguities and patriarchal ideations as he plans with them a major heist of antiquities. Incidentally, he falls in love with a naïve and innocent singer from the underworld, even though he experiences immediately the tragic impossibility of their affair. Soon one of the gangsters identifies him as the wrong 'dragon', which leads to Thomas's murder by the second prominent member of the group in one of the most memorable scenes in Greek cinema.

Around this basic plotline, Koundouros constructs a visual narrative that alternates between closed confined spaces full of claustrophobia and repression and the open landscapes of urban mystique, enhanced by Kostas Theodoridis's impressionist use of black-and-white cinematography. In the final scene, when the 'dragon' is stabbed to death, the nuances and shades of the chromatic juxtaposition become blurred, fusing with each other in an ingenious use of light as visual commentary on the story. In this film, Koundouros and Theodoridis establish a rhythmic montage, alternating between outside and inside spaces while moving the camera fast over the anxious human body, avoiding, however, the close-ups that we will see in the director's second film. Lakis Papastathis observed that in Koundouros's first film, 'the faces of actors are filmed from medium distance, without ever being isolated from their space, and without misuse of close-ups' (2014: 16).

Through such an amalgam and fusion of genres and styles, *The Ogre* appears like a visual palimpsest with an almost indeterminate and unfocused aesthetic and artistic *mise en scène*. In an interview for the television programme *Paraskinio*, Koundouros stressed that he did not have a specific purpose when he started making the film, and he thought that it would be 'a dark comedy' satirising the political atmosphere of the period. The scene when the main characters are arrested by the police and are photographed next to a female bra hanging on the line is probably the most important trace of Koundouros's original intention. The film, however, starts as an expressionist exploration of the 'state of emergency', as seen by the surveillance apparatuses of a repressive state. Then it evolves into a comedy of errors, with the misidentification of the main character and the hilarious scenes of chase in the streets of the city. Halfway, it is transformed into a traditional romance, and following that, it takes a turn towards being a crime story, with the selling of the stolen antiquities. Towards the end, it follows a pattern not actually anticipated by the previous narrative twists, opening up its formal structure into challenging political ambiguities and ethical dilemmas.

The final scene, with the dance of the underworld figures and the ritual execution of the supposed Ogre, foregrounds the moral antinomies and dark contradictions posited throughout the film. From a literary perspective, Kambanellis's story makes direct references to Nikolai Gogol's 'The Overcoat', Dostoevsky's *Notes from Underground* and Anton Chekhov's *The Story of a Nobody*, utilising the trope of the 'anti-hero' to frame the fact that the character is 'driven by motives that are obscure to everyone – even himself – and to behave in ways that appear to be against his material advantage and destructive of his happiness, but yet are felt by him to be overwhelmingly necessary' (Zinovieff and Hughes 2015: viii).

Theodoridis's camera moves through unpredictable stylistic angles to point out the ambiguities in the character and the ambivalence of the audience towards them. Within enclosed and confined spaces, it frames the faces and bodies of the main characters with the sharp contrasts and angular shadows of a proper film noir, in an almost expressionist intensity of violent close-ups (Figure 1.2). Yet, when out in the daylight, the sharp contours of human figures become fluid, diffused, lose their individuality and are transformed into impressions, illusory images of an incomprehensible reality. The only 'objects' that maintain their distinctiveness and solidity are those that have been purchased; in the case of *The Ogre*, the main character's coat. Thomas lives and dies in that coat; when he does not have his coat on, he becomes vulnerable, fragile and an easy prey, the victim of a system that has rendered him unable to understand its influence on his life. An interpretation, of course, of the coat as the fetishistic symbol of a repressed sexuality (in psychoanalytic terms, of masturbation, as prefigured by Gogol) could suggest another link to the noir since, in all films noirs, clothing as sexual fetishism is a leitmotif (Reader 1981: 56). This also indicates that the film, in many aspects, is structured around codes; in his brief description of his films, Koundouros revealed that, striving to avoid

Figure 1.2 Thomas the 'Ogre' (Dinos Iliopoulos) with Carmen (Maria Lekaki). Greek Film Archive collection. Courtesy of Sotiria Matziri.

censorship, 'with Kambanellis [they] wanted to construct a film in successive codes, the same as the ones prisoners use, knocking on the walls, once, twice or three times' (Koundouros 1998).

For Koundouros, however, the film goes far beyond the structural elements of its production. 'The *Ogre*', he wrote,

> far from accepting charges of formalism, intellectual pretensions etc. is pure cinema. It could not be either a manifesto or a play or a novel. I used, by exhausting all the potentialities of my material, the significance of the black and white image, of movement and sound. The two thirds of my symbols are visual and sonic. The dialogue is part of the film, but it is not the film. The idea is inextricably connected with the materials of its expression[,] and this consummation, this ideal marriage, makes the films convincing, even when ideological references do not energise the uninformed viewer. (Soldatos 2007: 52)

Antonia Voutsadaki (2006: 31) also addresses the 'lack of psychology' in Thomas's character, as we don't really get to know what is actually happening in his mind. In a sense, Thomas, whose surname, in a properly Kafkaesque and almost Orwellian manner, we are not told, is like a character from Robert Musil's book *The Man Without Qualities* (1930–43). Lefteris Xanthopoulos also stresses that

> the tragic hero now [at the end of the film] has no face anymore, he is not a person, his shadow has flown away and was lost, he is *Nobody*. The mask of the Ogre he had on, either by mistake or by misunderstanding, is also destroyed. Thomas cannot, he does not have the time to return even to his old worn-out self, which he had rejected and thrown away. (Xanthopoulos 2014: 55)

This is really indicative of Koundouros's approach to his character, the fact that he avoids any psychologisation, unlike what we find in American film noir of the period. This is extremely important for the structure of *The Ogre*, from which one of the main motifs of American film noir, the *femme fatale*, is also spectacularly absent. Alan Woolfolk (2007: 119) stresses that noir films are 'populated with male protagonists who encounter and probe their unconscious only to find a disturbing and deadly knowledge that frequently comes via a *femme fatale*'. Koundouros avoids such facile representations of women as a danger to the masculine world of social orthodoxy. Women are not sacrificial victims to the opaqueness of the patriarchal world. Like the men in the film, they are also 'nobodies', without complete and developed identities and self-perceptions.

Koundouros's approach is that of a post-gender, almost transhumanist, depoliticised representation of gender identity, framed by the complete neutralisation, indeed emotional numbing, of both genders under the oppression of political authoritarianism. It is the ubiquitous presence of power that overshadows and obscures both lived temporality and urban experience in this film. This can also be seen in the strange and deeply homoerotic dance at the end of the film, when, obviously intoxicated or under the influence of drugs, men create a circle of complete union and masculine solidarity with each other, as their oppression is abolished after they enter a collective Dionysian ritual. Koundouros visited Vassilis Tsitsanis and Manos Hatzidakis during the recording of the music and called it a 'sacred ritual' and 'a liturgy [...] which might lead to what somebody called national resurrection' (Soldatos 2007: 56).

The connection between Koundouros and noirness is, therefore, a very complex one and, to a certain degree, it raises a fundamental aporia about the genre. In his seminal text on the genre, Paul Schrader writes:

> The fundamental reason for film noir's neglect, however, is the fact that it depends more on choreography than sociology, and American critics have always been slow on the uptake when it comes to visual style. Like its protagonists, film noir is more interested in style than theme, whereas American critics have been traditionally more interested in theme than style. (Schrader 1972: 13)

Koundouros's approach to the genre can be encapsulated in this statement, although it is also completely contained by its pragmatic references, as Schrader predominantly had the American noir in mind. Koundouros borrowed from noir the choreography of space, especially of urban space as it experienced an interstitial fluidity and was transformed violently into a dark place of oppression, what the sociologist Max Weber (1930: 181) called 'the iron cage of the future', based on bureaucratisation and the mechanised petrification of society. In order to represent the dark sides of the transformation, Koundouros employed certain stylistic elements from noir, and cross-pollinated them with analogous imaginative structures originating from various sources, cinematic genres and visual styles of the local industry.

Furthermore, he wanted to avoid the aestheticisation of modernist violence and, as we have seen, later he abandoned the genre altogether. Schrader (1972: 13) stressed that 'film noir was first of all a style, because it worked out its conflicts visually rather than thematically, because it was aware of its own identity, it was able to create artistic solutions to sociological problems'. Within the confines of the Greek film industry and, of course, Greek film culture, *The Ogre* presented a personal and idiosyncratic style, and not a vision or a reimagining of reality: the style foregrounded the discrepancy between power structure and social reality. Koundouros addressed this in a brief notice:

> It is a melodrama which gave me the opportunity to develop a whole world, that world which was burdened by the post-occupation occupation, the occupation of the Right that is ... A peculiar Romanhood [*Romiosyni*], a world that was anxious and had the right to live, as it was oppressed, headless, directionless, decapitated, twitching like headless snake, in its effort to find one place and another. (Soldatos 2007: 65)

The noirness of *The Ogre* lies in the special use of the image, both fluid and motionless, photographic and cinematic at the same time. 'I admit my passion for the image', Koundouros stated, 'the frame, the settings, the costumes [. . .] I love the dissolution of life, and its reconstruction through the camera lens and the director's eye' (Koundouros 2009: 308). His film presents a hybrid approach to cinematic images, through a stylistic mishmash and a strange eclecticism that ultimately gave Greek cinema, in its golden age of production and spectatorship, a historical consciousness, which it was not aware that it possessed. 'I must add', Koundouros wrote,

> that only image is in no need for arguments, because it is itself the argument. It needs no other support, because it is self-sustainable. It defines precisely what is visible, it ignores provocatively what is not seen, it records and simultaneously invites its viewers to view it as the starting point, or as the end, of a narrative which preceded it. Image is motionless only if you don't want, or you are unable to, set it yourself in motion. (Koundouros 2009: 207)

Consequently, *The Ogre* does not really fit into a discursive category labelled 'film noir', although the category itself could be useful to delineate some of the film's aesthetic and pragmatic sources. As James Naremore (2019: 108) recently suggested: 'When we list any movie under the noir rubric, we invoke a network of ideas, moods, or themes as an organizing principle in place of other rubrics such as authors, movie studios, periods, genres, or national cinema (which we can also use).'

The Ogre exists in the in-between space of such categorisation without really being confined by any one of such heuristic and classificatory devices. Its interstitial visuality fuses regimes of seeing and practices of representing with unexpected and rather colliding significations within them. Definitely, *The Ogre* is an *un-canonical* film which, paradoxically enough, was used to define the canon of films in Greece, although a wider global reinscription of its visual semiotics is probably required for the full appreciation of its achievement.

The film ends with a very paradoxical statement: 'The Ogre was never arrested, cannot be arrested, will never be arrested.' Through the elusive optical stratagems of film noir, Koundouros made the cinematic screen the place out of which new social legends of urban dissent and repression were born; in a way, Thomas the Ogre is the only legend imagined in Greek cinema, the most elusive and accomplished cinematic figure, capturing a moment of transition towards a future without alternatives or opposition.[3] Its mythopoetic complexity is extremely ambiguous and frames the dark world of a society and its citizens in a state of profound panic; as Hirsch (2001: 208) notes about the American noir films of the period, *The Ogre* 'illuminated the night world of the other self that bedevils us all'. The darkness within and without is the most important dimension that connects the film to the wider phenomenon of the genre and its conceptualisation. Although the central element of his visual poetics remained until the very end what I have called 'his oppositional aesthetics' (Karalis 2012: 232), Koundouros left the atmosphere of the style behind with his next works, which were filmed in the open fields of the countryside, where the 'real' tragedy of history took place, and where the dark other self was exposed to the scrutiny of the Greek sun. His subsequent films, *The Outlaws* and *The River*, with their formal luminosity and linear geometry, stand in stark contrast to the claustrophobic and airless spaces of the adventures of Nobody.

Notes

1. The impact of such modernisation through cars can be also seen in Dinos Dimopoulos's *To amaxaki/Horse and Carriage* (1957), which addresses the transition from the personalised communitarianism to the possessive individualism of the new capitalist order.
2. Koundouros was also an iconographer with a personal style, akin to the visual appropriation of Byzantine iconography through the Renaissance perspective, as found in the paintings of Yannis Tsarouchis.
3. The other can probably be found in Cacoyannis's *To koritsi me ta mavra/A Girl in Black* (1956).

References

Biesen, Sheri Chinen (2005), *Blackout: World War II and the Origins of Film Noirs*, Baltimore, MD: Johns Hopkins University Press.
Borde, Raymond, and Chaumeton, Étienne ([1955] 2002), *A Panorama of American Film Noir 1941–1953*, San Francisco: City Lights.
Bould, Mark (2005), *Film Noir, From Berlin to Sin City*, London: Wallflower.
Bradshaw, Peter (2011), 'Franzen's *Freedom* Revives Legend of *The Dragon*', *The Guardian*, 13 October, <https://www.theguardian.com/film/filmblog/2011/oct/12/jonathan-franzen-freedom-the-dragon> (last accessed 20 July 2021).

Dermentzoglou, Alexis (ed.) (2007), *In a Dark Passage: Film Noir in Greek Cinema*, Athens: Erodios.
Fainaru, Dan (ed.) (2001), *Theo Angelopoulos, Interviews*, Jackson, MS: University Press of Mississippi.
Fotiou, Mikela, and Fessas, Nikitas (2017), 'Greek Neo-Noir: Reflecting a Narrative of Crisis', *Filmicon: Journal of Greek Film Studies*, 4, pp. 110–37.
Franklin, Stuart (2016), *The Documentary Impulse*, New York: Phaidon.
Hirsch, Foster (2001), *The Dark Side of the Screen*, New York: Da Capo.
Karalis, Vrasidas (2012), *A History of Greek Cinema*, London: Continuum.
Karalis, Vrasidas (2017), *Realism in Post-War Greek Cinema*, London: I.B. Tauris.
Kerr, Paul ([1979] 1996), 'Out of What Past? Notes on the B Film Noir', in Alain Silver and James Orsini (eds), *Film Noir Reader*, New York: Limelight, pp. 107–26.
Kokkalenios, Panos (2007), 'Tracing Film Noir in Greek Cinema 1954–1974', in Alexis Dermentzoglou (ed.), *In a Dark Passage: Film Noir in Greek Cinema*, Athens: Erodios, pp. 19–22.
Koundouros, Nikos (1998), 'Ego kai oi tainies mou' [Me and My Films], *Kathimerini*, 22 November, p. 12.
Koundouros, Nikos (2009), *Stop Carré*, Athens: Ergo.
Koundouros, Nikos (2016), *Mnimi apeitharhiti – Imerologio* [Undisciplined Memory – Diary], Athens: Agra.
Lukács, Georg ([1920] 1971), *The Theory of the Novel*, London: Merlin Press.
Maltby, Richard ([1995] 2003), *Hollywood Cinema*, Oxford: Blackwell.
Mitropoulou, Aglaia (2006), *Ellinikos kinimatografos* [Greek Cinema], Athens: Papazisis.
Mposkoitis, Antonis (2020), 'Thodoros Angelopoulos: I was always moved by the persistence of Eros', *Lifo*, 27 April, <https://www.lifo.gr/culture/cinema/thodoros-aggelopoylos-emena-pantote-me-sygkinoyse-i-emmoni-ston-erota> (last accessed 1 November 2020).
Naremore, James (1998), *More than Night, Film Noir in its Contexts*, Berkeley, CA: University of California Press.
Naremore, James (2019), *Film Noir: A Very Short Introduction*, Oxford: Oxford University Press.
Papastathis, Lakis (2012), *'O drakos' tou Nikou Koundourou/'Ogre of Athens' by Nikos Koundouros*, documentary for the TV programme *Paraskinio*, Cinetic/ERT, first shown 23 February.
Papastathis, Lakis (2014), 'O Nikos Koundouros sto xekinima' [Nikos Koundouros at the Beginning], in Lefteris Xanthopoulos (ed.), *Oi tesseris epoches tou Nikou Koundourou* [The Four Seasons of Nikos Koundouros], Athens: Gavriilides.
Reader, Keith (1981), *Cultures in Celluloid*, London: Quartet Books.
Schatz, Thomas (1981), *Hollywood Genres, Formulas, Filmmaking and the Studio System*, New York: Random House.
Schrader, Paul (1972), 'Notes on Film Noir', *Film Comment*, 8:1, pp. 8–13.
Soldatos, Yannis (2001), *Enas aionas ellinikos kinimatografos* [A Century of Greek Cinema], vol. 1, *(1900–1970)*, Athens: Kochlias.
Soldatos, Yannis (2007), *Odysseies somaton sto ergo tou Nikou Koundourou* [Corporeal Odysseys in the Work of Nikos Koundouros], Athens: Aigokeros.

Voutsadaki, Antonia (2006), *O drakos tou Nikou Koundourou: Enas politikos kinimagrafos* [*The Ogre of Athens* by Nikos Koundouros: A Political Cinema], Athens: Aigokeros.

Weber, Max (1930), *The Protestant Ethic and the Spirit of Capitalism*, London: Allen and Unwin.

Woolfolk, Alan (2007), 'The Horizon of Disenchantment: Film Noir, Camus and the Vicissitudes of Descent', in Mark T. Conard (ed.), *The Philosophy of Film Noir*, Lexington, KY: University Press of Kentucky, pp. 107–23.

Xanthopoulos, Lefteris (2014), *Oi tesseris epohes tou Nikou Koundourou* [The Four Seasons of Nikos Koundouros], Athens: Gavriilides.

Zinovieff, Kyril, and Hughes, John (2015), 'Introduction to Fyodor Dostoevsky', in Kyril Zinovieff and John Hughes (eds), *Notes from Underground*, London: Alma Classics.

2. OF MICE, MEN AND GREEK FILM NOIR: *THE LITTLE MOUSE*

Maria A. Stassinopoulou

Beginning with *Prosopa lismonimena/Forgotten Faces* (dir. Tzavellas, 1946), the immediate post-war years witnessed several noir productions in Greece. In this chapter I follow a timeline which sets the end of the first post-war noir phase with *O anthropos tou trainou/The Man on the Train* (dir. Dimopoulos, 1958), a film based on a screenplay by Yannis Maris. My discussion of this first phase focuses on *To Pontikaki/The Little Mouse* (1953).[1] Written and directed jointly by Giorgos Asimakopoulos and Nikos Tsiforos, and produced by Anzervos, then a major player in Greek cinema, the film has been recently 'rediscovered' through Greek television and social media. It attracts curious viewers, mostly because it features, for the first time in an ingénue role, Aliki Vougiouklaki (Lazaridis 1999: 298–301). She would later become the best-known star of Greek cinema, and certainly remains the best-remembered one. Her character, Krinoula, orphaned during the German Occupation and called by everyone *Pontikaki* ('little mouse'), gives the film its name. She has a substantial function in the plot development, saving the young criminal Loukis (Giorgos Lefteriotis). This is, nevertheless, not only a film about young love reaffirming what is best in the *condition humaine*, even amid a criminal milieu. By following the lives of an older and two young petty criminals in Piraeus, it also addresses in a realist, perhaps even neorealist way, broad social issues of its time: poverty, juvenile delinquency and overseas migration as consequences of the war.

Is Noir Greek Enough?

Questions of verisimilitude and film realism played a crucial role in discourses on post-war film, while current discussions of genre and European noir also inform the classification options when discussing a particular film (on European noir, see Spicer 2007; Broe 2014; Pillard 2014; for Greece: Poupou 2007; Dermentzoglou 2007; Fotiou and Fessas 2017). Critical rhetoric at the time and during the formative years of the New Greek Cinema consistently referred to an assumed escapism of Greek post-war cinema and to its silence vis-à-vis the realities of its spectators' lives. But the early post-war noir films offer enough material to demonstrate that cinema did engage with its surrounding society through relatable stories and characters, albeit in a different stylistic framework from that of mainstream cinema of the 1960s and of auteur cinema.

According to Pillard, '"film noir" does not constitute a specifically American phenomenon, but definitely a transnational form, that expresses itself in varied national and cultural historical contexts and is expressed in a variety of particular versions' (2014: 11).[2] In Greek cinema, as in European post-war film in general, dark street films including crime and law-enforcement scenes address at the same time political and social debates. Even in the German expressionistic *Straßenfilm* or in the excessive melodramatic narratives of interwar or post-war cinema, these issues would be immediately recognisable to contemporary local/national audiences, but more difficult for later spectators and film students to detect, as they require detailed historical contextualisation. The Greek noir films of the 1940s and early 1950s were in a position to easily establish communication with local audiences who had experience of international films of the genre – even during the heyday of Greek mainstream cinema in the 1960s, imported films represented the largest source of revenue at the box office. At the same time, Greek film noir embedded the plots firmly in the social surroundings of its audiences, through a few exterior scenes, well-known actors' faces and voices, and connotations of the Second World War and Occupation. It thus remained locked in what Jeancolas has called the 'inexportable' spatial and temporal complicity of 'national' popular film with its spectators, based on the presence of typecast actors, entertainment traditions outside cinema and specific locations (Jeancolas 1992: 141; Vincendeau 1998: 446).

As in other European post-war societies, Greek cinema stopped abruptly its short attempt at producing direct testimonials of the war, the Occupation and the Civil War trauma. Director Dinos Dimopoulos remembered in his memoir that, confronted with an idea of his to produce a film on the Civil War in 1953, producer Filopoimin Finos had compared Greece with France. There, in his opinion, right and left had embraced each other the moment the Germans left the country. In Greece, Finos thought, any production company engaging in the subject, along with the cinemas showing such a film, would face mob violence (Dimopoulos 1998: 154–5). The transition to more complex, hidden narratives, or even to rival myths about the retreating past of the Second World War during the 1950s, does not nevertheless constitute a Greek particularity. It belongs to a general European phenomenon, which can be interpreted in the context of the Cold War, of evolving memorial processes, and of style and genre change (Sorlin 1991: 70–80; Greffrath 1995; Stassinopoulou 2000c: 205–46; Eley 2001; Dominé 2008). Alongside the hiding, shooting and duelling scenes of the 'pastoral' or 'mountain' genre set in rural landscapes (Kymionis 2000; Dermentzopoulos 2002), the darkness of the Greek noir offers glimpses of urban violence and conflict in the controlled context of law and order, thus bypassing censorship regimes, which blocked the representation of violence and images of the injured human body.

As I have argued elsewhere, a detailed historical reading of Greek post-war feature films, which situates them in the complexity of their contemporary media and sources, can recognise more accurately their embeddedness in everyday realities and fluid mentalities, which later viewings fail to recognise (Stassinopoulou 2000c: 25–6). The lingering of filmic storytelling on small individual steps within large-scale phenomena (in *The Little Mouse*, for example, the difficulties of booking a passage to Australia as an individual story of post-war overseas migration) could be quite prominent for a viewer at the time, but does not form part of standard narratives about the period written later or in different communicative contexts and interested in broader perspectives. Like popular literature genres, mainstream film seems to react more rapidly to social trends, events and ideological phenomena of a medium duration than highbrow literature, drama, or academic publications. On the other hand, the slower rhythms – necessitated also by the production process – of the film industry in integrating everyday events into its own narrative complexities cause a delay, which sets film apart from the daily press. Cinema, to quote François Garçon, expresses better 'regular forms of sensibility and stable ceremonials of everyday life, in short the slower flux of the course of history' (1984: 199).[3] The reiteration of impulses from the social environment in popular narrative formulas does not change the fact that feature film is (and was even more so before television replaced it in this function) a historical narrator in its own right, and not simply a provider of supportive visualisation for textual sources (Kyrtsis 1994: 95; cf. Kassaveti 2017).

Greek noir variants also attest to the filmmakers' awareness of international trends in film aesthetics and style. Already in the 1930s *Koinoniki sapila/Social Decay* (dir. Tatasopoulos, 1932) engaged in its own right in an attempt to transfer the tropes of the Hollywood gangster film, German Expressionism and early French noir into Greek cinema. Its director Stelios Tatasopoulos had just returned from Paris, while its cameraman, Michalis Gaziadis, had been strongly influenced by his collaboration with his elder brother

Dimitris, who had studied and worked in Germany (Petris 1988; Arkolakis 2009; Delveroudi 2012). With *Forgotten Faces*, Greek post-war production reconnects with the crime film. *The Little Mouse* belongs to this group of films produced from the mid-1940s to the mid-1950s. They oscillate between noir, realism and melodrama, and apply elements that bring to mind the French *réalisme noir* of the years 1946–58 (Pillard 2014: 23): sombre visual style, inept male characters, young women who are innocent and/or susceptible to seduction, and older fallen female characters, a continuation of both visual and narrative elements from the 1930s, as well as an evocation of the characters' past, rooted in the Second World War and the Occupation. The films appear to have been relatively successful at the box office (always, however, behind imported films), at least in first-run cinemas, for which we have available numbers (Valoukos 1998). One should nevertheless take into account the fact that films remained for a long time in distribution packages, and could fill programme gaps in small cinemas all over Greece for many years (professional periodicals, such as *Kinimatografikos Astir* or *Ta Theamata*, report consistently and include open-air cinemas). *I Agni tou limaniou/Agnes of the Port* (dir. Tzavellas, 1952) was, for example, quite successful in the 1951–52 season while, on the other hand, *The Little Mouse* did not fare well in the 1953–54 season. In the perception of contemporary and later film criticism, Greek noir films occupy a mid-position between mainstream and art cinema, with the odd enthusiastic reception of individual films with a genre affinity, such as *O drakos/The Ogre of Athens* (dir. Koundouros, 1956). Towards the end of this first post-war noir phase, *Tzo o tromeros/Joe the Terrible* (dir. Dimopoulos, 1955) offers a parody of the genre (at least it was marketed as such). In its combination of fairytale sequences of the innocent girl and the overacting of the actors playing the petty criminals, it is close to the films which Pillard discusses under the label 'série noire pour rire' (2014: 111–84). By using actors such as Dionysis Papagiannopoulos and Nikos Rizos who, in this case, offer satirical reinterpretations of their roles in *The Little Mouse*, Dimopoulos converses with a knowing audience, which can appreciate his blend of suspense and parody (Figure 2.1).

Between the first and the second post-war noir phase stands *The Man on the Train*, produced by Olympos Film. It was to be the last film featuring Giorgos Pappas, the actor who had starred in the first post-war noir, *Forgotten Faces*. Produced by Pete Melas, Dimopoulos's film was also the first one based on a screenplay by Yannis Maris (Yannis Tsirimokos). It was followed by *Eglima sto Kolonaki/Murder in Kolonaki* (dir. Aliferis, 1959) and *Eglima sta paraskinia/Murder Backstage* (dir. Katsouridis, 1960), for which Maris also contributed the screenplays. The success of Maris's novels and films, with their secret-hidden-in-the-darkness-of-the-Occupation plots, inspired even Filopoimin Finos, who, after *Hamenoi angeloi/Fallen Angels* (dir. Tsiforos, 1948) and

Figure 2.1 Director Dinos Dimopoulos gives instructions to the actors Dinos Iliopoulos and Margarita Papageorgiou, during the shooting of *Joe the Terrible*. Greek Film Archive collection.

Agnes of the Port, had left the genre to smaller producers. It is indicative of Finos's long hesitation to invest in noir after 1951 that even trusted collaborators of his, such as Nikos Tsiforos and Dinos Dimopoulos, had to turn to other producers to finance their attempts at the genre throughout the 1950s. It was only in 1961 that Finos produced a film noir again: *O thanatos tha xanartheil/ Death Strikes Again* (dir. Thalassinos, 1961). This film offered a variation on the theme of solving a murder mystery related to the past of the characters by situating the crime scene in Cyprus, which had just become an independent state, and by making the victim a British officer. For this production, Finos Film employed partly newcomers among the crew. Thalassinos, who until then had worked for smaller companies such as Pergantis Films, directed the film, while Nikos Foskolos wrote his first screenplay to take place in an urban setting, after having provided screenplays for four 'pastoral genre' B-movies produced by small producers between 1959 and 1961. *Death Strikes Again* featured an all-star cast with well-known stage and film actors. But it seems that Finos Film had left the noir field open for too long to its rival companies such as Anzervos, but also to smaller ones such as Tzal Films or Pergantis Films. These producers seem to have formed a clearly defined niche during the 1950s, with low-cost productions and medium revenue. Finos Film's musical comedies of the same season *Aliki sto Naftiko/Alice in the Navy* (dir. Sakellarios, 1961, colour) and *Madalena* (dir. Dimopoulos, 1960, black and white) were far more successful than the studio's new noir. Once again Finos turned his back on the genre. During the 1960s and 1970s, noir would remain in the hands of second- and third-tier production companies (see also Kassaveti 2017).

Through substantial capital investment and a very strict production regime, Finos Film promoted the improvement of technical infrastructure in Greek cinema. The goal was clean, abundantly lit images and clearly audible sound. Through these technology and style standards, the company also largely defined what ought to be considered an 'appropriate' Greek visual canon after the Second World War. Critical opinion about early post-war noir films needs, in my view, to be read also in the context of the relations between certain film critics and particular Greek producers, while bearing in mind the unabashed promotion of Finos Film productions in the Greek media. In his regular film column, Marios Ploritis, who was a founding member of the Greek Union of Film Critics (Mitropoulou 1980: 123) and already highly influential, discarded in a short notice *The Little Mouse* as the futile attempt of a talented team to compete with American cinema in the 'gangster film', 'a genre that has become their [the Americans'] national product'. Watching the film, he wrote, he had missed the 'dynamism, speed and the verisimilitude which make American films of this genre tolerable'. He conceded, on the other hand, that the characters and the atmosphere were persuasive, but hoped that competent authors such as Asimakopoulos and Tsiforos would devote themselves to 'films with more Greekness' (Ploritis 1954). A couple of years earlier, when discussing *Agnes of the Port*, a film also set in Piraeus, Ploritis had dutifully stressed in a far longer text the technical progress of Finos Film's production before discussing content and style. This time, he attributed a closeness, not to the American gangster film, but to the French 'noir'. He wrote that, despite the definite progress in photography and lighting, the film was nothing more than an '"anthology" of the French "noir" films (*Quai des brumes/Port of Shadows, Dédée d'Anvers/ Dedee, La Marie du port/Marie of the Port*), without any of their substantial (not their superficial) truth' (Ploritis 1952).[4]

In his quest for 'Greekness', Ploritis, born in 1919 and shaped by the interwar intellectual debates on the subject (from the extensive bibliography, see indicatively Tziovas 1989; Papari 2018), argues thus against even the possibility of a Greek representative of an urban film genre, rephrasing a standard position of Greek intellectuals, who saw the potential of Greek film realism set in rural or semi-rural situations (on urban settings and Greek interwar and post-war cinema, see Stassinopoulou 2000b; Kartalou 2002; Poupou 2007). With statements such as those mentioned above, Ploritis follows the comedy author, filmmaker and critic Alekos Sakellarios, born in 1913. In 1946 *Forgotten Faces* had failed the 'Greekness' test for Sakellarios:

> The plot of the new film, much as the director tries to present it as Greek, with the assistance of a barrel organ, is too strongly American in tendency. The adventurer played by Mr. G. Pappas is more a gangster from Chicago and less a Greek crook; and in general, this whole case of blackmail, which could probably happen quite easily in America, is fairly improbable for Greece. (Aktsoglou and Kyriakidis 1994: 127)

In his review of *Agnes of the Port* for the newspaper *Fileleftheros*, Maris found no fault in drawing inspiration from French cinema; he also mentioned Marcel Carné as a particular source, and made the obvious reference to *Marie of the Port* (dir. Carné 1950), *Dedee* (dir. Allégret, 1948) and *Port of Shadows* (dir. Carné, 1938). What provoked his criticism was the directorial decision to stress 'cheap melodrama' instead of mining a 'beautiful subject, rich in potential: the fallen woman, the sailor, the port, its people'. Like Sakellarios and Ploritis, he too felt obliged to point out that spectators might relate to the plot and the characters not because they existed 'in Greek life', but because they recognised them, having previously seen them in similar foreign films (Aktsoglou and Kyriakidis 1994: 134–8). Maris's own answer to the quest for 'Greekness' in his take on the genre can be found in his serialised novellas in newspapers and in his screenplays. His characters are often involved in collaboration networks surviving the end of the war and in rapid enrichment during the German Occupation (Kalfopoulos 2016). Their close relation to French noir films of the 1950s evoking resistance and collaboration (Pillard 2014: 268–98) is further testament to the openness and transnationality of the genre.

How Two Lawyers and Comedy Writers Tackled Social Issues on Film

The screenwriters and directors of *The Little Mouse*, Nikos Tsiforos (Alexandria 1909–Athens 1970) and Giorgos Asimakopoulos (Akrata 1897–Athens 1970), were slightly older than the critics and filmmakers discussed above. They were experienced and successful comedy and revue authors for the stage, and joined forces in three film projects from 1952 to 1954, after having individually worked in Greek productions. They co-authored and co-directed two films, *O pyrgos ton ippoton*/*The Tower of Knights* and *The Little Mouse*, both produced by Anzervos in 1952 and 1953 respectively, while Tsiforos directed and Asimakopoulos wrote the screenplay for the third film, *O anemos tou misous*/ *Wind of Hate*, produced by Milas Film in 1954. Asimakopoulos wrote his first screenplay together with his standard revue theatre collaborators, Panagiotis

Papadoukas and Vasilis Spyropoulos, for the Anzervos production *Anna Roditi* (dir. Filippou and Gaziadis, 1948), a film set against the historical background of the Italian annexation of the Dodecanese after 1912, through the German Occupation in 1943, to the beginning of British rule in 1945 and, finally, the integration of the Dodecanese into the Greek state in 1947. Tsiforos, on the other hand, had written the screenplay for the melodrama *Ragismenes kardies/ Broken Hearts* (dir. Laskos, 1945), and had written and directed the noir *Fallen Angels* in 1948. After 1954 they did not join forces any more, but continued to contribute to Greek cinema, with successful screenplays or film adaptations based on their own plays, usually comedies of manners, while working with their established collaborators (Tsiforos with Polyvios Vasileiadis and Asimakopoulos with Spyropoulos and Papadoukas).

As authors, Asimakopoulos and Tsiforos have both been more appreciated for their comedies; Tsiforos's urge to write dramas for the screen has even been derided (Lazaridis 1999: 299). However, all three collaborative projects seem to bring to the fore, sometimes with surprising immediacy, subjects that the industry was afraid to touch. Both authors had studied law (as had Maris, Ploritis and Sakellarios). Asimakopoulos also practised law and became, due to this experience, a long-term and highly respected president of the Society of Greek Theatre Writers, until his death in 1970. Tsiforos, on the other hand, worked as a freelancer, writing political and social comments for dailies and magazines on a regular basis.[5] The first cooperation produced a rather bitter satire (despite its burlesque moments), the second a film noir, while the third resulted in a classical melodrama. The common feature of all three films is that they are close to the social fabric of their time and include commentary on contemporary issues. *The Tower of Knights* combines a Romeo and Juliet parody with clear references to money changing hands during and after the war. In an aside at the beginning of the film we witness one of the very few attempts in post-war Greek cinema to address the, mostly hostile and at best reluctant or indifferent, reactions of the greatest part of Greek society to post-war reporting about the Shoah, and its few Greek survivors (see indicatively Antoniou 2018; Králová 2018). A shop owner, Domenikos Dellarossa, uses the golden sovereigns of his former partner, a Greek Jew who had not returned after the war to reclaim his property. The rendition in the dialogue is shocking in its simplistic brutality: one feels the urge to read it as satire, as the postures of the wife (played by Smaro Stefanidou) who aspires to upper-class allures seem to indicate, but a very black satire it is, indeed.[6] According to an urgent letter received by Dellarossa, the former Jewish partner, Aaron Levidis, has died 'oven baked [*psitos eis ton fourno*] in Buchenwald in April 1944'. As Dellarossa reminisces fondly about his former partner, he remembers how Levidis had been better at making money 'because Jews are good at it'. *Wind of Hate*, on the other hand, relies on a *Count of Monte Cristo* type of plot with touches of *The Tempest*, and tells of an unfairly accused and jailed man who ends up a lighthouse keeper. The flashbacks to the life of the young merchant marine officer and the conflictual relation between ship owners and their crews reveal a keen interest on the part of the filmmakers in the relation between safety and profit in the maritime business world, a subject of much debate during the post-war rise of the new Greek ship-owning magnates.

The Little Mouse

Like *Forgotten Faces* and *Fallen Angels* before it, the noir film of Tsiforos and Asimakopoulos, the second of their three joint projects, focuses on the innocence of displaced post-war youth, and on the poverty and need that led to juvenile delinquency, which were major issues for European post-war societies. The Greek government and non-governmental organisations participated in international forums and sent their representatives to present the Greek case (Avdela 2019). Youth and juvenile delinquency remained on the agenda of both Greek society and cinema well into the 1970s (Katsapis 2013). The daily press reported regularly on parliamentary debates and legal initiatives, but also on more immediate measures. Alongside sensationalist reporting, for example, about two young thieves looking to finance their wedding (Anon. 1952a), or a 20-year-old robber of a cinema who was 'imitating gangsters' (Anon. 1952b), one can also find more substantial features on the subject (Anon. 1952c). At the same time, extensive coverage was given to underground communist activity, for example arrests in Piraeus (Anon. 1952d), the big trials and executions, but also to the trial of the allegedly communist air force officers (Stassinopoulou 2000a: 41–4). Law enforcement and the role of the police and of justice were furthermore intensely discussed in the press, whether with regard to the prevention of juvenile delinquency or investigative methods.

In the early post-war noir, the prominence of the educated, civil and almost paternal police officer in civilian clothes explaining to a young criminal the path to social reintegration certainly offers a filmic persona open to both protest and identification (cf. Davies 2009), depending on the experiences and political affiliations of the individual viewer. As opposed to the comical policeman of the late 1950s and 1960s, these are figures of authority; filmic policemen as villains are rarely found in the early Greek noir (cf. Mostafa 2018: 139–42).

The Little Mouse follows two young men trying to get out of the criminal activities into which they had been introduced by a gang leader. They will achieve a prospectively happy ending, with one serving time but being able to leave jail and rejoin his fiancée, and the other managing to go to Australia with the woman he loves, who finally leaves the gang leader for him. Shooting was announced in the press as scheduled to begin in September 1953, and the film must have been completed by the end of the same year. It reached Athenian cinemas in early February 1954. Probably due to the comic mannerisms of some of the cast who portrayed characters whose activities hovered between the legal and illegal (in particular Mimis Fotopoulos), the film has been classified as a comedy, which it definitely is not. Fotopoulos, featuring as the star of the film in initial newspaper advertisements, partly reproduced the sleazy character he had played in *Fallen Angels*. The important character roles of gang leader Kostas and the police superintendent were played by Dionysis Papagiannopoulos and Kostas Pappas respectively, both with a stage background in classical drama and boulevard theatre, and with some experience in film dramas. As in *The Tower of Knights*, Kostas Theodoridis was the cameraman in this Anzervos production, while the musical score was again written by Argyris Kounadis.[7]

In terms of style, *The Little Mouse* displays a series of crime scenes without dialogue, filmed in a rather expressionistic manner, with only the faces of the actors being highlighted, and supported by an impressive soundtrack. These include the opening scene, where we witness the breaking of a safe with an oxyacetylene cutter, a tool which came to prominence in burglaries after the Second World War – the scene is 'repeated' later in the film, with (probably) reused frames to depict the second burglary that Loukis performs with Kostas (Figure 2.2). The camera also visits – quite extensively for a Greek film of the period – the docks, the streets around the port, the main square of Piraeus,

Figure 2.2   The two burglars open a safe using an oxyacetylene cutter in the opening scene of *The Little Mouse*. Greek Film Archive collection.

and housing reminiscent of the refugee quarters on the outskirts of Piraeus. But the urban landscape remains mostly a background, without developing a strong agency of its own. The crime scenes are either immediately followed by police chase scenes, or else crime and policing are interconnected through montage. The police seem to be ever-present and vigilant, day and night, and the policemen, both in uniform and in civilian clothes, look benevolent, almost friendly. The dialogue, on the other hand, is ambiguous to say the least. What did audiences of the time make of the fatherly police superintendent? In his second appearance, quite early in the film (and as if to announce the plot twists that would follow), he declares in a mellow voice to the young burglar Loukis that, unlike his colleagues who would extricate confessions by torturing suspects, he prefers to wait and observe patiently until repentant suspects fall into his net. He adds that he would rather have people corrected, even if his colleagues thought him stupid. Correction is the goal of legal and penitentiary systems of modernity, but it was also the declared goal of the camps for communist detainees, while the use of torture as an illegal interrogation method could allude to several interwar, Occupation and Civil War contexts, about which there had been constant reporting in the press after 1944 and through to 1953.

The depiction of Kostas, the gang leader, as responsible for leading poor boys into criminal activity, while afterwards tricking them out of their fair share and making it impossible for them to leave crime behind, makes the superintendent and his correction methods seem, at first, the only viable option that young delinquents have for a way out. The role of Vangelis, the friend of Loukis, fulfils both the function of comic relief (albeit slight), but even more that of an alternative option for juvenile delinquents. Vangelis is never caught on the job and, in the end, he gets Christina, the woman of the gang leader, who, as we are told, had originally arrived from Hungary to sing in a nightclub (she speaks Greek with an accent, and uses Hungarian and German words). They both finally manage to embark for Australia, financing the expensive passage and passport costs with Vangelis's cut from a burglary. While walking towards the port, they witness Loukis being taken to jail. The two young men want to put an end to their conflict with the law and the film seems to offer a stark choice: either stay in the country and go to jail, or leave the country for a fresh start somewhere 'where nobody knows us', as the young characters repeatedly say to each other. Translated into the political setting of the early 1950s, this is a popular film narrative about post-war migration, the latter being explained here not only as the outcome of dire need, but also as an escape from marginalisation and discrimination. In that sense, in the Greek context, *The Little Mouse* constitutes one of the earliest filmic representations and one of the few mainstream attempts to discuss massive post-war migration without resorting to comedy (cf. Vamvakas 2004).

The Little Mouse approaches the world outside using realism. 'Realism is not a fixed group of textual attributes but a continuum of signifying potentialities, a range of strategies used by film-makers to mediate information about characters and their situations in reference to dominant conceptions of what constitutes reality' (Hallam and Marshment 2000: 123). In *The Little Mouse*, elements constituting a realist narrative framework include illegal card playing in the back rooms of a nightclub, and also of a travel agency; jail doors closing behind a young criminal; a queue of dock workers waiting to receive a week's wages; a police superintendent sitting in his office with the portraits of King Paul and Queen Frederica behind his back; a nasty ageing criminal being brutal towards his foreign girlfriend; migrants to Australia carrying a heavy suitcase; and a woman burning a shirt while ironing. Using the darkness of film noir, *The Little Mouse* tells a complex story of a society torn between competing perspectives on its traumatic past, and of a younger generation trying to escape from it. It is a film that rewards the discerning viewer with more insights than merely the answer to the question about the original hair colour of Aliki Vougiouklaki.

Notes

1. *To Pontikaki/The Little Mouse*, aka *To koritsi me ta louloudia/The Girl with the Flowers*, produced 1953, distributed 1954, 91 minutes; producer Anzervos; directors Giorgos Asimakopoulos and Nikos Tsiforos; screenwriters Giorgos Asimakopoulos and Nikos Tsiforos; photography Kostas Theodoridis; music Argyris Kounadis. Cast: Mimis Fotopoulos, *Babis*; Dionysis Papagiannopoulos, *Kostas*; Giorgos Levteriotis, *Loukis*; Aliki Vougiouklaki, *Krinoula/Pontikaki*; Kostas Pappas, *Astynomos/Police superintendent*; Mara Lanyie, *Christina*; Nikos Rizos, *Vangelis*; D. Sklavos, *Police detective Grigoris*. It has been suggested that the name Mara Lanyie, which never reappears in a Greek film cast, is a pseudonym for the then art student and later beauty contest participant, model and actress Rika Dialyna, whose participation in the Miss Universe contest in the United States in the summer of 1954 was almost cancelled because of visa difficulties, supposedly due to her political activism (see daily coverage in *Apogevmativini*, May–July 1954). In the film copies available to me, Dialyna appears for five seconds sitting alone, filmed in close up, smiling and smoking. The frames are at the beginning of the nightclub scene (at min. 37 approx.), and seem to me to have been introduced in a later montage.
2. My translation from the French: 'Le film noir ne constitue pas un phénomène spécifiquement américain, mais bien une forme transnationale, qui s'exprime dans des contextes historiques, nationaux et culturels variées et y connaît des déclinaisons particulières.'
3. My translation from the French: 'les formes régulières de sensibilité et les cérémonials stables de la vie quotidienne, bref un flux plus lent du cours historique'.
4. Ploritis refers to the films partly under their Greek distribution titles, for example *Limani ton Apokliron* for *Quai des brumes* and *I Parthena tou Limaniou* for *La*

57

Marie du port. Dédée d'Anvers, on the other hand, is mentioned only in a transliterated form of the original title, rather than under the Greek distribution titles *H Gynaika tis Amartias* aka *To Koritsi tou Dromou*; on distribution titles of foreign films, see Koliodimos ([1997] 2005).
5. We are still a long way from full-fledged biographies of contributors to the Greek movie industry. Alongside the standard encyclopedia and lexicon entries, one can refer for sparse biographical data on Asimakopoulos to the musical documentary made for television by Giorgos Papastefanou about the authors Asimakopoulos, Spyropoulos and Papadoukas's collective (*Mia fora thymamai/Once Upon a Time I Remember*, 1984, available at <http://yorgospapastefanou.gr/playlist/asemakopoulos-spuropoulos-papadoukas/> [last accessed 20 August 2021]); to Georgantopoulos (2000) and to theatrical programmes from the Greek Literary and Historical Archive [ELIA]; and on Tsiforos, to the TV biopics/documentaries *Nikos Tsiforos* (dir. Kesisoglou, 1987) (*Periskopio*, available at <https://archive.ert.gr/69852/> [last accessed 20 August 2021]) and *Nikos Tsiforos* (dir. Psarras, 2018) (*Epoches kai Syngrafeis*, available at <https://www.ertflix.gr/docs/epoxes-kai-sigrafeis/25fev2018-epoches-ke-syngrafis/> [last accessed 20 August 2021]); cf. also Mittler (2007).
6. Deriding 'humorous' references to the Shoah in a comedic context were, it seems, not uncommon. In 1955 the journal *Evraiki Estia* protested in its issue of July 1, against a 'joke' in the revue *Petrokerasa/Sour Cherries* of Takis Morakis and Christos Giannakopoulos. On July 15, the journal reported that the dialog had been taken out of the play after an intervention of the Greek Actors' Union. I would like to express my appreciation to Dimitris Varvaritis for pointing out the comments of *Evraiki Estia* and providing me with scans of the relevant issues.
7. The move to the studios of Milas Film in Egypt for the last joint project, *Wind of Hate*, led also to changes in the crew, and to a largely different cast.

References

Aktsoglou, Babis, and Kyriakidis, Achilleas (eds) (1994), *Yorgos Tzavellas*, Thessaloniki: 35th Thessaloniki Film Festival.
Anon. (1952a), 'Dyo nearoi diepraxan en mia nykti dyo klopas dia na exoikonomisoun ta exoda ton gamon ton' [A Young Couple Made Two Robberies in One Night . . . To Pay the Cost of their Wedding], *Eleftheria*, 8 January, p. 3.
Anon. (1952b), 'Mimitis ton gangksters' [Imitating Gangsters], *Eleftheria*, 29 March, p. 3.
Anon. (1952c), 'Oi sylifthentes eis ton Peiraia kommounistai' [The Arrested Communists in Piraeus], *Eleftheria*, 8 March, p. 3.
Anon. (1952d), 'Echei afxithei i paidiki englimatikotis en Elladi' [Juvenile Delinquency has Risen in Greece], *Eleftheria*, 5 July, p. 3.
Antoniou, Giorgos (2018), 'Bystanders, Rescuers, and Collaborators: A Microhistory of Christian–Jewish Relations, 1943–1944', in Giorgos Antoniou and A. Dirk Moses (eds), *The Holocaust in Greece*, Cambridge: Cambridge University Press, pp. 135–56.
Arkolakis, Manolis (2009), 'Ellinikos kinimatografos (1896–1939): syngriseis se evropaiko kai mesogeiako plaisio. Tropoi paragogis kai dianomis' [Greek Cinema (1896–1939):

Comparisons in a European and Mediterranean Context. Production and Distribution Modes], PhD dissertation, Hellenic Open University.

Avdela, Efi (2019), *When Juvenile Delinquency Became an International Post-War Concern. The United Nations, the Council of Europe and the Place of Greece*, Göttingen: Vienna University Press.

Broe, Dennis (2014), *Class, Crime and International Film Noir: Globalizing America's Dark Art*, New York: Palgrave Macmillan.

Davies, Ann (2009), 'Criminality and the Left in Spanish Retro Noir Films', *Journal of Iberian and Latin American Studies*, 15, pp. 15–28.

Delveroudi, Eliza Anna (2012), 'I oikogeneia Gaziadi kai i DAG Film Co' [Gaziadis Family and DAG Film Co.] in Theodorou Maria, Sakellaropoulos Tasos and Vatsaki Argyro (eds), *Eleftherios Venizelos kai Politistiki Politiki* [Eleftherios Venizelos and Cultural Politics], Athens and Chania: Benaki Museum and National Research Foundation 'Eleftherios K. Venizelos', pp. 244–69.

Dermentzoglou, Alexis (ed.) (2007), *In a Dark Passage: Film Noir in Greek Cinema*, Thessaloniki: Erodios.

Dermentzopoulos, Christos (2002), 'Paradosi kai neoterikotita ston elliniko kinimatografo. Oi tainies oreinis peripeteias' [Tradition and Modernity in Greek Cinema: Mountain Adventure Films], *Optikoakoustiki Koultoura*, 1, pp. 79–98.

Dimopoulos, Dinos (1998), *Enas skinothetis thymatai* [The Recollections of a Film Director], Athens: Proskinio.

Dominé, Jean-François (2008), 'Les représentations successives de la Résistance dans le cinéma français', *Revue historique des armées*, 252, pp. 41–53, <http://journals.openedition.org/rha/3173> (last accessed 20 August 2021).

Eley, Geoff (2001), 'Finding the People's War: Film, British Collective Memory, and World War II', *American Historical Review*, 106:3, pp. 818–38.

Fotiou, Mikela, and Fessas, Nikitas (2017), 'Greek Neo-Noir: Reflecting a Narrative of Crisis', *Filmicon: Journal of Greek Film Studies*, 4, pp. 110–37.

Garçon, François (1984), *De Blum à Petain: cinéma et société française (1936–1944)*, Paris: les éditions du Cerf.

Georgantopoulos, Tasos M. (2000), *Giorgos Asimakopoulos. O prigkipas tis satiras* [Giorgos Asimakopoulos: The Prince of Satire], Athens.

Greffrath, Bettina (1995), *Gesellschaftsbilder der Nachkriegszeit: deutsche Spielfilme 1945–1949*, Pfaffenweiler: Centaurus.

Hallam, Julia, and Marshment, Margaret (2000), *Realism and Popular Cinema*, Manchester: Manchester University Press.

Jeancolas, Jean-Pierre (1992), 'The Inexportable: The Case of French Cinema and Radio in the 1950s', in Richard Dyer and Ginette Vincendeau (eds), *Popular European Cinema*, London: Routledge, pp. 141–8.

Kalfopoulos, Kostas (ed.) (2016), *18 keimena gia ton Yanni Mari* [18 Essays for Yannis Maris], Athens: Patakis.

Kartalou, Athina (2002), 'Protasi gia ena plaisio anagnosis ton eidon ston elliniko kinimatografo' [A Suggestion for a Reading Framework of Genres in Greek Cinema], *Optikoakoustiki Koultoura*, 1, pp. 25–35.

Kassaveti, Ursula-Helen (2017), *Antestramena kosmoeidola. Dikastiko drama, melodrama, erotikos kinimatografos (1966–1974). Mia politismiki anagnosi* [Reversed

Worldviews: Courtroom Drama, Melodrama, Erotic Cinema (1966–1974): A Cultural Reading], Athens: Epikentro.

Katsapis, Kostas (2013), *To 'provlima-neolaia'. Modernoi neoi, paradosi kai amfisvitisi sti metapolemiki Ellada, 1964–1974* [The 'Youth Problem': Modern Youth, Tradition and Contestation in Post-war Greece, 1964–1974], Athens: Aprovleptes.

Koliodimos, Dimitris ([1997] 2005), *80 hronia xenos kinimatografos stin Ellada* [80 Years of Foreign Cinema in Greece], Athens: Oxy.

Králová, Kateřina (2018), 'Being a Holocaust Survivor in Greece: Narratives of the Postwar Period, 1944–1953', in Giorgos Antoniou and A. Dirk Moses (eds), *The Holocaust in Greece*, Cambridge: Cambridge University Press, pp. 304–26.

Kymionis, Stelios (2000), 'The Genre of Mountain Film: The Ideological Parameters of its Subgenres', *Journal of Modern Greek Studies*, 18:1, pp. 53–66.

Kyrtsis, Alexandros-Andreas (1994), 'Politismikes kai ideologikes ekfraseis tis metemfyliopolemikis neoterikotitas' [Cultural and Ideological Views of Post-Civil War Modernity], in *I elliniki koininia kata tin proti metapolemiki periodo (1945–1967)* [Greek Society during the First Post-War Period (1945–1965)], Athens: Sakis Karagiorgas Foundation, pp. 399–413.

Lazaridis, Giorgos (1999), *Flash Back: Mia zoi sinema* [Flash Back: A Life as Cinema], Athens: Nea Synora – Livanis.

Mitropoulou, Aglaia (1980), *Ellinikos kinimatografos* [Greek Cinema], Athens: Thymeli.

Mittler, Sylvia (2007), 'Subversive Storytelling: Popular Historiography, Alternative Cultural Memory, and Modern Greek Humorist Nikos Tsiforos', in Francisco Cota Fagundes and Irene Maria F. Blayer (eds), *Oral and Written Narratives and Cultural Identity*, New York: Peter Lang, pp. 175–88.

Mostafa, Dalia Said (2018), 'Shifting Narratives of the Police in Egyptian Cinema before and after the January 2011 Revolution', *Contemporary Levant*, 3:2, pp. 137–52.

Papari, Katerina (2018), 'The Plurality of Greeknesses in Interwar Greece: A Matter of Culture or Politics?', *Historein*, 17:2, <https://ejournals.epublishing.ekt.gr/pfiles/journals/14/editor-uploads/issues/735/main735.html?1=735&2=10833> (last accessed 10 August 2021).

Petris, Tasos N. (1988), *Stelios Tatasopoulos*, Athens: Etaireia Ellinon Skinotheton.

Pillard, Thomas (2014), *Le film noir français face aux bouleversements de la France d'après-guerre 1946–1960*, Paris: Joseph K.

Ploritis, Marios (1952), 'O kinimatografos: oi nees tainies' [Cinema: The New Movies], *Eleftheria*, 16 January, p. 2.

Ploritis, Marios (1954), 'O kinimatografos: oi nees tainies' [Cinema: The New Movies], *Eleftheria*, 17 February, p. 2.

Poupou, Anna (2007), "Représenter la reconstruction: le paysage urbain dans les films grecs de la période 1950–1974', PhD dissertation, Paris 3: Sorbonne Nouvelle.

Sorlin, Pierre (1991), *European Cinemas, European Societies 1939–1990*, London: Routledge.

Spicer, Andrew (ed.) (2007), *European Film Noir*, Manchester: Manchester University Press.

Stassinopoulou, Maria A. (2000a), 'Creating Distraction after Destruction: Representations of the Military in the Greek Film', *Journal of Modern Greek Studies*, 18:1, pp. 37–52.

Stassinopoulou, Maria A. (2000b), 'O kinimatografos ston elliniko astiko horo kai I kinimatografiki eikonografia tis ellinikis polis sto mesopolemo. Asymvates poreies, diaforetikes tachytites' [Cinema in Urban Space and the Cinematic Iconography of the Greek City during the Interwar Period: Incompatible Trajectories, Different Paces], in *I poli stous neoterous chronous, mesogeiakes kai valkanikes opseis (19os–20s ai.)* [The City in Modern Times: Mediterranean and Balkan Aspects (19th–20th Centuries)], Athens: Etaireia Meletis Neou Ellinismou, pp. 353–68.

Stassinopoulou, Maria A. (2000c), 'Reality Bites: A Feature Film History of Greece 1950–1963', unpublished habilitation thesis, University of Vienna.

Tziovas, Dimitris (1989), *Oi metamorfoseis tou ethnikou kai to ideologima tis ellinikotitas sto mesopolemo* [The Transformations of the National and the Ideology of Greekness during the Interwar Period], Athens: Odysseas.

Valoukos, Stathis (1998), *Filmografia ellinikou kinimatografou 1914–1998* [Filmography of Greek Cinema 1914–1998], Athens: Aigokeros.

Vamvakas, Vassilis (2004), 'I "metanastefsi" tou ellinikou kinimatografou apo to emporiko sto politiko stigma' [The Immigration of Greek Cinema from the Commercial to the Political Position], in Foteini Tomai-Konstantopoulou (ed.), *I metanastefsi ston kinimatografo* [Immigration in Cinema], Athens: Papazisis, pp. 41–62.

Vincendeau, Ginette (1998), 'Issues in European Cinema', in John Hill and Pamela Church Gibson (eds), *The Oxford Guide to Film Studies*, Oxford: Oxford University Press, pp. 440–8.

3. HISTORICAL COINCIDENCE OR GENERIC CROSS-POLLINATION? *THE ANGRY HILLS* AND THE BIRTH OF FILM NOIR IN GREECE

Yannis Tzioumakis

This chapter aims to contribute to the increasing scholarly interest in noir studies within a Greek film context, through an examination of *The Angry Hills* (dir. Aldrich, 1959), a British-American production that was shot for the most part in Greece in 1958. Produced by the British Raymond Stross Productions and released by Hollywood major MGM, *The Angry Hills* was the second Hollywood-sponsored 'runaway' film production in the country, after 20th Century-Fox's *Boy on a Dolphin* (dir. Negulesco, 1957). That film's success had opened the path for a wave of such productions by the rest of the Hollywood studios that lasted until the late 1960s, before a military coup in 1967 dramatically changed conditions in the country and discouraged the Hollywood majors from selecting Greece as a location for their international productions. The film told the convoluted story of a US Second World War correspondent who finds himself in Greece on the eve of the German Occupation of 1941, and becomes involved in a scheme to deliver a list of names of Greek Resistance spies to British intelligence. Branded by trade and popular press of the time as a 'war picture' (Rich. 1959), a 'cloak and dagger thriller' (A-MY-Y 1959), a 'melodrama' (Scott 1959) and 'a spy drama' (Harford 1959), and featuring as its main character an American in a foreign land who becomes gradually and reluctantly implicated in the war and the country's local politics, *The Angry Hills* has similarities with *Casablanca* (dir. Curtiz, 1942), although the latter was shot in the Warner Bros. studio backlot rather than on location.

Alongside this breadth of epithets chosen by contemporaneous critics to describe the film's generic identity, one cannot help but notice that both the story itself and the style in which it is told are characterised by strong noir elements, as these have been identified by a number of scholars and critics in numerous American films that cut across studios, genres and production trends (Walker 1994; Crowther 1990; Borde and Chaumeton 2002; Dickos 2002). Such elements, however, acquire an even greater significance when one considers that the film was directed by Robert Aldrich and scripted by Albert Isaac Bezzerides. Three years prior to the production of *The Angry Hills*, this duo had been lauded by critics for their collaboration on *Kiss Me Deadly* (1955). That film is considered a major contribution to the noir canon and, for some, is the last great title of the classic noir era in US cinema that extends from the early 1940s to the late 1950s (see, for instance, Borde and Chaumeton 2002: 155). Working separately, Aldrich and Bezzerides had also established a reputation for 'tough' pictures with strong noir elements, with the former responsible, within a short number of years, for such telling titles as *World for Ransom* (1954), *The Big Knife* (1955) and *The Garment Jungle* (1957). Greek-Armenian Bezzerides, on the other hand, had been a successful novelist whose fiction was adapted by other screenwriters in such well-known noirs as *They Drive by Night* (dir. Walsh, 1940), and who adapted his own work or wrote original screenplays for such classics as *Thieves' Highway* (dir. Dassin, 1949), *Sirocco* (dir. Bernhardt, 1951) and *On Dangerous Ground* (dir. Ray, 1951). Furthermore, *The Angry Hills* starred Robert Mitchum, a major Hollywood star with a significant presence in key noirs such as *Out of the Past* (dir. Tourneur, 1947) and *The Night of the Hunter* (dir. Laughton, 1955).

As this chapter will demonstrate, the presence of Aldrich and Bezzerides in Greece in 1958, collaborating for the first time since the success of *Kiss Me Deadly* on another film with a strong noir pedigree, was a historical accident. However, this presence also coincided with the starting point of a Greek film production trend with strong noir elements, which contemporary critics and scholars have identified as a noir film cycle that extended into the mid-1960s (see, in particular, Poupou 2018; Dermentzoglou 2007). The chapter, then, has two objectives. On the one hand, its main focus is an examination of the noir qualities of *The Angry Hills* on the textual level, focusing not only on the film's formal elements and the ways these mobilise the noir aesthetic, but also on the political implications of such mobilisation. As I will argue, the film functions as a potent allegory of the political climate in 1950s Greece by using an iconography that often invokes images associated with the Greek Civil War and reflects a spirit of political repression.

On the other hand, and beyond its emphasis on the film as text, the chapter also briefly explores the extent to which the presence of Aldrich and Bezzerides in Greece in the spring and summer of 1958 became a springboard for the emergence of the Greek film noir cycle of the late 1950s and early 1960s. Although the evidence for such an argument is inconclusive, the chapter shows that *The Angry Hills* production team did use Greek film resources and had encounters with Greek film talent that later became associated with the Greek noir films of the era. Besides suggesting the possibility of informal collaboration and knowledge exchange between Hollywood and the Greek film industry, such an argument also paves the way for understanding the establishment of noir in Greece as influenced by Hollywood in a more material way than has been accounted for.

Making *The Angry Hills* in Greece: A 'Gorilla Picture' with a Twist

Although the Hollywood film studios started practising 'runaway' film production in Europe and the rest of the world in the immediate post-WWII era (Steinhart 2019: 23), Greece remained outside their sphere of activity until well into the late 1950s. However, as this trend intensified in the 1950s, Greece finally became a destination for Hollywood when 20th Century-Fox decided to make *Boy on a Dolphin* in Greece, with exterior locations in Athens and on the picturesque island of Hydra. The film was a substantial box-office success, and introduced Greece to an international audience in glorious CinemaScope and Technicolor as an exotic location of rugged beauty with a revered ancient past, surrounded by the crystal clear waters of the Aegean and Ionian seas. It also paved the way, in the ensuing years, for other Hollywood runaway productions, with *The Guns of Navarone* (dir. Thompson, 1961), *America, America* (dir. Kazan, 1963) and *Zorba the Greek* (dir. Cacoyannis, 1964) being the most prominent.

Besides becoming a destination for ambitious productions that also became significant critical and commercial successes, Greece also welcomed other Hollywood-sponsored productions that were of more limited scope and ambition. First on this list was *The Angry Hills*, a film based on the titular novel by Leon Uris, which was first published in 1955. In the same year, Uris's first novel, *Battle Cry* (originally published in 1953), was adapted by the author for a film under the same title directed by Raoul Walsh and released by Warner Bros. *Battle Cry*, a Second World War adventure-romance that was partly shot on location in Puerto Rico, proved extremely successful at the North American box office (Finler 2003: 298). This success brought Uris a lot of attention and, not surprisingly, *The Angry Hills*, which also had a strong Second World War adventure-romance interest, was quickly optioned by British producer Raymond Stross. According to the trade press of the time, Stross bought the rights to the book in January 1957, before the release of *Boy on a Dolphin* in April 1957 put Greece on the map as a destination for international filmmaking (Anon. 1957).

Stross, however, was not directly related to the Hollywood majors. Through his company Raymond Stross Productions, he had managed to emerge in the 1950s as a significant force in British cinema, with a variety of pictures that ranged in terms of genre and quality. However, towards the end of the decade, Stross and other British producers benefited from MGM's opening up to the British film industry, which occurred at a time when the Hollywood major was transitioning from an old-fashioned studio to a financier and distributor of independent productions. As Britain continued to be Hollywood's most important overseas market (Balio 2018: 204), MGM made several deals with British producers, including Raymond Stross, who at that point was still a relatively small-time producer.

At the same time, Robert Aldrich, despite the success of *Kiss Me Deadly*, could not easily find employment in Hollywood and decided to leave the United States. As he explained in an interview, he had refused to soften aspects of his film *The Garment Jungle* and had been fired from that production by Columbia boss Harry Cohn (Silver 1970: 64). While in Europe, he quickly agreed to make two films for British producers, the war film *Ten Seconds to Hell* (1959) for Michael Carreras (a producer associated with Hammer Films), which was shot in Berlin and its famous UFA studios, and *The Angry Hills* for Raymond Stross (Sauvage 1976/1977: 104).

As is clear then, *The Angry Hills* was not a major production. However, it was not a small film either – the participation of Hollywood star Robert Mitchum in the lead role clearly attested to this – but rather a film of a particular scope, scale and ambition. The budget was set at a little more than $1 million,[1] it was shot in black and white, while the cast that surrounded Mitchum included minor stars such as Stanley Baker, Gia Scala and Elisabeth Mueller. With the exception of Greek actors Dimitris Nikolaidis and Kostas Gousgounis, and a cabaret singer under the name Marita Constantinou, no other person of Greek origin appears in the film's credits, with a number of non-Greek actors cast to play Greek bit parts, and all the crew positions occupied by British technicians. The film's interior scenes were shot at the MGM British studios in Borehamwood, UK,[2] while the exteriors were shot in Athens, on the nearby Mount Parnassos, and in villages in the region. In many ways the film was organised as an efficient production focused on Mitchum's stardom, and a genre story in an unusual location, overseen by a producer and a director with experience in genre films made with relatively limited resources.

On the other hand, both the film's director and the star seemed to be aware of the negative qualities of this kind of limited-ambition film, calling it retrospectively a 'gorilla picture', a kind of film that 'you wanted to work, labored hard to make work, but knew all along will never work no matter what you did' (Aldrich, quoted in Miller and Arnold 2004: xi). Looking back at his career, Aldrich disparaged *The Angry Hills* in a number of interviews, calling it a 'catastrophe' (Bogdanovich [1965] 2004: 37), a 'terrible picture' and a 'joke' (Petit and Combs [1977] 2004: 130), with critics largely agreeing with this summation and ignoring it in examinations of the filmmaker's rich oeuvre (see, for instance, Combs 1978; Williams 2004). However, as this chapter, which is the first sustained examination of the film, will argue, *The Angry Hills* has a number of interesting qualities, especially when considered in the context of Hollywood film production in Greece and its engagement with the then-nascent Greek film industry, as well as its potential contribution to the establishment of Greek film noir.

When pre-production started in late April 1958 (Ploritis 1958: 2), Aldrich quickly realised that Uris's screenplay contained elements that made the story unrealistic (Addison [1962] 2004: 16). Despite writing a novel in which the action takes place in Greece, Uris had never visited the country, and therefore his screenplay did not translate well in the context of staging scenes on location. Aldrich requested major changes and Stross tried to resolve the problem by sending Uris on a short trip to Greece to get a feel for the place and draw inspiration for the changes that needed to be made (Cameron and Shivas [1963] 2004: 25). However, Aldrich rejected Uris's follow-up notes that aimed to provide background, exposition and motivation for a number of scenes, and requested a new screenplay.[3] He convinced Stross to hire A. I. Bezzerides to undertake this task.

Compared to Uris, Bezzerides was a very different type of writer. While Uris became known for historical popular fiction, Bezzerides cut his teeth on 'pulp fiction modernism', with his stories and novels demonstrating an affinity for 'marginalised downtrodden ethnic' characters and 'life in the streets' of major American metropolises (Kalogeras 2004–05: 18). Not surprisingly, this kind of work made him a natural for films with noir elements, and he contributed to many such films in the 1940s and 1950s, both through adapting his own work and the work of others, as mentioned above. Indeed, Kalogeras highlights in Bezzerides's writing an ability 'to reproduce through dialogue an urban milieu, but also the ambiguity in human motives, especially of those who presumably stand for the law' (Kalogeras 2004–05: 29). Such elements tend to be central to the world of noir. They are also evident in the story of *The Angry Hills*, with the main character having to navigate through a foreign urban environment, and move amid an assemblage of Greek, German and British people, without knowing whom to trust.

On the other hand, despite his part-Greek ethnic background, Bezzerides had much more contact with his Armenian origins, and was therefore not that much better equipped than Uris to understand the particularities and peculiarities of Greece in the 1940s. Kalogeras asserts that Bezzerides was not knowledgeable on the topic of Greek history, and that 'he had no desire to go against the limitations of the movie storyline or of the Hollywood clichés and provide a more complex view of Greece' than the one expected from the type of production that *The Angry Hills* was (2004–05: 35). Still, his ability to come up with more realistic dialogue than Uris, in tandem with some references to politics that would be difficult to find in Greek films of the time, make his contribution to *The Angry Hills* a very important one. Indeed, his involvement in the film was such that in the end he was the only one credited as the screenwriter, with Uris receiving credit solely for being the author of the original source book.

The film's shooting also presented numerous problems, ranging from logistical issues pertaining to dealing with Greek organisations and authorities to Robert Mitchum's 'disengaged' performance (Addison [1962] 2004: 15). In the end, the production managed to complete all the unit work in Greece within a six-week period (Anon. 1959: 4), before moving to the United Kingdom for the interior scenes, while Freddy Germanos reports that the production received substantial technical support from Studio Alpha, a well-equipped, newly opened studio in Marousi, Athens (Germanos 1958: 3). Post-production proved to be equally problematic, with Stross taking the film away from Aldrich and implementing his own ideas in the editing process, which created a rift between director and producer (Silver 1970: 65). It is not surprising, then, that *The Angry Hills* got a lukewarm reception from critics and performed poorly at the global theatrical box office.[4] If one adds to this Aldrich's disparaging comments on the film's quality, it is no wonder that the film represents a tiny footnote in film history.

However, as the rest of this chapter will demonstrate, the film has a number of extremely interesting qualities if examined within a Greek cinema context, especially in relation to the Greek film noir cycle of the late 1950s and 1960s. The next section will discuss the film's noir characteristics, including its arguably most famous scene of a topless cabaret dancer. It will focus on its visual style, examining the ways it borrows from what critics have identified as noir codes. It will also attend to the film's narrative, highlighting the ways in which Aldrich uses aspects of what *The Angry Hills* reviewers saw as the 'adventure film in foreign setting' (Silver and Ursini 1995: 65) formula to create a dark world characterised by 'blackmail, informing, theft [. . .] brutality and murder', elements that have been associated routinely with the noir universe (Borde and Chaumeton 2002: 5). The chapter will then explore the extent to which the film – like all noirs of the 1940s and 1950s – can be read as an allegory of the political environment of the time. However, in this case it is not the environment of its country of origin that will be privileged, but that of its *host country*, Greece, an issue that has been raised by the limited Greek scholarly work on the film (see especially Kalogeras 2004–05; 2016). As the chapter will argue, it is through an examination as noir that the film finds its potency, presenting an unfamiliar Greece, a Greece unlike the one shown in the films of indigenous production or the one highlighted by other runaway film productions at that time.

In lieu of a conclusion, the chapter will end with an examination of the extent to which the film and its creative agents helped usher in the film noir cycle in Greece. Through an investigation of a number of events during its shooting, I will show that a proportion of Greek talent involved in the noir films of the late 1950s and early 1960s may have been close to the production of *The Angry Hills*, benefiting from Aldrich's and Bezzerides's experience in noir, and drawing inspiration for films such as *Eglima sto Kolonaki/Murder in Kolonaki* (dir. Aliferis, 1959) and *Eglima sta Paraskinia/Murder Backstage* (dir. Katsouridis, 1960) that spearheaded the cycle. It is in this dual fashion that *The Angry Hills* can amplify an understanding of film noir in the Greek context.

A Nightmare Greece

In his sweeping introduction to film noir, Michael Walker has approached the field generically by perceiving it as combining

> a number of elements in a way which makes it peculiarly complex and interesting: a distinctive and exciting visual style, an unusual narrative complexity, a generally more critical and subversive view of American ideology than the norm [. . .] [a] lack of sentimentality, [a] willingness to probe the darker areas of sexuality, [a presence of] rich subtexts, [the] emotional force of the downbeat. (1994: 8)

Despite *The Angry Hills*'s generic designation by contemporaneous reviewers as a 'war picture', a 'cloak and dagger thriller', a 'melodrama'[5] or 'a spy drama', one would be hard pressed not to notice that all the elements in Walker's definition of noir are integral to Aldrich's film. And even though a very substantial part of the film takes place away from the city, in the mountainous villages of the Greek countryside where protagonist Mike Morrison is fleeing the Nazis' persecution while recovering from an injury under the care of a beautiful young village girl, the world of noir is never too far away. As Dickos has argued of noir films in which part of the action takes place in the countryside, the protagonist's unsuccessful effort to 'find solace in the country' or to have his 'damaged li[fe] [. . .] nourished by rural peacefulness' is a sign of the continuous 'urban influence' on him, which brings him once again into the fold of a noir world (Dickos 2002: xii). He might well be talking about *The Angry Hills*'s protagonist who, after taking refuge in abandoned villages and hidden monasteries, has to return to the city, leaving behind Eleftheria, the Greek village girl who took care of him (and whose name means 'freedom' in Greek), who is quickly killed.

Like many noir heroes, Mike Morrison finds himself at the centre of the story in *The Angry Hills* by accident. As a war correspondent, he arrives in

Athens from Budapest, in transit to his next destination. 'What time's the last plane to London?', is the first question he asks the receptionist as soon as he arrives at the Athens landmark hotel, Grande Bretagne. He is informed that he has six hours, which is long enough to have a bath and check the 'local action', as he has heard that a beautiful singer is quite the attraction in one of the city's *tavernas*. But even before he makes his way to his room, it becomes clear that he is being watched by a man in a white suit. Morrison bumps into a British officer, Phillips, whom he knows from a previous mission. The next scene finds Morrison in a bathtub freshening up, when another man enters his room, his motives unclear. Thinking it is the hotel maid, Morrison invites her to rub his back. The intruder is revealed to be Stergiou, another of Morrison's old acquaintances. He is there to recruit the American for a mission that involves delivering a list of sixteen names to British intelligence. The names are of well-respected Greek people who will collaborate with the Germans when they occupy Greece, but who will also act as double agents by spying for the British government. The man in the white suit is outside the room listening to the conversation. Morrison tries to get out of this arrangement, but he is already 'involved'. Stergiou informs him that the enemy is already on his tail, and the only thing Stergiou can do is give him a financial incentive to carry out the mission. In the middle of their conversation, the phone rings. Phillips, the British officer Morrison had bumped into in the hotel lobby in the previous scene, gives him the details of where the 'local action' takes place. Morrison makes a note and then continues the negotiations with Stergiou. The importance of the mission cannot get in the way of the promise of Athens's night life, even on the eve of the German march into the city.

This scene early in the course of the narrative is very important in telegraphing as noir what, on the surface, looks like a war or a spy picture. The reluctant and cynical hero accepts the mission not because of his sense of duty, but because the price he will have to pay if he refuses to take it will be higher. When Stergiou starts talking to Morrison with the latter still in the bathtub, both men are lit in high contrast, which creates heavy shadows of Stergiou's figure against the walls of the hotel room. Such lighting suggests that the man's motives might be questionable, but Morrison, who is closer to the camera, is also covered by a heavy shadow, with his face hardly visible. When he finds out about Cleopatra, the beautiful *taverna* singer, in the middle of his negotiation with Stergiou, his instant switch to a lighter tone indicates that he (and the film) do not play fully by the (war and spy film genre) rules, paving the way for narrative and stylistic flourishes that contribute to the noir aesthetic. As it happens, the film's most prominent element of noir iconography and – depending on which version of the film one views – transgression can be found in the following few sequences. Meanwhile the narrative moves to establish Morrison's antagonists, continuing to sketch Greece as a country gripped by depravity and vice.

Stergiou leaves Morrison's room and the hotel. The mysterious man in the white suit nods to a uniformed man in the hotel lobby to follow Stergiou. Meanwhile, he makes his way along the dirt roads of Athens's neighbourhoods to the home of the chief of the Gestapo, Conrad Heisler. The latter shares the house with Maria Tassos, who is the sister of the man in the white suit, Dimitrios Tassos. As they wait for him to arrive, we see Heisler touching young Maria with a whip and asking her if she likes 'to be kissed'. It is obvious that Maria is Heisler's mistress or, worse, is in a sexually dependent relationship with him. The film's MPPA files reveal correspondence between the Production Code Administration and MGM about the depiction of this relationship in the screenplay, with the PCA understanding the relationship as prostitution, and seeing Dimitrios Tassos 'as a pimp for his sister', which contributes further to the increasingly unhealthy world of *The Angry Hills*.[6] However, despite the PCA's request that this representation be avoided, the scene leaves little to the imagination when Dimitrios arrives. Seeing his sister straightening her skimpy dress, he suggests that he should have come later.

The level of explicitness represented in this scene, however, pales in comparison to the next scene, which sees Morrison and Phillips in a Greek *taverna*, listening to Cleopatra singing and dancing. The young entertainer is wearing a long skirt, but her cropped top is open with her breasts on full display. She is singing an upbeat Greek song called 'Matia Stratigoi' (which loosely translates as 'Eyes that Look like an Army General'), while gyrating her hips suggestively and blowing kisses to Morrison, who seems to be in disbelief at the level of nudity in front of him. At some point she comes to sit at their table, asking for champagne. Morrison, however, is informed that there is a phone call for him, and leaves the table. The call brings Morrison back to the mission of taking the list out of the country and reveals some new details about where he can get his cash incentive. As these are negotiated, Cleopatra starts dancing and singing the same song again in the background. The film once again departs from the conventions of the war and adventure genres by emphasising instead mood and ambience as these are conveyed by Cleopatra's presence.

This scene could not have appeared either in the version of the film released in US cinemas by MGM, or that released by Damaskinos-Mihailidis, which represented MGM in Greece, in local cinemas. The Production Code Administration in the US and the censorship organisations in Greece forbade explicit nudity. Indeed, the PCA had already warned the production during the scriptwriting stage that the scene with Cleopatra would not be deemed 'acceptable', stating that 'the acceptability of the dance itself will depend entirely on the manner in which it is filmed in the finished picture'.[7] Under these circumstances, a scene with a semi-naked Cleopatra would have been impossible, so Aldrich shot two different versions of the scene, one as described above, and one with Cleopatra's cropped top covering her bust completely (Bogdanovich [1965]

2004: 37).[8] The singer was portrayed by Athens-born cabaret singer Marita Constantinou, who was announced in May 1958 as contracted to perform 'in a provocative nightclub scene [. . .] one of the most exciting routines ever to be filmed'. According to the press release that featured this quote, the singer was performing in the well-known Casanova Club in London when she was signed by Stross for *The Angry Hills*, and this was her only film credit.[9]

The cabaret scene with the topless entertainer locates the film firmly in the noir tradition. It reveals Athens at night as a city that is no different from the US film noir metropolises that have been described as 'sinful and polluting' (Hirsch 1981: 79), as places where the passions and obsessions of desperate characters 'drive them to upset a precarious moral ground' (Dickos 2002: xi). Even on the eve of the Nazis' march into Athens, the city has great pleasures and vices to offer. However, it is the following two scenes that stamp the film with an unmistakably noir visual style. The hallmarks of this style include 'the use of low-key lighting to create unusual shadows and chiaroscuro effects, a high proportion of night scenes [. . .] deep focus shots framing characters in cluttered, claustrophobic interiors, a greater or lesser extent of expressionistic distortion', especially staged in the city as 'a dangerous, hostile place', a place where 'the hero tends to take to the streets uneasily, aware of himself as an outsider' (Walker 1994: 25–6, 30), and one could not fail to see all these characteristics in action in *The Angry Hills*.

In the first of the two scenes, Morrison arrives in the office of American archaeologist Thackeray, who is supposed to give him the money Stergiou promised for taking on the mission, only to find him dead. To arrive at the scene of the crime, Morrison passes through a long corridor, and then a dark room full of marble figureheads, some of which are placed very close to the camera, creating a particularly strange environment. Indeed, at one point Morrison's head is confined among the heads of these statues, in a particularly cluttered image composition that very clearly signals the abnormality of the situation. Finding Thackeray dead on the floor, Morrison grabs a light hanging from the ceiling and swings it in the body's direction to see his surroundings more clearly. This creates a swirling and disorienting effect, making the room flash in flourishes of light and dark. Dickos suggests that Aldrich's heroes tend to be placed 'in a world disoriented by the vigor of amorality and violence' (2002: 130), and it looks like this scene is a literal example of this argument. To make things even more complex, Tassos, gun in hand, suddenly appears from behind a bookcase, taking Morrison by surprise. However, the scene quickly re-establishes the hero's ability to manage, momentarily at least, difficult situations as Morrison shows his tough-man skills. He knocks Tassos down with a punch, and then runs away. As is clear, the film is now in full noir territory as, alongside the visual style and iconography, Thackeray's murder adds another strong noir ingredient to the narrative.

However, visually, the film reaches its noir apogee in the following scene, which sees Morrison in the dark streets of Athens, trying to get away from Tassos, who has recovered quickly, and his gang of local thugs. The juxtaposition between hunted and hunters takes place under noir's trademark chiaroscuro, with parts of the dark streets marked by strong lighting, which creates impressive shadows that fall on the walls of the Athenian houses. The lights of Tassos's car, and a torchlight used by the gang members, contribute to the dramatic lighting of the scene, making for a truly exciting night chase sequence. It is also a rare opportunity to see Athens by night through the eyes of a foreign production in Greece that was much better resourced than Greek productions of the time. Athens looks dark and inhospitable, uninviting and dangerous, a true noir city. Besides Morrison and his adversaries, there is no one else on the streets. At some point Morrison is captured, but again he manages to escape (Figure 3.1). Tassos and his thugs close in on him again, but a military convoy appears as *deus ex machina* on one of the streets, and Morrison jumps into one of the vehicles, staging a last-minute escape. Although the audience does not see it, we learn later that the convoy was ambushed and that Morrison was badly injured.

It is at this point that the film changes mood and iconography, as the action now shifts to the Greek mountains and a typical village, where Morrison wakes up. As he recovers with the help of Eleftheria and her family, he becomes involved in the Resistance movement in the mountains, and participates in a mission to neutralise a German unit in a neighbouring village, while he also

Figure 3.1 The lead character Morrison (Robert Mitchum), filmed in noir's trademark chiaroscuro, escapes his chasers, but only momentarily. Digital still from *The Angry Hills*.

starts to become sexually involved with Eleftheria. But Heisler is on his tail and, through a spy, he learns of Morrison's whereabouts. When the Resistance group moves against the Germans, the latter are waiting for them. They kill most of the members of the group, though Morrison and another man escape. The Germans then go to Eleftheria's village and organise a mass execution in the village square. Eleftheria sacrifices herself by arranging for Morrison to leave before the Germans arrive. After hiding in a monastery in the mountains, Morrison returns to Athens where, with the help of Lisa Kyriakides, Heisler's former lover and one of the names on Morrison's list, he manages to escape together with Lisa's children, who had been used as leverage by Heisler to force Lisa to betray Morrison.

At first sight, the above summary might suggest that the film has largely eschewed the noir world, at least stylistically, given the change of scenery from the city to the countryside, and the much stronger presence of war-picture generic ingredients. On a closer look though, the increasingly convoluted narrative, the preponderance of sexually dependent relationships in which 'sex, greed and power tend to displace love as the motivating feature' (Walker 1994: 38), the strong manifestation of themes of 'pursuit and persecution' (Dickos 2002: 194), and the presence of a 'perpetual threat and contestation' (Dixon 2009: 4) that characterise films in the noir canon seem also to underpin every scene and action in this part of *The Angry Hills*. But perhaps the element that best links this part of the film with the world of noir is its potential for allegorical interpretation. I would like to argue that the scenes in the countryside strongly evoke themes and iconography associated with the Greek Civil War of 1944–49, a taboo topic for Greek film production of the time, and something that the reviews of the film in the foreign press were not in a position to identify.

Starting from iconography, one cannot ignore the film's focus on the rugged, mountainous Greek terrain, which not only hosted Resistance groups organised against the Nazis, such as the Greek People's Liberation Army, but also members of the Democratic Army of Greece, which represented forces supported by the Greek Communist Party that fought against the internationally recognised government of Greece led by right-wing and centre forces in the aftermath of the Second World War. Although none of these groups or parties are mentioned in the film, the barren landscape, the deserted villages with makeshift houses, the small guerrilla groups planning missions and the hiding of fighters in the mountains make the evocation of the Civil War inevitable, at least to a Greek audience. Furthermore, there is a scene where Morrison teasingly asks Eleftheria if he can call her 'Lefty', adding that, where he comes from, the word describes 'some very special people'. Whether this particular line of dialogue can be attributed to the left-wing politics of Bezzerides, or is Aldrich's homage to Clifford Odets, author of *Waiting for Lefty*, with whom he collaborated on the noir *The Big Knife* (1955) (Williams 2004: 17), it remains a potent and daring reference to partisan politics. The Hollywood blacklist was still in effect at the time of the film's making, while Greek left-wing politics had gone underground, with the Communist Party outlawed until the mid-1970s.

However, arguably the most potent scene in support of such an argument is the retaliatory execution of the male village population by the Nazis, and its aftermath. Helped by a villager, played by well-known Greek actor Dimitris Nikolaidis, Nazi troops, led by Tassos, gather all the people in Eleftheria's village, and parade them in the middle of the night in an alley. The mass execution is to avenge the villagers' 'sheltering troops of the enemy'. By that time Morrison has already left, making the execution scene not particularly integral to the narrative of the hero's escape from the Nazis. The scene also sees men of the village denouncing the local collaborator, who ends up being executed too. The SS officer calls the names of several men, who are executed one by one. After the third killing, the scene cuts to Eleftheria, who has managed to escape during the march of her compatriots, screaming in distress as she hears the shootings. Another cut moves the action to the next morning. Eleftheria comes out of the house, only to see a particularly 'Greek' picture: a number of dead men on the street, and old and young women over the men's bodies, crying and cursing the fate that has fallen upon them (Figure 3.2). One can even hear the unmistakable voice of an old Greek woman screaming in pain, as another cut brings the audience even closer to the mass mourning.

The fact that this scene is not especially integral to the narrative is perhaps a good reason to extol its potential for allegory. On the one hand, given its success in presenting a picture that would certainly resonate with Greek people, it

Figure 3.2 A particularly 'Greek' picture in a noir film. Digital still from *The Angry Hills*.

looks as though Aldrich and Bezzerides have managed to capture some of the essence of Greece that Uris had been unable to provide in his screenplay. On the other hand, the scene's emphasis on mass executions, collaborators and traitors, dead people on the streets and mass mourning operates well both in terms of the film's 'surface structure' and 'deep structure' (Stam et al. 1992: 66). As part of the former, it represents part of a story taking place during the Second World War. In terms of the latter, it mobilises images for a particular audience that relate to the national psyche, from Nazi atrocities to the Civil War killings on both sides that took place primarily in rural and mountainous Greek regions. With films, including noirs, implying continuities between the time they are set and the time they are made (Humphries 2004: 227), it is clear that these scenes have the potential for political interpretations, although this would probably be limited to Greek audiences of the time and contemporary ones.

Such interpretations of this part of *The Angry Hills* connect well with other scholarly efforts to understand the film's allegorical dimensions. Focusing primarily on the last thirty minutes of the film, when Morrison returns to Athens and is involved with Lisa Kyriakides, Kalogeras comments on the ways in which the film presents Athens, now mostly in daylight scenes, as a city that 'appears strangely silent and empty' (Kalogeras 2004–05: 34). Even though many of the film's scenes take place on the streets of the Greek capital, both in central locations and in Tourkolimano in Piraeus, very few people appear as passers-by. For Kalogeras, the silence on the city streets 'reflects the repressive political and social conditions prevalent in Greece at the time' (2004–05: 35), an argument he reiterates in his later work that focuses on Bezzerides's screenplays (2016: 79). In that later work, Kalogeras somewhat broadens the argument, by also taking into consideration the film's noir elements, especially its visual style, as contributing to such allegorical interpretations, with the shadowy world of the film corresponding to the ambiguous political atmosphere of 1950s Greece. Whether one approaches the film's allegorical dimensions through this focal point, or through its effort to mobilise Civil War memories, it is clear that *The Angry Hills* is a much more important film in a Greek context than it has been given credit for.

Conclusion: The Film that Inspired the Late 1950s/ Early 1960s Greek Noir Film Cycle?

In lieu of a conclusion, this chapter will briefly discuss the potential contribution of *The Angry Hills* to noir in Greece from a different angle, that is, the role that Aldrich and Bezzerides may have played in influencing directly or indirectly the Greek film noir cycle of the late 1950s and early 1960s, which contemporary Greek film scholars have noted emerging at that time. The presence of Aldrich and Bezzerides in Greece in the spring and summer of 1958 coincided with the making of *Murder in Kolonaki*, which was released in January 1959 and is often considered the first film in the Greek noir cycle, even though earlier films such as *O drakos/The Ogre of Athens* (dir. Koundouros, 1956) and especially *O anthropos tou trainou/The Man on the Train* (dir. Dimopoulos, 1958) have also been read as having noir elements (see Dermentzoglou 2007: 13). As mentioned in the introduction of this chapter, my research on this issue has been inconclusive. However, the production of *The Angry Hills*, and the creative team behind it, did come into contact on a number of levels with some of the talent that later participated in the Greek noirs, starting with *Murder in Kolonaki*, something that might suggest that the cycle's origins and inspiration might be traced, partially at least, to the presence of these US filmmakers in Greece.

One of the key Greek people who became involved in the production of *The Angry Hills*, even though he remained uncredited in the film, was the composer Mimis Plessas. At that time Plessas had returned from his studies in the US and had become a partner in the opening of Studio Alpha in Athens, with *The Angry Hills* being the first international production that used its facilities (Vainas 2009: 41). Furthermore, Aldrich's involvement with Studio Alpha and Plessas also led (allegedly) to the uncredited participation of Plessas as composer of the song 'Matia Stratigoi', which is sung by Cleopatra in the film's infamous cabaret scene, cited as the first song Plessas composed for the cinema (Vainas 2009: 41; see also Milesis 2019).[10] As discussed by Poupou (2018: 175), Plessas became integral to the late 1950s/ early 1960s Greek noir cycle, composing the music for two of the earliest and most important titles, *Murder Backstage* and *Efialtis/Nightmare* (dir. Andreou, 1961). He was also linked with the *Murder Backstage* director Dinos Katsouridis, since they had worked together in the Greek theatre prior to Plessas becoming involved in cinema.[11]

Actors Dimitris Nikolaidis and Michalis Nikolinakos also provide intriguing links between the production of *The Angry Hills* and the noir films of the time. Nikolaidis (who played the village informant in Aldrich's film) also appears in both *Murder Backstage* and *Nightmare*. Nikolinakos, on the other hand, did not make it to the final cut of *The Angry Hills*, even though he was mentioned as one of the Greek actors who participated in the film (Leotsakos 1958: 3). Nikolinakos was a leading figure in the noir films of the time, having appeared in *Murder in Kolonaki*, *Nightmare* and also in the earlier *The Man on the Train*. Furthermore, one of the several Greek assistant directors Aldrich hired to help with the logistics of the production in Greece was Marios Nousias. Following the end of the shooting of *The Angry Hills*, the second production hosted by Studio Alpha was a film directed by Nousias, *Na Petheros, Na Malama/Meet the Father-in-Law* (1959), with Dimitris Nikolaidis in a key role. Studio Alpha is also credited with providing technical support to both *Murder Backstage* and *Nightmare*, while the producer for the former title was Manolis Nikoloudis, one of the partners behind the establishment of Studio Alpha.

Given the positioning of so many Greek filmmakers, actors and other industry practitioners between the production of *The Angry Hills* and the beginning of the Greek film noir cycle of the late 1950s and early 1960s, it is not unlikely that they drew inspiration or even received direct advice and other kinds of support from Aldrich, Bezzerides and even Mitchum (whose photograph visiting the Studio Alpha facilities in the company of Mimis Plessas accompanies Freddy Germanos's above-mentioned article for *Eleftheria*).[12] If this was indeed the case, it would help scholars redefine the origins of Greek film noir in the late 1950s as a cycle of films that was influenced by US cinema in more *material* ways than at the textual level. It would also provide Greek film history with a fascinating example of knowledge transfer from a major to a small film industry at the threshold of a new era that is often referred to as the Golden Age of Greek cinema.

As this volume was going into production, Ericcos Andreou gave an interview to one of the editors. Asked whether he and other young Greek filmmakers doing noir films at the time were influenced in any way by the presence of the production of *The Angry Hills*, he thought that this might be an overstatement. Instead, he credits the production of low-quality comedies and melodramas as prompting young filmmakers to experiment and come up with new and interesting types of film, including noirs, while for his own *Efialtis* he cites Hitchcock rather than Aldrich as an inspiration. On the other hand, Andreou, who worked as assistant director in many Hollywood productions in Greece at the time, also stated in the interview that he had no professional connection with the production of *The Angry Hills* and no personal contact with Aldrich, Bezzerides or Mitchum during their time in Athens. Nonetheless, it is still plausible that other filmmakers and Greek film industry personnel were influenced in a material way by the making of this noir picture, especially as Andreou admitted that these productions were indeed an opportunity for young directors 'to learn the art of filmmaking' (Andreou 2021).

Whether future research on Greek film noir will be able to establish this with certainty remains to be seen. What is beyond any doubt is that *The Angry Hills* is a much more interesting film than reviewers, Aldrich scholars and even Aldrich himself have made it out to be. This is especially the case when one disregards the generic labels usually attached to it, and examines its many great noir qualities. It is also a much more important film than critics and scholars have argued, when one approaches it in the context of what Karalis calls 'the history of cinema in Greece' (2012: xvi). Within such a context, its noir qualities go beyond the aesthetic, and reach all the way into the nation's psyche. What more can one ask of a film!

Notes

1. The actual figure, as given on the film's IMDb page, was $1,190,000. Available at <https://www.imdb.com/title/tt0052563/> (last accessed 10 September 2021).
2. *The Angry Hills* is mentioned as one of the many films whose interior scenes were shot at the MGM British Studios (Pykett 2014).
3. Uris's eleven-page document is available in the Turner/MGM scripts collection, Folder 929, *The Angry Hills* (1959), The Margaret Herrick Library, Los Angeles, California.
4. According to the E.J. Mannix Ledger, which contains the box office figures, profits and losses for all MGM films between 1924 and 1962, *The Angry Hills* lost close to $500,000, following a global theatrical box office gross of $1,285,000 (Mannix 1962).
5. The term 'melodrama' was often used in reviews in the 1940s, 1950s and 1960s to describe films that were later identified as noir (Neale 2000: 168–70).
6. 'Letter from the PCA to MGM', 8 July 1958, MPAA Production Code Administration Records, *The Angry Hills*, The Margaret Herrick Library, Los Angeles, California.
7. Ibid.
8. Indeed, the poster that accompanied the film's release in France under the title *Trahison à Athènes* [Treason in Athens] features the scene from the tavern with Cleopatra's top covering her breasts. Interestingly, the poster's emphasis on the scene in the tavern and the choice by the French distributor of a title with the word *trahison* (treason, betrayal) in it highlight the film's noir qualities much more than the original US poster.
9. The information on Constantinou is taken from a press release that accompanies an image of her held in the Alamy database, available at <https://www.alamy.com/aug-08-1958-greek-cabaret-star-to-dance-in-the-angry-hills-nineteen-image69353021.html> (last accessed 10 September 2021).
10. Plessas's first official credit was for the Greek film *Meet the Father-in-Law*, which was made immediately after *The Angry Hills*. It has been very difficult to determine whether Plessas was actually the composer of the song (which remains uncredited in the film), with only contemporary sources confirming his credit. However, his involvement in Studio Alpha, and the fact that the film needed a Greek song, which the film's English composer Richard Bennett would not have been able to provide, make this a highly likely scenario. On the other hand, in a recent interview, Erricos Andreou, director of *Efialtis* (1961), for which Plessas wrote the music, disputes both his involvement in Studio Alpha as a partner and that he would agree to compose a song for *The Angry Hills* without credit (Andreou 2021). IMDb credits Yorgos Economides and Alekos Spathis as the composers of the song but there are no sources confirming this.
11. Plessas mentions his relationship with Katsouridis in Greek theatre in a television interview with Ahilleas Papadionysiou as part of *Anoihtes Selides* [Open Pages], a show for Aheloos TV, Part 2, 6 April 2012.
12. Indeed, in the 1985 Erricos Andreou-directed TV series *I exafanisi tou John Avlakioti/The Disappearance of John Avlakiotis* (ERT) the titular character is a WWII double agent who works with both the Germans and the British. The series was

based on the eponymous novel (his last one) by Yannis Maris, widely credited as a Greek noir master, whose stories provided the inspiration for such key Greek noirs of the late 1950s and early 1960s as *Murder Backstage* and *Murder in Kolonaki*. I am indebted to Nikitas Fessas for pointing out this connection to me.

References

Addison, George ([1962] 2004), 'Robert Aldrich', in Eugene L. Miller and Edwin T. Arnold (eds), *Robert Aldrich: Interviews*, Jackson, MS: University Press of Mississippi, pp. 10–19.
A-MY-Y (1959), 'The Angry Hills', *Green Sheet*, July.
Andreou, Erricos (2021), interview/personal communication with Nikitas Fessas.
Anon. (1957), 'Story Buys', *Daily Variety*, 14 January.
Anon. (1959), 'Depot "Squeezed" into Movie', *Mirror News*, 24 March, pp. 4–5.
Balio, Tino (2018), *MGM*, Abingdon: Routledge.
Bogdanovich, Peter ([1965] 2004), 'Robert Aldrich', in Eugene L. Miller and Edwin T. Arnold (eds), *Robert Aldrich: Interviews*, Jackson, MS: University Press of Mississippi, pp. 28-39.
Borde, Raymond, and Chaumeton, Étienne (2002), *A Panorama of American Film Noir, 1941–1953*, San Francisco: City Lights.
Cameron, Ian, and Shivas, Mark ([1963] 2004), 'Interview with Robert Aldrich', in Eugene L. Miller and Edwin T. Arnold (eds), *Robert Aldrich: Interviews*, Jackson, MS: University Press of Mississippi, pp. 20–7.
Combs, Richard (1978), *Robert Aldrich*, London: BFI.
Crowther, Bruce (1990), *Film Noir: Reflection in A Dark Mirror*, London: Virgin Books.
Dermentzoglou, Alexis (2007), 'They are ours, and you'd better believe it (them)', in Alexis Dermentzoglou (ed.), *In A Dark Passage: Film Noir in Greek Cinema*, Thessaloniki: Erodios, pp. 12–14.
Dickos, Andrew (2002), *Street with No Name: A History of the Classic American Film Noir*, Lexington, KY: University Press of Kentucky.
Dixon, Whiston Wheeler (2009), *Film Noir and the Cinema of Paranoia*, Edinburgh: Edinburgh University Press.
Finler, Joel W. (2003), *The Hollywood Story*, London: Wallflower.
Germanos, Freddy (1958), 'O ellinikos kinimatografos apokta tora gera themelia' [Greek Cinema is Now Getting Strong Foundations], *Eleftheria*, 16 July, p. 3.
Harford, M. (1959), '"Angry Hills" Spy Drama in Athens', *Mirror News*, 30 July.
Hirsch, Foster (1981), *Film Noir: The Dark Side of the Screen*, Cambridge: DaCapo.
Humphries, Reynold (2004), 'The Politics of Crime and the Crime of Politics: Postwar Noir, the Liberal Consensus and the Hollywood Left', in Alain Silver and James Ursini (eds), *Film Noir Reader 4*, New York: Limelight, pp. 227–45.
Kalogeras, Yiorgos D. (2004–05), 'Albert Isaac Bezzerides: Translating Ethnicity from Fiction to Film', *Journal of Modern Hellenism*, 21-2, pp. 17–41.
Kalogeras, Yiorgos D. (2016), 'Working Through and Against Conventions: The Hollywood Career of A.I. Bezzerides', *The Journal of Modern Hellenism*, 32, pp. 1–16.
Karalis, Vrasidas (2012), *A History of Greek Cinema*, New York: Bloomsbury.

Leotsakos, Yorgos (1958) 'Omilei o amerikanos skinothetis R. Aldrich dia tin nean tainia tou' [The American Director R. Aldrich Talks about his New Film], *I Kathimerini*, 26 July, p. 3.

Mannix, Eddie J. (1962), the E.J. Mannix Ledger, available in Margaret Herrick Library, Los Angeles, California.

Milesis, Stefanos (2019), 'O Robert Mitchum ston Peiraia tou 1958' [Robert Mitchum in Piraeus in 1958], *Pireorama*, 14 January, <https://pireorama.gr/o-robert-mitsam-ston-pirea-tou-1958/> (last accessed 10 September 2021).

Miller, Eugene L., and Arnold, Edwin T. (2004), 'Introduction', in Eugene L. Miller and Edwin T. Arnold (eds), *Robert Aldrich: Interviews*, Jackson, MS: University Press of Mississippi, pp. vii–xiv.

Neale, Steve (2000), *Genre and Hollywood*, Abingdon: Routledge.

Petit, Chris, and Combs, Richard ([1977] 2004), 'Interview with Robert Aldrich', in Eugene L. Miller and Edwin T. Arnold (eds), *Robert Aldrich: Interviews*, Jackson, MS: University Press of Mississippi, pp. 125–42.

Ploritis, Marios (1958), 'O Kinimatografos: Nees tainies – I arhi tou telous' [Cinema: New Films – The Beginning of the End], *Eleftheria*, 30 April, p. 2.

Poupou, Anna (2018), 'I periptosi tou ellinikou film noir ti dekaetia tou 1960' [The Case of Greek Film Noir in the 1960s], *Modern Greek Studies Australia & New Zealand*, 19, pp. 167–87.

Pykett, Derek (2014), *MGM British Film Studios: Hollywood in Borehamwood*, Albany, GA: BearManor Media.

Rich. (1959), 'The Angry Hills', *Weekly Variety*, 18 February.

Sauvage, Pierre (1976/1977), 'Aldrich Interview', in Eugene L. Miller and Edwin T. Arnold (eds), *Robert Aldrich: Interviews*, Jackson, MS: University Press of Mississippi, pp. 90–110.

Scott, John L. (1959), 'Intrigue, Beatniks, Share Bill', *Los Angeles Times*, 30 July.

Silver, Alain (1970), 'Interview with Robert Aldrich', in Eugene L. Miller and Edwin T. Arnold (eds), *Robert Aldrich: Interviews*, Jackson, MS: University Press of Mississippi, pp. 53–72.

Silver, Alain, and Ursini, James (1995), *Whatever Happened to Robert Aldrich? His Life and his Films*, New York: Limelight.

Stam, Robert, Burgoyne, Robert, and Flitterman-Lewis, Sandy (1992), *New Vocabularies in Film Semiotics: Structuralism, Post-Structuralism and beyond*, London: Routledge.

Steinhart, Daniel (2019), *Runaway Hollywood: Internationalizing Postwar Production and Location Shooting*, Berkeley, CA: University of California Press.

Vainas, Stavros (2009), 'Synantisi Tzaz kai Laikis Mousikis: I Periptosi to Mimi Plessa' [Where Jazz and Popular Music Meet: The Case of Mimis Plessas], Diploma dissertation, TEI Ipeirou.

Walker, Michael (1994), 'Film Noir: Introduction', in Ian Cameron (ed.), *The Movie Book of Film Noir*, London: Studio Vista, pp. 8–38.

Williams, Tony (2004), *Body and Soul: The Cinematic Vision of Robert Aldrich*, Oxford: Scarecrow Press.

4. NOIR BACKSTAGE: YANNIS MARIS FROM PAGE TO SCREEN

Thanassis Agathos

Yannis Maris and Film Noir

The fate of crime film in Greece would be different without Yannis Maris (1916–79), whose novels and scripts defined the genesis of the Greek film noir. Combining qualities of Hammett, Chandler and Simenon, Maris is considered the patriarch of the Greek crime novel, and the principal representative of an entire 'indigenous' school of 'light' crime fiction (Apostolidis 2009: 286). He was a pioneer writer who participated in the public discourse of the Athenian swinging 1960s by integrating elements of pulp fiction and pop culture into his work (Kalfopoulos 2016). Maris was a prominent newspaper journalist and editor-in-chief, as well as an avid cinephile and, from the late 1940s to the early 1950s, a professional film reviewer for the left-wing newspaper *I Machi* (Rangos 2016: 134–5). In this chapter I will focus on *Eglima sta paraskinia/Murder Backstage* (dir. Katsouridis, 1960), the film adaptation of Maris's eponymous novel, the screenplay of which was penned by the author himself. My aim is to provide a systematic comparison between the novel and the resulting film, which is a remarkably accomplished cinematic work and a seminal example of Greek film noir. By doing so, I will examine the narrative and representational strategies used by both the director and the (screen)writer in order to adapt the source material for the screen.

The first two noir films of Greek cinema, accepted today as the two emblematic examples of Greek film noir, were screened in 1960, five years after French critics Borde and Chaumeton (1955) defined the genre. These were *Eglima sto Kolonaki/Murder in Kolonaki* by Tzanis Aliferis and *Murder Backstage*, which were based on Maris's first two novels (published in 1953 and 1954 respectively), while notably their scripts were written by Maris (Figure 4.1). Two years earlier, in 1958, Dinos Dimopoulos had directed *O anthropos tou trainou/The Man on the Train*, based on Maris's third book, *O anthropos me to gkri kostoumi/The Man in the Grey Suit* (1955), a film that is considered by Dermentzoglou (2007: 13) as '[a] devastating allegory using the structures of film noir'.[1] Nevertheless, as I have argued elsewhere (Agathos 2018: 108–9), this film is mainly a romantic melodrama with elements of mystery and psychoanalytic implications. The view that the starting point of Greek film noir was *Murder in Kolonaki* is also supported by Anna Poupou (2018: 167–87), who discerns in the film a variety of influences including classic American noirs of the 1940s, the French classic *polar* of the 1940s and 1950s, as well as the work of younger directors such as Jean-Pierre Melville and Louis Malle.[2]

Maris is an easy-to-read, entertaining author, and a skilful screenwriter who, adapting his own novels, wrote the screenplays for six more noir films: *Horis taftotita/Without Identity* (dir. Dalianidis, 1963), *Amfivolies/Doubts* (dir. Grigoriou, 1964), *O teleftaios peirasmos/The Last Temptation* (dir. Kapsaskis, 1964), *Mia gynaika katigoreitai/A Woman is Accused* (dir. Grigoriou, 1966), *Zitima zois kai thanatou/A Matter of Life and Death* (dir. Serdaris, 1973) and *To hamogelo tis Pythias/Pythia's Smile* (dir. Bergonzelli, Soulis Georgiadis, 1979). All his novels first appeared in serialised form in newspapers (such as *Apogevmatini* and *Acropolis*) and magazines (such as *Theatis* and *Epikaira*), and several years later were reissued in book form, often with altered titles. This publishing strategy demonstrates Maris's deep commitment to journalism and his thorough knowledge of the needs and demands of the general public. Today, his contribution as an author and scriptwriter in the formation of the various expressions of Greek crime fiction is acknowledged by both film and literary critics.[3] The visual qualities of his writing have often been emphasised while, notably, the comic strips that originally accompanied Maris's serialised stories have been linked to their film adaptations (Marcou 2017: 112).

The plots of Maris's novels – and of the related films – are often set in the upper-class society of post-war Athens, far away from the daily struggle for survival (Spiliopoulos 1984: 39), although occasionally working-class settings and characters also appear. Maris's stories and screenplays offer not only suspense, but also images of a turbulent era, when Greece was struggling to come out of the ruins of the Civil War (1944–49). In his work, crime is usually associated with the guilty secrets of the cosmopolitan, so-called 'good society' of Athens, while the dark period of the Occupation and the persecution of the Jews by the Nazis are thematic motifs that recurrently surface. Both negative and positive characters populate Maris's fictional world: rotten industrialists,

Figure 4.1 Poster for *Murder in Kolonaki*. Greek Film Archive collection.

greedy businessmen, corrupt lawyers, gigolos, *femmes fatales*, ruthless heirs and Nazi collaborators, on the one hand; police inspectors, journalists, idealistic young men and innocent *ingénues*, on the other. The emblematic character of Maris is Inspector Bekas, a brilliant, reliable and serious police officer who guarantees safety, integrity and discretion, and who never uses violence. Bekas is often partnered with Yannis Makris, a well-known journalist, who can be read as Maris's alter ego.

From the Riddle to the Thriller: Dinos Katsouridis's *Murder Backstage*

Maris's crime novel *Murder Backstage* (1954) was originally published in serialised form in the newspaper *Apogevmatini*, while the resulting film can be seen as a serious and interesting attempt at a Greek whodunit movie with a noir atmosphere. It was the directorial debut of Dinos Katsouridis (1926–2011), a Greek Cypriot who moved to Athens in the mid-1940s to study cinema and, during the 1950s, worked as a cinematographer and film editor for Finos Film, Greece's major film production company of the time. The cast of *Murder Backstage* included well-known actors of the Greek stage and cinema (such as Alekos Alexandrakis), while established professionals contributed to the film. Interestingly, Aristeidis Karydis-Fuchs, who worked as the director of cinematography, had also shot the two previous film adaptations of Maris's novels (*The Man on the Train* and *Murder in Kolonaki*), while Marilena Aravantinou, an experienced set designer, was responsible for the noirish look and the settings of *The Man on the Train*. The jazz score was by composer Mimis Plessas, while the production company Damaskinos–Michaelidis assured relatively high production values by the standards of Greek commercial cinema.

When the film was first released, all Greek critics praised Katsouridis's professionalism and craftsmanship, emphasising his familiarity with the crime film (notably the term 'film noir' was not used in Greece at the time). Matsas (1960: 2), a reviewer for the newspaper *Ethnikos Kyrix*, described Maris's script as 'virtuoso', while Papamichalis (1960: 2), in *Acropolis*, believed that the film could be compared to the best foreign works of the crime film genre.[4] Savvidis (1960: 2), the influential reviewer of the newspaper *To Vima*, called *Murder Backstage* the 'best-made Greek crime film' to date, arguing that Katsouridis had chosen the crime film as a particularly suitable genre for a young director to practise, following a trend that originated among the young filmmakers of the French New Wave. Savvidis also noted that Maris's script hesitates at the end between the riddle and the thriller, thus pointing out the effort made by Katsouridis, and possibly Maris as a screenwriter, to strengthen the element of suspense in the film, and to avoid the feeling of a literary whodunit, even if the result was not entirely successful in this respect. Reviewing the film for the left-wing newspaper *I Avgi*, Stamatiou (1960: 2) noted that the director was a true connoisseur of the crime adventure genre, but he considered the subject matter 'foreign to Greek reality'. Finally Ploritis (1960: 2), the highly respected critic of the newspaper *Eleftheria*, described the film as 'the most accomplished crime film of Greek cinema'. Notably, the film won awards for Best Supporting Actress (Georges Sari) and Best Cinematography at the First Week of Greek Cinema (1960) held in Thessaloniki, and was a commercial hit, ranking seventh at the Greek box office that year, with 67,610 admissions in Athens and Piraeus (Soldatos 2001: 220).

Today Katsouridis's film holds a prominent place in the history of Greek cinema. Mikelides (1997: 35) considers it one of the best attempts to transpose film noir into the Greek context, Soldatos (2010: 265) describes it as 'the first remarkable and complete attempt at a Greek crime film consistent with the standards of the classic film noir', while Toulas (2007: 44) argues that Maris's book was first-rate material for the creation of a pure film noir. Similarly, Karalis (2012: 94) considers *Murder Backstage* 'one of the most atmospheric, expressionistic and dark films ever made in Greece', raving about its strange camera angles, rapid changes of scene and accelerating narrative rhythm. Finally, Chalkou (2008: 112) includes Katsouridis's film in a series of ambitious productions of the, powerful at the time, company of Damaskinos–Michaelidis, which exhibited a refreshing willingness to create 'quality films' that would appeal to international markets.

Katsouridis's Film as Commentary on Maris's Novel

Murder Backstage belongs to the category of film adaptations that Wagner (1975: 223) calls 'commentaries', where 'the original is either intentionally or inadvertently altered at some point and could also be called re-emphasis or re-structure'. Klein and Parker (1981: 9–10) argue that this form of adaptation 'retains the core of the structure of the narrative while significantly re-interpreting [. . .] the source text'. Andrew (1984: 98–104) uses the term 'intersecting', which means that 'the uniqueness of the original text is preserved to such an extent that it is intentionally left unassimilated in adaptation'. All these scholars emphasise the retaining of the basic elements of the narrative in the screen adaptation and highlight the importance of a cinematic reconstruction of the original text.

The film revolves around the efforts of police inspector Bekas (Titos Vandis) and the reputable journalist Makris (Alekos Alexandrakis) to catch the murderer of the notorious stage actress Roza Deli (Efi Mela), who has been found stabbed to death in her dressing room in the theatre, while the door was locked from the inside. The main suspects include Haris Apostolidis (Thanassis Mylonas), the *jeune premier* of the theatre company, who was heard quarrelling with the victim on the night of the murder; an unknown tough-looking man who visited Roza that same night and was seen by the stage-door keeper (Dimos Starenios); and Elena Pavlidi (Maro Kontou), a talented actress who had always hated Roza, since she was her main rival in the company. When Apostolidis disappears, his fiancée, young actress Mary Lamprinou (Aliki Georgouli), persuades Makris that her boyfriend is innocent. Makris begins to follow the veteran character actress Thaleia Chalkia (Georges Sari), who seems to be given money by the industrialist Pavlos Stephanou (Christos Tsaganeas), a lover and protector of Roza. Bekas and Makris investigate Roza's past and find out that the unknown man who visited her backstage was actually her ex-husband, Makis Angeloglou (Gikas Biniaris). Angeloglou, a wartime collaborator, was thought to have died during the German Occupation; however, he had merely assumed a fake identity. Bekas and Makris also discover the real murderer, Stephanou, who had been blackmailed by Chalkia and Angeloglou.

In his script, Maris retains some of the Barthesian 'cardinal functions',[5] the important events of his novel that directly contribute to the development of the story: the murder of Roza; the visit of Angeloglou to Roza's dressing room on the night of the murder; the interrogation of the actors by Bekas; the disappearance of the *jeune premier*; Roza's affair with the married industrialist; the involvement of Makris in the investigation; Angeloglou's past during the Occupation; and the monitoring of Chalkia's movements by Makris's young partner. In order to offer an idea of the film's 'commentary' on Maris's novel, I will present the scene where Chalkia meets Angeloglou in an old house in a poor neighbourhood as depicted in the novel and as visualised in the film.

> It was a working-class neighbourhood; a slum area. Roads without asphalt, small low houses, tiled roofs and desolation. Chalkia stood for a while in the middle of the road and then resolutely moved towards one of the houses. It seems that she had been waited for, because the door opened and closed quickly behind the actress once she entered. The moment the light from inside the house fell on the street outside, the young man thought he saw the silhouette of a man at the door. But he wasn't sure.
>
> He looked around. No one. People used to sleep early in this neighbourhood. He shuddered. The night was well advanced and only then did he realise that he felt cold. He went on, trying to make as little noise as possible. Outside the house where the actress had entered, he stopped. It was a small detached house, similar to almost all the other houses in the neighbourhood. Coming from the window, a low window with old shutters, a dim light fell on the road. The young man approached. His heart was pounding in his chest. What if the door suddenly opened and they caught him spying? He looked around again. No one. He dared. He

looked through the opening between the two shutters. The first thing he saw was the actress. She was talking to someone else, whom he could not see. He tried to listen, but in vain. Suddenly the actress opened her bag. She took a small long package out of it.

– The gold coins, the young man thought.

Indeed, there were coins. He saw Chalkia opening the package. The gold glowed in the candlelight. There was a table in front of her. The actress piled up the coins and shuffled them for a while with her hand. He saw her laughing. Then Chalkia's hand counted them, and assembled two smaller piles.

– They're dividing their share, he thought.

And then he saw the other man. First his hand. A thin though strong hand with long, wiry fingers. He entered the area which the young man could see, snatched the coins and disappeared for a while. Afterwards, the man appeared in full. He was tall, with a thin tough face and sparse blond hair. Neither young nor old. Between forty and fifty. He was saying something to the actress and she was listening to him carefully. (Maris 2016: 114–15)

This is one of the few passages in the novel where the action does not take place in the centre of Athens, in the theatre or in the offices of Makris's newspaper, but in a poor neighbourhood. Roads without asphalt and small low houses set the tone for a miserable, working-class district where people go to bed early. Maris makes the most of the strong contrasts between light and darkness, and between the shadows and the sounds of the night, while, at the same time, he offers an image that is common in American and French crime novels, the sharing of the loot between the two blackmailers. The whole scene is presented from the point of view of the young journalist who is Makris's assistant. Maris uses the literary motif of the window (Hamon 1981: 188; Jost 1987: 105), emphasising the fact that the description of Chalkia's and Angeloglou's movements is limited to the area of the young man's vision, to what he can see through the half-opened window of the old house, with the window functioning as a frame. Maris's language in the excerpt is, as usual, direct, precise and austere, and his style is edgy; he prefers brief sentences and very detailed descriptions of actions, feelings and thoughts.

The visual translation of this scene onscreen is quite interesting. Contrary to the novel's narrative, it is not Makris's young collaborator but Makris himself, and the actress Mary Lamprinou, who watch Chalkia. Thus, Maris and Katsouridis strengthen the role of Makris and highlight the journalist's bonding with the young actress, a friendship with a *soupçon* of romance. Another crucial difference is the place where Chalkia and Angeloglou meet: in the film we see an urban area instead of a poor neighbourhood, and the two blackmailers meet in an abandoned factory, while Makris and Lamprinou watch them share the money not through a window, but from a trapdoor in the upper floor of the building. This last detail connects the film with both the gothic and the film noir tradition, since the trapdoor, a key element in gothic literature (Evans 1947: 1), plays a pivotal role in a classic French noir, René Clément's *Au-delá les grilles/ Beyond the Gates* (1949). There is also a spiral staircase connecting the two floors, a possible reference to Robert Siodmak's gothic noir masterpiece *The Spiral Staircase* (1946). The gaze-centred narrative of the novel is retained in the film through several point-of-view shots, and the whole scene is underlit since, during the exchange between Chalkia and Angeloglou, the only light source is a lamp on the table, casting dark shadows on the faces of the four characters. The changes in the location and the plot, the background music by Plessas, the use of wide-angle lens and the combination of low-angle and high-angle shots create a noirish mood and a sense of absolute darkness.

From Page to Screen: Motifs, Changes and Omissions

Katsouridis's film retains the core events and all the dominant narrative motifs of the novel.[6] Thus, the Occupation holds a prominent place, with Angeloglou being a Nazi collaborator, and Elena Pavlidi describing her vain attempts to save her brother from the Nazis. Apostolidis (2012: 56) argues that 'the Occupation is the most widespread motif of Maris's fiction [. . .] one of his clichés', with *Murder Backstage* being part of a broader group of Greek films of the 1960s in which the Occupation appears in the narrative as a dark period of the past, where shady secrets and ambiguous identities are hidden or still-painful traumas are located (Chalkou 2008: 186). Any direct mention of Resistance organisations is notably absent from both the novel and the film, while the novel is more analytical in the description of Angeloglou's guilty past. Philippou (2016) relates Maris's insistence on referring to the Occupation and collaborationism only in flashbacks and narrations of the past to his reluctance to inflame political passions. In my view this is also connected to the novelist's firm belief that the Greek Resistance had been betrayed by the initiators of the foreign-driven Civil War. Collaborationism is often mentioned and always condemned in Maris's works, but there are no references to the Greek Civil War and the turbulent political life of Greece during the 1950s and 1960s, despite the fact that Maris had a leftist background (during the Occupation, he participated in the Resistance as a member of the powerful left-wing movement EAM; he was also a close relative of the socialist politician Ilias Tsirimokos, and was briefly imprisoned in 1949 for writing an article about communist political prisoners who were detained on Makronisos island).[7]

One of Maris's dominant motifs in the novel that is also kept in the film is that of impersonation and identity theft, with Angeloglou pretending to be murdered and changing his identity after the Occupation in order to escape punishment. Similarly central is the author's motif of the mystery of the 'locked room', with Bekas and Makris here constantly wondering how Roza's murderer came in and out of her dressing room, since it was locked from the inside. Finally, there is also the motif of the investigation (which can be encountered in Maris's fiction, and is here conducted by Bekas and Makris), which is decisive in the noir films.[8]

However, all of the episodes included in the third part of Maris's novel have been omitted from the film. Noteworthy is the absence of Bekas's journey to Larissa, a subplot foreshadowing Maris's future novels, which are set on the Thessalian Plain. The killing of Bekas's old colleague by Angeloglou, an episode which, in the novel, stresses the bonds of solidarity between cops, is another important omission, related perhaps to censorship restrictions, since harming the image of police officers on screen was forbidden. Likewise, Bekas's platonic affair with a chorus girl, his raid on the hotel room where Chalkia stays in Larissa, his trip to Thessaloniki and the excursion to Bachtse Tsiflik, where Angeloglou is found murdered, are excluded from the film. Thus, Bekas, who in Maris's novels 'does not just solve mystery crime riddles, but also attempts to penetrate the heroes' psyche' (Philippou 2018: 67), is reminiscent of Simenon's Inspector Maigret:[9] Bekas bases his investigative technique on understanding the personality of the different protagonists of a case and their interactions, while being guided by his instinct.

However, he is significantly reduced in Katsouridis's film. Because of these changes and omissions, the filmic Bekas, although he retains some of the character elements that he possesses in the novel (he is a man of principle with a sense of justice),[10] remains a two-dimensional and stereotypical character: he does not lead the investigation, he is deprived of the kindness and warmth he possesses in the novel – shown, for example, in the chapter where he encounters a group of young boys and girls travelling with a motorboat to Bachtse Tsiflik – and, most importantly, he is rather detached, reflecting the noir attitude. Instead, in the movie it is the character of the journalist Makris that dominates the narrative. A successful editor-in-chief of a major newspaper and personal friend of Bekas, Makris is presented in the film as an attractive bohemian young man (in contrast to the older, worldly wise, grey-haired, bespectacled man of the novel), equally adept at socialising with artists and industrialists, flirting with beautiful actresses, and helping the police with the investigation. In any case, the decision to make Makris the focus of the narrative is somewhat unsurprising, since he was played by Alekos Alexandrakis, one of the most popular Greek male stars of the early 1960s.

Another effect of the omission of Bekas's journeys is that the film's action is limited to the urban landscape of Athens. Like most films based on Maris's novels, *Murder Backstage* can be seen today as an accurate depiction of post-war Athens. The same impression is gained from the novel and most of Maris's fiction (Vatopoulos 2016: 93–101), where Athens, and especially its centre, is given a prominent role. In any case, 'the crime novel is undoubtedly the literature par excellence of the urban space' (Rangos 2018). Additionally, scholars emphasise the significance of the city in films noirs, 'explaining the metropolis as a transplantation from crime fiction, as a visual motif, as a determinant of ambience or mood, or an element of narrative causality' (Dimendberg 2004: 9). This emphasis on the Athenian cityscape provides the film with a firm noir look of urban modernism, and avoids a more traditional, picturesque, or even neo-realistic look that would perhaps undermine the noir impression; in this respect, *Murder Backstage* differs from Aliferis's *Murder in Kolonaki* or Katsouridis's later film *Oi adistaktoi/The Ruthless Ones* (1965), which include some scenes with neo-realistic elements.

Likewise, several characters from the book are absent from the film adaptation, such as Delios, an intellectual and politician, and Lili Greece, the young road-company actress Bekas meets in Larissa. Thus, the film lacks the emotional nuances that characterise the novel, as human relationships are presented as having a more detached, cynical dimension, common to film noir. Furthermore, it is clear that, by omitting all these episodes, places and characters, Katsouridis and Maris were seeking to make a relatively short film (just 83 minutes), a choice that possibly had to do with assuring dense editing – more suitable to the film noir typology – and a more economical budget.

Remarkable changes can also be found in relation to the film's ending. In the book, Angeloglou is killed by police officers at his hideout in Thessaloniki. In the film, Angeloglou is murdered by Stephanou in an industrial setting. The whole scene is reminiscent of the death of the painter Karnezis in the film adaptation of *Murder in Kolonaki*, which, in its turn, echoes the ending of the classic noir *White Heat* (dir. Walsh, 1949). Furthermore, in the novel Stephanou commits suicide after having confessed his crimes to Makris, while in the film Chalkia reveals everything to Makris, and the police patrol chase the guilty Stephanou by car, shine their headlights on him and immobilise him on the railings of a garden. The film's ending is much more intense and visually impressive than that of the book, since it combines a flashback (narrated by Chalkia) illuminating the circumstances of Roza's murder, a speedy chase scene and, above all, an apotheosis of the play between light and darkness, offering the symbolic image of the triumph of good over evil.

In the script, Maris made some changes in both catalyst and secondary actions. Thus, in the novel, the recognition of Angeloglou by actress Elena Pavlidi takes place during a dinner scene at Babis's tavern in Vathis Square, a late-night meeting point for journalists, actors and socialites. Against the familiar background of the bohemian tavern Pavlidi reveals to Makrio, his friend Delios and the theatre critic Canaris that she has known Angeloglou since the Occupation, offering useful information about his past as a Nazi collaborator. By contrast, in the movie Elena provides Makris with this same information during a private meeting at her apartment. This choice reflects Katsouridis's intention to avoid the rather old-fashioned space of the Athenian tavern and replace it with Elena's modern and sophisticated apartment, where she is seen half-naked, working out on a training bike, thus projecting the image of a modern and sexy young woman in the style of American or French noirs, while the decoration has an urban chic look. Moreover, in the film the *jeune premier* is not arrested, while in the book he surrenders himself to the police. The film ingeniously visualises a short sentence describing the agony of the young fugitive – 'Somewhere, in a house, or on a street, a young man would try to hide, like a hunted wild animal' (Maris 2016: 65) – with a few night scenes showing him, or his shadow, leaning on walls and trying to reach his fiancée's house.

As far as the Barthesian indices proper are concerned,[11] in the film Makris appears to be slightly attracted to the young *ingénue*, an indication absent from the novel. The film also omits the episode of the tender relationship between Bekas and Lili, who helps him in Larissa. This kind of ambiguous relationship between a middle-aged man and a young girl was still taboo subject matter in Greek cinema of the early 1960s,[12] and could potentially have raised problems with the censors.[13] Furthermore, in the film there is no presentation of the family life of the industrialist, which covers a few pages in the novel (Maris 2016: 92–4); Stephanou mentions only once that he has a wife and a daughter, when he asks Makris to be discreet about his affair with Roza, reminding us that the classic film noir presents family relationships as either absent or 'broken, perverted, peripheral or impossible' (Harvey 1998: 38). As for the informants, there are changes to several names, since Roza Vargi becomes Roza Deli in the film, the industrialist Karydis becomes Stephanou, the young *ingénue* Nelly Karzi is renamed Mary Lamprinou, and so on. An explanation might be that the names used in the literary text were reminiscent of well-known figures from the Greek theatre and cinema world of the period (stage star Elsa Vergi, director of photography Aristidis Karydis-Fuchs, who was married to actress Maro Kontou, one of the film's stars, and stage director Linos Karzis), and the creators of the film preferred to avoid any possible confusion. Similarly, the Rose-Rouge bar is renamed the Roxy in the film, indicating perhaps the dominance of American pop culture over French culture in Greece during the period in question.

There is also a major difference in the type of theatre that serves as a backdrop for each of the two works. In the novel, the crime takes place at the prestigious State Theatre, on the evening of the premiere of 'a modern adaptation of an old Spanish drama' (Maris 2016: 12). In the film, the murder is committed at the Gloria Theatre, where a revue, a big commercial hit, is being staged. The novel, like several works by Maris, contains many references to the theatre world.[14] The actor characters call attention to the fact that, in the past, Roza was an actress in 'light' theatre, as opposed to her later career in 'serious' *repertoire*, rehearsing for Eugene O'Neill's *Anna Christie*; they also mention the fact that Nelly Karzi had previously played Ophelia in Shakespeare's *Hamlet* (both plays were staged by the Greek National Theatre during the 1954–55 season, which coincided with the first publication of Maris's novel). None of these references were included in the film, which offers a rather superficial image of the theatrical world. This remarkable shift from a high-profile and prestigious theatre milieu, suitable to a traditional British-school whodunit, to a more commercial and light entertainment spectacle is probably linked to Katsouridis's intention of offering an image closer to the American-style noir of that period. Also omitted from the film is the depiction of the miserable working conditions of a group of travelling players who appear in a theatre located in Larissa, which 'seems to have been used mainly as a cinema, because its backstage was primitive' (Maris 2016: 164). This particular representation could have distracted the film from the noir imagery of urban modernity.

As a screenwriter, Maris makes extensive use of the addition technique, including several scenes that are absent from the novel.[15] In this context, the film's introductory scenes, presenting Angeloglou talking to the stage-door keeper and then walking towards Roza's dressing room, are interrupted by a musical revue scene performed by Roza's rival, actress Elena Pavlidi. These scenes create, from the very beginning, a suspenseful atmosphere, and prepare the viewer for something intense that is about to happen: the killing of Roza. At a later stage of the plot, Thaleia Chalkia appears to find shelter in her housemaid's house, hoping to escape from Stephanou's wrath; this addition brings more depth to the key character of Chalkia, and contributes to the reinforcement of the noir atmosphere, with some claustrophobic night shots presenting the terrified actress trying to ask for help from the police, as she realises that the menace is close at hand.

It is noticeable that Maris's novel is full of references to (crime) fiction as well as to cinema and crime films, often including self-reflexive comments about the thin line that separates reality from fiction: 'Such things happen only in novels and films!' (Maris 2016: 19); 'You will have enough material to write fine novels in your newspapers' (2016: 19); 'The case resembles a novel' (2016: 29); 'All this looked like a movie' (2016: 34); 'It is obvious that you have never read crime novels' (2016: 79); 'Life is not a novel' (2016: 150); 'I'm afraid you journalists love novels' (2016: 153); 'This unknown killer reminds me of one of a bad movie' (2016: 153); 'This whole story looked like a novel' (2016: 174); 'It is obvious that the young man thought himself as a crime-film hero' (2016: 194). Such references are rare in the film as, for example, when Bekas tells Makris that he doesn't like cases that resemble novels while, in another scene, the bartender tells Makris: 'You made a novel out of the crime!'

The Typology of Film Noir in *Murder Backstage*

Katsouridis seems to have thoroughly studied the typology of film noir.[16] As I have already noted, the presence of Athens as an attractive metropolis full of contradictions is dominant in the film. The city plays an important role in film noir, as everything takes place in it, while it symbolises the values of modern life (Dancyger and Rush 1995: 58–60). There is also a *femme fatale* type, both a victim and a victimiser: the beautiful Roza humiliates the industrialist, and leads him to crime and destruction. Furthermore, given that both American and French crime novels and films use bars and nightclubs as spaces of action,[17] both in Maris's novel and in Katsouridis's film some scenes, in which a barman informs Makris about Angeloglou's past, unfold in a cabaret. In the film, these scenes are filled with striptease dances that momentarily interrupt the suspenseful flow of the narrative.[18] Cabarets and nightclubs, such as Kalmazoo, Coq d'or or Acapulco, hold a prominent place in several of Maris's novels. In the film adaptations of *Murder Backstage*, *Murder in Kolonaki* and *To kokkino vazo* [The Red Vase], the musical numbers and the striptease scenes are narratively integrated into the main plot, since they are performed while important revelations take place.

Paradoxically, the use of flashback, a key narrative and stylistic component of film noir, is extremely limited in the film adaptation of *Murder Backstage*.[19] This can be partly attributed to the narrative structure of Maris's original novel, which contains very few analeptic narratives, compared to other works by the same author:[20] the bartender's narration of Angeloglou's dark past is preserved, but appears to be considerably abridged in the film, while Nelly's analeptic narration to Nina of what happened on the night of the murder is omitted in the movie, since the character of Nina has been eliminated. There is only one crucial flashback at the end of Katsouridis's film, when Chalkia reveals to Makris how the crime was committed, a flashback that works in an explanatory manner to fill various plot holes, as is often the case with American films noirs (Dix 2016: 118).[21]

Another structural strategy of film noir, the first-person narration in the form of a voiceover, is absent from *Murder Backstage*, following Maris's novel. The film retains the third-person narration and the zero focalisation of the novel (with the omniscient narrator knowing and telling more than any of the characters), using many panoramic shots where the camera knows and reveals more than any of the characters; this is consistent with the semi-documentary style of some of the scenes that were shot in outdoor spaces. It also gives the impression of a spontaneous recording.[22] The latter feature is compatible with the tag of 'crime novel-enigma' (Martinidis 1994: 254), which fits Maris's novel.

The main features of Karydis-Fuchs's exceptional expressionist black-and-white photography are the frenetic camera movements, especially in the surveillance scenes, the numerous indoor shots that create a claustrophobic impression, the use of wide-angle lens, the effectiveness of the night scenes which feature intense contrasts between white and black, or light and dark, as well as several shots of shadows.[23] Katsouridis's tight editing is noteworthy, especially in the first few scenes depicting the perpetration of the crime, as well as in the last scenes of the film, where the murderer is revealed. Finally, the creative use of Plessas's music, dominated by jazz motifs, is memorable.[24]

Katsouridis draws good performances from the actors who embody Maris's characters (Figure 4.2).[25] Titos Vandis, a character actor with a solid theatrical career – and a later Hollywood career with supporting roles in film (*The Exorcist*, dir. Friedkin, 1973) and television (in such iconic cop/crime TV shows as *Mannix*, CBS 1967–75, *Kojak*, CBS 1973–78 and *Hawaii Five-0*, CBS 1968–80) – is persuasive as Inspector Bekas. However, unlike the major star Jean Gabin, who was identified with Maigret in a series of French noirs of the 1950s and the 1960s based on Simenon's novels,[26] he would never play Bekas again, although he did play a police inspector in the 1964 noirish thriller *Apagogi/ Kidnapping* (dir. Karagiannis).[27] Alekos Alexandrakis, an important Greek star

Figure 4.2 Inspector Bekas (Titos Vandis) leading the murder investigation, assisted by journalist Makris (Alekos Alexandrakis). Digital still from *Murder Backstage*.

of the 1950s and 1960s, combines the dynamic and the bohemian side of journalist Makris, while Maro Kontou, on her way to cinema and stage stardom, projects sexiness and sophistication as Elena Pavlidi. Christos Tsaganeas, a noted stage actor who in films was typecast as an aristocrat, underlines Stephanou's duplicity, and Georges Sari, who later became one of the most important children's literature writers in Greece, is suitably gloomy in the nuanced role of Thaleia Chalkia. The character of Roza, who in the novel represents the usual type of Maris's *femme fatale*, is almost non-existent in the film.[28] In any case, the absence of a prominent female character is noteworthy in the film and its literary source, although others of Maris's novels and their respective film adaptations include such characters.[29] However, both the novel and the film *Murder Backstage* remain basically focused on male characters, while female characters, with the possible exception of Chalkia, are rather decorative.

The cinematic qualities of the film compensate for the gaps in Maris's script. Maris worked on source material (his novel) that was extremely rich in terms of plot. However, the film leaves several questions unanswered, especially with regard to the motives behind the actions of some of the characters. This ellipsis is a common narrative feature in film noir plots –in some cases it has to do with scenes omitted due to censorship – and this opaqueness is seen *a posteriori* as a stylistic trend of film noir, bringing it closer to the ambiguity of modernist cinema.

Katsouridis's film was influenced by two other Greek films noirs released earlier in 1960: *Murder in Kolonaki*, featuring Tsaganeas and Kontou,[30] and photographed again by Karydis-Fuchs; and Ion Daifas's *O dolofonos agapouse poly/The Murderer Loved Too Much*, which also focuses on a crime committed in the milieu of theatre and journalism – the murder victim is a theatre critic. It is also evident that Katsouridis was influenced by the French films noirs of the 1950s, particularly in the cabaret scenes of *Murder Backstage* that are reminiscent of Jacques Becker's *Touchez pas au grisbi/Honour Among Thieves* (1954), and in the street scenes, which bear echoes of both Jean-Pierre Melville's *Bob le flambeur/Fever Heat* (1956) and Louis Malle's *Ascenseur pour l'échafaud/Elevator to the Gallows* (1958).

As Maris's work was extremely underrated for several years, the novel *Murder Backstage* was not reviewed when it first appeared, and only recently has started to gain some academic recognition (Tonnet 2005; Marcou 2014). Likewise, it took a while before Maris attracted international scholarly attention as a novelist: in a recent European noir collection, Maris is described as 'the undisputed godfather of Greek crime-writing' (Forshaw 2014: 113), and it is mentioned that his 'well-plotted novels have only recently been accepted as classics of the genre' of pulp crime fiction (Forshaw 2014: 113). In any case, Maris's *Murder Backstage* is one of the author's most popular novels, thanks largely to the appeal of its film adaptation. Six decades after its first screening,

Katsouridis's *Murder Backstage* remains an absorbing piece of filmmaking, and an important film when it comes to the evolution of film noir in Greek cinema. It is a proof of Maris's flexibility, since he did not hesitate to alter his novel, adapting it to the demands of 1960s domestic movie production. It is also a sample of the mastery of the director Katsouridis and the cinematographer Karydis-Fuchs, who adopted the visual style of foreign films noirs, transferring it to the Greek context, with interesting formal features.

Acknowledgements

I want to express my gratitude to Maria Chalkou, Nikitas Fessas, Anna Poupou, Menelaos Karantzas and Spyridoula Bella, who helped me enormously with their thorough remarks and useful suggestions.

Notes

1. All translations from Greek are mine.
2. For a summary of the convergences and deviations between American and French film noir, see Dermentzoglou (2005: 45–9).
3. As Dermentzoglou (2007: 13) observes: 'We owe a number of fine scripts and powerful films to Yannis Maris'[s] skill as a writer.' Similarly, Philippou (2018: 150) comments: 'Maris's novels fuelled for years, until his death, domestic cinema, which exploited to the fullest extent readers' love for his crime novels.'
4. However, some of the reviewers of the time were not impressed with Maris's script (for example, Ploritis 1960: 2). According to Matsas (1960: 2), Katsouridis's direction 'has some coldness and lacks inspiration, but is technically flawless'. Vlachou (1960: 2) admired the rapid pace of the film and Plessas's score, which supported the 'atmosphere of mystery'; nevertheless, she found gaps in Maris's script; Mitropoulou (1960: 2) was less enthusiastic about the film, merely calling it 'well-made', featuring 'unoriginal, but well-photographed shots', while she pointed out the thematic similarity between Maris's script and the one for *Murder in Kolonaki*.
5. The main/cardinal functions (in French, *fonctions cardinales* or *noyaux*) and catalysts are the two sub-categories of the narrative functions mentioned by Barthes ([1966] 1985: 167–206) and adopted by McFarlane (1996: 14–15) and Whelehan (1999: 10). 'The cardinal functions refer to important events that are directly related to the development of the story, while catalysts refer to minor acts that assist in the evolution of cardinal functions. The above functions are transported directly from literature to cinema, as they refer to acts and facts that can be visualized' (Kaklamanidou 2006: 38).
6. On Maris's dominant thematic motifs, see Apostolidis (2012: 53–7).
7. For a detailed description of Maris's personal and professional life, see Leondaritis (2013).
8. Park (2011: 26) notes: 'Whether it leads to punishment and doom or redemption is not as important to the genre as there being an investigation. Such then are the

components which make up the genre of film noir: a crime, a fallible protagonist, a contemporary setting and, usually, an investigation by someone or some agency, not necessarily the protagonist.'
9. On Simenon's Maigret, see Alder (2013); Wenger and Trussel (2017). For comparisons between Maigret and Bekas, see Apostolidis (2012: 119); Philippou (2018: 244–6).
10. 'With Bekas we have the best example of a man of value. He is not selfish, like many of the current heroes of crime novels. He does not drag his personal problems in front of us' (Foster 2016: 15). Contemporary Greek crime author Petros Markaris (2016: 51) notes: 'Maris understood very early on that police officers involved in solving crimes are neither ingenious, nor curious. They are simple people, usually petty bourgeois, who are in a profession, which they strengthen with a sense of justice.'
11. The indices proper and the informants are the two sub-categories of the indices, the second category of narrative functions recorded by Barthes ([1966] 1985: 167–206), adopted and transferred to the analysis of films by McFarlane (1996: 14–15) and Whelehan (1999: 10). The indices proper refer to psychological information about the characters, as well as to the narrative atmosphere. Informants are data of immediate signification, such as names of characters, their ages, professions, etc. (Kaklamanidou 2006: 38).
12. Although five years later, in 1965, Giorgos Papakostas directed *Lolites tis Athinas/Athens Lolitas*, also based on a pulp novel (by Nikos Marakis).
13. According to Andritsos (2016: 36), 'cinema was a privileged field of censorship in Greece from 1945 to 1974'. See also Chalkou (2018).
14. See, for instance, stage star Dimitris Apergis, a main character in *O Thanatos tou Timotheou Konsta* [The Killing of Timotheos Konstas] (1961), or Liza Perri, a young actress of the Art Theatre in *Zitima empistosynis* [A Matter of Confidence] (1955).
15. On practices in film adaptations of novels, see Moraitis (1990: 13–15); Garcia (1990); Serceau (1999).
16. On the features of film noir, see Valoukos and Spiliopoulos (1985: 19–28); Dancyger and Rush (1995: 58–60).
17. For example, Roy William Neill's 1946 noir *Black Angel*, adapted from a novel by Cornell Woolrich.
18. See McDonnell's observation that in such scenes in noir films the narrative is interrupted in order for the spectator to appreciate the spectacle (2007: 76).
19. On the use of flashbacks in film noir, see Menegaldo (2004).
20. For the narrative analepses in Maris's prose, see Ioakeimidou (2005: 47–56).
21. As Poupou (2018: 181) observes, in Greek noir 'the theme of the dark past does not appear in a flashback'.
22. See Neale's observation that third-person narration is more often found in semi-documentary style noir films (2000: 166–7, n. 5).
23. Commenting on Karydis-Fuchs's stylistic coherence in *Murder Backstage* and *Murder in Kolonaki*, Poupou (2018: 182) observes: 'In his films we have a strong contrast, the use of a strong light source, deep shadows, stark outlines, nighttime rain-shots and wet roads that reflect the light.'

24. Mylonas (2001: 64) notes of Plessas's music: 'The scenes of mystery and suspense in this crime thriller are emphasized by the music, the role of which emerges as one of the most important expressive means of the film.' On the use of jazz music in the noir film, see Butler (2002).
25. W. H. Auden (1948: 408) comments: 'Greek tragedy and the detective story have one characteristic in common, in which they both differ from modern tragedy, namely, the characters are not changed in or by their actions: in Greek tragedy because their actions are fated, in the detective story because the decisive event, the murder, has already occurred.' However, this is not always the case, and Maris's characters are often far from static, offering interesting challenges to actors.
26. Gabin starred as Maigret in *Maigret tend un piège/Maigret Sets a Trap* (dir. Delannoy, 1958), *Maigret et l'affaire Saint-Fiacre* (dir. Delannoy, 1959) and *Maigret voit rouge* (dir. Grangier, 1963).
27. The character of Bekas appeared in two more big-screen adaptations of Maris's novels, *Murder in Kolonaki* and *Amfivolies/Doubts* (dir. Grigoriou, 1964), in which he was played by the character actors Yannis Bertos and Liakos Christoyannopoulos respectively.
28. Despite her extremely limited screen time, Roza is the film's *femme fatale*, the dangerous and lustful woman who threatens normative masculinity and must be punished by the end of the narrative. See Fessas and Kosma's remarks on how Greek noir, similarly to American noir of the 1940s, presents the anxieties of Greek society of its time (2017: 83–109).
29. For an overview of images of women in film noir, see Kaplan (1998).
30. According to Fotiou and Fessas (2017: 113), Tsaganeas and Kontou belong to the group of actors who were identified with the early attempts at noir in Greek cinema.

References

Agathos, Thanassis (2018), 'Eglima sto Kolonaki: to athinaiko astynomiko mythistorima tou Yanni Mari stis ellinikes othones tou 1960' [Murder in Kolonaki: An Athenian Detective Story by Yannis Maris on the Greek Screens of 1960], *Modern Greek Studies Australia & New Zealand*, 19, pp. 105–20.

Alder, Bill (2013), *Maigret, Simenon and France: Social Dimensions of the Novels and Stories*, Jefferson, NC: McFarland.

Andrew, J. Dudley (1984), *Concepts in Film Theory*, Oxford: Oxford University Press.

Andritsos, Giorgos (2016), 'I logokrisia ston elliniko kinimatografo (1945–1974)' [Censorship in Greek Cinema (1945–1974)], in Penelope Petsini and Christopoulos Dimitris (eds), *I logokrisia stin Ellada* [Censorship in Greece], Athens: Idryma Rosa Luxenburg, pp. 35–42.

Apostolidis, Andreas (2009), *Ta polla prosopa tou astynomikou mythistorimatos* [The Many Faces of the Crime Novel], Athens: Agra.

Apostolidis, Andreas (2012), *O kosmos tou Yanni Mari* [Yannis Maris's World], Athens: Agra.

Auden, W. H. (1948), 'The Guilty Vicarage: Notes on the Detective Story, by an Addict', *Harper's Magazine*, May 1948, pp. 406–12 <harpers.org/archive/1948/05/the-guilty-vicarage/1/> (last accessed 27 February 2019).

Barthes, Roland ([1966] 1985), 'Introduction à l'analyse structural des récits', in Roland Barthes, *L'aventure sémiologique*, Paris: Seuil, pp. 167–206.

Borde, Raymond, and Chaumeton, Étienne (1955), *Panorama du film noir américain 1941–1953*, Paris: Les Editions de Minuit.

Butler, David (2002), *Jazz Noir: Listening to Music from Phantom Lady to The Last Seduction*, Westport, CT: Greenwood Publishing.

Chalkou, Maria (2008), 'Towards the Creation of "Quality" Greek National Cinema in the 1960s', PhD dissertation, University of Glasgow.

Chalkou, Maria (2018), 'Kinimatografos kai logokrisia stin Ellada apo ta prota chronia eos ti metapolitefsi' [Cinema and Censorship in Greece from the First Years to Metapolitefsi], in Penelope Petsini and Dimitris Christopoulos (eds), *Lexiko logokrisias stin Ellada* [Dictionary of Censorship in Greece], Athens: Kastaniotis, pp. 82–99.

Dancyger, Ken, and Rush, Jeff (1995), *Alternative Scriptwriting: Successfully Breaking the Rules*, Boston: Focal Press.

Dermentzoglou, Alexis (2005), *To petagma tou anaptira. Sygritiki matia sto evropaiko kai sto amerikaniko nouar* [The Flying of the Lighter: A Comparative Look at European and American Noir], Thessaloniki: Erodios.

Dermentzoglou, Alexis (2007), 'They are ours, and you'd better believe it (them)', in Alexis Dermentzoglou (ed.), *In a Dark Passage: Film Noir in Greek Cinema*, Thessaloniki: Erodios, pp. 9–11.

Dimendberg, Edward (2004), *Film Noir and the Spaces of Modernity*, Cambridge, MA: Harvard University Press.

Dix, Andrew (2016), *Beginning Film Studies*, Oxford: Oxford University Press.

Evans, Bertrand (1947), *Gothic Drama from Walpole to Shelley*, Berkeley, CA: University of California Press.

Fessas, Nikitas, and Kosma, Yvonne (2017), 'The Crisis of Gender Identity in the Greek Film Noir: Sexuality, Paranoia and the Unconscious in *Efialtis/Nightmare* (1961) and *O Ergenis/The Bachelor* (1997)', *Filmicon: Journal of Greek Film Studies*, 4, pp. 83–109.

Forshaw, Barry (2014), *Euro Noir: The Pocket Essential Guide to European Crime Fiction, Film & TV*, Herts: Pocket Essentials.

Foster, Nick (2016), 'Enas Anglos diavazei Mari stin Ellada' [An Englishman Reads Maris in Greece], *CLM (The Crimes and Letters Magazine)*, 1, pp. 14–15.

Fotiou, Mikela, and Fessas, Nikitas (2017), 'Greek Neo-Noir: Reflecting a Narrative of Crisis', *Filmicon: Journal of Greek Film Studies*, 4, pp. 110–37.

Garcia, Alain (1990), *L'adaptation du roman au film*, Paris: Paris IF Diffusion-Dujarric.

Hamon, Philippe (1981), *Introduction à l'analyse du descriptif*, Paris: Hachette.

Harvey, Sylvia (1998), 'Woman's Place: The Absent Family of Film Noir', in E. Ann Kaplan (ed.), *Women in Film Noir*, London: BFI and Palgrave Macmillan, pp. 35–46.

Herbert, Rosemary (2003), *Whodunit? A Who's Who in Crime & Mystery Writing*, Oxford: Oxford University Press.

Ioakeimidou, Lito (2005), 'Aisthitika criteria paralogotechnikotitas sto ergo tou Yanni Mari kai tou Andrea Apostolidi. I arsi tis amfisimias kai o anagnostis' [Aesthetic Criteria of Paraliterature in the Work of Yannis Maris and Andreas Apostolidis: The Removal of Ambiguity and the Reader], *Dia-Keimena*, 7, pp. 47–56.

Jost, François (1987), *L'oeil-camera*, Lyon: Presses Universitaires de Lyon.

Kaklamanidou, Despoina (2006), *Otan to mythistorima synantise ton kinimatografo* [When the Novel Met the Cinema], Athens: Aigokeros.
Kalfopoulos, Kostas (2016), 'Y. Maris-Tsirimokos, i aioniotita enos patriarchi' [Y. Maris-Tsirimokos, the Eternity of a Patriarch], *I Kathimerini*, 15 February, <http://www.kathimerini.gr/859496/article/politismos/vivlio/g-marhs--tsirimwkos-h-aiwniothta-enos-patriarxh> (last accessed 27 February 2019).
Kaplan, E. Ann (ed.) (1998), *Women in Film Noir*, London: BFI and Palgrave Macmillan.
Karalis, Vrasidas (2012), *A History of Greek Cinema*, London: Continuum.
Klein, Michael, and Parker, Gillian (1981), *The English Novel and the Movies*, New York: Ungar.
Leondaritis, Giorgos (2013), *O Yannis Maris kai i epochi tou* [Yannis Maris and his Era], Athens: Agra.
Marcou, Loïc (2014), 'Le roman policier grec (1953–2013): les enjeux littéraires du genre policier en Grèce', PhD dissertation, Université Paris-Sorbonne.
Marcou, Loïc (2017), 'Roman policier, littérature médiatique, et transferts culturels franco-grecs (1865–1965)', *The Historical Review/La Revue Historique*, XIV, pp. 95–124.
Maris, Yannis (1953), 'Eglima sto Kolonaki' [Murder in Kolonaki], *Oikogeneia*, 2, 29 July.
Maris, Yannis (1979), 'Mia afigisi' [A Narrative], *Anti*, 28 September, pp. 30–1.
Maris, Yannis (2012), *Eglima sto Kolonaki* [Murder in Kolonaki], Athens: Alter-Ego MME A.E.
Maris, Yannis (2016), *Eglima sta paraskinia* [Murder Backstage], Athens: Atlantis.
Maris, Yannis (2011), *To kokkino vazo* [The Red Vase], Athens: Atlantis.
Markaris, Petros (2016), 'Simeioseis pano sto fainomeno Yannis Maris' [Notes on the Phenomenon Yannis Maris], in Kostas Kalfopoulos (ed.), *18 keimena gia ton Yanni Mari* [18 Texts about Yannis Maris], Athens: Patakis, pp. 49–57.
Martinidis, Petros (1994), *Synigoria tis paralogotehnias* [In Defence of Paraliterature], Athens: Ypodomi.
Matsas, Nestoras (1960), 'Oi tainies tis evdomados' [The Films of the Week], *Ethnikos Kyrix*, 15 November, p. 2.
McDonnell, Brian (2007), 'Film Noir Style', in Geoff Mayer and Brian McDonnell (eds), *Encyclopedia of Film Noir*, Westport, CT: Greenwood Press, pp. 70–84.
McFarlane, Brian (1996), *Novel to Film. An Introduction to the Theory of Adaptation*, Oxford: Clarendon Press.
Menegaldo, Gilles (2004), 'Flashbacks in *Film Noir*', *Sillages critiques*, 6, <http://journals.openedition.org/sillagescritiques/1561> (last accessed 27 February 2019).
Mikelides, Ninos Fenek (1997), *Istoria tou kinimatografou: 100 xronia ellinikes tainies* [History of Cinema: 100 Years of Greek Films], vol. 3, Athens: Maniateas.
Mitropoulou, Aglaia (1960), 'Nees tainies' [New Films], *Athinaiki*, 15 November, p. 2.
Moraitis, Makis (1990), *To mythistorima ston kinimatografo* [The Novel in the Cinema], Athens: Alexandreia.
Mylonas, Kostas (2001), *I mousiki ston elliniko kinimatografo* [Music in Greek Cinema], Athens: Kedros.
Neale, Steve (2000), *Genre and Hollywood*, Abingdon: Routledge.

Papamichalis, Vion (1960), 'Oi tainies tis evdomados' [The Films of the Week], *Acropolis*, 15 November, p. 2.
Park, William (2011), *What is Film Noir?*, Lewisburg, PA: Bucknell University Press.
Philippou, Philippos (2016), '100 chronia apo ti gennisi tou Yanni Mari' [100 Years since Yannis Maris's Birth], *To Vima*, 10 January, <https://www.tovima.gr/2016/01/09/culture/100-xronia-apo-ti-gennisi-toy-gianni-mari/> (last accessed 27 February 2019).
Philippou, Philippos (2018), *Istoria tis ellinikis astynomikis logotechnias. O Yannis Maris kai oi alloi* [History of Greek Crime Fiction: Yannis Maris and the Others], Athens: Patakis.
Ploritis, Marios (1960), 'Oi nees tainies' [The New Movies], *Eleftheria*, 16 November, p. 2.
Poupou, Anna (2018), 'The Case of Greek Film Noir in the 1960s', *Modern Greek Studies Australia & New Zealand*, 19, pp. 167–87.
Rangos, Yannis (2016), '"Poios skotose ton theati?" Ta erga tou Yanni Mari ston kinimatografo kai tin tileorasi' ['Who killed the spectator?' Yannis Maris's Works in Cinema and Television], in Kostas Kalfopoulos (ed.), *18 keimena gia ton Yanni Mari* [18 Texts about Yannis Maris], Athens: Patakis, pp. 133–9.
Rangos, Yannis (2018), 'Athina kai astynomiki logotechnia' [Athens and Crime Fiction], *I Poli Zei*, 61, <https://ipolizei.gr/athina-kai-astunomikh-logotexnia/> (last accessed 27 February 2019).
Savvidis, Giorgos (1960), 'Oi nees tainies tis evdomados' [The New Films of the Week], *To Vima*, 15 November, p. 2.
Serceau, Michel (1999), *L'adaptation cinématographique des textes littéraires: théories et lectures*, Paris: Editions du CEFAL.
Soldatos, Yannis (2001), *Enas aionas Ellinikos kinimatografos* [A Century of Greek Cinema], vol. 1 *(1900-1970)*, Athens: Kochlias.
Soldatos, Yannis (2010), *Istoria tou Ellinikou kinimatografou* [History of Greek Cinema], vol. 1, Athens: Aigokeros.
Spiliopoulos, Vasilis (1984), 'Anichnevontas ton kosmo tou Yanni Mari' [Tracing Yannis Maris's World], *Diavazo*, 86, pp. 39–45.
Stamatiou, Kostas (1960), 'O kinimatografos' [Cinema], *I Avgi*, 16 November, p. 2.
Tonnet, Henri (2005), 'Skepseis gia tin exelixi tou neoellinikou astynomikou mythistorimatos' [Thoughts on the Evolution of the Modern Greek Crime Novel], in Mike Mairy, Miltos Pechlivanos and Lizy Tsirimokou (eds), *O logos tis parousias. Timitikos tomos gia ton Pan. Moulla* [The Speech of Presence: Honorary Volume for Pan. Moullas], Athens: Sokolis, pp. 329–41.
Toulas, Giorgos (2007), 'Eglima sta paraskinia' [Murder Backstage], in Alexis Dermentzoglou (ed.), *In a Dark Passage: Film Noir in Greek Cinema*, Thessaloniki: Erodios, pp. 43–5.
Valoukos, Stathis, and Spiliopoulos, Vasilis (1985), *To film noir* [Film Noir], Athens: Nea Synora–A. A. Livanis.
Vanoye, Francis (1989), *Récit écrit, récit filmique*, Paris: Nathan.
Vatopoulos, Nikos (2016), 'I Athina tou Yanni Mari' [Yannis Maris's Athens], in Kostas Kalfopoulos (ed.), *18 keimena gia ton Yanni Mari* [18 Texts about Yannis Maris], Athens: Patakis, pp. 93–101.

Vlachou, Eleni (1960), 'I kinimatografiki evdomas' [The Film Week], *I Kathimerini*, 17 January, p. 2.
Wagner, Geoffrey (1975), *The Novel and the Cinema*, Rutherford, NJ: Fairleigh Dickinson University Press.
Wenger, Murielle, and Trussel, Stephen (2017), *Maigret's World: A Reader's Companion to Simenon's Famous Detective*, Jefferson, NC: McFarland.
Whelehan, Imelda (1999), 'Adaptations: The Contemporary Dilemmas', in Deborah Cartmell and Imelda Whelehan (eds), *Adaptations, From Text to Screen, Screen to Text*, New York: Routledge, pp. 3–19.

5. DARK CINEMA, DARK SOUNDS: MIMIS PLESSAS AND THE INTEGRATION OF JAZZ INTO GREEK FILM NOIR

Nick Poulakis

> Music is placed where it's needed in the film for only one reason: to make the viewer believe and at the same time let him dream!
>
> Mimis Plessas (2005)[1]

Music of the so-called 'Old Greek Cinema'[2] of the 1950s to the early 1970s plays a fundamental role not only in the construction of the films' narrative milieu, but also in the formation of a distinctive, hybrid cinematic soundscape, which is characteristic of Greek film and popular music production of the period, and crucial for their perception and reception by the audience (Poulakis 2017). Particularly, in line with neo-noir film music of the post-classical era, Greek film noir depends heavily on the incorporation of jazz music styles, textures and practices. Mimis Plessas has been acknowledged as a remarkably prolific composer for mainstream cinema, having scored more than sixty films during the 1960s (Papadimitriou 2006: 177). Furthermore, he has been widely acclaimed as the composer who integrated a jazz feeling into Greek film music of the aforementioned period (Stavrinides 2011: 63; Baskozos 2014; Troussas 2019; Tziritas 2019). Bearing in mind that the relationship between jazz and cinema has not been investigated with regard to Greek film noir, my goal is to highlight diverse aspects of Plessas's music for this genre. The score for *Eglima sta paraskinia/Murder Backstage* (dir. Katsouridis, 1960) was the first of his three noir soundtracks of the 1960s – along with those for *Efialtis/Nightmare* (dir. Andreou, 1961) and *Pyretos stin asfalto/The Asphalt Fever* (dir. Dimopoulos, 1967) – as well as one of his first challenges in scoring films for Greek genre cinema and offering a characteristic mood of noir music contrary to other Greek film composers. By providing a critical examination of *Murder Backstage*,[3] this chapter draws attention to the performative practices of audiovisual representation in early Greek film noir and the ambiguous qualities of Plessas's scores as a means to explore mixed cultural identities, collective memories, personal emotional situations, and the osmosis between everyday life and the social imaginary during the early 1960s in Greece.[4]

Music in Film Noir

Drawing from German Expressionism and using pulp crime novels as its literary basis, film noir of the 1940s, 1950s and 1960s is still the subject of academic debate: should it be considered a special film genre or is it just a particular cinematic style? In any case, film noir is essentially a theoretical creation, a post-constructed term that was not extensively in use at the time these films were produced. Although it was introduced in the mid-1940s by French scholars, it was not until the late 1960s and the early 1970s that the term was widespread (Mercer and Shingler 2004: 5–6).[5] However, as a specific category these movies shared a number of common features, most of which underlined a sense of 'otherness'; for example, the extensive use of black-and-white cinematography, optical contrasts, subdued lighting, reflections and shadows; the emphasis on filming both inner and outer urban spaces; the ambiguous narrative development using flashbacks and voiceovers; the thematic focus on crime detection, moral decay, psychopathology and conspiracies; as well as the prominence of *femme fatale* and 'private eye' characters in the plot (Brookes 2017).

In particular, the soundtracks of noir films have been historically, stylistically and culturally linked to the incorporation of the jazz musical genre into American cinema, although this observation has received some criticism regarding its accuracy. Following Meeker's (1981) compendium cataloguing appearances by jazz musicians in films, Butler talks about the 'jazz noir cliché', a misread (stereotypical) aspect of jazz presence in noir films, affirming that 'although the number of films noir to employ jazz in their scores was relatively small it was still notable' and could be encountered in 'films noir from the 1940s but almost always as source music' (2013: 309) – an alternative term used in film industry for 'diegetic' music.[6] While many people identify jazz as the classic film noir sound, we might argue that this only included a few instances of source music. A substantial changeover occurred from the 1950s onwards, when 'jazz was used more prominently in film scoring' (Butler 2013: 311). Spotting the shift from diegetic to non-diegetic jazz music in the film noir genre could further delineate, to some extent, the intermediate phase of switching from classic film noir to neo-noir. If this approach was applied to the study of music in Greek noir films,

Murder Backstage could be considered a classic Greek noir with neo-noir elements since, first, it incorporates Plessas's background jazz score and, secondly, noir films in Greece appeared later than their foreign counterparts.[7]

In their discussion of jazz music in early film noir, Buhler, Neumeyer and Deemer (2002: 356) claim that jazz was a narrative tool that often served as a manifestation of 'seedy urban settings' or 'the dangerous world of crime'. Addressing either personal or collective attributes, '[n]oir filmmakers employed jazz as a gateway to invisible segments of society, in the process unveiling various suspicious character types and exposing hidden corners of postwar cultural consciousness' (Osteen 2013: 154). In the broadest sense, all indicative components of noir films imply or, better still, accentuate the element of fear. As Richardson (2010: 85) mentions, taking into consideration the traumatic consequences of the Second World War and the difficult circumstances that followed, in film noir '[f]ear is everywhere, and this fear is a fear primarily of otherness, an otherness that is ever present, contained in everything, even within oneself'. This remark lines up with Kalinak's assumption that the 'classical score frequently encoded otherness through the common denominator of jazz' and, thus, 'used jazz as a musical trope for otherness' (1992: 167). Or, in the particular case of scores for Hitchcock's films, jazz stands for 'an exuberant surface [that] barely hides a feeling of danger' – a risky 'but also liberating' filmic feature (Sullivan 2006: 211). Jazz scores for noir films underlined an atmosphere of 'displacement by defying the tonal tradition of classical Hollywood film scoring, with its emphasis on melody and the dominance of a home tone' (Ness 2008: 52).

Plessas's Early Career and his Jazz Grooves in Film Music

The Greek film noir *Murder Backstage* was directed by emerging filmmaker Dinos Katsouridis. Its script was based on Yannis Maris's novel of the same title, first published in 1954. Maris was a celebrated writer of crime and detective fiction stories, many of which have been adapted for the big screen. The film's action takes place several years after the Axis Occupation of Greece during the Second World War. The plot revolves around the murder of an actress, Roza Deli, infamous for her erotic scandals, who is found stabbed in her dressing room in the Gloria Theatre. Inspector Bekas undertakes the investigation, while Yorgos Makris, a strong-willed reporter from *Proini* newspaper, who also tries to solve the crime, teams up with Bekas in investigating the mystery of the murder. Who killed Roza? How was the murder committed since the door of Roza's dressing room was found locked from the inside? There are three prime suspects: leading actor Haris Apostolidis, who had quarrelled with Roza on the night of the murder and is defended by his fiancée, Mary Lamprinou; an unknown man who had visited Roza on the same day; and, finally, Elena Pavlidi, another actress from the theatre group who had always disliked Roza.

In the end, Roza's patron Pavlos Stephanou is revealed as her murderer. He had been blackmailed by the unknown visitor – identified as Roza's husband, Makis Angeloglou, who had been presumed dead – and Roza's colleague Thaleia Chalkia. Although the film did not fare particularly well at the box office on its initial release, over the years it has gained a cult classic status as 'one of the most atmospheric, expressionistic and dark films ever made in Greece' that 'brought Hitchcock's style into Greek cinema' (Karalis 2012: 94). *Murder Backstage* participated in the First Week of Greek Cinema (1960) held in Thessaloniki – winning two prizes, namely Best Cinematography (Aristeidis Karydis-Fuchs) and Best Supporting Actress (Georges Sari) – and was unofficially screened at the Cannes Film Festival.

A unique quality of the film is its soundtrack by Mimis Plessas, a vastly skilled and inventive musician who dominated Greek film music production. Plessas's early professional years are quite enlightening about his later career in Greek discography and cinema. He started as a self-taught musician playing the piano. He was very talented in memorising diverse melodies and repeating them by heart. Although he could not read sheet music, he managed to become the leading soloist in the National Radio Foundation of Greece at the age of 15. His dedication to the piano stimulated him to study music intensely and to begin composing. While an undergraduate at the School of Physicomathematics at the National and Kapodistrian University of Athens, Plessas made his living as a pianist in the capital's nightclubs and cabarets with his established jazz quartet. He was a huge fan of the bebop revolution and a keen collector of records, which served as his educational and training tool for digging into the particular characteristics of jazz.

In the late 1940s, during his stay in the United States where he had settled to finish his doctoral thesis in chemistry at Cornell University, Plessas took part in a students' piano contest at the University of Minnesota, winning the first prize and the opportunity for a scholarship in music.[8] However, he preferred to complete his PhD, and to have music as an avocation. The following year he was nominated as the fifth best pianist in the US. During his stay in New York, Plessas had the privilege of performing with a selection of celebrated jazz personalities, such as Dizzy Gillespie, Quincy Jones, Sarah Vaughan, Lester Young and Coleman Hawkins, who recognised that Plessas invested an esoteric 'black', groovy feeling in his performance that made him stand apart from other white jazz musicians (Haronitis 2005: 24).[9] Known as the 'Greek Gershwin' (Happel 2011) or the 'King of Balkan Jazz' (Vardaki 2016), Plessas concentrated mostly on modern jazz style, although at that point jazz was considered to be a subordinate kind of music in Greece, in comparison with other music genres such as classical, folk or even rock music.[10] Although he was honoured on several occasions as a gifted pianist and improviser, he had never composed and never been paid for his work before his return to Greece in the early 1950s.

By the mid-1950s, although a number of Greek composers of 'light' music for cinema, theatre, radio and revue had already drawn on the jazz idiom, the reputation of this popular music genre had diminished as a result of the Greek Civil War.

> After the American implication, and the left party's defeat, part of the jazz public became suspicious of American imperialism. It was under this suspicion, accompanied by conspiracy theories, that the concerts of Dizzy Gillespie in 1956 and Louis Armstrong in 1959 were hosted in Athens [and jazz] was linked to local conservative elites and American cultural dominancy. (Anagnostou 2016: 71)

As Troussas (2005: 28) comments, 'the precepts, techniques and aesthetics of jazz found ways to reach the wider audience [in Greece] primarily through the light song of that period'. Occasionally, jazz was also confused with rock and roll or Latin American music, considered to be either underground or low-quality music. Under these circumstances, when Plessas came back to Greece from the US, he had initially to conceal his love for jazz and be very careful with his future projects, even though he had always believed that '[j]azz is not what we play, but how we play it!' (Rouben 2011).

Just a few years later, Plessas started to write music professionally for Greek films. This was an excellent opportunity for him to experiment with the integration of jazz into the broadly accessible audiovisual medium of cinema.[11] In an interview, Plessas (2005) stated that '[m]usic is placed where it's needed in the film for only one reason: to make the viewer believe and at the same time let him dream!' Plessas's statement is a first-class example of a composer's reflection on the relationship between the main functions of a film's music and the audience in the cinema. Furthermore, this account is quite pertinent, since it reveals not only the experience-based practice of film scoring, but also particular analytical formulas that contemporary film musicology has now highly systematised. It echoes the viewers' interaction with the music and sounds that accompany the moving images projected on to the big screen. Plessas's vivid description of people's complex engagement with film music embodies Kassabian's (2001: 2–3) methodological distinction between 'assimilating' and 'affiliating identification'. These are two types of audience identification with a film's soundtrack, which correspond either to a firmly controlled connection ('assimilating identification') or to an open-ended dialogical interchange ('affiliating identification'), according to the spectators' perceptions.

In the following sections, after discussing in detail Plessas's music for *Murder Backstage*, I will present further interpretations of this soundtrack and put forward some arguments about the integration of jazz into Greek film noir.

Murder Backstage: A Scene-by-Scene Analysis of the Film's Music

Murder Backstage begins with an exterior night shot of the street outside the Gloria Theatre. In the beginning there is no music, but we can clearly hear the sound of a car and the echo of a man's footsteps as he gets out of the car, walks to the theatre and enters through the backstage door. He has a brief discussion with the theatre's doorman and afterwards with Roza Deli on the phone. The doorman gives the unknown man directions on how to get to Roza's dressing room. This is when the music starts. In the background, we hear the offscreen diegetic sound of the theatre's orchestra playing light dance music during the rehearsal for the show. The music connects, via overlaying, different shots that introduce three of the main characters of the film: Deli, Makris and Stephanou. Moreover, the music heard can be categorised as a standard instrumental tune from a variety show of that period, since we can identify the performance of a theatrical jazz ensemble consisting of rhythm, woodwind, brass and string sections. The film continues with a music and dance act, in which Elena Pavlidi sings one of Plessas's songs during her realistic onscreen performance supervised by Yannis Flery – a prized choreographer of Old Greek Cinema and subsequent contributor to successful Greek musicals of the 1960s. The actress is accompanied by a group of three young male dancers.

Background diegetic music from the theatrical rehearsal continues to be heard offscreen, when suddenly a creepy scream breaks the music continuum. A woman announces the terrible news: 'Roza . . . They killed Roza!' Theatre personnel gather outside Roza's room, trying to understand what has happened, the mysterious guy leaves the building, and the film's opening titles appear on the screen. Plessas's non-diegetic jazz score begins, accompanying the opening credits: its vibrant orchestral character is emphasised by the use of brass, percussion and string *pizzicato* sounds. The scene also features tracking shots from a car driving around the centre of Athens at night. While music continues to be heard and the opening titles, along with the 'Athens-by-night' car scene, finish, a new sequence begins with Inspector Bekas entering the theatre and heading to Roza's dressing room. In this case, music apparently connects, in a smoother manner, the film's credits and the outdoor scene with the next one, in which Bekas arrives. After breaking down the door, another non-diegetic music clip appears at the time Bekas and Makris discover Roza's dead body. This short piece of jazz music could be considered a typical paradigm of scoring the psychological tension of a scene, as it begins with a 'stinger', that is an all-together-playing *sforzando* (a sudden and strong musical emphasis), punctuating dramatic moments of unexpected suspense and parallelling image and vision with music and sound.[12]

As Bekas and Makris set up their side-by-side investigation of the murder, the journalist discusses with another actress Apostolidis's earlier quarrel with

Roza. Jazz music begins. It is a short, lyrical, non-diegetic cue that operates as a narrative comment on the theatre's leading actor, his possible connection to the murder, and Makris's thoughts on this possibility. During the next scene Bekas interrogates Chalkia and, soon after that, Makris bumps into Apostolidis. Once again, jazz music is heard, serving as a sonic background that reinforces the abovementioned speculations. Bekas also questions Pavlidi, the theatre's doorman and Lamprinou, while Apostolidis disappears. Here there are two small non-diegetic music cues that support the film's onscreen action and emotional tension. The first is quite common and underpins Lamprinou's declaration: 'I killed Roza Deli.' The subsequent one illustrates Bekas's mysterious but steadfast expression and is musically imposed through brass orchestration.

The film continues with two scenes, one inside Makris's office and another on the street, without music underscore. The echoes of footsteps throughout the outdoor scene function as a supplementary soundscape for the film's black-and-white visual play between the lights and shadows of the night and the heroes' ghost-like movements. The second music-and-dance sequence of the film includes a sexy striptease act (Figure 5.1). This is the second instance when jazz music is employed as a diegetic element, either onscreen or offscreen, and

Figure 5.1 A jazz band playing diegetic music, while a dancer performs a striptease act. Digital still from *Murder Backstage*.

it begins with Makris's entrance into the nightclub. In the foreground, an Italian stripper swings and undresses on the dance floor while, in the background, the club's orchestra plays and the customers sit around and enjoy the sensual spectacle. The orchestra is a typical jazz band that consists of five members: two saxophonists, pianist, contrabassist and drummer. Although a vibraphone is also heard playing a melodic improvisation, it does not appear on screen. This is a familiar film music practice in Greek mainstream cinema of the 1960s that causes a quasi-realistic sound effect, since the music heard by the film's audience does not match the instrumentation presented on screen. The timbre of the saxophones, sometimes passionate, other times soft, stands out while playing the musical theme accompanied by piano chords, bass *pizzicato* and the rhythm of the drums. During his conversation with the manager of the bar, Makris finds out that Roza was married, and in the next scene he discusses this with Bekas.

The scene that follows shows Makris in his home turning on the radio, relaxing in an armchair and reading about Roza's murder in the newspaper. Lighthearted music orchestrated with accordion, piano, guitar, bass and percussion floods the room, supposed to be coming from the radio. This is also a case of artificially diegetic (pseudo-diegetic) music, since both the quality and the volume of the radio sound create an unbalanced environment. Makris receives a visit from Lamprinou, they talk about the murder, and he turns the radio off. A non-diegetic jazz music cue with *tremolo* strings and brass section climax conveys their astonishment about Roza's locked dressing room. Their meeting continues in the next outdoor scene, where non-diegetic jazz music, based on trombone, vibraphone, piano and bass *pizzicato*, accentuates their surveillance by a covert agent.

Makris drops by Pavlidi's home and, later on, he reaches his office, where Stephanou is waiting for him. The reporter gathers material relating to Roza's assassination. One of Makris's colleagues secretly traces Chalkia in the streets of Athens. Chalkia's shadowing is underscored by non-diegetic jazz music with saxophones, flute, vibraphone, piano, drums and bongos playing an atmospheric improvisation of the film's characteristic melody, while supporting the underlying sense of tension. The transition between indoor (without music) and outdoor (with music) shots heightens the anxiety, but also links the related settings. During the next sequence, the camera captures Makris going back to the theatre and meeting Chalkia and Lamprinou. When Makris and Lamprinou get out of the theatre, a short music cue is introduced. Its improvisational aura is counterbalanced by the role of the orchestral strings, operating as an overall musical nexus. The two protagonists start following Chalkia from a distance, by taxi. A similar non-diegetic mood music cue takes up the film's audio channel, in conjunction with various diegetic road sound effects. When they finally arrive at an old factory, where Chalkia meets the strange man who had visited

Roza on the day of her murder, Plessas's dramatic scoring adds more suspense to the scene. Plessas uses woodwind in the upper registers, strings either in *legato* or in *pizzicato* style, and brass in several dynamic music entrances. There are also some instances with total synchronisation between the modernistic symphonic music composition, ambient sounds, silence and the visual action, increasing the film's tension. At the end of this sequence, Lamprinou meets Apostolidis, and their encounter is lavishly scored with a full orchestral love melody with smooth strings *glissandi* and a climaxing finale.

Makris returns to the nightspot to find its manager and ask him about Roza's supposedly dead husband. This is the third music-and-dance scene in the film when (offscreen) diegetic jazz music is performed. Couples are dancing in the ballroom, but we cannot see the band playing; yet, we can link this scene to the previous one with the stripper at the same club and featuring the same ensemble. Although this is undoubtedly a cheerful piece of source film music, it is principally perceived as a backdrop to the discussion between the two men. Makris comes back to interrogate the theatre's porter and Pavlidi to find out more about Roza's secret marriage. He also asks them about the strange man who had visited Roza – probably her husband, Makis Angeloglou, who has faked his own death. Makris lastly meets Inspector Bekas, and together they decide to investigate the abandoned industrial site where Makris had previously seen the mysterious man. They arrive at the deserted place, where absolute silence reigns. We can only hear the sounds of the men's footsteps and their discussion, a dog barking in the distance, and the door opening. Just as Makris and Bekas find Angeloglou's dead body, the music bursts out with a 'stinger' composed of sudden percussion and brass dissonance, which is transfigured into timpani roll and violin *tremolo* in high notes. Afterwards, the music continues with a mixture of unmelodic but powerfully orchestrated rhythmic phrases that build a dialogue between the brass, the woodwind and the strings. Two more musical *crescendos* illustrate the drama of this scene: one when Makris and Bekas come across Angeloglou's uncle, and the other when Chalkia appears out of hiding behind a corner.

The next part of the film begins with a jazz music cue of solo vibraphone improvisation, along with cool hi-hat rhythmic accompaniment that gradually becomes more obscure, referring once more to undercover surveillance, and operating as a 'sound bridge' that connects different shots via music. Chalkia finds out that she is considered a missing person related to the murders of Roza and her husband. She calls Makris anonymously and hangs up on him. That is when another short, non-diegetic thrill music episode emerges – quite similar to the previous ones – and eventually fades out. Back in the newspaper office, Makris and Bekas make assumptions about the case, and set off to find Chalkia and solve the mystery. At this crucial moment, non-diegetic music starts, being not just a supporting component of the scene, but a critical and enhancing factor, until the policemen finally catch the real murderer. Dissonant brass chords and deep-toned melodic lines, in contrast to high-pitched violin *tremolo* with harmonics, frame a background musical commentary to the dramatic peak and emotional intensity of the scene. Unexpected volume variations, rhythmic accelerations and large pauses in the music, followed by a progressive orchestral *tutti*, rapid improvised sections played by the percussion, and the sounds of the police sirens add more suspense to the already stressful narrative of the film. Chalkia reveals everything to Makris (Figure 5.2). During a flashback, the decisive points of the murder are exposed. Bekas arrests Stephanou, while Makris gets all the information needed from Chalkia. In the closing scene, as the cops put her in the police car, Makris and Bekas start back, discussing the details of the murder and the motives of Roza's murderer. An upbeat jazz variation of the film's musical theme is heard, emerging in a completely different mood that creates a joyful and triumphant ending.

To sum up, Plessas's overall score for *Murder Backstage* might be described as a 'dark' and 'dense' progressive jazz soundtrack, although it also contains some 'lighter' musical moments that, however, do not alter the general impression. Some film musicology scholars underpin the 'inaudibility' (Gorbman

Figure 5.2 Chalkia's confession scene: psychologically intense non-diegetic music, mixed with realistic sounds of police sirens. Digital still from *Murder Backstage*.

1987: 73) of the classical film score, that is its 'inherent necessity not to draw attention to itself' (Sabaneev 1935: 22) as 'a stimulus that we hear but, by and large, fail to listen to' (Kalinak 1992: 3). As opposed to the above considerations, I argue that the music in *Murder Backstage* is not a conventional score, as it moves between Kassabian's 'assimilating' and 'affiliating' identifications, and intrinsically operates as an 'added value' to the film's visual narrative, revealing 'the expressive and informative value with which a sound enriches a given image' (Chion 1994: 5).

Plessas's Soundtrack for *Murder Backstage* as a Musical Trope for Otherness

Plessas's soundtrack for *Murder Backstage* represents his early attempt at scoring for the mainstream cinema, in which he incorporates his personal jazz style, distancing himself considerably from other classical, popular and folk approaches that dominated Greek film music of the time, including his future compositions for Finos Film. Plessas (2005) notes:

> At some point, [Greek] cinema tried to break away from the symphonic style imposed by the syndicalist classical orchestra musicians [. . .] This is where I learned, first recorded and played music that was harmonically modern. This is where we managed to establish the jazz harmonies of tetrads. All these were sounds from the US, but also modern sounds from my childhood.

Along the same lines, Kostas Klavvas (2001), another film music pioneer of Old Greek Cinema, appraised Plessas's obsession with modern American music and the introduction of jazz into his film soundtracks:

> Mimis Plessas, a great composer, wrote sheet music that you cannot understand [. . .] At that time, it was not common for us to use big bands – three saxophones, two trumpets and a trombone [. . .] Mimis Plessas did use them [. . .] Jazz idiom was employed at every opportunity! [. . .] We were smug about jazz. It was something we lived in and we knew it. And it was something rich. To be precise, we were playing the standard music tracks during our everyday jobs and we were enjoying it. Using lush harmony and improvisation [. . .] We were playing music in the orchestras, or we were orchestrating for bigger ensembles or smaller bands and we were improvising. We put our heart and soul into that!

Murder Backstage gave Plessas the opportunity to introduce his own music preferences into mainstream cinema, although jazz, especially 'noir jazz' or 'crime jazz',[13] had never been exploited in a systematic and creative way in Greek genre films; instead, it had been mostly used as a musical 'condiment' in conjunction with other popular music styles.[14] As designated by Poupou (2018: 175), all ten noir films of the Greek commercial cinema released between 1960 and 1967 contain jazz elements of some kind, as opposed to the music of other genres. Poupou identifies three distinguished composers with active contributions to scoring noir films during this period: Mimis Plessas, Yorgos Katsaros and Kostas Kapnisis. However, there are significant musicological differences between these three composers' scores for Greek noir films. Katsaros's music arrangements for *O dolofonos agapouse poly/The Murderer Who Loved a Lot* (dir. Daifas, 1960) and *Kravgi.../Cry...* (dir. Andritsos, 1964) rely heavily on simple melodies and rhythms with extensive use of saxophone and vibraphone, incorporating a fairly large number of Greek elements – a sort of jazzy music that one could easily encounter as an interposed cue in various scenes from other Greek dramatic and police/crime movies of the 1960s. Mixing classical European and jazz music features, Kapnisis's music for *Eglima sto Kolonaki/Murder in Kolonaki* (dir. Aliferis, 1959) and *Ligo prin ximerosi/Just Before the Crack of Dawn* (dir. Kosteletos, 1963) is much closer to the soft mood style of earlier Greek composers such as Takis Morakis and Yorgos Mouzakis. Kapnisis usually employs a homophonic accompaniment approach of a melodramatic string background coupled with easy-listening piano and acoustic guitar sections. He follows an organised development of his musical themes, often encompassing Greek music scales and thick instrumental textures. In addition, both Katsaros's and Kapnisis's film noir music includes several diegetic songs in Greek light, popular and light-popular music genres.

On the contrary, Plessas's scores for the noir films *Murder Backstage*, *Nightmare* and *The Asphalt Fever* – albeit the latter to a much lesser degree – seem to operate differently from the film noir soundtracks of the two aforementioned composers. Regardless of whether he is composing musical cues to establish the entire ambiance of a film noir scene or is 'playing to the details',[15] Plessas inherits an improvised jazz mood – effortlessly modernist and free from other European or Greek music (con)textual references. This leaves the audience with the general feeling of a jazz music film score, although determining music genres with absolute precision has never been an easy task. As Plessas's collaborator Nikos Avgeris (2001) affirmed in an interview,

> Plessas could improvise and write down the music afterwards. But when he did write it down, it was not exactly as he had played it [...] Plessas had a different style, besides his irregular music writing [...] He was influenced by American jazz. He tried to integrate Greek elements in his music and this attracted a certain audience.

In fact, although Avgeris's last comment could be true of other Plessas's soundtracks, we hardly encounter any 'Greek' musical features in Plessas's non-diegetic score for *Murder Backstage*.

David Butler (2002: 116–17) identifies three categories of jazz included in noir films: the jazz-inflected non-diegetic score, live performances by jazz bands and jazz recordings heard diegetically. Music in *Murder Backstage* belongs mainly to the first of the above examples. This is what is generally called 'mood music', that is, music that matches the audience's acoustic perception with their visual experience, functioning as an additional commentary on the drama. The second and third patterns of jazz presence in *Murder Backstage* are rather limited or less obvious, occurring only in cases of 'realistic representations of the film's "actual world"' – hence in 'actual music' (diegetic or source music).[16] On the other hand, it is a common method in film production to employ background scoring, thus ensuring structural and stylistic unity within a film. In Old Greek Cinema, this feature was dominant and of a particular intensity, when comparing either different films scored by the same composer, or other films directed according to the norms of a specific cinematic genre (Poulakis 2017: 81). Plessas's music for *Murder Backstage* functions in this specific way, since the greater part of the film's jazzy score is consistent with non-diegetic music–image association, while source music is limited to the theatre and nightclub 'live' performances, providing a meta-diegetic soundscape of 'direct address' that exceeds the characteristic diegetic/non-diegetic dichotomy, as defined by Stilwell (2007: 196–7).

Ness (2008: 52–4) has argued that film noir not only included particular optical and narrative themes, but also introduced a 'specific sound', which was equivalent to its visuals and drama, and consisted of the elimination of the classic neo-romantic tradition and the use of contemporary techniques, qualities and instrumentation. In this case study, it is obvious that the music and sound mood of *Murder Backstage* construct an analogy with its visual and dramatic tropes – such as *femmes fatales*, cool detectives, nightlife and chiaroscuro lighting – building up the audience's expectations. This is what Frith (1996: 120) calls 'musical shorthand' in cinema – a semiotic dimension of film music that frequently employs 'generic conventions', and derives from Gorbman's (1987: 2–3) attempt to define theoretically the involvement of music in a film's 'cultural codes'. Apart from the broader jazz ambiance of *Murder Backstage*, Plessas does not avoid an overused film music cultural marker that makes a strong connection between 'sexy saxophone' sounds and a hedonistic female dance, when he chooses to provide a typical 'luscious' score for the striptease number in the nightclub.

Jazz music style has been characterised by its freedom and innovation in expression, articulated through various practices and techniques, such as the imitation of the sounds of the human voice (mumbles, sighs, *glissando*, *tremolo*) by the instruments; the unconventional syncopated and polyrhythmic (offbeat) measures; the driving and swinging tempos; the European-guided (romantic and impressionistic) principles of music scales and harmonic modes that embrace chromaticism, 'dirty tones', 'blue notes' and 'hot intonation'; the structural forms of call-and-response, variations and improvisation; and the heterophonic, pseudo-polyphonic or fully contrapuntal textures of musical composition (Hardie 2013: 78). One can indicate numerous of the above qualities of jazz in Plessas's music for *Murder Backstage*. A progressive, unconventional, experimental and cosmopolitan perspective on free jazz music, in conjunction with modernist textures of dissonance, atonality, timbral experimentation and rhythmic autonomy, dominate the soundtrack, emphasising the 'darker' sides of the film's multiple juxtaposed realities, and giving rise to novel trends in mainstream Greek film music from the 1960s onwards.

Nowadays, Plessas remains incredibly active both in composing and performing his jazz music in numerous live concerts and shows worldwide. As a testimony to his work's continuing cultural relevance and significance, some of Plessas's scores – among them the ones for *Murder Backstage*, *Nightmare* and other Greek films of the time that feature noir elements – were later remastered and released both on vinyl and CD (Troussas 2019). In a recent article on Plessas's film soundtracks, contemporary Greek film critic Thodoris Koutsogiannopoulos (2020) claims that the most impressive feature of Plessas's film scores for Old Greek Cinema is that he managed to integrate 'jazz sounds and his experiences of American popular music [. . .] into [indigenous] films that had multiple needs, either cosmopolitan or narrowly Greek, [that is] accompanying music for long episodes or short fill-in cues, background scores of punctual detail and atmospheric emphasis'. The evaluation of Plessas's music for Greek noir films of the early 1960s justifies previous general studies of noir film soundtracks (Butler 2002; Ness 2008; Wager 2017) that analyse jazz not as an absolute, standardised or taken-for-granted formula but, in Kalinak's terms, as a 'musical trope' (1992: 167). In this sense, the aura of otherness in Plessas's dark music for *Murder Backstage* lies particularly in his ambivalence in being a 'white' European composer with a 'black' American sound.

Notes

1. Unless otherwise noted, all translations from Greek are the author's.
2. The term 'Old Greek Cinema' refers to Greek commercial film production from 1950 to 1970 approximately. These mainstream films were extremely popular among native audiences, but rarely crossed the national frontier, while the notion of genre was central to them (Papadimitriou 2006: 13–27).
3. I would like to express my appreciation to Louise Stefanidaki for her immense help in the analysis of the film.

4. Several Greek cinema scholars, such as Dermentzoglou (2007), Karalis (2012) and Poupou (2018), agree in categorising this as a film noir. For further discussion on the definition and taxonomy of Greek film noir and neo-noir, see Fotiou and Fessas (2017).
5. As Naremore ([1998] 2008: 11) states, the term 'film noir' falls both into the 'history of ideas' and into the 'history of cinema'. Therefore, it concerns both a set of artefacts and a discourse about them – an analysis associated with a 'dark' past.
6. For an analytical description of the terms 'diegetic', 'non-diegetic' and 'metadiegetic' concerning cinematic music and sound in relation to the visual, logical and spatio-temporal context of a film, see Gorbman (1987: 11–30).
7. In this case, the result is quite similar to Poupou's (2020) recent categorisation of Greek noir cinema. Poupou proposes a quadripartite classification, namely: 1) early Greek noir, 2) classic Greek noir, 3) Greek neo-noir and 4) Greek post-classic noir. Greek film noir of the second phase – covering roughly the 1960s – differentiates itself from classic American noir by thematically moving away from gender/sex-based phobias towards anxieties related to the cultural/social change of Westernisation and urbanisation.
8. For a first-hand account of the life and times of Mimis Plessas, see Plessas (1996) and Delaportas (2002).
9. Plessas recounts a story of when, during one of his performances in a US club, he was told: 'Dimitris, there is something with your blood!', meaning that he was playing the piano like a proficient black jazzman (Haronitis 2005: 24).
10. For a historical and contextual overview of jazz in Greece since the 1920s, see Papadimitriou (2018).
11. From the very beginning of his involvement with film scoring, Plessas expressed his willingness to introduce fresh musical ideas into his soundtracks: 'On every occasion, I also pumped jazz into the cinema – where, at least, I knew that the film allowed it and where it would not be heard so much as to . . . disturb the producers!' (Haronitis 2005: 25).
12. For the use of 'stinger' as a cliché in film music scoring and narrative interpretation, see Audissino (2017: 147).
13. For an explanation of these terms, see Butler (2016).
14. As already stated, Plessas was largely a self-educated musician. On one of the few occasions when he went to a music teacher, he was bumped from the class by the second lesson. Plessas explains: 'Because, instead of bringing him the written exercises, I gave him my score for *Murder Backstage*, where I had used everything that he taught me. He kissed me and told me: "You don't need to come back for this class because, against my will, I could deprive you of the advantage to perceive music as something you already know, as a déjà vu". It turns out he was right [. . .]' (Haronitis 2005: 25).
15. Buhler, Neumeyer and Deemer (2002: 322) specify two basic methods that had been inherited from the silent era: 'playing the overall mood of a scene, which had been associated especially with the orchestral practice of the picture palace, and playing to the details, which had been associated with improvising keyboard players. Both methods continued in the sound era, with overall mood being favored for

establishing, spectacle, and montage sequences and playing to details being favored for underscoring dialogue, especially in melodramatic scenes.'
16. See, for instance, the film's music and dance numbers in the nightclub.

References

Anagnostou, Panagiota (2016), 'Towards a History of Jazz in Greece in the Interwar Era', *Jazz Research Journal*, 10:1–2, pp. 54–74.

Audissino, Emilio (2017), *Film/Music Analysis: A Film Studies Approach*, Cham: Palgrave Macmillan.

Avgeris, Nikos (2001), personal interview with Nick Poulakis, 17 December.

Baskozos, Yannis N. (2014), 'Jazz: I elliniki peripeteia' [Jazz: The Greek Adventure], *O Anagnostis*, 29 April, <https://www.oanagnostis.gr/τζαζ-η-ελληνική-περιπέτεια> (last accessed 1 July 2021).

Brookes, Ian (2017), *Film Noir: A Critical Introduction*, London: Bloomsbury Academic.

Buhler, James, Neumeyer, David, and Deemer, Rob (2002), *Hearing the Movies: Music and Sound in Film History*, New York: Oxford University Press.

Butler, David (2002), *Jazz Noir: Listening to Music from Phantom Lady to The Last Seduction*, Westport, CT: Praeger.

Butler, David (2013), 'In a Lonely Tone: Music in Film Noir', in Andrew Spicer and Helen Hanson (eds), *A Companion to Film Noir*, Chichester: Wiley-Blackwell, pp. 302–17.

Butler, David (2016), 'Film Noir and Music', in Mervyn Cooke and Fiona Ford (eds), *The Cambridge Companion to Film Music*, Cambridge: Cambridge University Press, pp. 175–86.

Chion, Michel (1994), *Audio-Vision: Sound on Screen*, New York: Columbia University Press.

Delaportas, Makis (2002), *Mimis Plessas: Enas dromos, hilies notes* [Mimis Plessas: One Route, A Thousand Notes], Athens: Angkyra.

Dermentzoglou, Alexis (ed.) (2007), *In a Dark Passage: Film Noir in Greek Cinema*, Thessaloniki: Erodios.

Fotiou, Mikela, and Fessas, Nikitas (2017), 'Greek Neo-Noir: Reflecting a Narrative of Crisis', *Filmicon: Journal of Greek Film Studies*, 4, pp. 110–37.

Frith, Simon (1996), *Performing Rites: On the Value of Popular Music*, Cambridge, MA: Harvard University Press.

Gorbman, Claudia (1987), *Unheard Melodies: Narrative Film Music*, Bloomington, IN and London: Indiana University Press and British Film Institute.

Happel, Frans (2011), 'Mimis Plessas (86), de Gershwin van Griekenland' [Mimis Plessas (86), the Gershwin of Greece], *Lychnari*, 25:1, pp. 6–9.

Hardie, Daniel (2013), *Jazz Historiography: The Story of Jazz History Writing*, Bloomington, IN: iUniverse.

Haronitis, Yorgos (2005), 'Mimis Plessas: The Jazz Side', *Jazz & Tzaz*, 148–9, pp. 22–5.

Kalinak, Kathryn (1992), *Settling the Score: Music and the Classical Hollywood Film*, Madison, WI: University of Wisconsin Press.

Karalis, Vrasidas (2012), *A History of Greek Cinema*, London: Continuum.
Kassabian, Anahid (2001), *Hearing Film: Tracking Identifications in Contemporary Hollywood Film Music*, New York: Routledge.
Klavvas, Kostas (2001), personal interview with Nick Poulakis, 28 November.
Koutsogiannopoulos, Thodoris (2020), 'Mimis Plessas: O prigkipas tou ellhnikou soundtrack' [Mimis Plessas: Prince of Greek Soundtrack], *LiFO*, 24 May, <https://www.lifo.gr/articles/music_articles/283352/mimis-plessas-o-prigkipas-toy-ellinikoy-saoyntrak> (last accessed 1 July 2021).
Meeker, David (1981), *Jazz in the Movies*, New York: Da Capo.
Mercer, John, and Shingler, Martin (2004), *Melodrama: Genre, Style and Sensibility*, London: Wallflower.
Naremore, James ([1998] 2008), *More than Night: Film Noir in its Contexts*, Berkeley, CA: University of California Press.
Ness, Richard R. (2008), 'A Lotta Night Music: The Sound of Film Noir', *Cinema Journal*, 47:2, pp. 52–73.
Osteen, Mark (2013), *Nightmare Alley: Film Noir and the American Dream*, Baltimore, MD: Johns Hopkins University Press.
Papadimitriou, Lydia (2006), *The Greek Film Musical: A Critical and Cultural History*, Jefferson, NC: McFarland.
Papadimitriou, Sakis (2018), 'Greece', in Francesco Martinelli (ed.), *The History of European Jazz: The Music, Musicians and Audience in Context*, Sheffield: Equinox, pp. 560–70.
Plessas, Mimis (1996), *Mimis Plessas: Autoviografia* [Mimis Plessas: Autobiography], Athens: Kaktos.
Plessas, Mimis (2005), personal interview with Nick Poulakis, 1 March.
Poulakis, Nick (2017), 'I mousiki ston palio elliniko kinhmatografo tis dekaetias tou 1960: Zitimata esthitikis, analysis kai ermineias stis tainies tis Finos Film' [Music in the Old Greek Cinema of the 1960s: Issues of Aesthetics, Analysis, and Interpretation in Finos Films' Movies], in Maria Paradeisi and Afroditi Nikolaidou (eds), *Apo ton proimo sto syghrono elliniko kinimatografo* [From Early to Modern Greek Cinema], Athens: Gutenberg, pp. 76–103.
Poupou, Anna (2018), 'The Case of Greek Film Noir in the 1960s', *Modern Greek Studies (Australia and New Zealand): A Journal for Greek Letters*, 19, pp. 167–87.
Poupou, Anna (2020), 'I elliniki ekdochi tou film noir: Skoteines afigiseis kai politikes alligories se periodous krisis' [The Greek Version of Film Noir: Dark Narratives and Political Allegories in Periods of Crisis], in Vassilios Sabatakakis (ed.), *The Greek World in Periods of Crisis and Recovery, 1204–2018*, Athens: European Society of Modern Greek Studies, pp. 29–52.
Richardson, Michael (2010), *Otherness in Hollywood Cinema*, London: Bloomsbury Academic.
Rouben, Elli (2011), 'Mimis Plessas: Mia monadiki mousiki synevresi me to Yiorgo Psychoyio sto Athenaeum' [Mimis Plessas: A Unique Music Encounter with Yorgos Psychogios at the Athenaeum Conservatory], *Orfeas*, 6 April, <https://web.archive.org/web/20170701204507/http://www.e-orfeas.gr/artists/interviews/3290-μιμης-πλεσσας-γιωργος-ψυχογιος-athenaeum.html> (last accessed 1 July 2021).

Sabaneev, Leonid (1935), *Music for the Films: A Handbook for Composer and Conductors*, London: Sir Isaac Pitman and Sons.

Stavrinides, Christos (2011), 'National Identity in Greek Cinema: Gender Representation and Rebetiko', PhD dissertation, University of Sheffield.

Stilwell, Robynn J. (2007), 'The Fantastical Gap between Diegetic and Nondiegetic', in Daniel Goldmark, Lawrence Kramer and Richard Leppert (eds), *Beyond the Soundtrack: Representing Music in Cinema*, Berkeley, CA: University of California Press, pp. 184–202.

Sullivan, Jack (2006), *Hitchcock's Music*, New Haven, CT: Yale University Press.

Troussas, Phontas (2005), 'Mimis Plessas: Jazz Activities', *Jazz & Tzaz*, 148–9, pp. 28–9.

Troussas, Phontas (2019), 'Gia proti fora se vinylio 5 exoha soundtrack tou Mimi Plessa ap' ta 60s' [Five of Mimis Plessas's Fabulous Soundtracks from the 1960s Released on Vinyl for the First Time Ever], *LiFO*, 20 June, <https://www.lifo.gr/articles/music_articles/241483/gia-proti-fora-se-vinylio-5-eksoxa-saoyntrak-toy-mimi-plessa-apo-ta-60s> (last accessed 1 July 2021).

Tziritas, Stylianos (2019), 'Mimis Plessas: Ependyontas efialtes kai iligous' [Mimis Plessas: Scoring Nightmares and Vertigos], *MiC*, 11 December, <http://www.mic.gr/thema/mimis-plessas-ependyontas-efialtes-kai-iliggoys> (last accessed 1 July 2021).

Vardaki, Eri (2016), 'Mimis Plessas: "An den eisai trelos, den kaneis gia ayti ti douleia"' [Mimis Plessas: 'Can't Do this Job, if You Ain't Crazy'], *VIMAgazino*, 14 November, <https://www.tovima.gr/2016/11/14/vimagazino/mimis-plessas-an-den-eisai-trelos-den-kaneis-ayti-ti-doyleia> (last accessed 1 July 2021).

Wager, Jans B. (2017), *Jazz and Cocktails: Rethinking Race and the Sound of Film Noir*, Austin, TX: University of Texas Press.

6. FATAL ABSENCES AND FEMALE GAZES: ALTERNATIVE FEMININITIES IN GREEK FILM NOIR AND THE PSYCHOLOGICAL THRILLER

Anna Poupou

If someone asks, 'Who is the most iconic *femme fatale* character in the classic Hollywood noir?', we would hurry to choose between Phyllis, or Cora, or Gilda; among characters played by Elizabeth Scott or Veronica Lake, and so on. If someone asks us to name the most typical *femme fatale* in Greek film noir, it would not be so easy to come up with an immediate answer. Only a few film buffs would remember Irene Papas in her first screen appearance in 1948, in the film *Hamenoi angeloi/Fallen Angels* by Tsiforos, or a couple of dangerous women who appear in Greek noir of the 1960s.[1] One could also think of the imposing, catastrophic protagonists in the films *Eva* (dir. Plyta, 1953) and *Phaedra* (dir. Dassin, 1962), but these examples could not be offered without stretching the limits of film noir, as they fall more closely into the category of melodrama or gothic thriller. This chapter thus starts with the question: Are there any 'real' *femmes fatales* in Greek film noir? 'Real' not in the sense of being faithful to a stereotypical model, or fulfilling a handful of diegetic criteria regarding their participation in the film's plot, but mostly as iconic characters that remain forged in the memory of the spectator and create a cinephilic image.

Recent academic work on film noir, such as that of Sheri Chinen Biesen (2005) and Helen Hanson (2007), which continues Steve Neale's argument (2000), have shown that the *femme fatale* is not exclusive to the film noir genre, but can equally be found in melodramas and other genres contemporary with film noir. In the following pages, I will put forward the argument that women who represent power, enigma, menace and sexual aura are not the main focus of Greek film noir of the classic period.[2] I will discuss the absences and presences regarding female representations in the sociohistorical context of the Greek late 1950s and 1960s, taking also into consideration the reception of US and French films noirs in Greece. To address these issues, I will study the range of interesting female characters to be found in Greek film noir, and I will focus on the issue of the female gaze, as it appears in the film O *anthropos tou trenou*/*The Man on the Train* (dir. Dimopoulos, 1958). Finally, I will address the issue of the participation of female professionals in the production of Greek films and its impact on the construction of female film characters.

FEMMES FATALES AND OTHER STEREOTYPES

The figure of the *femme fatale* was not invented by film noir, nor even by the cinematic art. The archetype of the evil and catastrophic woman is common in Greek and Roman mythology, literature and theatre, with characters such as Medea and Pandora, and in biblical fables, with characters such as Eve and Salome. This archetype survived and became quite popular in the second half of the nineteenth century, mostly in poetry and opera. Incarnated by famous actresses and singers, this image was associated with an over-representation of the female body as the opposite of maternal – the figures of the prostitute, the sterile woman, the lesbian and the androgyne (Buci-Glucksmann [1984] 1994: 93–7). Characters from famous operas such as Carmen and Lulu who express the diversity of the shock of modernity attune to this archetype and bring it closer to the cinematic expressions of the *femme fatale* in the 1910s and 1920s, embodied by the 'vamp' types of Theda Bara and Marlene Dietrich, or *filles fatales*, such as Louise Brooks and Lillian Gish. For Mary Ann Doane, the representation of the *femme fatale* in this period is 'a potential epistemological trauma', as she presents a 'threat which is not entirely legible, predictable or manageable'; she is transformed into a secret that must be aggressively 'revealed, unmasked, discovered' through a hermeneutic process (Doane 1991: 1), a venture in tune with the rise of psychoanalysis and positivism at the beginning of the twentieth century.

In American film reviews of the 1940s, when the label 'film noir' had not yet been established but the concept was already something tangible and recognisable by both spectators and producers, film critics were talking about 'dark crime melodramas with Freudian implications' (Spicer 2002: 1). The pessimistic eroticism of these thrillers, their suggestive filmic codes and a tendency towards the popularisation of psychoanalytical themes that revolved around sexual and gender anxieties were labelled as trademarks of a filmic group that would be later known under the label of film noir. Nino Frank ([1946] 1999: 17) traces the 'misogyny' in the films he discusses (*The Maltese Falcon*, dir. Huston 1941; *Murder, my Sweet*, dir. Dmytryk, 1944), stating that 'It cannot be by accident that the films end in the same manner, the cruellest way in the world, with the heroines paying the full price'; he mentions again 'this hardness, this misogyny' with regard to the film *Double Indemnity* (dir. Wilder, 1944). Film reviewer Jean-Pierre Chartier ([1946] 1999: 23) writes that in these films, 'the females are particularly monstrous' and traces the 'pessimism and despair which radiates from these characters'. He continues: 'Women as insatiable as Empress Messalina, animalistic or senile husbands, young guys ready to kill for the sexual favors of a *femme fatale* [. . .] these are the charming types of the films we've discussed', concluding that in contrast to these US thrillers, the French film noir always leaves room for the spectator to feel sympathy and pity for the characters.[3]

In Greece, films such as *Double Indemnity*, *The Maltese Falcon*, *The Woman in the Window* (dir. Lang, 1944), *The Shanghai Gesture* (dir. Sternberg, 1941) and many other iconic films noirs were shown in the midst of the Greek Civil War, during the seasons 1945–46 and 1946–47; the film critic Eleni Vlachou wrote in her review of the melodrama *In This Our Life* (dir. Huston, 1942) that the film is based on a specific 'type' of woman. 'Lately, there is a trend for heroine-monsters. The dashing, jealous and lying Stanley, with her hypocrisy and her criminal selfishness, not only she is not an obnoxious character, but on the contrary a very interesting one' (Vlachou 1947: 2). After 1945 the American and French films noirs produced during the Second World War were distributed regularly in cinemas, so the Greek audience became acquainted with the conventions of this new kind of crime film and its stereotypical characters no later than French and other European spectators.

In the first scholarly accounts of the genre in the 1950s from French critics Raymond Borde and Étienne Chaumeton, the *femme fatale* derived from the dominant pattern of moral ambivalence and ambiguity of the characters (both male and female) becomes one of the key concepts of film noir:

> Finally there is ambiguity surrounding the woman: the femme fatale who is fatal for herself. Frustrated and deviant, half predator, half prey, detached yet ensnared, she falls victim to her own traps [. . .] This new type of woman, manipulative and evasive, as hard bitten as her environment, ready to shake down or to trade shots with anyone – and probably frigid – has put her mark on 'noir' eroticism which may be at times nothing more than violence eroticized. (Borde and Chaumeton [1955] 1996: 22)

This wave of misogyny, which becomes harder in the thrillers of the 1950s, did not go unnoticed by Greek critics: an example of the critical response can be traced back to a 1954 article in *Empros*, entitled 'The Raid of the Killers'. The author writes that 'this year the crime film, the film of shadows, blood, infamous bars and knives will reign over the Athenian cinemas, filling with awe and horror the souls of the unlucky spectators'. He reports that the major trend of these American and French films is their misogyny, as the feminine characters are sadistically beaten, tortured and slaughtered, and he mentions as an example *The Big Heat* (dir. Lang, 1953). The article is illustrated with a photo from *Les femmes s'en balançent/The Women Couldn't Care Less* (dir. Borderie, 1954), showing Eddie Constantine hitting Dominique Wilms. Finally, the author seems concerned about the role models presented to the young men who watch these violent films (Foskolos 1954: 7). It is noteworthy that the author of this article was Nikos Foskolos who, in the years that followed, became one of the major screenwriters and directors of Greek crime films, thrillers and police procedural TV series.

The theoretical discussion of the nature of film noir was revived in the early 1970s, in tune with the appearance of neo-noir films by the generation of the New Hollywood, who decided to paint it black. Paul Schrader, in his wide-ranging essay, provides one of the most influential accounts of this old Hollywood genre that reflects contemporary fears and anxieties. Schrader highlights post-war disillusionment as a condition for the emergence of these films, and traces the reasons for the shift in the representation of both male and female characters to the return of soldiers to a peacetime economy and the return of female factory employees and businesswomen to the domestic activities of their household sphere (Schrader [1972] 2006: 53–63). Similar sociological and psychological interpretations regarding the female workforce in the 1940s and the male anxieties it caused became more common in the discourse on film noir,[4] and took the place of the sensational and somewhat moralistic descriptions of the *femme fatale* by male film critics of the 1940s and 1950s.

It was in the 1970s that the most important shift in the study of film noir occurred, through the theoretical approaches of second wave feminism. In 1975, in her seminal essay 'Visual Pleasure and Narrative Cinema', Laura Mulvey makes clear that psychoanalytic theory is used as a 'political weapon, demonstrating the way the unconscious of patriarchal society has structured film form' (1989: 14).[5] The volume edited in 1978 by E. Ann Kaplan, *Women in Film Noir*, encapsulates the dominant psychoanalytical and sociological discourses that make film noir a privileged playground for feminist film theory. The authors, from different points of view, propose a turn in the conceptualisation of the *femme fatale* and reconsider her as a positive icon of female empowerment rather than a phallocratic and misogynistic projection (Dyer [1978] 1998). Janey Place, in one of the most revisited essays of this collection, notes:

> Film noir is a male fantasy, as is most of our art [. . .] Film noir is hardly 'progressive' in these terms – it does not present us with role models who defy their fate and triumph over it. But it does gives us one of the few periods of film in which women are active, not static symbols, are intelligent

and powerful, if destructively so, and derive power, not weakness, from their sexuality. (Place [1978] 1998: 47)

From the 1990s onwards a more detailed historical examination of the industry of wartime Hollywood, focusing on women's professional participation in film noir as screenwriters and producers, gaining control and power in creative positions (Martin 1998; Biesen 2005; Wilt 2013), led to a reconsideration of film noir as a totally male-centred genre, or at least as an expression of a hegemonic male gaze. Theories on generic hybridity and the fluidity between film noir and the melodrama (Neale 2000), the women's film (Park 2011: 42–50) and the gothic thriller (Hanson 2007) underline the above assumptions. Despite the essentialist stereotype that considered tough thrillers as a male genre, films noirs were very popular among female audiences. According to a 1946 poll '54% of female respondents preferred "romantic dramas" and 29% "mystery" film types' that, according to Hanson, encompassed both the noir crime thriller and the female gothic film. The 'woman's angle' has been particularly stressed, in order to address the female homefront audience during the war years (Hanson 2007: 9). Presenting the complexities of a gender-segregated audience during the war and its consequences for Hollywood production, Biesen (2005: 126) writes: 'Films noir featured the savvy strategy to target market, and appeal to an audience stratified by gender with audacious romantic female lead characters aimed at a 1940s home-front audience and brazen sex appeal with heightened violence for combat troops abroad.'

Biesen and Hanson discuss a wide range of female characters who inhabited the classic film noir, but remained in the shadow of the *femme fatale*. One of the most important is the female investigator, whether she operates by herself, is appointed by the police, like Kansas (Ella Raines) in *Phantom Lady* (dir. Siodmak, 1944), or works as a team with her male partner (Lauren Bacall in *The Big Sleep*, dir. Hawks, 1946). A scrutiny of many classic films shows that 'good girls' who help the investigation, or female characters who prove to be innocent despite first impressions, are equally as numerous as the dark ladies and spider women; behind them we can often find a female scriptwriter or producer. Working girls and career women, secretaries, professionals in managerial posts, creative executives and businesswomen, as for example in the films *Mildred Pierce* (dir. Curtiz, 1945), *The Strange Case of Martha Ivers* (dir. Milestone, 1946), *Laura* (dir. Preminger, 1944) and *Phantom Lady*, also follow a common pattern in the classic film noir period.

WOMEN IN GREEK FILM NOIR

In the earliest examples of Greek crime films that initiate the film noir tradition, the stereotype of the *femme fatale* is almost absent; an exception is a secondary character played by Irene Papas, in a film that could be best characterised as a courtroom melodrama with noir elements, *Fallen Angels* (1948); despite the clumsy performance of the 22-year-old actress in her first screen appearance, her intense gaze and statuesque figure, dressed in lush furs and sporting a Joan Crawford-like hairdo, create an imposing image that is probably the most interesting feature of this forgotten film. Papas never again appeared in a crime film in a similar role, but this part gives her the title of the first Greek noir *femme fatale*. More common is the figure of the *ingénue*, who might be revealed as a threat to the main male character despite her good intentions. Interestingly, these characters are referred to by their nicknames: 'Pussycat' ('*Psipsina*', in *Magiki polis/The Magic City*, dir. Koundouros, 1954), 'Mousy' ('*Pontikaki*', in *To Pontikaki/The Little Mouse*, dir. Asimakopoulos and Tsiforos, 1954) and 'Baby' ('*Moro*' in *O drakos/The Ogre of Athens*, dir. Koundouros, 1956). These women have a remote resemblance to the feminine figures of 'fallen angels' from pre-Code gangster films; they are closer to the desperate characters found in the dark French melodramas of the 1930s; prostitutes, victims of harassment or low-life artists hoping to change their lives with the help of the main (male) hero. Together they form doomed couples reflecting the fatality, pessimism and impossibility of a happy romantic end for both characters, something that also constitutes the main tone of the post-1936 French crime films. Many of these French films of the late 1930s were distributed in Greece after 1946 and had significant success, so we can suppose that there was a direct influence on the Greek directors of the time. Even if in these Greek cases the tone is not so bleak and the level of desperation not so deep, one can see the similarities between these young heroines and their French counterparts.

After 1958 a cycle of psychological thrillers and detective stories established crime film as a common genre in the context of commercial Greek cinema. Many of them were based on the pulp novels of Yannis Maris, whose serialised detective stories were published in newspapers and specialist crime fiction magazines. His first novel, set in Athens, *Eglima sto Kolonaki* [Murder in Kolonaki] (1953), was a big success that established him as one of the leading crime fiction novelists, and paved the way for 'the Athenian novel' – as Maris called it – a mixture of classic whodunit plots with sentimental and erotic themes, combined with a strong sense of social observation of Athens during the reconstruction era.

In these films of the late 1950s and 1960s we trace a female figure who is close to the stereotype of the *femme fatale*: the 'luxurious woman' as she has been called by Apostolidis (2012: 69–81). This character represents power and wealth; she is often the young wife or mistress of a rich senile husband and is one of the few women in Greek noirs who can produce a feeling of awe in the male lead character. Nevertheless, her involvement in the narration is not usually crucial; she often plays a secondary part, or she appears as a 'red herring' in the plot. While she bears most of the external signs of a potentially dynamic female figure, she can be described as a superficial imitation of the *femme fatale*, and she is rarely constructed as a strong character. These characters are also ineffective because of the actresses who usually play them, such as Maro Kontou and Mary Chronopoulou: while these actresses were known and very popular in commercially successful films, they never became 'A list' film stars like Elli Lambeti, Melina Merkouri or even Zoe Laskari. They were typified by numerous shallow roles – maternal figures, 'good girls' or 'rich bitches' in popular comedies, musicals or melodramas – such that they lose any aura of superiority.

A good example of the 'luxurious woman' is the character of Juliette in the film *Murder in Kolonaki* (dir. Aliferis, 1959), played by Maro Kontou. At first, she appears as the trigger of the plot, being the mistress of the allegedly murdered painter Karnezis; however, after the first twenty minutes of the film she is almost forgotten, as the investigation follows other paths that lead away from the hypothesis of a crime of passion. Her character is associated with overt sexuality; in the first sequence of the film she is flirting with Karnezis, a friend of her husband, luring him away from the others to ask him to paint her portrait naked. In the first five minutes of the film we seen her posing in her underwear, while Maris's prose on the first pages of the novel is also promising and revealing – it reminds us that the novel was published serially, so the first part is meant to gain the reader's attention as a sensual cliff-hanger. One could note here that the sensual scene arrives too soon in the plot, as it doesn't construct any sense of emotional suspense or give the character a dark, mysterious background; as a result, the character remains too superficial and there is no attempt to put her in the centre of the action. Restricted to the role of the object of the male gaze (of the painter, of the investigator, of the spectator) – objectified as a nude portrait – she is deprived of any real agency in the narration.

In the first pages of the novel, the recurrent adjective used to describe Juliette and her world is 'luxurious': 'Her oblique mysterious eyes, her exquisite body [. . .] the luxury that surrounded her'. In the eyes of the police officer Bekas, she is a 'silly, insatiable, empty woman', a 'shameless doll', a 'luxurious doll' (Maris [1953] 2011: 30, 32). In other places, Maris highlights the social difference between the characters: 'Surrounded by these luxurious carpets, expensive furniture, lace and artefacts that decorated the wealthy apartments, Bekas's red and fat face was a dissonance' (Maris [1953] 2011: 25). The instinctual police officer immediately expresses his dislike of her. However, in the film this sense of 'luxury' and abundance is not so pronounced due to the low production values: the set for the living room represents a typical middle-class apartment with modern Danish furniture – far from the heavily decorated apartment located near the Palace that Maris describes. However, Juliette is a typical Maris character, whose power derives from wealth, upward social mobility and social class, and she is associated with a series of venues (beauty and hair salons, gyms) and consumerist practices (expensive cars, impressive jewellery, travelling, designer clothes) that highlight her class difference from the other characters.

One more reason for this absence of the *femme fatale* is the fact that in the late 1950s the feminine models in Greek cinema were different from those that we find in classic Hollywood. The films of the 1940s were shown in Greece after 1945, and they stimulated articles in fashion or gossip columns about the lives of star actresses who played *femmes fatales* (Lauren Bacall, Rita Hayworth, Joan Crawford), their lifestyles and relationships, with particular emphasis on their divorces. But what was in vogue in the late 1940s in the US was just out of fashion in the mid-1950s. Maris describes it very well in *The Lady of the Night*, perhaps his only novel based on a strong lead *femme fatale* character, Liana Perez:

> Lisa said: A friend of my father claimed that Perez is very seductive. Like a cinematic fatale. Nassie laughed.
> – The fashion of the femme fatale is long gone. Now, my dear, it's the time of Brigitte Bardot and Audrey Hepburn. The time of the young girls! (Maris [1955] 2012: 283)

In this vein, an unexpected character who can be found in Greek film noir is the girl-investigator: in *O thanatos tha xanarthei/Death Strikes Again* (dir. Thalassinos, 1961), for example, we have 'Miss Detective' Vivi, who is the assistant of a criminologist and helps him solve the case. In other cases, the girl-investigator is not a police professional, but teams up with the male protagonist. In both *Murder in Kolonaki* and *Eglima stin Omonoia/Crime at Omonoia* (dir. Lathouropoulos, 1962), the character played by Gelly Mavropoulou works in tandem with the male investigator played by Andreas Barkoulis. In general, female helpers and 'good girls' who assist the police or the detectives appear more often in Greek film noir than the *femme fatale*. Conversely, one could add to a list of lethal women the criminal mastermind (*Amfivolies/Doubts*, dir. Grigoriou, 1964) who at the beginning of the film appears as an autonomous career woman, or the psychopathic serial killer, such as the schizophrenic Anna in *Efialtis/Nightmare* (dir. Andreou, 1961) or the sociopath heroine of *To koritsi tou 17/The Girl of 17* (dir. Lykas, 1969).

Interestingly, we can add two figures who could be easily described as *femmes fatales*, in two melodramas that cannot be classified as films noirs: the first is *Phaedra* (1962) by Jules Dassin, a modern adaptation of the Euripides myth. Merkouri, as the lead character, possesses the special aura of the *femme fatale*, seductive, mysterious, controlling and excessive, and she maintains her superiority, in terms of characterisation and imagery, over Raf Vallone and Anthony Perkins. The image of Phaedra owes much to the Oscar-nominated costume designer Deni Vahlioti, while the complexity of the character is due to the scriptwriter, Margarita Lymberaki. The second example is the heroine of *Eva* (1953) by Maria Plyta, one of the few Greek women filmmakers. *Eva* is a gothic melodrama about an illicit and fatal love affair that takes place on an isolated island, featuring a married seductress who turns out to be catastrophic for everyone, herself included. One of the most interesting features of the film is the construction of the subjectivity of the heroine, through point-of-view shots, especially when she admires the body of her young lover, Antiochos. This construction of female subjectivity, the expression of desire and the enhanced woman's angle is a characteristic of Plyta's filmmaking, and it is also obvious in her film *Mono gia mia nyhta/Only for One Night* (1958), which combines the generic conventions of crime films with the female melodrama in a doomed love story between a burglar and a prostitute. In these few examples, one can see that the participation of female professionals results in more complex, convincing and dynamic female protagonists that are related to film noir.

FEMALE GAZE AND SUBJECTIVITY IN THE PSYCHOLOGICAL THRILLER: *THE MAN ON THE TRAIN*

While the figure of the *femme fatale* has been associated with women's involvement in the labour force and veterans' anxieties after the war was over, women began to be described as excess labour and would be soon pushed back into their domestic roles (Martin 1998: 203). This shift, from films that highlight a woman's point of view through strong, 'Rosie the Riveter' style career-driven women (Biesen 2004: 168) to films that put forward the figure of the redeemer and the victim, can be read as an expression of the gender distress that characterised Hollywood in the immediate post-war period. The gothic thriller can be described as a mirror of the film noir, in which the gender patterns are reversed; it is based on the construction of a female subjectivity, through flashbacks and voiceovers, in a movement of the character towards empowerment and emancipation from a 'fatal' male hero. A dominant motif in the psychological thriller of the late 1940s and 1950s – a heroine distressed by a house, or by her husband – refers to anxieties about the domestication of women and their reinsertion into maternal and family-centred roles.

In the years between 1945 and 1950, thrillers and crime films with a strong female lead character, such as *Laura*, *Mildred Pierce*, *Phantom Lady*, *Tangier* (dir. Waggner, 1946), *A Woman's Face* (dir. Cukor, 1941) and others, were distributed in Greece and shown in cinemas for many months. At the same time, psychological thrillers such as *Rebecca* (dir. Hitchcock, 1940), *Gaslight* (dir. Cukor, 1944), *Man of Evil* (dir. Asquith, 1944), *Suspicion* (dir. Hitchcock, 1941) and many others enjoyed no less popularity. Few were the Greek films that qualified as 'gothic' psychological thrillers or as 'prestige horror films' (Hutchings 2013: 117); however, we can trace influences and generic features – imposing castles and ruins, scary households, *'hommes fatales'* using gaslighting practices, uncanny presences and wild landscapes, mirrors, doubles and ghosts – in the melodrama and the crime film. A film by Dinos Dimopoulos, *The Man on the Train* (1958), is one of the few examples that successfully transfers the conventions of the gothic psychological thriller to the Greek landscape and social context.

The Man on the Train is one of the most controversial films in the discussion of Greek film noir: at the time of its release it was a film of modest success and fair critical acclaim. It premiered in February 1958 and was continuously screened in multiple cinemas until October. The generic ambiguity of the film, which did not fit the taxonomies of the well-known genres of popular cinema, as well as its fluidity between commercial cinema and artistic quality, placed it outside the canon and the established narratives of Greek cinema. The film was mostly remembered for its impressive cast of characters, as it featured theatre actress Anna Synodinou, famous for her performances in ancient Greek drama, in one of her few screen appearances, and also the last appearance of lead actor Giorgos Pappas, who died at the age of 55 just after shooting was completed. A key collaborator was the established set designer Marilena Aravantinou, who was responsible for the overall look of the film: One of the most impressive attributes of the film is the choice of shooting locations, the use of the cityscape and the scenography, which highlight the psychological state of the heroine, and the costumes that underline the relationship of the characters. *The Man on the Train* was 'rediscovered' in the last twenty years, as it was screened in retrospectives of Greek film noir; film scholars discussed the theme of historical trauma that lies at the centre of the plot (Chalkou 2008: 213–32; Karalis 2012: 84), and its complex narrative devices make the film an interesting case of overlapping genre conventions and a singular exception to the standards of Greek cinema in the 1950s (Thanouli 2012).

This film was based on Maris's novel *O anthropos me to gkri kostoumi* [The Man with the Grey Suit], published in instalments in the newspaper *Acropolis* in 1955. During the same year, it was published in Pechlivanidis's 'dime' editions under the new title *The Man on the Train*, while versions of the story were recycled under various titles in magazines in the following years. This is not considered one of Maris's major novels, and it would probably not be remembered today if the film had not assured its longevity. The film was promoted as a suspenseful thriller, something that was a novelty for Greek cinema (Figure 6.1). Maris, in an interview during the film's promotion, talked about its particularities. When asked if it was a 'police film' (*astynomiko*) he answered 'not exactly, but it has elements of anxiety, mystery and action': he underscored that 'suspense' films that were so common in foreign film production had never been made in Greece (Maris 1958). At the same time, the film was advertised as 'The sentimental tragedy of a woman who

Figure 6.1 Actress Maro Kontou, who specialised in the type of the 'luxurious woman' in Greek noirs, with Inspector Bekas (Titos Vandis). Digital still from *Murder Backstage*.

saw the face of a dead man in the window of a train, and totally changed her life' (Apostolidis 2012: 150). This pitch prepares the spectator for a romantic thriller with a twist of metaphysical terror; however, it is deceiving in a double way: the 'dead man' is not actually dead, nor does the heroine's life change. Indeed, some critics, despite the generally positive reception of the film, complained that the element of suspense and mystery was not so heightened as the promotional campaign led one to imagine (Sokou 1958). Other critics stressed the feeling of 'anxiety' that the spectator shares with the heroine, showing that the film achieved the sense of identification and subjectivity (Papamichalis 1958). In any case, the generic fluidity of the film between romance, thriller, melodrama and crime film triggered a debate among film critics at the time of its release.

The main character is Mando (Synodinou), a woman in her thirties, mother of two and wife of a middle-aged man called Dimitris (Pappas). They belong to the wealthy middle class of Athens. The couple, with a group of friends, leave for a weekend excursion to the town of Nafplion. When the cars make a stop at a level crossing, Mando sees the face of a man in the window of the train; this sudden event causes her great distress, and she enters a strange state of depression, grief and silence. When she sees him again, she dares to speak to him, but he seems not to recognise her, saying that he is not the person she is looking for. Mando then confesses to her friend Eleni (Georges Sari) that the man bears a resemblance to her lover during the German Occupation. He was a spy on a mission in the Middle East, and she witnessed his murder in a street fight in Athens back in 1942. Mando becomes distant from her husband and acts as if she is ready to give up everything. But the unknown man hides his identity until the last moment and doesn't acknowledge knowing her. Finally, Mando lets him go away, and returns to the safety of family life.

One of the particularities of the film, which shows the successful collaboration between Aravantinou and the director of photography Karydis-Fuchs, is that it is visually based on two different regimes of the *mise en scène*. The major part of the film belongs to the general tradition of realism, with a few details that could be inscribed in the realm of late neorealism (for example, *Viaggio in Italia/Journey to Italy*, dir. Rossellini, 1954, or *Cronaca di un amore/Story of a Love Affair*, dir. Antonioni, 1950). There is an emphasis on real locations, natural lighting, depictions of everyday life, the use of the natural and urban landscape to reflect the psychological state of the characters, long takes, long shots and deep focus organisation of space. During Mando's flashback, when she recalls the love story she lived through in 1943, the features of the *mise en scène* totally change, and the film takes on the look of a film noir. These sequences are shot at night and are underlit, with strong chiaroscuro and key lighting. There is a clear choice here of medium framing and close-ups, dense continuity editing that shares Mando's perspective. There are scenes of surveillance, persecution and gunshots in the streets of Athens, wet cobblestones that reflect the light, and unexpected flashes of light in the dark, use of *contre-plongée* framing and wide-angle lens perspective. The characters are dressed in raincoats, and Mando wears a beret in Lauren Bacall fashion. Most importantly, during the flashback we hear Mando's voiceover in first person, emphasising her impressions, implying the feeling of ambiguity or the possibility of a false interpretation. Phrases such as 'I didn't know then' or 'I later understood' are recurrent motifs of uncertainty in her narration. She meets a man who is hiding from a Gestapo raid, and they have a love affair that lasts a few days, before she witnesses him dying in a street fight from police gunshots. From the moment of the flashback onwards, the heroine's subjectivity is enhanced by voiceovers, close-ups and POV shots, so it is clear that the director stresses the woman's angle.

In the novel, the story unfolds in third-person narration; however, Maris uses multiple perspectives of the characters as the narration goes on. In the beginning the story tends to put forward the point of view of Mando's husband Nikos (Dimitris in the film); in the following chapters, the principal point of view becomes that of Eleni, who appears almost as the investigator of the enigma that Mando represents. The novel opens with a description of the husband looking at his wife and expressing his love and tenderness towards her. The film, on the contrary, starts with two female gazes towards another woman: at a party Mando and her friend Eleni are looking at the astonishing Ms Zerbini, the former with admiration and the latter with jealousy. Ms Zerbini is a character in the vein of the 'luxurious woman', who is used, in typical Maris fashion, as a 'red herring'. This character reveals the feelings of Eleni, who becomes not only very affectionate but also very possessive and jealous towards Mando, who instead seems amused by Ms Zerbini. In the novel, Maris, in characteristic voyeuristic style, gives a slight hint of eroticism between the two women, something not uncommon for this author, who in many novels suggests nuances of female homosexuality, usually including a male point of view, in order to excite the reader's interest. This tension is also discernible in the film, as Eleni shows an excessive will to investigate, understand and even control Mando's thoughts and desires. She is the catalyst of the plot, as she tries to convince Dimitris to be more strict with his wife, and also tries to convince the stranger to leave Mando alone. Finally, Eleni is the *confidante*, the person who takes Mando out of the state of muteness and initiates the process of her narration; like a psychoanalyst, she helps her recall the forgotten trauma. According to Hanson (2007), this character of an older woman – a good friend, a partner, a midwife, an ancestor or even a ghost or a figure in a portrait – who operates as a guide for the heroine, helping her to find her voice and articulate her subjectivity, is one of the most common motifs in gothic female thrillers.

One of the most interesting aspects of the film is the choice of location and the organisation of space. Aravantinou and Karydis-Fuchs create an atmospheric 'Mediterranean gothic' universe, combining images of ruins and impressive monuments with sun-drenched summer seascapes (Figure 6.2). The hotel where the characters are staying is the fortress-island of Bourdji, or Castello dello Soglio, a Venetian fortress of the fifteenth century. Once used as a prison and residence of the guillotine executioners during the nineteenth century, the fortress was renovated in the 1930s to become a luxurious hotel resort. In the newspapers of that time, we find sensational articles that present the legends surrounding this 'haunted' and 'bloody' location. In the novel and the film, the characters playfully mention the 'chilling' atmosphere of the hotel and describe their stay there as an uncanny experience. In a similar way, the group of friends visit the medieval fortress of Palamidi, which overlooks the city: 'these ruins are full of ghosts', Eleni says, just before the mysterious man makes a fugitive appearance – we don't know if he is real or a figment of Mando's imagination. The figure of the ghost appears throughout the dialogues: Dimitris confesses to Eleni that this 'shadow' of the dead lover is more alive than anyone else, and that he can never beat 'a ghost, a chimera, a phantasy'.

Figure 6.2 Photo from the film shooting at the Bourdji Castle island in Nafplion. From Yannis Maris's archive. Courtesy of Angelos Tsirimokos.

The third location that Dimopoulos masterfully shoots in is the theatre of Epidaurus; the characters go on a weekend excursion in order to watch a performance of *Medea* at the ancient theatre. The Festival of Epidaurus was inaugurated in 1954, so during the summer of 1956 – when the film was shot – it represented a brand new experience for the Athenian middle class, which combined a cultural activity at an archaeological space and a weekend stay at the nearby town of Nafplion. It is during this performance that Mando sees for an instant the man who she assumed dead, sitting in the dark among fourteen thousand spectators. Dimopoulos recreates, in a Hitchcockian vein, the choking feeling and the sense of claustrophobia generated by this packed open-air amphitheatre, from which there is no way out until the end of the spectacle, where visual contact cannot be obtruded, and where all the 'high society' of Athens is gathered for this highly advertised theatrical event, as Maris's novel describes ([1955] 2011: 94).

What make this film so peculiar and controversial, in my opinion, is the fact that it is somehow incomplete. It raises expectations that are not fulfilled; it builds to a climax of suspense that does not manage to reach its goal. The audience is prepared for a dramatic event, for the revelation of a dark secret, a crime maybe, a twist, or a burst of feeling that never comes. Something is missing and something is never mentioned: the lack of any reference to the Resistance and the Greek Civil War functions as a structural absence that inevitably leads to allegorical interpretations. The ex-spy who hides his past, lives under a new identity and works as a respectful engineer, and the passing reference to 'prisons and camps' without other details in his brief talk with Eleni, make an allusion to the period of the Civil War, a restricted topic in cinema for the audience of that time, and one that was avoided in public discourse during the post-war era. *The Man on the Train* bears similarities to *Muerte de un ciclista/Death of a Cyclist* (dir. Bardem, 1955), a film that also uses the trope of a love affair and the disclosure of a crime in order to talk, in a fragmented and elliptical way, about the crimes of the Franco era.

This lack of reference to the political context of the recent past is contrasted to what the film emphatically shows, to its 'cinematic excess' (Thompson 1977): the iconography of the film is loaded with images of a prosperous upper middle class; of a wealthy lifestyle of consumerism; of moderate luxuries that were at that moment accessible to emerging middle financial strata due to the post-war financial boom; images of visitors at historical locations of high cultural status and shots of shiny cars on the coastal roads of Corinth, at Epidaurus, in Nafplion. Despite the fact that the train appears in the title of the film, representing the past – the repressed memory that resurfaces in a violent way – the film highlights in an unusual way the image of the automobile as the sign of a wealthy present, which can be achieved only on one condition: the repression of the radicalism of the past (a theme also explored in the previously mentioned films by Bardem and Antonioni). The film concludes with this exact dilemma for the heroine, who is asked to choose between an absence – a shadow of the past – on the one hand, and the security of family life and her wealthy lifestyle on the other. The last shot of the film, showing the heroine directing her steps towards her husband instead of the man without identity, can be seen as one of the best cinematic depictions of the post-Civil War social 'consensus' that condemned the memory of the Resistance and the Civil War to be repressed into oblivion, at least for a large part of the upcoming 'petty bourgeoisie' of Greece.

So even if *The Man on the Train* fails to deliver the suspense and thrilling excitement that it promises, it succeeds as one of the most daring and profound expressions of the trauma of the Civil War, confirming that the film noir is not a mere whodunit but a 'trauma' genre, born out of the anxieties of post-war disillusionment. At the same time, it makes the contemporary audience think that women's representation, even in the patriarchal and conservative context of Greek cinema, can be more complex and profound than a superficial imitation of the *femme fatale*.

Conclusion

The absence of strong *femmes fatales* in Greek noir does not mean that women are less lethal than men. A quick overview shows that women in film noir are equally as murderous as men: they appear as masterminds, partners in crime, killers, blackmailers as well as victims. However, the image of the *femme fatale* derives from the dynamics of their relationship with their male partners: in Greek film noir, we rarely see male characters who feel disempowered and emasculated under the spell of a powerful woman; we also rarely see male protagonists overshadowed by their fellow actresses. Apparently Greek films did not have a problem showing women pulling the trigger; but they hesitated in showing weak, inadequate and ineffective men, characters who don't really know their societal place, or reflect a rejection of the established order. This reluctance to portray male characters who are insecure, unsociable and detached from dominant values simultaneously leaves no room for a more serious development of the *femme fatale*. This lack is also a result of the belatedness of Greek film noir, in a period when feminine models had left behind the imagery of the emancipated and dangerous woman of the 1940s. Finally, one could argue that a stronger representation of female professionals in crucial creative positions in the film industry could have resulted in the construction of more substantial female characters, as the examples of Maria Plyta, Marilena Aravantinou and Margarita Lymberaki let us glimpse.

Notes

1. Examples are Anna Margot (Voula Harilaou) in *Efialtis/Nightmare* (dir. Andreou, 1962), or Martha Foka (Betty Arvaniti) in *O Zestos Minas Avgoustos/The Hot Month of August* (dir. Kapsaskis, 1966).
2. I consider 1946 to 1966 to be the 'classic period' of Greek film noir; from 1966 onwards we have a mediated, modernist and self-reflexive production of neo-noirs. In the late 1960s, Greek filmmakers dealing with crime narratives turned their gaze inwards, in the process of fabricating the film noir myth, as well as outwards to the international influences of modernist versions of the genre. The plots and characters tend to be more intertextual, ironic or deliberately stereotyped in order to appeal to the new wave cinephilia of the era. Thus, it is easier to trace *femmes fatales* in films after 1966, as their symbolic, ironic or even mythological function is enhanced through cinephilia and intertextuality.
3. One could argue that the figure of the devouring and monstrous *femme fatale* was also not uncommon in the French films of the 1930s and 1940s, such as *La Chienne/The Bitch* (dir. Renoir, 1931).
4. Farber ([1974] 1999: 49) connects the appearance of the *femme fatale* with a 'crisis of masculinity': 'During the war years, another psychological dimension was added to this anxiety – fear of the evil, overpowering woman with a shocking ability to humiliate and emasculate her men.' See also Krutnik (1991).
5. Based on the Freudian concepts of lack of penis and castration anxiety, Mulvey (1989: 14–26) distinguishes two forms of 'escaping avenues' for the male unconscious regarding the pleasurable structures of looking: the pleasure of sadistic voyeurism (which is associated with film noir, and is expressed through the devaluation

or punishment of the guilty object – the *femme fatale*) and the pleasure of fetishistic scopophilia (which breaks the privileged look of the male protagonist in favour of the direct look of the spectator, best exemplified in the work of Sternberg).

REFERENCES

Apostolidis, Andreas (2012), *O kosmos tou Yanni Mari* [Yannis Maris's World], Athens: Agra.
Biesen, Sheri Chinen (2004), 'Manufacturing Heroines: Gothic Victims and Working Women in Classic Noir Films', in Alain Silver and James Ursini (eds), *Film Noir Reader 4. The Crucial Films and Themes*, New York: Limelight, pp. 161–74.
Biesen, Sheri Chinen (2005), *Blackout: World War II and the Origins of Film Noir*, Baltimore, MD: Johns Hopkins University Press.
Borde, Raymond, and Chaumeton, Étienne ([1955] 1996), 'Towards a Definition of Film Noir', in Alain Silver and James Ursini (eds), *Film Noir Reader*, New York: Limelight, pp. 17–26.
Buci-Glucksmann, Christine ([1984] 1994), *Baroque Reason: The Aesthetics of Modernity*, London: Sage.
Chalkou, Maria (2008), 'Towards the Creation of Quality Greek National Cinema in the 1960s', PhD dissertation, University of Glasgow.
Chartier, Jean-Pierre ([1946] 1999), 'American are also Making Noir Films', in Alain Silver and James Ursini (eds), *Film Noir Reader 2*, New York: Limelight, pp. 21–5.
Doane, Mary Ann (1991), *Femmes Fatales: Feminism, Film Theory, Psychoanalysis*, London: Routledge.
Dyer, Richard ([1978] 1998), 'Resistance through Charisma: Rita Hayworth and *Gilda*', in E. Ann Kaplan (ed.), *Women in Film Noir*, London: BFI and Palgrave Macmillan, pp. 115–22.
Farber, Stephen ([1974] 1999), 'Violence and the Bitch Goddess', in Alain Silver and James Ursini (eds), *Film Noir Reader 2*, New York: Limelight, pp. 45–56.
Foskolos, Nikos (1954), 'Nea epidromi ton dolofonon' [The New Raid of the Killers], *Empros*, 11 September.
Frank, Nino ([1946] 1999), 'A New Kind of Police Drama: The Criminal Adventure', in Alain Silver and James Ursini (eds), *Film Noir Reader 2*, New York: Limelight, pp. 15–20.
Hanson, Helen (2007), *Hollywood Heroines: Women in Film Noir and the Female Gothic Film*, London: I.B. Tauris.
Hutchings, Peter (2013), 'Film Noir and Horror', in Helen Hanson and Andrew Spicer (eds), *A Companion to Film Noir*, Chichester: Wiley-Blackwell.
Karalis, Vrasidas (2012), *A History of Greek Cinema*, London: Continuum.
Krutnik, Frank (1991), *In a Lonely Street: Film Noir, Genre, Masculinity*, New York: Routledge.
Maris, Yannis (1958), 'Mythistorima tis "Acropoleos" egine prototypo film mystiriou' [A Novel of 'Acropolis' Became an Original Mystery Film], *Acropolis*, 20 January.
Maris, Yannis ([1953] 2011), *Eglima sto Kolonaki* [Murder in Kolonaki], Athens: Atlantis.
Maris, Yannis ([1955] 2011), *O Anthropos tou trenou* [The Man on the Train], Athens: Atlantis.

Maris, Yannis ([1955] 2012), *I Kyria tis Nychtas* [The Lady of the Night], Athens: Agra.

Martin, Angela (1998), 'Gilda Didn't Do Any of Those Things You've Been Losing Sleep Over! The Central Woman of 40s Films Noirs', in E. Ann Kaplan (ed.), *Women in Film Noir*, London: BFI and Palgrave Macmillan, pp. 202–28.

Mulvey, Laura (1989), *Visual and other Pleasures*, New York: Palgrave, pp. 14–26.

Neale, Steve (2000), *Genre and Hollywood*, Abingdon: Routledge.

Papamichalis, Vion (1958), 'Kritiki ton tainion tis evdomados' [Review of the Film Week], *Apogevmatini*, 21 January.

Park, William (2011), *What is Film Noir?*, Lewisburg, PA: Bucknell University Press.

Place, Janey ([1978] 1998), 'Women in Film Noir', in E. Ann Kaplan (ed.), *Women in Film Noir*, London: BFI and Palgrave Macmillan, pp. 47–68.

Schrader, Paul ([1972] 1996), 'Notes on Film Noir', in Alain Silver and James Ursini (eds), *Film Noir Reader*, New York: Limelight, pp. 53–63.

Sokou, Rosita (1958), 'I kinimatografiki zoi' [Cinema Life], *Kathimerini*, 22 January.

Spicer, Andrew (2002), *Film Noir*, Abingdon: Routledge.

Thanouli, Eleftheria (2012), 'Film Style in Old Greek Cinema: The Case of Dinos Dimopoulos', in Lydia Papadimitriou and Yannis Tzioumakis (eds), *Greek Cinema: Texts, Histories Identities*, Bristol: Intellect, pp. 221–39.

Thompson, Kristine (1977), 'The Concept of Cinematic Excess', *Cine-Tracts*, 1:2, pp. 54–64, special issue, 'Theoretical Perspectives in Cinema', edited by David Allen and Teresa de Lauretis.

Vlachou, Eleni (1947), 'I kinimatografiki evdomas' [The Film Week], *Kathimerini*, 22 January.

Vrassidas, Karalis (2012), *A History of Greek Cinema*, London: Bloomsbury.

Wilt, David (2013), 'The Black Typewriter. Who Wrote Film Noir?', in Helen Hanson and Andrew Spicer (eds), *A Companion to Film Noir*, Chichester: Wiley-Blackwell, pp. 193–210.

7. BUMS AND DARK ALLEYS: CONSTRUCTING QUEERNESS IN A MID-1960S GREEK NOIR

Nikitas Fessas

Film noir is (in)famous for its representations of gender and sexuality: neurotic men, voracious women and, last but not least, flamboyant (male) queens, such as Joel Cairo in *The Maltese Falcon* (dir. Huston, 1941) and Waldo Lydecker in *Laura* (dir. Preminger, 1944). Important scholars see noirs as being about thinly veiled homoerotic relations between men (Krutnik 1991: 143; Dyer 1998a: 117–18; 2002: 110, 113, n. 20; Apostolidis 2009: 73, 93). Furthermore, in films such as Hitchcock's *Strangers on a Train* (1951) and noir director Otto Preminger's 1962 adaptation of Allen Drury's 1959 novel *Advise and Consent*, homosexuality was constructed in a paranoid fashion as a threat to the US security state, while recent works have brought to the fore Raymond Chandler's unacknowledged homosexuality (Fuller 2020).[1] In the 1964 Greek noir *Amfivolies/Doubts* (dir. Grigoriou), the character of the villainous Koronelos is basically played as a queen by Paris Alexander.

Kyriakos (2016) categorises the 1965 B-movie *To remali tis Fokionos Negri/The Bum of Fokionos Negri* (dir. Karagiannis) under 'masculinity'. The film features stylistic and thematic elements today identified with noir: cynicism, nihilism, pessimism, fatalism, lust, greed, sexual perversion, corruption, obsession, betrayal, crime and murder. The ending is dark. The film employs the noir underworld milieu, including recognisable noir character types, one (at least) *homme fatale*[2] and the male noir queer. The same year *The Bum* was released, one of the few texts on male homosexuality in Greece of the time was published in a mainstream Greek magazine. The film and the article discussed in this chapter taxonomise specific masculinities and sexual identities as 'deviant', while discursively constructing the Greek male queer.[3]

Karagiannis's film narrates the story of Alekos (Alkis Yannakas), a handsome young hustler and member of a group of no-goods. Alekos becomes involved in a scheme in which he has to seduce a 30-year-old virgin, Mary (Alexandra Ladikou), and swindle her out of her money. Mary becomes obsessed with Alekos. Her friend Dina (Efi Economou) and Mary's middle-aged suitor, the lawyer Nikolaidis (Andreas Filippides), unsuccessfully try to talk sense into her. Alekos's behaviour towards Mary quickly turns sadistic. To avoid losing him, she showers him with gifts and money. Yet no amount can satisfy his decadent lifestyle. A queer young man named Miltos (Alekos Kouris), also obsessed with Alekos, and the brightest among the group of conmen, comes up with ideas to trick Mary out of the rest of her fortune. Miltos becomes increasingly vindictive towards Alekos, who mistreats him. He devises a plan involving Alekos's initiation into the debauched circles of Athenian high society. Miltos pimps up Alekos, who has to seduce a supposedly very wealthy older woman, Dora (Despo Diamantidou). However, Dora is in fact a hustler, paid by the double-crossing Miltos. When Mary discovers that Alekos has lost every penny she gave him playing poker[4] and has hit on Dina, she shoots him. Unbeknownst to her, Alekos has replaced the bullets in her gun with blanks. Mary is tricked by the gang into bringing them more money, supposedly to save Alekos's life. Alekos's jealous but honest ex-girlfriend, the platinum-blonde, strip-dancing bombshell Thaleia (Zeta Apostolou), helps Mary to realise that she has been duped again. Mary finds the hotel where Alekos is staying with Dora. She empties her revolver into his body. Nikolaidis considerately takes Mary away, probably to the authorities, while Alekos's mother (Elli Xanthaki) mourns over her dead son, blaming modern society and contemporary lifestyle for his downfall.

The Noir Love that Dare not Speak its Name

According to *The Bum*, in mid-1960s Greece there were two main, antithetical modes of male courtship of women. One was the old-fashioned, chivalric, 'civilised' method that involved dating or meeting with the object of romantic interest at parties and other social events. Middle-aged, upper-middle-class Greek gentlemen such as Nikolaidis represent this school. Alekos belongs to a different breed: he is animalistic, unlike Nikolaidis, who is no 'caveman' (*agrianthropos*).[5] Men like Nikolaidis drive their dates home without expecting sex before marriage; they bring flowers and address their dates formally. The code of the suit-wearing gentleman requires being there for the woman you love, supporting her financially, and protecting her by fending off antagonists and gold-diggers.

By contrast, young Greek men and women in Karagiannis's film are represented as sexually aggressive, having multiple sexual partners. This approach to flirting and (hetero)sexual relations is considered modern and is much more direct, raw and 'vulgar'. In this scenario, the man seduces the woman and asks for sex immediately, dropping any romantic pretence. A gigolo expects women to support him financially. He does not feel emasculated; as Alekos says, this is part of how the 'new [modern] tricks' and the 'new rules of the game' work.

The modern Greek man walks around naked, not minding being sexually objectified or derided by bourgeois Greek society, which he considers hypocritical. Alekos calls men like Nikolaidis *floroi*, meaning lesser/not 'real' men, too sophisticated, wimpy, soft, pampered, flabby, fussy, effeminate and easily manipulated by women (*floros* is still used as a derogatory substitute for 'homosexual').[6] Nevertheless, Dora considers Alekos 'chic' on the only occasion we see him in black tie. These opposite types of masculinity are connoted through the film's music: romantic, melodramatic music for Nikolaidis, and modern sounds with African drums for Alekos.

The occurrence of sexual relations between men was not news in mid-1960s Athens. My intention is neither merely to read a character as gay or queer, nor to simply compare the textual homosexual to the 'real' thing. Instead, I study the ways in which identities are constructed through various strategies (framing, *mise en scène*, dialogue). Miltos is treated by other men in the film with varying degrees of respect: sometimes with sarcasm, at other times with empathy for his 'perversion' (he pays to peep through keyholes in order to watch the man he desires having sex with women), occasionally with violence. Greek queers are represented as part of homosocial companies of men. They are the 'brains' in the planning of scams; they dress fastidiously in suits, sport 'Caesar' haircuts, are well-mannered and eloquent. Miltos belongs to the lumpenproletariat. As in Huston's *The Maltese Falcon*, as well as Preminger's *Laura*, in Karagiannis's film women treat male queers with disgust and contempt, far less sympathetically than heterosexual Greek men do.

Although they remain unnamed, male homosexuality and the queer male sexual identity play a central role in *The Bum*'s noir narrative. The text makes clear that Miltos is gay when he refuses to buy Thaleia a drink, declaring that he already does that for Alekos. When a half-naked Thaleia catches him outside her bedroom, peeping through the keyhole, she asks 'What do you want in the middle of the night?', to which Miltos replies: 'Not you'. In the film, queer male sexual identity is linked to impotence and various perversions, including voyeurism, fetishism, sadism and masochism. Voyeurism is represented as a re-enactment of the primal scene, in which the 'normal' (meaning, in an orthodox psychoanalytic context, heterosexual) resolution of the Oedipus complex fails: Miltos ends up desiring the Father (Alekos), instead of the Mother (substitute), Thaleia. The text synecdochically proposes this as the 'cause' of Miltos's homosexuality, while conflating male homosexuality and male queerness with misogyny.[7] Male homosexuality is also connected to modern gender and sexual norms, as part of an imported, corrupting, immoral lifestyle.

In Greek genre cinema of the 1950s and 1960s, male homosexuals are caricatured and ridiculed (Delveroudi 2004: 238–43) for their effeminate manners and clothes, or professions that carry feminine connotations. Hadjikyriacou notes that in Greek comedies of the time, gay male characters

> are restricted to auxiliary roles [. . .], [they are] connected with specific 'feminine' professions such as hairdressers, teachers of good manners, nurses and beauticians, or artists [. . .] They never appear in blue-collar professions or in rural environments. Their attire and appearance almost uniformly had elements of the feminine dress code, usually a scarf or a bag, an obvious connotation to their queer sexuality [. . .] [S]uch characters from whom the audience expected to see an imitation of female voice or a female body movement, as well as naivety, self-sarcasm, oversensitivity, over-politeness, indications of their true sexual desires towards handsome men, and a tendency to undertake female tasks such as cleaning the house, knitting, or cooking [. . .] were sexually sole features, never shown in the presence of other gay men or with a male partner. (2013: 90–1)[8]

As part of stereotypical representations of male queerness or homosexuality in Greek comedies of the 1960s, Delveroudi (2004: 239–40) also lists the squeaky voice accompanied by characteristic hand-gesturing, the hysterical reactions and cowardice, and the tendency of the male queer/homosexual to cry easily. Greek actors of the period were typecast in roles of 'effeminate', implicitly homosexual men (Delveroudi 2004: 238).[9]

Nevertheless, as Dyer (2002: 100) notes, 'there are no queenly [. . .] hairdressers or couturiers' in film noir. In *The Bum*, gay men are not caricatured. However, male homosexuality and the male queer are identified with effeminacy and, therefore, according to the noir codes (see, for example, Tasker 2013: 353, 361), with duplicity, insidiousness, manipulative behaviour and villainy.[10] The same reactionary representation grants visibility to an identity which was ignored or ridiculed in Greek genre films of earlier periods.[11] The complex portrayal is facilitated by the nature of the cinematic medium, and the particular overdetermined polysemy of noir, with its formal play of dark and shadow, as well as its ambiguous character types, read simultaneously as embodiments of social and cultural fears and as projected, transgressive, repressed desires. The characterisation and image of Miltos are more nuanced, as the body of the Greek male homosexual is discursively produced.

The Greek male queer is represented here as both a victim and a perpetrator of male violence. He oscillates between the sadistic and masochistic positions that structure his sexual identity. As part of a homosocial male group, Miltos seems slightly marginalised, but not explicitly mocked. He is treated as one among equals. In contrast to the large, heterosexual oafs, he possesses superior intelligence. He controls his drives, sublimating them into schemes. He is also much more rational and cunning than the female candidates for the *fatale* role, Mary and Thaleia – who are revealed as decent and kind-hearted. Miltos outsmarts everyone, wreaking revenge on his abusing object of desire, Alekos, and thus avenging the patriarchy that marginalises him for his sexuality. The representation is reactionary insofar as Miltos puts his intelligence to 'bad', anti-social use.

Nevertheless, in comparison with genre films of earlier years, Greek society is represented as much more tolerant towards male homosexuality. Heterosexual men treat Miltos with understanding and relative empathy. This does not sound very progressive, but Miltos is neither bullied nor beaten up, as might have been the case in the Greek context of the time.[12] His comrades even allow him (for a price) to indulge his 'vices'. Narcissistic Alekos seems to enjoy being Miltos's object of desire. However, by being placed in the position typically reserved for the *femme fatale*, and thus being effeminised by the text, Miltos can be read as condemned by the homophobic and misogynistic Greek patriarchy. Nonetheless, the latter treats him much better than it treats Thaleia. Miltos goes unpunished while Mary faces a heavy prison sentence for killing her abuser. This could be read as a wider tendency in (especially classic) noir to punish women's desires harshly, while being less concerned with male 'deviancy'.[13]

Furthermore, and following the genre's tradition, *The Bum* is subversive in blurring the boundaries between 'normal' and 'abnormal' sexualities: sexuality is entangled with perversion, and 'straight' sexuality is represented as an uncontrollable disease. The male protagonist's sexuality is part of a new hegemonic masculinity[14] that is a far cry from the traditional Greek gender ideals of *pallikari* and *leventis*; Alekos fits the physical description of *pallikari*[15] – tall, dark, handsome, with a frame that contrasts with Miltos's tiny, 'girly' physique. However, Alekos completely lacks the code of honour of *pallikari*, or of *mangas*.[16]

Alekos is constantly effeminised, objectified through his long hair that hedonistically falls over his eyes – the 'Teddy boy'[17] haircut – and that distinguishes him from the other men in the film. His body is filmed in the way women's bodies were filmed up to that moment in Greek genre cinema.[18] The boxing match scene (another noir motif) serves purely as spectacle to stimulate female, but also queer male, desire, showcasing Yannakas's sweaty, athletic body. Apart from being a sadist, Alekos is also represented as masochistic: he takes multiple beatings and encourages his male friends to beat him hard.[19] He enjoys being the object of a queer man's desire. All this bends traditional Greek standards of masculinity to a point that it becomes very difficult to talk about a heteronormative/heterosexual male identity to which Miltos can be contrasted. Upholding such binaries becomes impossible.

The stagedness of the beating, Alekos's assumption of a chivalric/romantic male identity to get Mary to fall for him, and his duplicity highlight the performativity, constructedness and instability of his gender, sexual and class identities: he pretends to be a student, a boxer, a working-class man; he masquerades as a bourgeois; and he pretends to be in love; he might as well have been pretending to like women to begin with. Alekos is reminiscent of Patricia Highsmith's Ripley.

Dyer (1998b: 125–6) writes that noir queers, like the *femme fatale*, 'keep the hero from the woman in a sickly bonding over the faintly eroticised arts of fashion, jewellery, *savoir-faire* and scents, and are part of the confusion, uncertainty [and] deeply untrustworthy character of the appearances of this world' (see also Dyer 2002: 100). As Abbott notes, in noirs and hardboiled fiction, male homosexuality might be 'allied' with 'high culture, which is gendered feminine', dandy looks and 'conflated with [. . .] rarefied taste[s]' (2002: 70). These remarks echo the process of refinement and sophistication and, therefore, feminisation through which Miltos puts Alekos. He dresses him up, teaches him good manners and introduces him into a world where nothing is what it seems and nobody is to be trusted, a world in which everyone, including 'straight' men, performs an identity. Ultimately, what is foregrounded is the fact that there is no 'real' heterosexual male identity, no essence behind the performance; the performance is all we are left with.[20] In the noir world of deadly dames and duplicitous male queens, there is no redemptive model of untroubled masculinity in which the male spectator can take refuge.

In *The Bum*, the male spectator is often positioned as identifying with the queer gaze – which, in turn, crosses gender lines, identifying with the heterosexual female gaze – enjoying the body of Alekos. Queering the (male) gaze is an accomplishment for a commercial Greek text of the time. The male spectator is rendered a voyeur/eavesdropper, 'perversely' enjoying Alekos's narcissistic, self-glorifying narration of his seduction of Mary, being explicit about his sexual prowess to his male buddies (including a visibly turned-on, salivating Miltos in the front row) standing in for the male audience/viewer. Alekos is a pervert, as this is one of the few, if any, occasions when he seems to draw pleasure from dealing sexually with women. Elsewhere he is cynical, doing it only for the money, or is shown as rather passive, simply going through the motions in an uncanny, mechanical way, like an automaton. All this agrees with Dyer's comment that it is femininity, including that of queers, which threatens the male heroes' 'sense of security, selfhood and knowledge of the world in film noir', and that noir male heroes seem actually to be relieved 'to fall back on the bonds of loving homosociality' (1998b: 127).

The only representation that could, through identification, 'cure' the male spectator of his queerness is that of Nikolaidis. However, he is impotent, basically called a pussy on multiple occasions. Dina, in disgust, describes Nikolaidis's flaccid type of masculinity as 'lukewarm'. When Mary says that she might enjoy a little danger walking alone in Athens at night, Nikolaidis comments that this could be unfortunate for the man accompanying her; as already mentioned, cowardice was typically linked to queerness in other Greek film genres of the period. Nikolaidis is unable to avenge Mary's honour, as the traditional Greek father, brother or husband would do. He can only provide her with bullets and let her pay the price for transgressing the patriarchal Law.

The male spectator is left to identify with Alekos, a narcissistic, sexually deviant sociopath; a sex-starved, reluctant *femme fatale*; or a queer peeping Tom. He is, thus, unavoidably 'effeminised'. However, as Dyer notes,

> Film noir is interesting not because it resolves this conundrum, but because it foregrounds it, and not least by the presence of its queers. Film noir queerness suggests that the feminine is not coterminous with womanhood – that there are different ways of being feminine, that some men can be feminine, that some women can be effeminate [. . .] [I]t may make us wonder what is so very masculine and straight about heterosexual male sexual desire for the feminine [. . .] unsettling the notion that there are, clearly and separately, queers and straights, winkling out the queerness of everything [. . .] [M]ost culture works to hold the line of sexual differentiation, but not film noir, or at any rate not always definitely. (1998b: 129)

In *The Bum*, gender and sexual identities form dialectical pairs:

Alekos/Nikolaidis
Alekos/Miltos
Alekos/Mary
Alekos/Thaleia
Mary/Alekos
Mary/Miltos
Mary/Dina
Mary/Thaleia
Mary/Dora
Mary/Alekos's mother
Thaleia/Alekos's mother
Dora/Alekos's mother
Miltos/Mary
Miltos/Thaleia
Miltos/Dora

Alekos's modern image is opposed to Nikolaidis, whose hegemonic masculinity also mixes traditional elements. In 1950s and 1960s Greek noirs, the main agent of an imported, corrupting modernity is a woman.[21] In *The Bum*, it is a man. Alekos's modern, vulgar masculinity is also contrasted with the more sophisticated version of Miltos.[22] Alekos forms a queer, or at least homosocial, 'couple' with Miltos, the only person Alekos seems to trust and admire. He is shown enjoying Miltos's company. Dyer (1998b: 127) writes that 'film noir heroes trust no one, but if it's going to be anyone, it will be another man'. Miltos and Alekos seem made for each other, much more than Alekos is made for Mary, Thaleia, Dina or Dora. Alekos and Miltos 'get' each other. Miltos is never jealous; he is the ideal partner for Alekos. A scene with the two of them physically very close to each other in Alekos's room, and Thaleia being angry at the other end of it, is full of *doubles entendres*:

ALEKOS.	[naked from the waist up] In a few days, we are going to have the little bird[23] [Mary] in the cage...
MILTOS.	Are you sure? What are you going to do?
ALEKOS.	[smiling cheekily, while caressing Miltos's head and neck] Why? Are you interested?
MILTOS.	Well . . . I love you. . .
ALEKOS.	Do you really love me? Or are you in a hurry for me to earn some money, so that I can pay you back?
MILTOS.	Alekos, you got me all wrong...[24]

The Bum is an alarmist moral tale about the dangers of modernity and modernisation with regard to gender embodiments and sexualities. However, it does not offer any viable traditional alternatives. A return to the pre-modern past would possibly mean complete sexual repression and a vow of celibacy for unmarried women such as Mary and, thus, failure and castration for men (Nikolaidis). Under the old, traditional gender status quo, Miltos would be invisible, possibly in prison simply because of his sexuality, murdered, or marginalised. The film's vision is pitch-black.

Queer Pseudoscience and Noir Discourse

The publication of an article about the Greek homosexual scene in 1965 (Anon. 1965) was a seemingly radical move. However, as Papanikolaou (2014: 160, 169, n. 22) observes, articles with titles describing a sexually debauched scene that involved (implied) lesbianism, effeminate young men and transvestite youths could be found in Greek newspapers as early as the late 1920s/early 1930s. What makes the article in *Athinaia* different is how its various discourses coalesce to delineate a particular *identity* (cf. Chaudhuri 2006: 77).[25] The article spreads over multiple pages, presenting itself as a piece of 'social research'. A text on Greek male homosexuals appearing in a women's magazine[26] places them closer to the feminine 'pole' of the heteronormative gender binary: according to such a view, a man who desires men is basically an *ersatz* woman. Here are the main points of this extraordinary article.

Its title, '"[The] THIRD SEX": Through the Prism of Science', establishes science as the ultimate authoritative power discourse constructing gendered sexual identities. However, the text opens with a description of Athens by night that reads like the pages of a hard-boiled novel or a crime story. Cold, desolate and narrow streets, passers-by 'enveloped in deep darkness', the sound of 'shaky steps' on the sidewalk, suspicious figures, dingy and disreputable hotels, the occasional 'cheap' prostitute, neon lights and fast cars. Most of the photographs (Figures 7.1, 7.2 and 7.3) in the article look strikingly *noir-esque* today: smoke and shadowy silhouettes of people lit from behind and underneath. We are immediately introduced to the Greek male queer, through a description of his strange clothing, 'odd' gestures and 'peculiar' manner of speech. The Greek queer male body is objectified, fetishised, taxonomised and marginalised. The journalist/author presents a queer mapping and topography that includes the centre of Athens, Piraeus and the suburbs, noting the areas that Greek male queers populate, and that 'the police know about'.[27]

Despite the title promising a scientific text, the article is full of suspense, criminal underworld (arche)types, poorly lit places, seedy bars and nightclubs, and a general atmosphere of danger, unease, moral and sexual depravity mixed with perverse fascination. The sex/gender of the anonymous narrator remains

Figure 7.1 & 7.2 Cruising: some of the original images that accompanied the *Athinaia* article in 1965; the low-key lighting/photography, the framing, camera angle, as well as the particular choice of settings contribute to a strikingly noir visual aesthetic.

Figure 7.3 Neon lights, disreputable backstreets: the construction of a queer noir Athens, both alluring and dangerous.

unclear. We might assume it is a man, as there were fewer female reporters in Greece at the time; however, a small detail in the text might persuasively be read as suggesting it is a woman, when the author describes how male transvestites flirtatiously and hedonistically turn their eyes towards the men of the company 'escorting' the journalist. In any case, early on the journalist positions him or herself as a pervert, by admitting that he or she was drawn to the particular story out of voyeuristic interest.

The description of transvestite Greek men could have been penned by Yannis Maris (the 'patriarch' of Greek crime fiction) for one of his *femmes fatales*: extravagant dresses and hairdos, heavy make-up, especially around the eyes. These men are initially identified by the patriarchal gaze as women and 'ladies', but at the end of the paragraph the narrator reveals it is a *tromp l'oeil*. 'They belong to the THIRD SEX!' (capitals in the original). It is the voice that 'betrays' them, an uncanny male voice coming from the body of a woman. Since the text links sexuality to gender, Greek male transvestites and transsexuals disturb gender binaries and dichotomies in both exciting and unnerving ways. As the journalist puts it in essentialist terms, they are merely 'the bad copy of a woman', the parody of a woman, a masquerade of femininity, not the real deal. In terms of posture and gesture, the narrator contrasts the 'colourful' Greek male transvestites with the hegemonic masculinity of *laika paidia*, young working-class men.[28] According to the author, the latter are not extravagant, and hold their cigarettes in a 'manly' way. In an ideological move, the text represents this type of 'folk' masculinity as unadorned and 'natural', supposedly outside performativity.

Similar to what happens in the noir slasher *Efialtis/Nightmare* (dir. Andreou, 1961), in which, however, male homosexuality remains unnameable, the *Athinaia* article presents Greek male homosexuals and queers as populating 'another "society" entirely of their own, with mores, customs, unwritten laws, and even their own language, which only they know'.[29] This world exists at the margin of daytime, heterosexual, bourgeois society. It is the world we know from films noirs,[30] and from what the French call the *demi-monde*.[31]

The journalist describes Greek male homosexuals with some sympathy, admiration, even a latent lust for their 'well-shaped, adolescent bodies' and, at the same time, an exoticising fascination with their androgynous hairdos that 'turn' them into 'young women'. In the context of noir, Dyer has noted that

> [t]he effeminate aestheticism of queers is an exaggeration or parody of femininity, in effect a foregrounded performance of it [. . .] Womanhood [but also queerness] in film noir most often [. . .] figures as over-elaborate or sheened coiffure, strikingly perfected couture, sophisticated mannerisms – in short, the product of the queenly arts [. . .] [E]ffeminacy [in film noir], whether of the kind bespeaking male queerness or of the performative, artificial kind so dependent on the queenly arts [. . .] femininity (including that of queers) [. . .] (1998b: 125, 127)[32]

In the *Athinaia* article, just as in film noir, queer masculinity is linked to art of all kinds, and to sophisticated manners and tastes; a 'real' man cannot be interested in art or fussy clothing, which are read as unmistakable signs of effeminacy. Greek queer men are seen by the journalist, and by the Greek scientists whose views are presented in the article, as slaves to their 'passions', perverted drives and vices, and thus implicitly contrasted with the rational heterosexual man. However, the male noir hero can be both.

The caption under one of the photos identifies the movies – one of the most popular among the imported means of entertainment in Greece at that time (Hadjikyriacou 2013: 65, 243) – and cinemas as among the darkened spaces that generate perverted desires, a place where Greek (male) homosexuals supposedly manipulate and 'seduce their victims'. Homosexuality is thus linked to one of the most iconic signifiers of modernity: cinema.[33] Likewise, the imported modern nightclub becomes a space of vice and depravity in the article, as happens in Greek crime fiction and films noirs of the time, including *The Bum*.

Greek male homosexuality is referred to by the journalist as an 'increasingly gaping, bleeding wound' for Greek society. A thousand Greek homosexuals are allegedly known to the vice division, and another 5,000 are estimated to be 'the closeted ones'. After these introductory descriptions and data, the largest part of the article features the opinions/'diagnoses' of Greek 'specialists', scientists who explain, in the most authoritative manner, the 'causes of this personality change', as male homosexuality is called in large type in one of the subheadings. First, the journalist offers their 'layman' opinion of the reasons behind this 'disquieting' social phenomenon of 'men becoming women', based on empirical observation: since it is more frequent to find male homosexuals following professions such as fashion designer, dancer or hairdresser, it might be their 'constant contact with the female sex' that has 'contribute[d] to this distortion' (this agrees with the stereotypical representation of gay men in Greek comedies of the time).

Immediately afterwards, the article cites the scientific/professional opinion of a Greek (child) psychiatrist and university professor.[34] For him, the main reason for male homosexuality is a lack of parental care and attention during childhood and (pre)adolescence. When the mother dresses up a male child in a 'girly manner' and the boy is involved in the mother's activities such as sewing (this echoes gay male caricatures in Greek comedies), or exhibits narcissistic behaviour while, simultaneously, being the recipient of 'too much caressing and pampering', he might grow up to be a homosexual. Parents should also always keep an eye on their children and be careful of dangerous places such as billiard halls (also featured in *The Bum*). For the child psychiatrist, the causes of male homosexuality, which he describes as a 'symptom' and a 'real illness', can potentially be found in hereditary biological factors – in which case he claims that 'there is absolutely no cure'. At other times this 'psychological perversion' and 'disability is caused by the family environment': divorces, broken homes and the lack of emotional bond between the (male) child and his parents lead to juvenile delinquency and (male) child-'bums' wandering around aimlessly. (Male) homosexuality is described as a deviation from the 'normal'/'natural' path of sexual development, 'an acquired perversion, a corruption/alteration of the direction of the instinct of the natural sexual tendency' and 'a dangerous vice', with many male homosexuals also having, according to the psychiatrist, 'an inclination towards' criminal activity. This agrees with the representation of Miltos as a sociopathic queer criminal mastermind (cf. Stoddart 2004).

Next, we read the equally ultra-conservative 'scientific' opinion of a Greek coroner. He preposterously includes Surrealism and Freudianism among the causes behind 'various intellectual deviances and the dangerous increase of sexual perversions' such as homosexuality.[35] In an alarmist tone, the coroner calls for the attention of psychiatrists, sociologists and criminologists to protect Greek youth from these corrupting influences; people 'exhibiting any sexual perversion [that is] typically considered slightly pathological and of a particular type' should not 'be worthy of mercy or of sympathy'.[36] For him, 'these types', the homosexuals, especially the male 'passive' (meaning here, via connotation, the 'effeminised')[37] ones, are 'dangerous to society' and to 'normal [young] people' of 'both sexes', as they are sociopathic supreme egotists with an inferiority complex and delusions of grandeur.[38] He also includes male homosexuality among other sexual perversions such as '[e]xhibitionism, hyper-eroticism, fetishism, bestiality, necrophilia, sadism and masochism'. For him, male homosexuals have, as 'sexually perverted individuals a truly diabolical capability to seduce and convert [heterosexual male] youths'. The coroner concludes that, 'according to statistics', and compared to the United States and England, homosexuality in Greece is linked less to sex crimes than to sexual and 'moral offences', while 'there is a wide spread of sexually transmitted diseases among homosexuals'. Male homosexuals are represented here as a mortal danger to Greek public health and morals. All this has basically to be taken at face value, as no specific scientific research is actually cited.[39]

The article concludes with the opinion of the Greek 'president of the Organization for Crime Prevention' and 'director of the Centre for Criminology Research', Nikodotis. He calls (male) homosexuality 'a disease', spreading on a global level. He seems regretful that the hands of the police in Greece are supposedly tied, and implicitly advocates harsher (legal) treatment of homosexuals.[40] He agrees with the coroner about the alleged wide spread of STDs among homosexuals. He links male homosexuality to criminal activity and pederasty. A class dimension is introduced, as Nikodotis claims that many poor young Greeks coming from the countryside to the capital are corrupted by the prospect of making a quick buck, and are manipulated by rich homosexual patrons, who trick them into a life of prostitution, 'homosexual passion' and 'perversion' that becomes a form of addiction, to the point that these young men 'lose any drop of humanity'. This sounds like a plot summary of *The Bum*.

Although sexual relations between people of the same sex have obviously always existed, Foucault noted how, at a specific point in historical time, the homosexual started to be seen as a separate 'species', an abnormal, deviant type of human being defined by his – Foucault refers to the male homosexual – perverse sexuality (Foucault [1976] 1978: 43; Nixon 1997: 297; Spargo 1999: 17–18).[41] The homosexual becomes the topic/product of various modern discourses (Hall 1997: 46), including the legal/juridical, the demographic, the educational, the psychiatric and modern literary ones (see Kosyfologou 2013: 15–16), discourses concerned with the protection of public health and the purity of the population (Spargo 1999: 19, 21). (Male) homosexuality begins to be seen as a (pathological) condition linked to arrested development, a deviation from the norm to be examined and treated (Spargo 1999: 19–20). The body of the male homosexual is immediately marginalised and has to be disciplined through various discourses and regimes (Spargo 1999: 20).

Sedgwick has, perhaps somewhat exaggeratedly, argued that, as Edwards (2009: 44) sums it up, 'every important debate in twentieth-century Western thought' has been structured around issues of defining the modern homo-/heterosexual. Such debates include '[c]onceptions of secrecy and disclosure [. . .] privacy and publicity, masculinity and femininity [. . .] innocence and initiation, new and old, [. . .] wholeness and decadence, urbanity and provincialism, the domestic and foreign, health and illness'. In the *Athinaia* article, the body of the Greek male queer represents all the 'depravities' introduced by an imported modernity. The pathological, criminal, contagious, unclean, sexualised body of the homosexual, the transvestite or the Greek queer man should be disciplined, examined, probed, imprisoned, beaten, punished, (mis)treated, 'cured'.

The scientists in the article are presented as embodying/employing what Foucault ([1963] 2003: 155) calls the 'clinical gaze': supposedly distanced, neutral and dispassionate. However, the body of the Greek queer man obviously excites this same gaze in a voyeuristic, fetishising way.[42] Parker et al. write that language (or, in this case, discourse – the two often overlap, but are not identical)

> does not merely describe or explain, but [. . .] constructs its object. Psychiatric language, embedded in research and clinical practices, constitutes the very 'pathological phenomena' it seeks to explain. Psychiatry, however, pretends to be scientific. It pretends to study and classify what is out there, in individuals' minds and bodies, in a neutral and objective way. (1995: 93)

The body of the (Greek) male homosexual rises as an object as it is constructed in discourses such as the aforementioned ones (see Yannakopoulos 2016: 173; c.f. Salih 2002: 110–12). These discourses present themselves as what Lacan calls 'discourses of the University'. However, in the form they take in the *Athinaia* article, they are merely discourses of the Master. In Lacan, the discourse of the Master can be summarised as 'do as you are told, simply because I said so' (Salecl 1994: 168; Bracher 1994: 12; Bracher 1993: 59–63). It does not need to refer to some prior knowledge in order to gain justification (Salecl 1994: 163, 169). The discourse of the Analyst exposes the empty kernel of the discourse of the Master, but also, ultimately, of the discourse of the University too (Bracher 1994: 8–9, 117; Bracher 1993: 60–1, n. 6). By assuming the position of the subject-*supposed-to-know*, the analyst hystericises the subject/*analysand*, as he or she encourages them to confront their unsymbolisable *jouissance* (Bracher 1994: 121, 124–5; Braunstein 1994: 152–3; Bracher 1993: 69, 71–3, 163). Within the discourse of the Analyst, the (male) scientists, the subjects representing supposedly 'objective' knowledge (Braunstein 1994: 154), are forced to face, as Bracher (1994: 123) would note, 'their own alienation [and] anxiety', the abyss of their own traumatic desire. Within the heteronormative discourse of the Master, the repressed desire is the homoerotic/homosexual one: here the exclusion of the same-sex object of desire is the condition for this discourse of the Master to exist. For the 'specialists' in *Athinaia*, acknowledging their *jouissance* would mean them coming face to face with their fragile male heterosexual identity.

This confrontation, this liberating 'comeuppance' of desire that shatters stable notions of identity, is partially achieved in a noir text such as *The Bum*. It produces an (unconscious) knowledge that 'offers not absolute, clearly established, self-referential identities, but rather a system of oppositions embodied in images and fantasies that offer no unequivocal identities, meanings, or values', as Bracher (1994: 125–6) notes of the discourse of the Analyst. Hence, I argue that the noir text itself assumes the position of the Lacanian 'subject-supposed-to-know'. And if noir functions as a type of analytic discourse,[43] it makes sense that it produces what Bracher (1994: 124) describes as 'a master signifier that is a little less oppressive, because it is of a different style [. . .] that [. . .] is less absolute, exclusive, and rigid in its establishment of the subject's identity, and more open, fluid, processual – constituted, in a word, by relativity and textuality'. Isn't 'queer' (another name for) such a master signifier?

Conclusion

As a noir, Karagiannis's text offers a more complex negotiation of homosexual identities and queer masculinities when compared to other Greek genre films of the time. It does so by problematising traditional and modern hegemonic models of masculinity, while exposing the ideological mechanisms behind the naturalisation of specific gender and sexual identities and the marginalisation of others. In a noir such as *The Bum* there is no redeeming 'straight' model of masculinity with which the (male) spectator can identify, something that has allowed me to talk about the film's subversive potential.

Nevertheless, the same text vilifies male homosexuality. Similar representations can be found in the *Athinaia* article. Through essentialist arguments and rhetorical strategies, Greek queer male identities and sexualities are delineated in both texts as symptoms of a degenerating, imported modernity. Homosexuality is represented as a modern wound for Greek society, categorised as a perversion, and identified with modern crime.[44] However, even though, in this respect, such representations are blatantly reactionary, they acquire a form that both excites and stimulates, while it irrevocably queers the desire of the spectator/reader. It is a form that we have come to identify with/as 'the noir style'.

Acknowledgements

I would like to thank Daniel Biltereyst, Sofie Van Bauwel, Frederik Dhaenens, Annette Kuhn, Philippe Meers, Mélisande Leventopoulos and Mario Slugan for their feedback on early versions of this chapter as part of my doctoral thesis; Dennis Broe for his expert remarks; Mark Bracher for his generous encouraging comments; Dimitris Papanikolaou for his erudite suggestions; Aliki Kosyfologou for her productive notes; and Robert Hensley-King for his invaluable help. Special thanks to Achilleas Hadjikyriacou and Maria Arvanitaki of the Greek Literary and Historical Archive (ELIA) for providing me with copies of the *Athinaia* article. I am grateful to Mary Tsouloufa for digitally restoring some of the original photos that accompanied the article, which are reproduced here.

Notes

1. I am indebted to Dennis Broe for pointing this out to me.
2. Regarding the *homme fatale*, see Krutnik (1991: 153); Wager (2005: 20, 51–2).
3. See also chapter 6 in Weeks (2012). In the initial drafts of this chapter, I drew partially and loosely from Yvonne-Alexia Kosma's (2007) and Aliki Kosyfologou's (2013) methodological applications of the model proposed by Kyrkos Doxiadis (2011), based on his systematised reading of Foucault's writings in *The Archaeology of Knowledge* (1972). Eventually my model deviated significantly, by looking at various media and types of representations simultaneously (cf. Rose 2001: 10, 151), and by mixing Lacanian discourse theory (Seminar XVII, 1969–70). When designing my methodological model, I also drew on Griffin's (2013) succinct account and examples.
4. For a queer reading of the theme of the compulsive gambler and his double life in film noir, see Dyer (2002: 95, 106).
5. Importantly, Benshoff (1997: 55) notes that male homosexuality 'was (and still is) often conceived of within the popular gestalt as a form of degeneration or regression to baser, animalistic instincts'; see also Benshoff (1997: 112).
6. See <https://el.wiktionary.org/wiki/%CF%86%CE%BB%CF%8E%CF%81%CE%BF%CF%82> (last accessed 16 September 2021). *Floroi* is translated as pansies by Kostis (in Yannakopoulos 2016: 187, n. 39).
7. See also Dyer (2002: 113, n. 10).
8. Delveroudi (2004: 240–1) notes exceptions to this rule.
9. The 'cinematic reportage' *Nyhtoperpatimata/Night Wanderings* (dir. Zervoulakos, 1964) – a mix of urban documentary and fiction – features an interesting case of queer performativity and self-conscious gender (self-)parody (see also Kassaveti 2019: 87) by including the famous 'fterou' (Andreas Nomikos [*MihanitouXronou*]), a real-life, acerbic, flamboyant seller of feather dusters and queer icon, who plays himself. Constantly moving, 'fterou' virtually ties together the various vignettes of the movie, a seemingly ubiquitous, riotous, anarchic presence traversing various modern(ist) spaces of mid-1960s Athens by night. Interestingly, in one of the scenes he crashes the shooting of a strongly noir-looking fictional film within the actual film.

10. Yannis Maris's 1961 crime story *O thanatos tou Timotheou Konsta* [The Death of Timotheos Konstas] features the murderous, and unmistakably queer, Alex Argyris.
11. Onscreen representations of female homosexuality during this period are notably rarer, with few bold exceptions such as the prison noir *Stefania* (dir. Dalianidis, 1966) and, by the end of the decade, the exploitation (neo-)noirs *Katigoro to kormi mou/I Blame My Body* (dir. Andreou, 1969) and *Akoma mia fora . . . prin xepsyhiso* aka *Gynaikes polyteleias/One More Time Before I Die* aka *Luxury Women* (dir. Papakostas, 1970).
12. See also Delveroudi (2004: 241).
13. Dennis Broe suggested this possibility to me.
14. For this term, see Connell ([1995] 2005: 77).
15. Campbell (1964: 278–80); Hadjikyriacou (2013: 15–16); Peristiany (1965: 181).
16. For the masculinity of *mangas*, see Campbell (1964: 283); Cowan (1990); Hadjikyriacou (2013: 17–18). Some traditional remnants, such as *philotimo* and a variation of the Greek/Mediterranean code of honour/shame, persist in the film. In this model, it is the woman who should feel ashamed of her sexuality. However, in *The Bum* the gendered version of *philotimo* is linked to honest, low-paid jobs. Moreover, before the end and his complete embrace of modern, amoral ideals, Alekos seems to be ashamed to face his elderly mother.
17. For the Teddy boy culture in Greece, see Hadjikyriacou (2013: 49–50).
18. See also Kartalou's observation (2005: 303–4, n. 29).
19. A similar scene can be found in the 1963 Greek melodrama with noir elements *To katharma/The Scum* (dir. Andritsos). The male hero being beaten is a recurring image in noir film/fiction (see, for example, Abbott 2002: 75–6; Apostolidis 2009: 75), and has been read as an instance of the effeminisation/problematisation of fragile hard-boiled masculinity.
20. Recall Rivière: '[t]he reader may now ask [. . .] where I draw the line between genuine womanliness and the "masquerade". My suggestion is [. . .] [that] they are the same thing' (in Doane 1991: 25).
21. For female characters as 'agents of modernization' in other Greek film genres of the time, see Stassinopoulou (2000: 140).
22. Alekos is linked to Thaleia through their shared modern, animalistic sexuality and promiscuity, and through their common class identity and outsider status. This couple is contrasted with the respectable, bourgeois Nikolaidis and Mary.
23. In modern Greek, 'bird' is also a slang term for a penis.
24. All translations from Greek are mine.
25. Chronologically, this claim, and the article in *Athinaia* in general, seem to partially go against Yannakopoulos's narratives (2016: 180–1; 2019: 27–8). My chapter could be situated between what Papanikolaou (2018: 174–5) has described as 'two distinct critical projects. On the one hand, an archaeology of Greek gay (pre)histories of the nineteenth and twentieth century, an effort to search for concrete identities of sexual dissidence in the Greek past, and a critique of institutional culture for their disavowal [. . .] the re-visiting of past homosexual groups, subcultures and practices; the various histories of gay cultural expression or the representation of homosexuality in mainstream media [. . .] the histories of homosexual suppression

[. . .] all these [. . .] attempts to reconstruct a "Greek gay past"'; and '[o]n the other hand, [. . .] the historical persistence of queer modes of relationality and sociability in Greek society that have existed outside the contours of concrete sexual identities [. . .] Various practices of accepted homosociality, or of acknowledging sexual/gender difference without concrete identitarian politics [. . .] used as a caveat for the normativity [. . .] the tradition of homosociality present in canonical cultural genres [. . .]'. Papanikolaou (2018: 175) insists that these two projects 'are haunted by each other'.

26. The name of the magazine means a female resident of Athens, highlighting the urban element of the modern capital.
27. Papanikolaou offers a type of deconstruction/genealogy of such an approach. He also makes a distinction between a homosexual and a queer Athens, 'between the gay city and the queer city, the mappable urban place of non-normative sexual identities and the unmapped space of non-normative desire' (2014: 153, 166).
28. See *laika tekna* (Yannakopoulos 2016: 176).
29. Six years later, cultural ethnographer Elias Petropoulos clandestinely published his infamous *Ta Kaliarnta* (1971), the first Greek queer dictionary, for which he was imprisoned by the junta regime (see also Papanikolaou 2014: 154). Interestingly, Papanikolaou notes how Petropoulos mixes research, autobiography and *crime fiction* (my emphasis), while he asked 'for the help of members of the vice squad' to produce what, according to Papanikolaou, is 'the earliest cartographic account of a homosexual subculture of Athens, the first graphic map of Athens as a city containing a queer geography' (2014: 155).
30. According to Papanikolaou (2014: 155), '[h]omosexual lifestyles would become more visible from the late 1960s onwards'. For Papanikolaou (2014: 156), Petropoulos's view 'of Greek queer lifestyle in the 1960s as subcultural and hidden [. . .] overdoes the description of how completely marginal, sealed off and clandestine it was. Equally problematic is the fact that this account was produced with the collusion/help of state control, while also aiming to titillate a wider middle class audience [. . .]' The same can be argued of *The Bum* and the *Athinaia* article.
31. Dennis Broe pointed this out to me.
32. See also Dyer (2002: 96); Fay and Nieland (2010: 150–7); Abbott (2002: 69–71).
33. See also Avdela (2013: 309, 312, 315–17, 320); Papanikolaou (2014: 165); Yannakopoulos (2016: 179; 2019: 30). According to Theodorakopoulos (in Papanikolaou 2014: 158), since as early as the late 1940s in some central cinemas in Athens, 'men picked up men in the back rows while families enjoyed the film in front rows'.
34. For similar views and debates in the USA, see Benshoff (1997: 31–3, 38, 83, 123–5, 139–41, 178, 182, 242).
35. (Freudian) psychoanalysis as a signifier of an imported, corrosive modernity and modernisation can also be found in the film with noir elements *Katiforos/The Decline* (dir. Dalianidis, 1961) (see Kosyfologou 2013: 49, 58; Atzina 2004: 257, 264–6).
36. According to Tzanaki (2019: 11), Greek psychiatrists and coroners embraced such ideas almost a hundred years before the release of *The Bum*.
37. Sedgwick notes that (homo)sexuality has often been conceptualised 'along the axis of who penetrate[s] who' (Edwards 2009: 21).

38. Dennis Broe remarked to me that 'this might be closer to the American depiction in *The Maltese Falcon* and *Laura*, with the added veneer of the upper-class characterisation'.
39. These views are reminiscent of J. Edgar Hoover and the 1950 Senate Subcommittee's Report on the 'pervert problem' (Stoddart 2004). Dennis Broe has mentioned to me that, in the McCarthy era, the homosexual (man) was seen as a danger to the state and the Cold War 'consensus'.
40. Homosexuality was illegal in Greece until 1951. According to Papanikolaou (2014: 160–1), 'most [Greek] newspaper pieces in the 1930s called for the authorities not to let Athens become "debauched Paris", while at the same time rejoicing in the act of fully describing queer scandals, or the nocturnal activity in the central parks'. For Greek representations of homosociality or queer desire during the interwar years, before the establishment of a homosexual identity, see Papanikolaou (2014).
41. For a genealogy in the Greek context, see Tzanaki (2019).
42. Cf. Holmberg (2012: 7, 20, 113, 130, 134–5, 138, 141, 148, 154).
43. For the view of film noir as discourse, see Fay and Nieland (2010: 147).
44. In *Nightmare* (1961), male homosexuality is linked to perversions, paraphiliae, criminal activity, prostitution and pornography. However, unlike *The Bum*, in Andreou's film the (disabled) male homosexual/queer is represented as being in desperate need of treatment for his 'disease' (see also Avdela 2013: 326).

References

Abbott, Megan E. (2002), *The Street Was Mine: White Masculinity in Hardboiled Fiction and Film Noir*, New York: Palgrave Macmillan.

Anon. (1965), '"Trito fylo": Ypo to prisma tis epistimis: 6,000 omofylofiloi kykloforoun stin periohi tis protevousis' ['[The] Third Sex': Through the Prism of Science: 6,000 Homosexuals Wander around the Area of the Capital], *Athinaia*, 5, pp. 22–5.

Anon. (2021), '"Fterou, fteraaaa, parte kala fteraaa". Andreas Nomikos I "fterou". O pio sympathitikos andras tis Athinas synehizei na anastatonei me tis atakes tou' ['Feather lady, feathers, good feathers.' Andreas Nomikos or 'fterou'. The Most Likeable Man in Athens Continues to Excite with his Lines], *Mixanitouxronou.gr*, <https://www.mixanitouxronou.gr/fterou-fteraaaa-parte-kala-fteraaaa-andreas-nomikos-i-fterou-o-pio-simpathitikos-andras-tis-athinas-sinechizi-na-anastatoni-me-tis-atakes-tou/> (last accessed 15 March 2021).

Apostolidis, Andreas (2009), *Ta polla prosopa tou astynomikou mythistorimatos: Dokimia gia tin istoria kai tis synchrones taseis tou* [The Many Faces of the Crime Novel: Essays on the History and its Contemporary Trends], Athens: Agra.

Atzina, Lena (2004), *I makra eisagogi tis psychanalysis stin Ellada* [The Long Introduction of Psychoanalysis in Greece], Athens: Exantas.

Avdela, Efi (2013), *'Neoi en kindyno': Epitirisi, anamorfosi kai dikaiosini anilikon meta ton polemo* ['Youth in Danger': Surveillance, Reformation and Juvenile Justice after the War], Athens: Polis.

Benshoff, Harry. M. (1997), *Monsters in the Closet: Homosexuality and the Horror Film*, Manchester: Manchester University Press.
Bracher, Mark (1993), *Lacan, Discourse, and Social Change: A Psychoanalytic Cultural Criticism*, New York: Cornell University Press.
Bracher, Mark (1994), 'Introduction', in Mark Bracher, Marshall W. Alcorn Jr, Ronald J. Corthell and Françoise Massardier Kenney (eds), *Lacanian Theory of Discourse: Subject, Structure, and Society*, New York: New York University Press, pp. 1–16.
Braunstein, Nestor A. (1994), 'Con-jugating and Playing-with the Fantasy: The Utterances of the Analyst', in Mark Bracher, Marshall W. Alcorn Jr, Ronald J. Corthell and Françoise Massardier Kenney (eds), *Lacanian Theory of Discourse: Subject, Structure, and Society*, New York: New York University Press, pp. 151–9.
Campbell, John K. (1964), *Honor, Family and Patronage: A Study of Institutions and Moral Values in a Greek Mountain Community*, Oxford: Oxford University Press.
Chaudhuri, Shohini (2006), *Feminist Film Theorists: Laura Mulvey, Kaja Silverman, Teresa de Lauretis, Barbara Creed*, New York: Routledge.
Connell, R. W. ([1995] 2005), *Masculinities*, Berkeley, CA: University of California Press.
Cowan, Jane K. (1990), *Dance and the Body Politic in Northern Greece*, Princeton, NJ: Princeton University Press.
Delveroudi, Eliza-Anna (2004), *Oi neoi stis komodies tou ellinikou kinimatografou: 1948–1974* [Young People in the Comedies of Greek Cinema: 1948–1974], Athens: National Hellenic Research Foundation.
Doane, Mary Ann (1991), *Femmes Fatales: Feminism, Film Theory, Psychoanalysis*, London: Routledge.
Doxiadis, Kyrkos (2011), *Discourse Analysis: A Social-Philosophical Grounding*, Champaign, IL: Common Ground.
Dyer, Richard (1998a), 'Resistance through Charisma: Rita Hayworth and *Gilda*', in E. Ann Kaplan (ed.), *Women in Film Noir*, London: BFI, pp. 115–22.
Dyer, Richard (1998b), 'Postscript: Queers and Women in Film Noir', in E. Ann Kaplan (ed.), *Women in Film Noir*, London: BFI, pp. 123–9.
Dyer, Richard (2002), *The Culture of Queers*, Abingdon: Routledge.
Edwards, Jason (2009), *Eve Kosofsky Sedgwick*, New York: Routledge.
Fay, Jennifer, and Nieland, Justus (2010), *Film Noir: Hard-Boiled Modernity and the Cultures of Globalization*, Abingdon: Routledge.
Foucault, Michel ([1969] 1972), *The Archaeology of Knowledge and the Discourse on Language*, New York: Pantheon.
Foucault, Michel ([1976] 1978), *The History of Sexuality: Vol. I.*, trans. R. Hurley, New York: Pantheon.
Foucault, Michel ([1963] 2003), *The Birth of the Clinic: An Archaeology of Medical Perception*, Abingdon: Routledge.
Fuller, Ken (2020), *Raymond Chandler: The Man Behind the Mask*, privately published.
Griffin, Gabriele (ed.) (2013), *Research Methods for English Studies*, Edinburgh: Edinburgh University Press.
Hadjikyriacou, Achilleas (2013), *Masculinity and Gender in Greek Cinema: 1949–1967*, New York: Bloomsbury.

Hall, Stuart (1997), 'The Work of Representation', in Stuart Hall (ed.), *Representation: Cultural Representations and Signifying Practices*, London: Sage, pp. 13–74.

Holmberg, David Thomas (2012), 'Prying, Peeping, Peering: The Voyeuristic Gaze in Late Nineteenth-Century American Literary Naturalism', PhD dissertation, University of Washington, <https://digital.lib.washington.edu/researchworks/bitstream/handle/1773/20721/Holmberg_washington_0250E_10223.pdf?sequence=1> (last accessed 14 September 2021).

Kartalou, Athena (2005), 'To anekpliroto eidos: Oi tainies koinonikis katangelias tis Finos Film' [The Uncompleted Genre: Finos's Films of Social Denunciation], PhD dissertation, Panteion University.

Kassaveti, Ursula-Helen (2019), 'Nyhtes horis eglima sti dekaetia tou 1960: I athinaiki kinimatografiki revue' [Nights without Crime in the 1960s: The Athenian Film Revue], *Polar*, 5, pp. 86–9.

Kosma, Yvonne-Alexia (2007), 'Eikones gia to fylo mesa apo ton elliniko kinimatografo sti dekaetia tou '60: Fylo kai sexualikotita sto eidos tis aisthimatikis comedi (1959–1967)' [Images of Gender in Greek Cinema of the Sixties: Gender and Sexuality in the Romantic Comedy Genre (1959–1967)], PhD dissertation, National and Kapodistrian University of Athens.

Kosyfologou, Aliki (2013), 'I ideologia tis gynaikeias sexualikotitas: Anaparastaseis kai sygrotisi protypon ston elliniko erotiko kinimatografo tis dekaetias tou '60' [The Ideology of Female Sexuality: Representations and the Construction of Role Models in Erotic Greek Cinema of the 1960s], PhD dissertation, National and Kapodistrian University of Athens.

Krutnik, Frank (1991), *In a Lonely Street: Film Noir, Genre, Masculinity*, London: Routledge.

Kyriakos, Konstantinos (2016), *Epithymies kai politiki: I queer istoria tou ellinikou kinimatografou (1924–2016)* [Desires and Politics: The Queer History of Greek Cinema (1924–2016)], Athens: Aigokeros.

Lacan, Jacques ([1969–70] 2007), *The Seminar of Jacques Lacan: The Other Side of Psychoanalysis, Book XVII*, New York: W. W. Norton.

Nixon, Sean (1997), 'Exhibiting Masculinity', in Stuart Hall (ed.), *Representation: Cultural Representations and Signifying Practices*, London: Sage, pp. 291–336.

Papanikolaou, Dimitris (2014), 'Mapping/Unmapping: The Making of Queer Athens', in Matt Cook and Jennifer V. Evans (eds), *Queer Cities, Queer Cultures: Europe since 1945*, London: Bloomsbury, pp. 151–70.

Papanikolaou, Dimitris (2018), 'Critically Queer and Haunted: Greek Identity, Crisiscapes and Doing Queer History in the Present', *Journal of Greek Media & Culture*, 4:2, pp. 167–86.

Parker, Ian, Georgaca, Eugenie, Harper, David, McLaughlin, Terence, and Stowell Smith, Mark (1995), *Deconstructing Psychopathology*, London: Sage.

Peristiany, John (1965), 'Honour and Shame in a Cypriot Highland Village', in John Peristiany (ed.), *Honour and Shame: The Values of Mediterranean Society*, London: Weidenfeld and Nicolson, pp. 171–90.

Petropoulos, Elias (1971), *Ta Kaliarnta*, Athens: Digamma.

Rose, Gillian (2001), *Visual Methodologies: An Introduction to Researching with Visual Materials*, London: Sage.
Salecl, Renata (1994), 'Deference to the Great Other: The Discourse of Education', in Mark Bracher, Marshall W. Alcorn Jr, Ronald J. Corthell and Françoise Massardier Kenney (eds), *Lacanian Theory of Discourse: Subject, Structure, and Society*, New York: New York University Press, pp. 163–75.
Spargo, Tamsin (1999), *Foucault and Queer Theory*, Cambridge: Icon.
Stassinopoulou, Maria A. (2000), 'Reality Bites: A Feature Film History of Greece, 1950–1963', unpublished habilitation thesis, University of Vienna.
Stoddart, Scott F. (2004), '"Queer Eye" for a "Straight Dick": Contextualized Homosexuals in Film Noir', <https://case.edu/affil/sce/Texts_2004/stoddart.htm?fbclid=IwAR0cGQ8VIO4x0YYmMdKEX78H8L6LZiSfaKWPrzYcQ1kKuFB6AgGRJy04Eis> (last accessed 25 May 2020).
Tasker, Yvonne (2013), 'Women in Film Noir', in Andrew Spicer and Helen Hanson (eds), *A Companion to Film Noir*, Chichester: Wiley-Blackwell, pp. 353–68.
Tzanaki, Dimitra (2019), 'Apo to 1871 mehri to 1950: Genealogia fylou kai sexualikotitas' [From 1871 to 1950: Genealogy of Gender and Sexuality], in Nancy Papathanassiou and Elena-Olga Christidi (eds), *Taftotita fylou: Simeioseis gia to mathima* [Gender Identity: Course Notes], pp. 9–13, <http://www.kordoutis.gr/panteion/images/pdf/sexualid/Notesgenderid.pdf> (last accessed 30 May 2020).
Wager, Jans B. (2005), *Dames in the Driver's Seat: Rereading Film Noir*, Austin, TX: University of Texas Press.
Weeks, Jeffrey (2012), *Sex, Politics and Society: The Regulation of Sexuality since 1800*, New York: Routledge.
Yannakopoulos, Kostas (2016), '"Naked Piazza". Male (Homo)Sexualities, Masculinities and Consumer Cultures in Greece since the 1960', in Kostis Kornetis, Eirini Kotsovili and Nikolaos Papadogiannis (eds), *Consumption and Gender in Southern Europe since the Long 1960s*, London: Bloomsbury Academic, pp. 173–89.
Yannakopoulos, Kostas (2019), 'Mia diahyti omofylofilia sti metapolemiki Ellada' [A Diffuse Homosexuality in Post-War Greece], in Nancy Papathanassiou and Elena-Olga Christidi (eds), *Taftotita fylou: Simeioseis gia to mathima* [Gender Identity: Course Notes], pp. 26–31, <http://www.kordoutis.gr/panteion/images/pdf/sexualid/Notesgenderid.pdf>, (last accessed 30 May 2020).

PART II

POLITICAL ASPECTS AND TRANSNATIONAL DYNAMICS OF THE GREEK NEO-NOIR

8. A DARK INTRIGUE OF MURDER: *KIERION* AND *RECONSTRUCTION*, OR FILM NOIR AS POLITICS

Maria Chalkou

This chapter discusses Dimos Theos and Theo Angelopoulos's debut feature films, *Kierion* (1967–74) and *Anaparastasi/Reconstruction* (1970) respectively, through the lens of film noir. This may seem paradoxical since the two films are typically considered as the starting points of New Greek Cinema, a politically engaged, auteur-driven and arthouse movement that turned away from the thematic, stylistic and genre conventions of the mainstream Old Greek Cinema of the 1950s and 1960s. Kovács, however, argues for the transitional character of film noir, which prepared the way for modernist film narration, drawing attention to the phenomenon that many great auteurs such as Visconti, Antonioni, Godard and Truffaut, at the beginning of their careers, 'constructed their films on film noir structure' (2007: 246). 'The investigation pattern', according to Kovács, 'may dominate even the most esoteric European modernist art films' (2007: 245). Moreover, film noir and other classical genres became central to modernist cinema as 'forms to be interrogated, rewritten, subjectivised and transformed, from films of genre to films of *auteurs*' (Rohdie 2015: 28). The main aim of the chapter is thus to examine how *Kierion* and *Reconstruction*, made by two major auteurs of New Greek Cinema from left-wing perspectives and in a turbulent era – on the verge of and during the military junta of the Colonels (1967–74) – while being comfortably placed within the modernist film tradition, employ 'noir' patterns in order to deal with authoritarianism and the bleak sociopolitical reality in Greece.

KIERION: POLITICAL CONSPIRACY AND THE DARK SIDE OF THE URBAN

Theos in the 1960s was a highly politicised filmmaker as he was committed to the left-wing party EDA.[1] His interest in politics and film noir aesthetics can be traced back to 1963–64 when he co-directed with Fotos Lambrinos the short *Ekato ores tou Mai/100 Hours of May* about the assassination of the EDA deputy Grigoris Lambrakis by parastate extremists in May 1963. This radical documentary uses iconographic, thematic and narrative tropes derived from the film noir: it opens with a crime announced by the press; it adopts a journalistic investigative format and a complex flashback structure to reveal hidden truths; its dark and violent plot exposes the links between common crime and the deep state; there is an emphasis on night-time city scenes, while the noir atmosphere is emphasised by the soundtrack, punctuated by the beat of a metronome and Henry Mancini's musical theme from the *Peter Gunn* police series heard over clashes between protesters and police (Chalkou 2021). *100 Hours of May* clearly anticipated the political content and the dark aesthetics of Theos's first feature film three years later.

Kierion was filmed in April 1967, just before and in the early days of the dictatorship, initially with a censorship permit granted to a fake script and, after the coup, completely illegally.[2] Shot entirely on location and in sharp black-and-white cinematography, it used a mix of professional and amateur actors, including future filmmakers such as Theo Angelopoulos, Tonia Marketaki, Stavros Tornes, Kostas Sfikas, Nikos Nikolaidis, Pantelis Voulgaris and Costas Ferris, among others, who were later to be recognised as the founders of New Greek Cinema. Inspired by recent developments in European cinema and during a period of sociopolitical unrest, the making of *Kierion* was marked by a spirit of comradeship, offering a model for improvised, oppositional, collective and low-budget filmmaking.

Kierion is loosely based on a notorious actual case, the unsolved murder of the American journalist George Polk in Thessaloniki in 1948, during the Greek Civil War, which was attributed by the authorities to the left. Set in Athens, the story takes place in the 1960s and revolves around the murder of George Morgan, an American journalist visiting Greece to meet Ervin Goss, an Englishman working for oil cartels. Similarly to Polk, Morgan disappears and his dead body is found floating in the sea. The film gradually unfolds the villainous activities of a shadowy apparatus of international and local power in its attempt to cover up the crime by fabricating suspects and culprits. At the same time, it features the unsuccessful struggles of the investigative reporter Aimos Vagenas to uncover the hidden truth behind the fabricated one, always being confronted with dead ends and extreme violence.

Following the noir pattern (Studlar 2013), Vagenas, played by Anestis Vlahos – an idiosyncratic actor with a damaged eye, usually cast as a psychologically fragile villain or pervert – is a troubled and not necessarily sympathetic character. As a journalist he usually covers political topics, such as demonstrations and the radicalised university student movement, which are mostly illegal and underground affairs. He also secretly collaborates with Morgan in writing a book on the economic and political impact of oil corporations on the wider area of Mediterranean Sea. Despite his extrovert, upper-middle-class and cosmopolitan lifestyle, his sociopolitical position is unstable, as he crosses the boundaries between the established elites and the underside of society, often being tailed by the police, not always supported by his newspaper and distrusted by the students. Vagenas seems alienated and depressed, recovering from a nervous breakdown caused by losing control over investigations in the past, while his alienation is further underscored by his disintegrating marriage. The initial emotional drifting between Vagenas and his wife, who resorts to alcohol and sleeping pills, is followed by her complete absence, as early on in the film she disappears from the screen without mention, leaving Vagenas deprived of any intimacy and psychological support. As highlighted by his first-person voiceover narration, Vagenas is an existential character, always questioning himself, his profession and his surroundings, while also philosophising on the concept of truth.

Vagenas, who collects Morgan from the airport and drives him to his hotel, is unwittingly trapped in a vicious conspiracy. After waiting in vain to meet Morgan in a bar, he and a Marxist student named Leo Zadik are arrested as suspects for Morgan's murder and violently interrogated by the police. Vagenas is set free due to lack of evidence, while Zadik is jailed as he appears to have confessed. Trying to clear his name, as the police accuse him of being Zadik's accomplice, and convinced of the student's innocence, Vagenas embarks on a horrific investigation. Soon he finds himself isolated as his compromised newspaper editor-in-chief refuses to back him up. Having only the support of a colleague named 'Theo' – played by Theo Angelopoulos – he works on the crime independently, becoming thus the archetypical wandering loner of film noir.

The film constructs an extremely dark, corrupt and dangerous noir milieu preoccupied with politics. This embraces Greece's political scene and institutional system – the police, the judiciary and partly the press – while also having strong international tentacles. Ervin Goss, a wartime British secret agent who acted as a liaison between the Greek Resistance and the Middle East headquarters, is now a consultant to oil cartels. The pro-Arab Morgan, who supports the nationalisation of oil supplies and is investigating the shadowy activities of the cartels to secure their interests by precipitating a war, has to be silenced before he makes any revelations. Zadik is a convenient and convincing culprit as his ethnic origin – he is Jewish – allows him to be presented as a secret Zionist who is acting on behalf of his country, defaming at the same time the left-wing radicals.

From the outset the narrative establishes links between the international and the local, creating a cosmopolitan atmosphere while presenting Greece as being strongly dependent on foreign financial and political powers. The film opens with an American technocrat, interviewed by Greek journalists, among them Vagenas, developing his vision of the future capitalist growth and consumer society in Greece. The very title *Kierion* ('Cierium'), the name of an ancient town that lost its freedom and name under successive occupations – as a brief excerpt from Strabo's *Geography* informs us at the beginning of the film – functions as a metonymy for Greece, suggesting its politico-economic dependency and lost cultural identity. The notion of 'occupation' forms a dominant narrative subtext. The distant views of the war cemetery for the Allied Forces of the Second World War and the Athens Memorial – seen during Vagenas and Morgan's ride towards Athens – revive traumatic war memories, while the Occupation, in accordance with a popular motif in Greek crime novels and films of the time, appears as a dark area of the past where shady secrets and ambiguous identities are hidden (Chalkou 2008: 186).

Kierion, like many noirs, is marked by widespread violence. Morgan is shot and thrown into the sea, although the crime is never shown onscreen. Daring depictions of Vagenas and Zadik being brutally tortured articulate a strong criticism of the political regime and the police practices of the time. In a dark, claustrophobic basement Vagenas is restrained in a chair and beaten while strong light is shone in his face – a common iconography of film noir (Figure 8.1). The severity of the torture is reflected in Vagenas's intense vomiting and in the piercing sounds of a jackhammer used to cover Zadik's cries. The marks of violence are evident on Zadik's face when after a haemoptysis – officially explained as an allergic reaction to interrogation – he is hospitalised. Later on, Zadik is found dead in his cell in a pool of blood, without it being clear whether he was murdered or committed suicide. In the course of the investigation Vagenas eventually discovers Pelagia, a young prostitute, who was present at a dinner attended by Morgan in Goss's villa, where the journalist was murdered. Vagenas secures a passport for her to flee the country after testifying as a witness. While he is on his way to meet her, Pelagia is thrown from the window of her hotel room by unknown men hidden in the dark, making her death appear as suicide.

The violation of privacy and private spaces by state and parastate forces is a recurrent motif in the film: police invade the student hideout, seizing left-wing books as evidence of Zadik's political commitment while criminalising him by putting a gun on his desk. Similarly, they infringe on the private territory of Vagenas's apartment, messing up his things and reading his letters. Thus, the state and public institutions of post-Civil War and dictatorial Greece protect neither the public nor the individual, but are omnipresent forces of evil. This is highlighted further by the anonymous group of corrupt and cynical judges who cancel the reconstruction of the crime because they are afraid

A DARK INTRIGUE OF MURDER

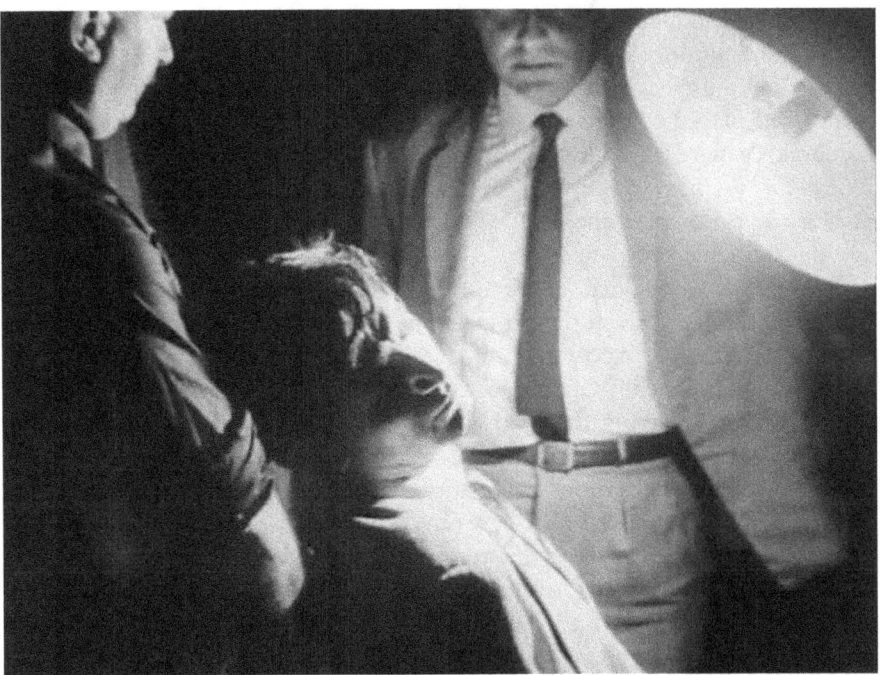

Figure 8.1 Vagenas (Anestis Vlahos) is tortured by the police. Digital still from *Kierion*.

of the truth. Following a tradition of films noirs that explore the corruption of power (Mortenson 2016), in *Kierion* a dense network of dark and invisible power mechanisms does everything to protect its interests, indifferent to human life and the values of freedom, justice and truth.

The film was made during and reflected on a turbulent period in Greek political life when the Lambrakis assassination, the subsequent notorious trial, the so-called *Apostasia* ('Apostasy') that caused the overturn of Papandreou's democratic government, the 'ASPIDA' military scandal and rumours of an impending dictatorship brought parastate violence, deep state machinations, political intrigue and conspiracy to the fore. It was the same sociopolitical background that inspired *Z* (1969) by Costa Gavras, which largely launched and popularised a new genre in the late 1960s, the political thriller (Wayne 2001: 68). *Kierion* predates the genre, situating itself somewhere between film noir, political thriller and political conspiracy film – the latter two flourishing in the 1970s. The impact of current political realities on the film's content is traced also in the figure of the prosecutor, who is singled out by the narrative as a decent individual who doubts the official version of the truth. Played by future avant-garde filmmaker Kostas Sfikas, he is an allusion to the real prosecutor Christos

Sartzetakis, who later in Z, played by Jean-Louis Trintignant, was depicted as a hero. The film's belief in independent journalism as an idealistic force that struggles to unravel corruption and truth seems also to have its origins in the crucial role played by the press at the time in uncovering the hidden plot behind Lambrakis's murder.

Kierion employs the investigative but not the typical flashback structure of films noirs. Its plot appears to be linear although still confusing, elliptical and often fragmented (Spicer 2002: 74–83), as open patterns are never closed, narrative gaps never filled, and questions never answered. However, the story is vaguely displaced from the present. The whole film is a single flashback as Vagenas's narrating voiceover – another recognisable film noir trait – reflects on the past, occasionally challenging narrative linearity by predating events (for example, we learn about the death of Zadik several scenes before it happens). Key indicators of the timeframe of the story include an impending dictatorship in Greece and an Arab–Israeli war, anticipating the junta that came to power in April 1967 and the Six-Day War between Arab and Israeli forces that took place in June of the same year. Thus the story is firmly located in the time of the film's making, evoking the fears of the period and its climate of upheaval. Importantly, the voiceover, as we know it today, was recorded and the dialogue dubbed much later, as *Kierion* was first released abroad in 1968, while in 1974 the soundtrack – including Vagenas's narration and the dubbing of the actors – was remade for the film's release in Greece after the fall of the junta (Rentzis 2006: 74).[3] Thus there is an actual distance of time between the filmed material and the voiceover narration, which was thus able to incorporate afterthoughts and retrospective knowledge. From 1967 to 1974 a succession of traumatic events took place resulting in political disenchantment: the dictatorship that put an abrupt halt to hopes for democratisation and to the cultural flourishing of the 1960s (interestingly, Morgan's murder takes place on 21 April, the day of the coup, establishing a link between the fictional loss and the actual historical trauma); the split of the Greek left in 1968; and the Turkish invasion of Cyprus in 1974.

Thus Vagenas's subjective narration is a post-traumatic interior monologue emotionally detached from his depicted self. A slight discord is traced between the dispassionate but still struggling Vagenas onscreen and the defeated Vagenas who narrates. His stream of consciousness is deprived of hope and prospects, as he is now aware that he was overwhelmed by the events – a typical noir trait; aware of his failure to uncover the truth and the vicious underground powers he faced. From the beginning to the end an all-pervasive sense of helplessness and defeat, of isolation and entrapment, of frustration and grief, of shame and guilt – for the death of Pelagia and perhaps of Zadik – saturates his narration. The tone of Vagenas's voice is one of disillusionment and profound pessimism.

Moreover, there is a typical noir focus on the dark side of the urban (Smith 2011: 19–33). As Vagenas wanders around the city, initially as a journalist and in the process of solving the murder, he is exposed to a sinister cityscape. The period of modernisation and urban sprawl of Athens is registered in the film. 'I see a lot of changes around here', Morgan observes upon arriving in Athens, receiving Vagenas's cynical reply: 'We built a lot of hotels, prisons, concentration camps', a comment on massive, faceless and distorted growth motivated by the values of consumer society and political authoritarianism. The film offers authentic views of peripheral locations that function as symbols of modernity: the airport, vast industrial buildings, newly built apartment blocks and piles of rubble, highways, bridges and roundabouts, Goss's modern villa in a high-class suburb. These, however, are not pictured as sites of progress and affluence but rather as bleak and barren places pervaded by a strong sense of dislocation. Even a brief seaside scene at the periphery of the city does not offer escapist views but is another site of crime.

Furthermore, the film anonymises the urban setting, completely avoiding tourist Athens and its historic centre, focusing instead on an abstract, modernised city centre at night, in the tradition of noir. It pictures Omonoia, Athens's central square, and its underground station marked by escalators and busy crowds; neon lights, cars and reflective streets; nightclubs, bars and cafés; the newspaper's office and printing house; store windows, a modern gym and urban consumer cultures. Moreover, pursuing the truth, Vagenas, either on foot, on a train or by car, embarks on a journey beyond the city centre towards the marginal spaces and fringes of society: poor neighbourhoods, impoverished slums, dirty and unhealthy refugee tenements – Vagenas on entering the apartments covers his face with a handkerchief to protect himself from unpleasant smells – and cheap hotels, all miserable places inhabited by the outcasts of society. Working-class settings, such as a clothing factory crowded with female workers, and vacant industrial sites with dirt roads, such as the area around the gasworks of Athens dominated by smoking chimneys, are also part of this alienating trip.

The urban thus embodies the class stratifications of Greek society. Theos adopted documentary aesthetics to explore the city's dense and diversified social fabric, often using observational shots through the windows of moving cars. A recurrent motif of the film is a quick glance from a window or a balcony at the outside world, capturing minor real-life situations that insert into the plot the non-fictional world, tightly linking fiction to reality while disrupting narrative coherence:[4] a political demonstration, boys playing football, workers loading a truck in a narrow back street, people packed into a bus station, a man mopping the wet floor of the underground station, a passing train. At other moments, and in a style as much neorealist as surrealist, underdogs inhabit the cinematic image, such as the blind street musicians whose distant song breaks the silence of an empty industrial space or the chatting beggars – who momentarily are given voice – resting on the steps of a church. The cinematic gaze is constantly diverted from the political intrigue to social problems and vice versa, as Vagenas's investigation of the crime is a journey through, and a visual inspection of, the socio-spatial environment.

At the same time outdoor and indoor spaces seem to internalise the intricacies and perils of the plot as they appear labyrinthine and claustrophobic. There is an emphasis on enclosed and underground locations, underscoring a sense of confinement and entrapment. Characters are exposed to threatening transitional spaces, suggesting their precarious position. They arrive at the airport, occupy hotel rooms, walk along corridors or up and down stairs, while they are also restricted within tight interiors: the terrifying police basement, Zadik's prison cell, the student hideout, a packed elevator, Pelagia's unlit hotel room – a death trap. Doors open and close, restlessly fragmenting the interior spaces, while the actors are visually entrapped by frame and composition as they are filmed behind bars and other visual obstacles, seen through glasses and reflections, framed by windows and doors. Moreover, the ceilings in the rooms are often visible, enhancing the overwhelming sense of menace and suffocation. Cinematographer and future film director Giorgos Panousopoulos's expressive lighting techniques and fluid camerawork contribute greatly to this noir atmosphere of uneasiness and enclosure: expressionistic and deep-focus photography, hand-held cameras, minimal light sources, backlighting, long shadows cast on to walls and floors, high-angle shots diminishing human figures, faces half-hidden in the dark, reflective surfaces. Darkness appears as much expressive as symbolic, as, for example, in the scene where the amoral judges, surrounded by complete, uncanny darkness, cancel the reconstruction of the crime. This sinister atmosphere is further increased by the use of enhanced natural or mechanical sounds – the sounds of modernity – such as footsteps, a typewriter, a siren, alarming door bells and telephone calls, while voices are often mechanically reproduced through telephone speakers and tape recorders, creating an alienating effect. Indicatively, a disembodied voice on the telephone warns Zadik of his imminent arrest and, several scenes later, we see Vagenas listening to Zadik's recorded confession.

In the noir tradition, exterior and interior spaces convey a sense of surveillance: Vagenas is being watched at the airport, his car tailed, his discussion with Pelagia eavesdropped, while in the underground station he is followed by uniformed men. Photographs are carefully examined as Goss inspects surveillance photos of Morgan and Vagenas, and Vagenas scrutinises a wartime picture of Goss with a magnifying glass. Suspect noises are heard behind the wall of Morgan's hotel room, and faceless killers are hidden in the shadows of Pelagia's room. Suspicion, distrust and fear lurk everywhere: Vagenas meets the students secretly in the dark, and the students suspect a traitor among them. In this suffocating atmosphere, however, interior and exterior settings articulate a cry of protest. There is a feverish tension in the city at night as the distant roar of political demonstrations evokes a climate of turmoil and unrest. In daylight a political graffito on the ground attributes responsibility, and demands: 'Foreigners go home'. Posters, photos and newspaper snippets on the wall of the student hideout and Zadik's bourgeois home – showing Malcolm X, Martin Luther King, Che Guevara and an injured child in the Vietnam War, among others – are evidence of highly politicised times and of a world in upheaval. These are also striking political statements expressing the civil rights, emancipation and anti-war demands of the 1960s. Furthermore, the recurring appearance of Picasso's *Guernica* on the wall of the hideout and in Vagenas's apartment is a central visual motif of the film, connecting, via its powerful anti-fascist and anti-war message, the liberal journalist with the Marxist students, while clearly demarcating them from the forces of evil: a cop in Vagenas's house inspects *Guernica* with evident stupidity and incomprehension.

Athens, therefore, is pictured as an alienating, suffocating and demoralised wasteland and as a city of contrasts. Besides, for the spectator, the film creates a highly alienating and contrasting visual experience of the city itself. At night it is exceedingly dark, with a few scattered lights surrounded by deep, unbroken blackness. During daytime it is a sun-scorched place, almost bleached under the Mediterranean sunlight. The city seems to lose its materiality, fading away in the darkness of the night and in the brightness of the day, becoming more of an apparition than a physical presence. Its darkness is political and moral, its extreme brightness suggests disintegration; it is a city dissolving into decay. Corruption and degeneration, however, are not only part of the political regime, but also involve everyday people who are supporters and servants of the establishment. Thus the concierge of Pelagia's hotel shares responsibility for the crime: she fakes illness and does not warn Pelagia of the danger, letting her enter the room and meet her death, while soon afterwards she confirms that Pelagia committed suicide. Corruption and amorality lie deep in Greek society, which is not innocent.

The narrative of *Kierion* follows a 'circular trajectory', a practice often encountered in modernist cinema, in which 'the story comes back to its starting point without a solution to end there' (Kovács 2007: 76). The film opens and closes with an identical sequence of documentary shots of an apathetic crowd of people, restlessly moving around the city centre as automata, either leisurely or self-absorbed. The opening sequence is accompanied by the menacing sound of *scacciapensieri* (jaw harp), a Sicilian musical instrument heard in *Salvatore Giuliano* (dir. Rosi, 1962), a film that highly impressed Theos at the time, influencing his work (Kersanidis 2006b: 11).[5] In the final sequence *scacciapensieri* is replaced by neurotic jazz scores,[6] characteristic of films noirs, and Vagenas's subjective narration. Traumatised individual consciousness is juxtaposed to that of the ignorant crowd, with Vagenas's voiceover stressing the innocence of the victims – Pelagia and Zadik – and his own guilt, together with his obligation to continue the investigation in the dark, entrapped in an unsolved problem that needs clarification.[7]

RECONSTRUCTION: THE REBELLION OF THE FEMME FATALE

The fascination of Theo Angelopoulos with detective stories, 'be they novels or films' (Fainaru [1999] 2001: 125), has been openly declared in his interviews, in which he describes his obsession with the American classics, drawing particular attention to Curtiz's *Angels with Dirty Faces* (1938) as the first film he ever saw. It has also been confirmed in his writing as a film critic (1964–67) for the left-wing newspaper *Dimokratiki Allagi* [Democratic Change], where he reviewed around fifty crime-related movies, displaying a thorough knowledge of the relevant literature and genres, while giving enthusiastic reviews of contemporary noirs such as *The Killers* (dir. Siegel, 1964) and *Le deuxieme souffle/ Second Breath* (dir. Melville, 1966) (Chalkou 2015: 26–7). It is evident also in his early attempts at filmmaking: *En Blanc et Noir*, his lost short set in Paris, was 'a black-and-white nod to film noir' (Horton 1997a: 20), while the never completed *Forminx Story* employed a police plot written by Angelopoulos.

Set in a remote and almost deserted village in rural and mountainous Epirus, one of the poorest regions of Greece at the time, Angelopoulos's first feature film *Anapaparastasi/Reconstruction* (1970) retells a 1968 true crime story widely discussed in the press: Eleni, a mother of three, and her lover, a married rural policeman, murder Eleni's husband after he returns from Germany, where he had gone to work. They bury the body in the house's yard, stage a trip by the dead husband to the nearby town of Ioannina and to Athens, and post a letter supposedly from him saying that he has left, making it appear that he has returned to Germany. After the murder is revealed, they accuse each other. Angelopoulos based the film's storyline on personal and journalistic research, and on court records (Hopf [1971] 2001: 3). As he felt it would be dishonest to turn the story into a fictional account, *Reconstruction*, in his own words, 'offers as accurate a version as possible of the events' (Hopf [1971] 2001: 3). Thus, as well as the major events of the actual story, *Reconstruction* includes meticulous real-life details, such as the small tavern run by Eleni, the oiled rope used as the murder weapon, the bedsheet used to wrap the body, Eleni's suggestion that the body be cut into pieces, the spring onions she planted in the yard to cover the traces of the grave, the wrong name given by mistake at the hotel in Ioannina that finally exposed them, and the village women attacking Eleni. The film even restages scenes derived from photographs published in the press, such as the incident with Eleni's son pointing to the trapdoor through which the two lovers threw the dead body to hide it from Eleni's children when they suddenly returned from school.[8] The film's title, therefore, although character names and the actual locations have been changed, does not simply refer to the reconstruction of the crime by the police in the film's plot, but also describes the film itself. Thus, at first sight, *Reconstruction* can be seen as a docudrama.

The relationship of *Reconstruction* to film noir, although only briefly discussed, has been widely noticed by critics and scholars, who stress mainly its differences from the genre. Horton, for example, notes that Angelopoulos switched 'the location from a city to a village' and made 'a "tough woman" the center of attention instead of a male detective or criminal' (1997a: 93). As Angelopoulos shot *Reconstruction* under the authoritarian regime of the Colonels, analogies have also been traced between the film and the work of Hollywood left-leaning filmmakers who made noirs during McCarthyism (Wilmington 1997: 60). The film has been also understood as part of a wider trend among young European filmmakers who introduced themselves with crime plots. David Bordwell has pointed out that *Reconstruction*, like Bertolucci's *La commare secca/The Grim Reaper* (1962), recasts the plot dynamics of *Citizen Kane* (dir. Welles, 1941) and *The Killers* (dir. Siodmak, 1946), 'rework[ing] a narrative template characteristic of European art cinema since the 1950s: the police-investigation-plus-flashbacks that affords a chance to juggle time and point of view' (1997: 11).

Reconstruction both relates to and destabilises the conventions of film noir. In terms of narrative, there is a crime plot of a love triangle and a crime of passion reminiscent of James M. Cain's classic *The Postman Always Rings Twice*. Furthermore, the film adopts a double investigation pattern: one conducted by the police and another by a TV crew and journalists headed by Angelopoulos himself, as if he slipped from the narrative of *Kierion* into *Reconstruction*. The official investigation, including intense interrogations and the reconstruction of the crime, is conducted by a prosecutor and uniformed men in Eleni's house – the crime scene – where the two lovers are questioned. Here, there is not the police brutality and secrecy of *Kierion*, while the whole process is openly recorded by the media so that the story becomes public. Central to the reconstruction of the crime is an obsessive whodunit question, with the interrogation being performed by the authorities in a routine, although still authoritative manner. However, the forces of law and order fail to resolve the details of the crime, lacking the skill to reveal the motives, who was really the murderer and how things actually happened, as their questions remain unanswered or inadequately replied to. Apart from their professional insufficiency, the figures of authority are further ridiculed: the camera captures the austere interrogator while exiting the cramped toilet in the house's yard and tidying his clothes. Later on, Eleni physically assaults him and he cannot deal with her strength and anger: he is saved by the policemen and, exhausted, he collapses in a chair. If in *Kierion* the police and justice were pictured as forces of evil, with some hope still surviving in the dignity of the individual, here they are narrow-minded and incompetent public servants, deprived of real authority.

On the other hand, the investigation by the journalists focuses mainly on the village and its inhabitants. Reporters, after taking pictures and recording interviews, move away from the violated privacy of the house to focus on the public sphere. They meet the villagers, mainly elderly people who have been left behind, and discuss migration and living conditions with them. As representatives of modernity, both state officials and journalists are strangers, outsiders to the village. Their city clothes – Angelopoulos wears a trenchcoat and a comic fedora hat, parodying the figure of detective – make them look alien, uncomfortably placed both in the crime scene and the village setting. After briefly disturbing village's weird, incomprehensible life, which has to be disciplined and clinically examined, they will return to where they belong.

The film uses a flashback structure, a key narrative device of film noir. A series of flashbacks and fragments of the reconstruction of the crime alternate and momentarily fuse: after the opening credits, from inside the house, through a window and from Eleni's perspective, we witness the return of her husband and, as he enters the room, a rope being suddenly put around his neck. In this plot twist and brief moment of narrative disorientation we discover that the unfolding events are not a crime taking place in the present but a re-enactment of the past. Elliptical, fragmentary and – in the abovementioned scene – unreliable narrative fractures the story, undermining its continuity and occasionally also its sense of reality. If subjective narration is a staple of film noir, in *Reconstruction* objectivity and subjectivity are fused, as it is not always clear whether the flashbacks are subjective, narrated by the interrogated lovers, or objective representations introduced by an omnipresent narrator. Multiple narrators, retellings and points of views – another trait of film noir – provide fragmentary and incomplete information or contradict each other. Importantly, neither flashbacks nor the reconstruction process illuminate the actual details of the crime, as like *Kierion* the murder remains absent from the screen. Instead, the narrative focuses exclusively on the agonised attempts of the two lovers to escape. From the outset, however, we are aware that they are doomed to fail – their actions and plots to cover up the crime lead them to dead ends – enhancing thus the omnipresent sense of entrapment and the impossibility of escape characteristic of film noir.

'[C]entral to the intrigue' (Kaplan 1998: 16) of *Reconstruction* is an adulterous, seductive and murderous woman, although, in contrast to a typical noir, her presence on screen is entirely desexualised. With her common looks and unflattering village clothes, Eleni does not represent a glamorous *femme fatale*. Yet she is still defined by her sexuality as 'desirable but dangerous to men' (Kaplan 1998: 16). The overwhelming sexual attraction is stressed by her lover who tries to convince the persecutor that he was manipulated and destroyed by her spell: 'and then she bewitched me'. Nevertheless, although Eleni is deprived of an 'exciting sexuality' (Place 1998: 48) onscreen, as in film noir she produces 'a remarkably potent image of woman' (Place 1998: 48) since, in contrast to the male characters, she possesses a strong individuality. The returning husband is the first character to be introduced, but he is not the protagonist, as the film is marked by his absence. He was away, already forgotten – his five-year-old son does not recognise him when he returns home – almost a ghost figure. The arriving man with the suitcase looks like a passer-by, displaced, alien and alienated; he does not belong there any more, and by murdering him, the lovers send him back into oblivion. The rural policeman, on the other hand, has a masculine and robust physical appearance, but he also appears weak. He blames the woman and attempts to avoid responsibility. During the interrogation his answers are defensive, accented by negations and sentimental explosions, while he swears his innocence on the life of his children.

Eleni, by contrast, is presented as the most active, determined and consistent character in the film, dominating the narrative time. We follow her lonely struggles to cover up the traces of the murder (by planting onions, posting the letter, breaking her husband's suitcase and burning his clothes), but we also observe her skilfully coping with everyday tasks such as house and shop keeping, caring for the children, serving and handling soldiers and other customers. In the beginning she was willing to take all the blame, and she endured the violent explosions of her frightened and – in the course of the film – distant lover. During the interrogation her answers are straight and cold-blooded, and when the authoritative gaze is directed towards her, she can return it. In the final stage of the reconstruction, when the two lovers are examined together, although the rural policeman has betrayed her and she is overwhelmed by anger, she remains silent, not accusing him any more. Eleni dominates men by initiative, strength and character as much as she visually dominates the frame with her vitality. Regardless of Angelopoulos's preference for distant framing and long shots, the cinematic image is often structured around her body and powerful physicality.

Both authorities and community attempt to restore the broken social order 'through the exposure and then destruction of the sexual, manipulating woman' (Kaplan 1998: 16). In the context of the patriarchal society, the Law and the community are convinced of Eleni's guilt: according to the interrogator the motive behind the crime is her 'promiscuous character'; when the two lovers are being taken away by the police in a jeep, screaming village women, internalising and sustaining the patriarchal structure, attack Eleni – and not the rural policeman – with an animalistic urge for the destruction of the evil woman. However, the exposure and destruction of Eleni is not the ideological stance of the film. If film noir is a male fantasy, the story of *Reconstruction*, by contrast, as Angelopoulos has pointed out, 'is told from the perspective of the woman' (Horton [1992] 2001: 86), occasionally also allowing the spectator's gaze to merge with Eleni's subjective point of view (views from windows and from inside the jeep followed by the attacking women). *Reconstruction* is never judgemental about Eleni – 'I will have no one judge me', she cries to her brother – instead sympathising with her. She is not shown as a perpetrator but as a victim herself of a repressive sociopolitical reality, as seen in several films noirs (Grossman 2009: 2). The narrative attempts to shift the focus of interest from the evil of the woman (and of her lover as well) towards the decay of the wider society. As Angelopoulos argued in an interview, 'It is rather [. . .] her environment that is the real murderer, that has murdered her spirit' (Horton 1997b: 108). In a dying village, he explains, and with no possibility of escape from her life, the woman revolts against what she thinks keeps her tied to that miserable life. 'She does not kill because of love', but as a way to escape and free herself (Rafaelides 1969: 24).

At the end of the film Eleni refuses to obey. She is neither exposed by the authorities nor broken and controlled. Eleni performs a double rebellion: first by attacking the interrogator, and later by throwing away the rope she is given to re-enact the murder.[9] The rope, the key murder weapon – *To skoini* [The Rope] was the working title of the film (Angelopoulos 1969) – is transformed from a dark instrumental prop into an emancipatory metaphorical one.[10] Eleni, breathing heavily like an animal, externalising but still controlling her accumulating anger, and being faithful to her own sense of justice – 'nobody is responsible, things happened that way' – throws away all her ties with repressive social rules and the roles reserved for her within patriarchy.

Films noirs commonly take place in urban settings, although there are a notable number set in desolate regions beyond the city (Smith 2011). What *Reconstruction*'s setting – a small and secluded village against a rocky and mountainous landscape – shares with film noir is that it is bleak, inhospitable and extremely claustrophobic. The village has been almost abandoned by the villagers, who have extensively migrated to Germany. With its small, low, grey houses – many of them in ruins – and its narrow streets, this ghost village is built exclusively in stone and is completely absorbed by the surrounding mountains. Dark, barren and enormous, the mountains prevent any escapist view of the horizon while heavy clouds, repressive high-angle shots and the frequent use of the frame to exclude the sky construct a powerful sense of confinement and claustrophobia. *Reconstruction* opens with the road – a transition place – leading to the village. The remoteness and inaccessibility of the village, which seems to exist beyond the borderline of civilisation, is stressed by the old bus being stuck in the mud, and the driver's laborious efforts to make it move in the rain. The whole setting is rainy, misty and muddy, emanating a strong feeling of decay. It is a wild, primordial space, as if it has existed from before the creation of the world, an empty wasteland, a no man's land, a place of exile. The village in *Reconstruction* bears the ancient Greek name Tymphaea, which does not refer to an actual village but metonymically to the whole area of Epirus – and by extension of Greece – where the ancient territory of Tymphaea was located.

Angelopoulos, like Theos, links the national past to the present, using an ancient *topos* as a political metaphor. Angelopoulos implies the degeneration of the place, underscoring a lost bond and an alienating relation with the past.

If in *Kierion* the narrative temporarily escapes to marginal spaces pointing to impoverished slums that recall pre-modern village life, *Reconstruction* allows brief glimpses of the city. The two lovers cross a lake by boat – another crossing of a borderline and an indication of the remoteness of the village – to reach Ioannina, the biggest town in the region. Having left Eleni in a miserable hotel room, the rural policeman, completely alienated and self-absorbed, wanders alone around the city, allowing thus noiresque night-time images to appear on screen: cinemas, hotels, bars, cafés, busy streets and night life. The iconography of the film also includes highways that, however, lead nowhere: the policeman, pretending to be Eleni's husband, takes the bus to Athens, but he never arrives, as he fakes not only his identity but also his journey, and comes back. The road does not lead to a possible escape.

The film is shot in gloomy black-and-white with composition and framing emphasising the claustrophobia of the space, and at the same time connecting characters with their surroundings. The overwhelming presence of the natural setting – its roughness, emptiness and sense of alienation – which functions also as a metaphor of the suffocating sociopolitical context, is highlighted by Angelopoulos's practice of using long shots: he locates the characters in their spatial and sociocultural environment, exposing the organic link between them, so that their repressed desires and desperate actions are contextualised. A telling shot is when at the top of a rocky hill, and next to the abyss, Eleni burns her husband's clothes and suitcase to eliminate any traces of him. As the camera zooms out, it reveals her tiny figure against the immense landscape, surrounded by barren and monumental mountains. The apparently empty and awe-provoking shot, on the one hand, perhaps explains her behaviour, and on the other, becomes a psychic reflection of the woman, powerfully suggesting her entrapment, loneliness, inner emptiness and ethical annihilation, but also, as Bakoyiannopoulos (1981: 40) points out, her physical and psychic strength.

Bordwell (1997: 19) argues that Angelopoulos uses 'architecture to shape the frame space' as a central tactic to handle 'empty' shots. He uses '[r]ecessive diagonals [that] can carve a locale into zones which different characters occupy', a practice that expresses 'division and incommunicability among characters'. Bordwell also states that 'Gates, doors or other features can mark distant figures or incidents as important' (1997: 19). In *Reconstruction*, the use of architecture as well as framing and composition methods not only alienate and highlight but also, like *Kierion*, visually and symbolically confine and entrap the characters. Eleni often appears next to or behind a window, either caged by the window bars, as if in a prison cell, or watching the outdoor space. She is mostly filmed in cramped interiors – especially in her house – and restricting spaces, behind diagonal and other visual obstacles, through doors and windows, framed within the frame, diminished by the volume and the complexity of the surrounding space, which appears fractured and repressive. Low-key night-time scenes, darkened and semi-darkened rooms with shadows falling on the walls, the faces and the bodies of the characters, further add to the general sense of entrapment and dead end.

It has often been pointed out that *Reconstruction* draws on *Salvatore Giuliano* – which is an acknowledged influence on the work of Theos – not only in the mixture of neorealism and film noir aesthetics but also in the fact that it keeps the identity of the person who actually committed the murder unclear (Schütte 2012: 112). Angelopoulos follows the same track as Rosi, oscillating between fiction and authenticity: location shooting in a mountainous setting, non-professional actors, an investigation of a crime through a flashback-structured plot, the observational approach of the camera and emotional distance from the events. Angelopoulos emphasises documentary practices – as previously did Theos – to shift attention to social reality. His approach is not only visual – the documentation of the village itself and the images of Ioannina by night are of particular documentary value – but he also uses audio techniques. In the opening shot of the film he employs a brief informational voiceover – we hear his voice – commenting on the geographical and historical background of Tymphaea and the radical reduction of its population from 1,250 inhabitants in 1939 to 85 in 1965. Since Angelopoulos in the film appears as the head of the group of journalists, his voiceover framing the story is conceived retrospectively as part of the journalistic investigation. Later on, we listen to recorded interviews of villagers, both male and female, that describe migratory experiences. They compare life in Germany and Greece, stressing the poverty and the hardships of village life, while elderly men reflect on the neglect of the countryside. These authentic testimonies of limited opportunities, hard work and lack of choice further contextualise the crime story.

Like *Kierion*, *Reconstruction* follows a 'circular trajectory' (see Koutsourakis 2015: 71–2). The final sequence shot goes back in time to retell the act of the murder, mirroring the first police attempt at its re-enactment after the film's opening credits. Now the camera is positioned outdoors, in front of Eleni's house, observing the events from outside. We witness the same movements of the actors and listen to the same sounds and words from the opposite perspective, but the crime takes place behind the closed door, not allowing visual access to the actual details. Thus at the end of the film the initial problem has not been solved. The unresolved narrative of *Kierion* is primarily concerned with the manipulation of truth, while in the judges' cancellation of the reconstruction of the crime it sees a lost opportunity for uncovering the real events. In Angelopoulos's film, however, although the official reconstruction of the crime does take place, the truth still remains hidden. *Reconstruction* does not care about the private secret of the individual, keeping it wilfully undisclosed, as the real crime is not the one that took place within the privacy of the domestic space but that of the wider sociopolitical structures generating it.

It is precisely the meticulous scrutiny and conscious exposition of the deteriorating sociopolitical and cultural framework, through reworked noir tropes, that make *Kierion* and *Reconstruction* political. Concurrently this redirection of the genre's focus of attention away from 'finding the solution to the initial problem' and towards a range of sociopolitical issues, according to Kovács's perspective (2007: 99), clearly differentiates both films from classical film noir, placing them in the territory of the 'modernist investigation film'.

Notes

1. Eniaia Dimokratiki Aristera [United Democratic Left)].
2. Information from an interview with Theos given to the author in 2004.
3. Ibid.
4. On the deconstruction of narrative coherence through random documentary incidents, see also Gerasis (2006: 29–30).
5. Information from the abovementioned interview with Theos.
6. According to Theos, in the initial soundtrack of the film, jazz music played a more central role (interview with Theos).
7. For further discussions of *Kierion*, see Kolonias et al. (1974); Gerasis (2003–04); Kersanidis (2006a); Anastopoulos (2019).
8. For details of the crime and photographs published in the press of the time, see Ragkos (2010).
9. For further analysis of Eleni's character and her revolt, see Bakoyiannopoulos (1981).
10. For the terms 'instrumental' and 'metaphorical' prop, see Corrigan and White (2012: 72).

References

Anastopoulos, Thanos (2019), '*Kierion*, Dimos Theos, 1968', in Afroditi Nikolaidou and Anna Poupou (eds) (2019), *I hameni leoforos tou ellinikou cinema* [The Lost Highway of Greek Cinema], Athens: Nefeli, pp. 172–83.
Angelopoulos, Theo (1969), *To skoini* [The Rope], script available at General State Archives, Athens, section 'Greek screenplays', 8 August 1969.
Bakoyiannopoulos, Yannis (1981), 'Anaparastasi' [Reconstruction], *Film*, 21, pp. 27–62.
Bordwell, David (1997), 'Modernism, Minimalism, Melancholy: Angelopoulos and Visual Style', in Andrew Horton (ed.), *The Last Modernist: The Films of Theo Angelopoulos*, Wiltshire: Flicks Books, pp. 11–26.
Chalkou, Maria (2008), 'Towards the Creation of "Quality" Greek National Cinema in the 1960s', PhD dissertation, University of Glasgow.
Chalkou, Maria (2015), 'Theo Angelopoulos as Film Critic', in Angelos Koutsourakis and Mark Steven (eds), *The Cinema of Theo Angelopoulos*, Edinburgh: Edinburgh University Press, pp. 23–38.

Chalkou, Maria (2021), '*Ekato ores tou Mai*: Ena rizospastiko, politiko dokimanter kai i apopeira eksafanisis tou apo ti dimosia sfaira' [*100 Hours of May*: A Radical, Political Documentary and the Attempt at its Extinction from the Public Sphere], in Andreas Maratos (ed.), *1821–2021: Mnimes technon – thravsmata istorias* [1821–2021: Memories of Art – Fragments of History], Athens: Nicos Poulantzas Institute and Nisos, pp. 551–68.

Corrigan, Timothy, and White, Patricia (2012), *The Film Experience: An Introduction*, Basingstoke: Bedford/St Martin's.

Fainaru, Dan ([1999] 2001), '. . .And about All the Rest', in Dan Fainaru (ed.), *Theo Angelopoulos: Interviews*, Jackson, MS: University Press of Mississippi, pp. 123–49.

Gerasis, Yiannis (ed.) (2003–04), *Monokeros*, 14, special issue, 'Kierion'.

Gerasis, Yiannis (2006), 'Domiki afstirotita kai poiitiki eleftheria sto ergo tou Dimou Theou' [Structural Austerity and Poetic Freedom in Dimos Theos's Work], in Stavros Kersanidis (ed.), *Dimos Theos*, Athens: Aigokeros, pp. 26–30.

Grossman, Julie (2009), *Rethinking the Femme Fatale in Film Noir*, Basingstoke: Palgrave Macmillan.

Hopf, Florian ([1971] 2001), 'An Elegy for a Land Rotting Away: *Reconstruction*', in Dan Fainaru (ed.), *Theo Angelopoulos: Interviews*, Jackson, MS: University Press of Mississippi, pp. 3–8.

Horton, Andrew ([1992] 2001), 'National Culture and Individual Vision', in Dan Fainaru (ed.), *Theo Angelopoulos: Interviews*, Jackson, MS: University Press of Mississippi, pp. 83–8.

Horton, Andrew (1997a), *The Films of Theo Angelopoulos: A Cinema of Contemplation*, Princeton, NJ: Princeton University Press.

Horton, Andrew (1997b), '"What do our souls seek?": An Interview with Theo Angelopoulos', in Andrew Horton (ed.), *The Last Modernist: The Films of Theo Angelopoulos*, Flicks Books, pp. 96–111.

Kaplan, E. Ann (1998) (ed.), *Women in Film Noir*, London: BFI.

Kersanidis, Stavros (ed.) (2006a), *Dimos Theos*, Athens: Aigokeros.

Kersanidis, Stavros (2006b), 'Mia synentefxi me ton Dimo Theo' [An Interview with Dimos Theos], in Stavros Kersanidis (ed.), *Dimos Theos*, Athens: Aigokeros, pp. 11–14.

Kolonias, Babis, Liappa, Frieda, and Nikolakopoulou, Maria (1974), 'Mia syzitisi me ton Dimo Theo gia tin tainia tou Kierion' [A Conversation with Dimos Theos about his Film *Kierion*), *Synchronos Kinimatografos*, 2–3, pp. 34–41.

Koutsourakis, Angelos (2015), 'The *Gestus* of Showing: Brecht, Tableau, and Early Cinema in Angelopoulos' Political Period (1970–80)', in Angelos Koutsourakis and Mark Steven (eds), *The Cinema of Theo Angelopoulos*, Edinburgh: Edinburgh University Press, pp. 64–79.

Kovács, András Bálint (2007), *Screening Modernism: European Art Cinema, 1950–1980*, Chicago: University of Chicago Press.

Mortenson, Erik (2016), *Ambiguous Borderlands: Shadow Imagery in Cold War American Culture*, Carbondale, IL: Southern Illinois University Press.

Place, Janey (1998), 'Women in Film Noir', in E. Ann Kaplan (ed.), *Women in Film Noir*, London: BFI, pp. 47–68.

Rafaelides, Vassilis (1969), 'Poreia pros to avevaio mellon, mia syzitisi tou Thodorou Angelopoulou me ton Vassili Rafaelidi' [Towards the Uncertain Future, a Conversation between Theo Angelopoulos and Vassilis Rafaelides], *Synchronos Kinimatografos*, 3, pp. 20–9.

Ragkos, Yiannis (2010), 'To ekglima piso apo tin "Anaparastasi"' [The Crime behind 'Reconstruction'], I & II, *Crime and Punishment*, <https://eglima.wordpress.com/2010/02/27/anaparastassi1/> and <https://eglima.wordpress.com/2010/03/06/anaparastassi2/> (last accessed 27 July 2021).

Rentzis, Thanasis (2006), 'I gnorimia mou me ton Dimo Theo' [My Encounter with Dimos Theos], in Stavros Kersanidis (ed.), *Dimos Theos*, Athens: Aigokeros, pp. 72–4.

Rohdie, Sam (2015), *Film Modernism*, Manchester: Manchester University Press.

Smith, Imogen Sara (2011), *In Lonely Places: Film Noir beyond the City*, Jefferson, NC: McFarland.

Schütte, Wolfram (2012), 'Land-surveyor & Time Traveller', in Eirini Stathi (ed.), *Theo Angelopoulos*, 53rd Thessaloniki International Film Festival, pp. 111–18.

Spicer, Andrew (2002), *Film Noir*, Abingdon: Routledge.

Studlar, Gaylyn (2013), '"The Corpse on Reprieve": Film Noir's Cautionary Tales of "Tough Guy" Masculinity', in Andrew Spicer and Helen Hanson (eds), *A Companion to Film Noir*, Malden, MA: Wiley-Blackwell, pp. 369–86.

Wayne, Mike (2001), *Political Film: The Dialectics of Third Cinema*, London: Pluto.

Wilmington, Michael (1997), 'Theo Angelopoulos: Landscapes, Players, Mist', in Andrew Horton (ed.), *The Last Modernist: The Films of Theo Angelopoulos*, Wiltshire: Flicks Books, pp. 57–68.

9. NEO-NOIR AND 'BECOMING-MURDERER' IN TONIA MARKETAKI'S *JOHN THE VIOLENT*

Ioulia Mermigka

Ioannis o Viaios/John the Violent is a 1973 black-and-white film written and directed by the renowned Greek auteur Tonia Marketaki. It was made just before the fall of the Greek junta (1967–74) and in line with the modernist aesthetics and politics of New Greek Cinema. This chapter explores *John the Violent* in the breach between Gilles Deleuze's movement-images and time-images, and attempts to make readable the intersection between the neo-noir aesthetics and the existential and political power of the film. I argue that the neo-noir sensibility of the film lies not in the classic noir presentation, investigation and solution of a crime, but in the multiple fascination with the 'powers of the false' (Deleuze 2005b: 122–50) in crime and cinema. John, the psychologically troubled but charming protagonist, seems to have murdered a woman, as he willingly confesses to the police. While this might or might not be true in the fictional narrative, I will attempt to illustrate how Marketaki undermines narrative verisimilitude and how *John the Violent* is less the story of a psycho-killer and more a neo-noir about the existential and political processes of a becoming-murderer.

The film opens with a crime committed around midnight in a street in Athens: a young woman is stabbed to death by someone who disappears in the dark. During the interrogation of the witnesses by the police, the spectator gets bits of contradictory information about when and how the murder was committed. The witnesses expose in flashbacks and voiceovers different versions of what happened. Then the victim is identified and presented: Eleni worked as an assistant in a woman's underwear shop, and had a fiancé who lived with his mother and sister whom she used to visit and attend on every day. Through police interrogations of Eleni's colleagues, relatives and friends, who are similarly presented through voiceovers and flashbacks, with increasing curiosity we learn about her financial situation, intimate life and sexual habits. In the next few days, parts of this information hit the newspapers, spiced up with rumours and hearsay. The witnesses' and the press's narratives reflect, in a crude way, all the dominant gender and class stereotypes of the time. The filmic strategy of presenting the facts through fragmented narratives and different points of view, often used in noir and neo-noir films, questions from the very beginning the possibility of accessing the truth.

John, an intelligent young man in a fragile psychological state who lives with his grandmother and aunt, is introduced twenty minutes into the film while reading about the crime in the newspaper. He becomes fascinated by the crime and starts fantasising himself as a murderer. It is not clear whether John is imagining being a murderer, or if he really is. The character's transformation takes place in what Marketaki describes in her synopsis of the film as 'the dream-world of cathartic violence' (Kyriakidis 1994: 26). When John confesses that he committed the crime, the police are relieved at finding the criminal, and the press cultivates an obscure fascination with John's psychological profile and intimate life. Despite the efforts of judges, psychiatrists and police officers as they seek the truth, the trial does not answer the question whether John committed the crime or not. In an atmosphere of general relief, he avoids prison and is sentenced to confinement in a psychiatric asylum.

I consider this film a neo-noir and not a mere crime film because John's existential transformation is not conveyed in purely psychological terms, but is shown as being explicitly entangled in the social and cultural semiotic regimes of Greece in the late 1960s and early 1970s. John's 'becoming-murderer' intersects with a series of social and cultural phenomena, such as the repressive police force and the interpersonal culture of suspicion and snitching; the press and the cultivation of fascination with sex crimes and moral panics; the transformation of Athens into an alienating metropolis; the sociocultural regimes of gender, marriage and sexuality; as well as the juridical regimes of truth and judgement regarding crime and madness. Even though conventional neo-noir films are typically made in colour, *John the Violent* is black-and-white. I will attempt to illustrate how this marks out the blackness of John's impulses, the grey uncertainty of his confession and its resonance in a public sphere both shocked and fascinated by the crime, as well as the existential light of choice and becoming, barely visible, against the psychiatric whiteness (Figure 9.1).

In what follows, before I elaborate more closely on a reading of the film, I will present my approach, that is, how I reconsider the auteurist approach of Marketaki, and how I use the Deleuzian cine-semiotic in a neo-noir genre perspective.

Figure 9.1 John (Manolis Logiadis) and an officer (Minas Chatzisavvas) at the police station. Still from *John the Violent*. Greek Film Archive collection.

Auteurism and Neo-Noir's Time-Image

A new generation of Greek film scholars has criticised the auteur canon that for several years has dominated Greek film studies, in that it has neglected genre and has limited the study of New Greek Cinema to a somewhat superficial praise of the 'great Greek auteurs' (Nikolaidou and Poupou 2019: 17). In this context Tonia Marketaki was, and still is, often explicitly acclaimed as a woman auteur. While I understand the feminist political expediency of approaching Marketaki as a woman director, I hold that her work deserves to be studied from other perspectives as well.

In the early 1960s Marketaki managed to study cinema in the male-dominated Parisian IDHEC. Back in Greece, she worked as a film critic (Chalkou 2008: 39, 44) and in 1967 she made her first short film, *O Yannis kai o dromos/John and the Road*. With this short, which Deleuze would call 'a trip/ballad' film (2005a: 213), Marketaki introduced herself as an artist who would comply neither with the junta, nor with a stagnant petty-bourgeois ideology. Shortly afterwards she was arrested for her left-wing views, but she managed to escape and leave Greece in self-exile. Later on, as a militant socialist, she undertook the production of agricultural documentaries for the post-colonial nation-state of Algeria, while in 1971 she returned to Greece because, as she said, she preferred her 'own fascists' (Kyriakidis 1994: 21). Marketaki, controversially, used money from a Ford Foundation grant[1] to produce her first feature film, *John the Violent*, which made a great impact at the Thessaloniki Film Festival in 1973.[2]

While her first two films have male protagonists, both named with the typical Greek name Ioannis/Yannis – a choice that indicates that Marketaki at the time was negotiating the cultural changes in Greek masculinities – her last two films, *I timi tis agapis/The Price of Love* (1984) and *Krystallines nychtes/Crystal Nights* (1992), focus on female protagonists. Especially after the *Price of Love*, a costume drama about the changing position of women at the beginning of the twentieth century, Marketaki was acclaimed as a 'woman auteur'. Against such a classification, in an interview she explicitly said: 'Yes I am a woman . . . a woman director no' (Kyriakidis 1994: 43). However, even today, apart from some recent exceptions (Nikolaidou and Poupou 2019; Mermigka 2015), she is invoked first and foremost as a woman director, and not as an auteur.

In my approach, I will consider seriously Marketaki's assertion, as well as a comment by Deleuze. He notes:

> My ideal, when I write about an author, would be to write nothing that could cause him sadness, or if he is dead, that might make him weep in his grave [. . .] Give back to an author a little of the joy, the energy, the life of love and politics that he knew how to give and invent. (Deleuze and Parnet 1987: 119)

Thus, I will refrain from a one-dimensional woman's perspective to critically engage with Marketaki's radical reworking of neo-noir generic conventions in *John the Violent*. The revision of the politics of authorship through genre considerations can shed new light on the New Greek Cinema and show that art cinema in Greece was in a creative dialogue with popular genres such as noir and neo-noir. Moreover, in the case of *John the Violent*, I will enrich neo-noir approaches with Deleuzian perspectives, as I find them suitable for an analysis that intersects at both the level of images and the level of cultural meanings.

Reconstructing mainly the semiotics of Peirce and the philosophy of Bergson and Nietzsche, Deleuze discerned and elaborated on two major categories of cinematic images, the movement-image and the time-image. In broad terms, the movement-image and its varieties refer to the triumph of realism, the classic narrative cinema and its major genres. The three basic varieties of the movement-image are the perception-image, the affection-image and the action-image, with the latter being dominant in classic narrative cinema. Drawing from psychoanalysis, only in this case among other sub-variants of the affection-image and the action-image, Deleuze invents the impulse-image. Although a thorough presentation of these concepts is beyond the scope of this chapter, it can be said that the narrative and realistic cinema of the movement-image, which is dominated by the action-image, is based on the so-called sensory-motor schema of cinematic perception. The perception of cinematic narrative uses the conventional functions of human perception in general, which is oriented towards action and actuality in order to draw mental conclusions about the plot – about what happened, what will happen and what is happening. It can be argued that for Deleuze, the triumph of narrative realism lies not merely in the fictional representation of reality, but in the sublimation in the cinematic art of this basic human sensory-motor form of perception oriented towards action (Deleuze 2005a).

Without considering the narrative cinema of the movement-image as inferior or extinct, Deleuze argues that the conventional sensory-motor schema of the action/movement-image has been largely surpassed by the emergence of modern cinema's time-image. Starting with Italian neorealism, the movement-image fell into crisis, and afterwards new auteurs and cinematic waves emerged to undermine the narrative of the sensory-motor schema that until then dictated that a film's duration and editing were just the means to the end of a plausible narrative. In other words, a cinema emerged between the cracks of realism, the purpose of which was not to tell plausible stories only with images, but with virtual images, in the sense of time's virtuality and contingency, to audiovisually present and open up stories to the philosophical, political and aesthetic enigmas of time (Deleuze 2005b). If, as Deleuze argues, 'time has always put the notion of truth in crisis' (2005b: 126), the modern cinema of the time-image has been preoccupied with the contestation of truth and, consequently, with its social and cultural representations.

Among the other basic variations of the time-image – such as the crystal, the sheets of past and the peaks of present, which concern the orders of time, that is, the games of simultaneity and coexistence of the past, present and future – the image of the powers of the false concerns the very nature of time, as it is sublimated in cinema, as a force of falsification, creation and metamorphosis. According to Deleuze, the powers of the false do not concern so much the lie, the error or the doubt, but rather how time unites and simultaneously traverses the before and the after instead of separating them. The powers of the false should be conceived as a multiple series of powers that present contingencies and virtualities rather than actualities and closures. That is why, for Deleuze, they should be understood beyond the notions of truth and falsehood, as a multiple processual force of becoming and creation: 'beyond the true or the false, becoming as power of the false' (2005b: 264). Moreover, in the cinema of the powers of the false, artists are not inspired by the quest for realism and truthfulness, but by the will to create and forge their own truths and cinematic becomings (Deleuze 2005b: 122–49, 150, 264).

Deleuze's elaborate philosophical taxonomy has not always rested comfortably alongside more established practices in film studies. The question of genre presents a particular point of tension in this regard. However, there have been efforts by Deleuzian scholars to draw attention to genre and, alongside Deleuze's classification, to expand the understanding of the functionality of generic categories (Conley 2000; Herzog 2012; del Río 2012). Deleuze classified noir within the domain of the action-image, signalling the triumph of narrative realism, verisimilitude and artistic 'will to truth' (Deleuze 2005a: 145; Deleuze 2005b: 142–3). In his diagnosis of the crisis of the action-image, he observed that 'the great genres of cinema, the psycho-social film, the noir, the western, the American comedy, collapse and yet maintain their empty frame' (Deleuze 2005a: 215). It is interesting how del Río interprets Deleuze and contends that noir also put the action-image in crisis: 'the noir genre [is] the specifically American counterpart to Italian neorealism's transitional role in marking a psycho-moral crisis in the post-war period' (del Río 2012: 155). Deleuze did not refer to neo-noir; however, it could be argued that the processes of repetition and differentiation in genre theory (Neale 2000: 165–7), namely the conventions and differentiating creativity of singular works and auteurs, discerned both in noir and neo-noir, could be read as symptoms of a crisis in noir's action-images, and as the emergence of noir's and/or neo-noir's time-images.

In what follows, I will attempt to illustrate how, in *John the Violent*, Marketaki undermines the sensory-motor narrative and brings to the fore a neo-noir version of the cinematic powers of the false. The reading of the film is divided into three parts. In the first, I argue that, from the beginning of the film, the non-conventional flashbacks, the recollection-images in Deleuzian terms, and the multiple use of voiceover in the testimonies serve to undermine a plausible narrative and, at the same time, to provide a neo-noir cinematic tapestry of the contested sociocultural realities of Greece in the early 1970s. In the second part, the character's portrayal is explicated through the varieties of the movement-image, the affection-image and impulse-image, taking into consideration their dynamic qualities and how they lead to John's transformation. Finally, in the third part, John's confession and his trial are read as neither true nor false, but as a neo-noir becoming-murderer in its own right.

A Crime in Athens

As aforementioned, the crime and its investigation are presented through flashbacks, voiceovers and disjunctive editing of sound and image. Marketaki uses these devices not only to undermine the reliability of the police investigation, but also to pull together a neo-noir tapestry linked to the social and cultural dynamics of Greek society of the time. At the beginning of the film, shots of the scene of the crime from the different perspectives of eyewitnesses, sometimes compounded with their off-camera voices reading their typed official testimonies, are flashbacks from their actual oral statements to the police. Their statements are conflicting. For example, some witnesses insist that they are 'absolutely sure' that the victim screamed for help, while others say that the victim remained silent. For Deleuze, the conventional function of the flashback is to go back to the present tense of the narrative action and explain it. Nevertheless, the flashback can also be a recollection-image: it can only insinuate a time-image, rather than be one (Deleuze 2005b: 45–52), and it can also undermine a single explanatory perspective and the reliability of personal memory, as in Kurosawa's *Rashomon* (1950). Marketaki deploys the flashbacks in the latter, more unconventional way, as they do not serve the singular point of view of an investigating character, but are presented as a series of multiple and contrasting points of view of the testifying eyewitnesses. Right from the start, the contradictory and unreliable flashbacks sow the seeds of uncertainty regarding the outcome of the search for the truth about the crime.

Moreover, noir and neo-noir often explore disjunctions in voiceover and flashback structures, a fact that shows that noir undermines classical realism, utilising sound and speech-acts separately from the image (Harris 2003: 12). According to Deleuze, the cinematic image must be grasped intrinsically in its internal relations between sight and sound. With the advent of sound in cinema, human interactions and communication through speech-acts, especially rumour, hearsay and deceit, became not only visible, but also sociologically and culturally legible, while the disjunction of image and sound elevated cinema to its full potential as a double audiovisual art (Deleuze 2005b: 218–19, 21). In this context, another aspect of Marketaki's innovative approach is the way she uses speech, text and music, that is, sound as an image, in its own right.

For example, the official reports that are heard over the flashbacks are in katharevousa, a purist form of modern Greek, which until 1976 was the official written language of Greece, and was used in government, police and judiciary documents, as well as in education and most newspapers. With these linguistic signs, Marketaki signals the policing of politics through language, since katharevousa was used by the conservative status quo to transmit and impose the hegemonic rhetoric of right-wing nationalistic legitimacy and anti-communism in the post-Civil War period, and until the fall of the junta in 1974 (Fragkoudaki 2001).

Between the flashbacks, Marketaki depicts the circulation of rumours about the murder and, by extension, the fascination with it. In a traditional coffee-house, someone spreads the news of a neighbourhood girl who has been stabbed to death, while a group of men rush to the scene of the crime. There, a crowd is gathered, including alerted journalists and photographers. Interestingly, these shots are silent. Then John is introduced, silently reading about the crime in the newspaper; we hear his voiceover reciting the article, and afterwards we see him chatting about it with his grandmother and cousin. Later, the official testimony of a willing woman, keen to present herself as an informant to the police, is heard over her flashback. It is mixed with the sound of a typewriter. The woman states that on the night of the murder she saw the victim with a man and that she recognised her from the photograph in the newspaper.

One of the two occasions when music is heard in the film is just before Eleni's fiancé, detained as a suspect, is confronted by this woman. In the police lock-up, a group of prostitutes sing the rebetiko song 'Nichtose horis feggari' [Night Fell without a Moon], which, before being censored, referred to the imprisoned communists during the Greek Civil War (1944–49) (Kaldaras 2017). In this audiovisual way, Marketaki not only conveys the handling of the case by the police, but also makes legible the police as a repressive state apparatus. Furthermore, she again hints at Greek anti-communism and nationalism, and to what Belantis (2004: 84) refers to as the molecular levels of repression, surveillance and control, such as the eagerness of the citizens to become informants for the police.

As the police investigation continues, more flashbacks/testimonies prevent any conclusion from being drawn, as well as composing an image of the fluctuating social and cultural regimes of gender and sexuality. The fiancé recounts how he had to sell his property and postpone his marriage to Eleni: in order to safeguard the honour of his sister, who got pregnant and had to get married, he needed money for her dowry. Using noir chiaroscuro in nocturnal images of Athens in the flashbacks from the scene of the crime, Marketaki, along with cinematographers Giorgos Arvanitis and Giorgos Panousopoulos, now transposes the narrative high-contrast realism of noir to the observational and documentary-style realism of neo-noir (Conard 2007: 2) (Figure 9.2). The rural area around the family home is filmed in long, low-contrast shots, and the family is shown contemplating, in silent shots, the ruined house that is about to be sold. Using documentary-style images, the film opens up the crime narrative into anthropological layers of marriage rules and strategies. What can be noted on a cultural level is that marital transactions, such as the dowry, should not be considered as traditional customs that survived into the perceived belated modernisation of Greece. As Karapostolis has shown (1993: 105–8), in the moulding regimes of heteronormativity and patriarchy, these marital strategies were functional to the modernisation of Greek society (since they were related to the entry of women into the labour force), urbanisation and more generally the reinvention of tradition in emerging post-war capitalist relations. In her parents' flashbacks, Eleni is presented as performing unpaid housework for her future mother-in-law, while she also has to earn a living and save money for her dowry and marriage.

In a twist, the forensic report confirms that Eleni had sex on the day of the crime. Her fiancé reveals that, at the beginning of their relationship, they had

Figure 9.2 At the police station during the investigation. Still from *John the Violent*. Greek Film Archive collection.

anal sex in order to conform to the premarital virginity rule; he adds that, when they eventually broke the rule, he suspected that Eleni was not a virgin after all, and actually forced her to have a gynaecological examination to prove her virginity. The testimony of a bragging sex partner of Eleni contributes even more to the perception of her as a woman of questionable morality. All this is again filmed in an observational documentary style. On a cultural level, the rule of female chastity is related to religious and moral value-systems, and such issues were often found to be the motive for so-called 'crimes for reasons of honour'. In the post-war period, the Greek orthodox value-system was weakened by the new urban sexual economies and the ambiguous position of women in them. As a reaction to discourses and practices of sexual emancipation, discourses regarding the prevention of vice and the protection of virtue were intensified (Avdela 2002: 183).

The cultural transformations of both sexuality and criminality are also made readable in the film through the discursive, reflexive and audiovisual images of the press. In her research on violence, affects and values in post-Civil War Greece, historian Efi Avdela indexed newspapers from the 1950s and 1960s, observing that the public discourses regarding premeditated interpersonal crimes, related to the anthropological Mediterranean 'code of honour and shame', gradually gave way to discourses on crimes of passion and sexual crimes, linked more to internal migration and an alienating urbanisation. The rhetorical tropes or hegemonic stereotypes of female vice were still in circulation, but were now embedded in moral panics about ogres and lonely psychopath killers (Avdela 2002: 29–44, 232). It is through inclusive neo-noir disjunctions or alternations of sight, voice and text, regarding the representation of the crime in the newspaper, that Marketaki unravels both the fascination with the crime in the public sphere and John's own gradual fascination and transformation. She intersects images of the central Omonoia square, with its newspaper stands and thronging crowds, with images of John silent in his room, reading aloud in voiceover the newspaper reports, spiced up with rumours and hearsay about the victim's 'depraved' sexual life. These observational images radiate a sense of high irony about the stereotypes used in journalistic sensationalism, as well as the complicity of the press in producing affects, namely adjusting the urban surveillance and control mechanisms regarding sociability, gender, sexuality and criminality.

While the audiovisually disjointed flashbacks of the eyewitnesses at the beginning of the film provide a sense of their unreliability and the inaccessibility of the truth of the crime, the flashbacks concerning the victim's life and social circle perform a higher function. Their purpose seems to go beyond the solving of the crime into a neo-noir audiovisual stratigraphy of the social and cultural dynamics of the time. Their function is similar to what Deleuze argues about the flashbacks in *Citizen Kane* (dir. Welles, 1941): they are direct time-images of 'sheets of past', that is images of time independent of action, in which the past is not merely a former present but coexists contemporaneously with the present of Kane's becoming (2005b: 96–114). Moreover, while flashbacks are very common in film noir, more often as explanatory narrative devices, for example in *Killers* (dir. Siodmak, 1946), the flashbacks are fascinating (Harris 2003) less because they unravel the mystery of the murder, and more because they give, from a Deleuzean perspective, a philosophical dimension of a becoming-suicidal.

While a few years earlier, in his debut feature film *Anaparastasi/Reconstruction* (1970), Theo Angelopoulos, using also flashbacks, excavated sheets of past that were still functional in the present of 1970s rural Greece,[3] Marketaki utilises more the neo-noir discontents regarding the urbanisation (Dimendberg 2004) of Athens. The flashbacks about the victim's life serve more as an anatomy of how old value-systems are contested and surpassed despite being still present in the city's life, how old and new stereotypes and crimes are negotiated, and how all these are component series of powers that bring about John's transformation and becoming-murderer. Even though Marketaki approaches John more closely, with the passing from the affection-image to the darker impulse-image, as is argued in the next section, his neo-noir becoming-murderer is not purely subjective.

John

Having presented in the first part of the film a wider social and cultural symptomatology, urban grey zones of indeterminacy and obscure fascination with the crime, Marketaki now offers more detailed images of John. I argue that, although she scans John's psychic black hole, she does not succumb to a psychoanalytic composition of symptom-images of primordial death and sex drives. She uses the varieties of the movement-image, the affection-image and the impulse-image for the higher purpose of traversing his becoming. Almost all Deleuze's images have a dual aspect to them – one aspect towards framing and the other towards editing. The introductory close-ups of John, reading about the crime in the press, show him being affected by its resonance and gradually becoming obsessed with it. Marketaki traverses the intensities of his feelings of both power and powerlessness, while the cinematography becomes darker.

In his dark room, through the closed curtains, John leers at a woman in the opposite window. He attempts to stalk her, but soon gives up. Inspired by the forensic report he has read in the newspaper, he draws female breasts, stabs them and looks at them as they look back at him, like a pair of eyes. He dresses up as Dracula and frightens his nagging grandmother. Seen through the eyes of his cousin, John is portrayed among his cats, his drawings of monsters, books on science, politics, art and occultism. The filmic space of his dark room generates images of John's faces of agony and lust, wherein affects – which according to Deleuze are 'expressive entities in their own right' (2005a: 97) – emerge. John is shaded in bleak tones of fear and repressed sexuality.

These affection-images gradually give way to creeping impulse-images. In Deleuze's psychoanalytic take on the dual aspect of the impulse-image, on the side of framing there are fetishes that, in editing, create impulse-images of symptoms. Death and sexual drives lurk in John's dark room and take hold of him. He becomes obsessed with his knives and increasingly suffers from symptoms caused by his repressed sexuality. With his fetish-knife John cuts his hand, smashes his mirror reflection, and calls the shattered reflection of himself 'a eunuch'. He has sexual hallucinations and dreams of himself trapped in a white void, which enhances the darkness of his impulses.

As aforementioned, the impulse-image is situated between affect and action. John walks the streets of Athens at night engulfed in his desire to kill. He carries his knife around, and looks as though he is challenging himself to step into action. Marketaki, however, once again, reconnects him with the wider social symptomatology. His strangeness attracts the attention of the omnipresent police. He is brought to the police station and, again, through a sound-image, Marketaki points to howls of torture behind a closed door. Torture along with snitching and corruption have always been the police's powers of the false (Deleuze 2004: 03), and Marketaki, with this subtle sound-image, also refers to the methods of the Greek junta.

One of the most insinuating features of Marketaki exiting the psychological domain and summoning the powers of the false of the time-image is when John admits to his cousin that he committed the murder. The confession is more a performative speech-act that allows him a simulation or a fabulation (Deleuze 2005b: 233) of a desired action, than an actual indisputable confession. The strangeness of John's confession is obvious from the way he talks about his supposed deed, and presents his lack of alibi in a small-talk context: he childishly tries to persuade his cousin that he is capable of murder and he even says to her that she does not believe him because she is a virgin. This peculiar confession, however, disturbs the cousin, who talks about it with John's aunt, who is a stage-actress. In a disorienting neo-noir gesture, Marketaki then shows John wandering around at night. In a dark street he attempts to stab a woman, but the headlights of a passing car impede the viewer from seeing him committing the act. When he returns home, the police, called by his aunt, are waiting for him.

Powers of the False, Regimes of Truth and Becoming-Other

While conducting my research, I had the honour of talking with the renowned cineaste Yannis Bakoyiannopoulos, who plays a forensic psychiatrist in the film. When I expressed the opinion that Marketaki, throughout the film, undermines the certainty that John is actually the murderer, Bakoyiannopoulos asserted that there was no doubt about it, and that his generation's fascination with the film came from the portrayal of an actual murderer. Moreover, he argued that things must be so, since Marketaki was inspired by a real-life crime (Ragkos 2018). In what follows, I attempt to highlight the difference between the cinematic image of an actual murderer and the cinematic image of a becoming-murderer, and relate it to Marketaki's reworking of noir conventions towards a more processual neo-noir awareness and sensibility.

For Deleuze, the triumph of the movement/action-image lies in the common-sense perception, where truth is claimed even in fiction (2005b: 123). A major contribution of Deleuze's cine-philosophy is that he demonstrated the struggle in the evolution of cinema over and beyond the ideals of truth, reality and representation. Deleuze's movement-images are governed by sensory-motor schemata, namely by perceptions that, one way or another, must pass into action and a conventional narrative closure. In this vein, *John the Violent*, with its chronological anomalies in the flashbacks, its intervals using affection-images, impulse-images and dream sequences, is prone to be read more as a plausible noir narration. This also cunningly allows a sympathetic identification with the protagonist. John the guilty is only so because of his psychic illness. However, as Deleuze warns, this kind of mental schema, intrinsic to the forms of cinema, makes us complicit with an overall dominant system of judgement, in which the form of the true, even in fiction, being reassuringly unifying for our perception (2005b: 129), prevents us from conceiving the workings of the regimes of truth and judgement.

In my view, the film's heightened neo-noir sensibility contests the truthfulness of fiction, with the presupposition that the spectator disengages from any verdict about John's guilt or innocence, or from any causal truthful conclusion. My aim is not to engage in sophistry about the character's guilt or innocence, or to give John the benefit of the doubt, an approach that would overshadow a proper cinematic analysis, but to cast light on the short-circuiting and breaking of the narrative sensory-motor schema that the film performs. Rather than forming a realist representation, the film constructs a more reflexive type of neo-noir image, inasmuch as it relates thinking to a perception that no longer passes into action (Alliez 2000: 298). Since Marketaki brilliantly avoids any reconstruction image of the crime, the hypothesis that John has committed the murder is as possible as the one that he has not committed it. The strangeness of his confession to his cousin and then his ambiguous testimony to the police and before the court make palpable the emergence of a paradoxical time-image: the possibility that he did it cannot be distinguished from the possibility that he did not, and the two possibilities are fused into one. At one point after his confession to the police, John is interviewed by journalists. One of them is troubled by his willingness to confess, and asks him what he will do if the actual murderer is detected. John replies: 'If he has more proof . . .', a speech-act that shows Marketaki's irony about factual fiction.

Marketaki, along with the editor Giorgos Korras, did not join images for plain narrative integration. Instead, the montage of the film manifests itself as a higher cinematic act, not in the cuts, but as Deleuze argues, in the interstices and re-linkages it creates between images (2005b: 179–81). The film's editing gaps create this paradoxical forking time 'of incompossible presents, returning to not-necessarily true pasts' (Deleuze 2005b: 127). In the film's gaps, the cinematic character of John is neither a liar nor a representation of a psychopath killer, but a cinematic forger of spatio-temporal perceptions (Deleuze 2005b: 128). To the detriment of a truthful narration, the extended and intensive moment of his confession, a time-image that permeates the whole film and reconnects repetitively with the images of a cultural symptomatology, provokes undecidable alternatives and inexplicable differences between the real and the imaginary, as well as between the true and the false. As in Deleuze's powers of the false, these falsifying neo-noir powers of the film tell more than the story of an actual murderer. They illustrate how Marketaki's cine-thinking was related to the philosophical problem of time as a haunting multidimensional, yet singular, contemporaneous and simultaneous virtuality of the past, the present and the future, and overall as a creative power that fuses its partial dimensions into a will for metamorphosis. They illustrate the processes of John's becoming, as entangled in a controversial Nietzschean will to power and will to change.

In the breach between the movement-images of the first part of the film and the signs of becoming in John's confession, the previous affection- and impulse-images, and the subsequent testimony-flashbacks to John's disturbed childhood, lose even more of their spatio-temporal causality, and they become expressive audiovisual rhythms. John's affects, impulses and memories become, in their own right, virtual, that is doubled, chiasmatic and temporal/transversal entities that forward cine-thinking to the indiscernibility and fusion between the real and the imaginary, the true and the false. What is made cinematically perceivable is the paradoxical encompassing moment of the exchange between John's active traumatic memories and sexual and morbid fancies, and the virtuality of actually releasing them, making them real. Thus, his cinematic becoming-murderer is neither an imitation nor a representation, but a transversal presentation running the circuits of actuality and virtuality. Regarding the character in the fiction, he can be, and eventually is, judged leniently for summoning a nihilist and self-destructive will to power, a will to kill that stems from his mental illness and psychic black hole. However, the empathetic and intuitive way Marketaki shades John's becoming, in lucid existential tones beyond a tragic nihilism, as well as the way she makes the onscreen and offscreen audience become fascinated with him, as in the scenes of crowds outside the court waiting for him, raises another ethical issue. If we allow ourselves to tune into the cinematic making of John, we sense his metamorphosis. In order to break out from a petty and ill life, John gathers the powers, albeit nihilist and self-destructive, to transform his life, opening the possibility of becoming-other, becoming-someone, becoming-murderer. In this sense, and in an affirmative Nietzschean vein that indicates a path beyond good and evil, the film takes us beyond judgement. In Deleuze's Nietzschean words: 'it is clear that becoming is always innocent, even in crime, even in the exhausted life in so far as it is still a becoming' (2005b: 137).

However, the non-subjective neo-noir merits of the film lie in how it invites us to reconnect the existential transformation of John to shaky cultural and political regimes of truth. As the film is permeated with the time-image of John's becoming, a series of interstitial images emerge. His becoming-murderer is not purely subjective, but its powers of the false burst through the multiscalar perspective of a series of social powers of the false. The truth in the series of eyewitnesses' testimonies/flashbacks is intrinsically falsified by their different perspectives. The victim had falsified her virginity to conform to marital norms. The press falsifies the truth about her life, so as to cultivate fascination and moral panic. John's aunt hands him over to the police, more as an act of duty within the overall culture of snitching than by persuasion. The police, in fear of being accused of inefficiency, are relieved by his confession. Overall, the transitional political and cultural regimes are permeated with falsifications in order to maintain discipline and control. John is surrounded by people of the truth, who nevertheless falsify it.

The powers of the false become legible in John's trial as well: professionals of truth, judges, prosecutors, attorneys and forensic psychiatrists perform commanding speech-acts, each of them in accordance with the disciplinary intentions of their sciences, their regimes of truth. While Deleuze's philosophy is permeated with Foucault's critical thought about the notion of truth, it can be said that a Foucauldian genealogy of law and its rivalries and synergies – forensic psychiatry, medico-legal judgement and the discursive construction of the abnormal individual (Foucault 2010) – is dramatised in the film. According to the classical notions of natural law and punishment, John is considered a debased freak of nature who, as such, deserves to be punished severely. Representatives of more modern positivist approaches to jurisprudence admit that his motives are incomprehensible; he is thus absolved from responsibility and is sentenced to psychiatric confinement. Before that, in the trial, forensic psychiatrists explicate their truth claims on the crime in relation to questionable modern medical discourses of heredity, instincts, psychopathological sexuality, deviance and the overall indeterminacy of madness. Paraphrasing Deleuze, madness, like time, had always put truth in crisis.

The public prosecutor is a proponent of the classical school of natural law. While John is smiling in the background, the public prosecutor fires utterances at the jury against any expression of mercy. Interestingly employing the powers of the false in arguments about John's forgery, the prosecutor asserts that he is not paranoiac, but an impeccable actor who has inherited his aunt's acting talent and intends to deceive everybody by pretending to be ill. Furthermore, the prosecutor maintains that he is not questioning the science of psychiatry; nevertheless, safeguarding nationalism, he says that the jury's judgement should not be guided by chaotic psychology, but by the vocation of securing, from John's criminal monstrous soul, 'the sublime and heroic Greek society, with its thousands of years of glorious and brilliant history'. The documentary-style, grey-toned cinematography of the trial can now be read as permeated by a stochastic cinematic light that makes visible how and to what extent the system of judgement is traversed by scientific and social powers of the false and how these are fused in John's becoming-murderer.

At the end of the film, Marketaki shows images from the quadrangle and the corridors of a psychiatric asylum, with patients walking in circles. John is filmed in a plain white room, looking out of a window. Against the clinical psychiatric white, an imperceptible light comes in from a radical outside, which also means a radical inside (Deleuze 2005b: 173), and folds out into a close-up of John's face. It is the same stochastic cinematic light that lyrically abstracted John's face from his dark subjective affects and impulses, and illuminated his existential domain of the selection of choice and becoming. It is the observational, but also purely thinking and creative light, with which Marketaki's film has scanned transitional political, juridical and cultural regimes, and has made visible the invisible powers of the false crossing them. This neo-noir stochastic light that permeates the whole film consists not just in showing a portrait of a psycho-killer in Greek society during the junta, but in demonstrating the extent to which pure becoming lies beneath, while evading, the domains of the visible and the spoken.

This chapter has attempted to explicate Marketaki's *John the Violent* as a neo-noir Deleuzian time-image that traverses social, cultural, scientific, as well as existential powers of falsification and, in this sense, makes visible a serial 'becoming-murderer'. The film belongs to a philosophical neo-noir cinema of forging radical Otherness. From an 'outside', which also means immanently within interstices of social and cultural significations and subjectivations, Marketaki creates an image of the Other not in relation to the self, identity and representation, but insofar as this Other refers 'to the existence of a possible world' (Deleuze and Guattari 2004: 24). John appears neither as an idealised murderer nor as a medico-legal case study but, within the images of social and cultural dynamics, as the temporal/transversal possibility of a frightening world, uncannily familiar and charming. The artistic value of the film, then, lies not just in reflecting the historical psycho-social and moral crisis of Greek society, but in its self-contained, temporal/transversal neo-noir cinematic expression both of becoming and of radical Otherness.

Notes

1. Marketaki rejoined the radical cineastes of the journal *Synchronos Kinimatografos* [Contemporary Cinema], who criticised commercial cinema and censorship while trying to bring cinephilia and auteur cinema to Greece (Chalkou 2008: 63–99). The Ford Foundation grant – something that was considered 'dirty' American money – that chief editor Rafaelidis received to support the journal and the work of young filmmakers ignited furious debates among the left-wing radicals (Karalis 2012: 160).
2. The film won the award for best direction, screenplay and male lead. From 1969 to 1975 Thessaloniki Film Festival became the major platform for dedicated cinephiles to promote their cultural politics, using cinema as a political weapon.
3. The film *Di'asimanton aformin/The Reason Why* (dir. Psarras, 1974) is also worth mentioning for its flashbacks, which reveal that the real reasons behind a crime lie in the cooperative tobacco workers' movement in northern Greece of the 1950s.

References

Alliez, Éric (2000), 'Midday, Midnight: The Emergence of Cine-Thinking', in Gregory Flaxman (ed.), *The Brain is the Screen*, Minneapolis, MN: University of Minnesota Press, pp. 293–303.

Avdela, Efi (2002), *Dia logous timis: Via, synaisthimata kai axies sti metemfyliaki Ellada* [For Reasons of Honour: Violence, Emotions and Values in Post-Civil War Greece], Athens: Nefeli.

Belantis, Dimitris (2004), *Anazitontas ton esoteriko ehthro. Diastaseis tis antitromokratikis politikis* [Seeking the Enemy Within: Dimensions of Anti-terrorist Policy], Athens: Proskinio.

Chalkou, Maria (2008), 'Towards the Creation of "Quality" Greek National Cinema in the 1960s', PhD dissertation, University of Glasgow.
Conard, Mark T. (ed.) (2007), *The Philosophy of Neo-Noir*, Lexington, KY: University of Kentucky Press.
Conley, Tom (2000), 'Noir in the Red and the Nineties in the Black', in Wheeler W. Dixon (ed.), *Film Genre 2000*, Albany, NY: SUNY Press, pp. 193–210.
Deleuze, Gilles (2004), 'The Philosophy of Crime Novels', in Gilles Deleuze, *Desert Islands and Other Texts, 1953–1974*, Los Angeles: Semiotexte, pp. 81–6.
Deleuze, Gilles (2005a), *Cinema 1. The Movement-Image*, London: Continuum.
Deleuze, Gilles (2005b), *Cinema 2. The Time-Image*, London: Continuum.
Deleuze, Gilles, and Guattari, Felix (2004), *What is Philosophy*, Athens: Kalentis.
Deleuze, Gilles, and Parnet, Claire (1987), *Dialogues*, New York: Columbia University Press.
del Río, Elena (2012), 'Feminine Energies, or the Outside of Noir', in David Martin-Jones and William Brown (eds), *Deleuze and Film*, Edinburgh: Edinburgh University Press, pp. 155–72.
Dimendberg, Edward (2004), *Film Noir and the Spaces of Modernity*, Cambridge, MA: Harvard University Press.
Foucault, Michel (2010), *I mi kanoniki: Paradoseis sto Kollegio tis Gallias, 1974–1975* [Abnormal: Lectures at the College de France, 1974–1975], Athens: Estia.
Fragkoudaki, Anna (2001), *I glossa kai to ethnos, 1880–1980* [Language and the Nation 1880–1980], Athens: Alexandria.
Harris, Oliver (2003), 'Film Noir Fascination: Outside History, but Historically So', *Cinema Journal*, 43:1, pp. 3–24.
Herzog, Amy (2012), 'Fictions of the Imagination: Habit, Genre and the Powers of the False', in David Martin-Jones and William Brown (eds), *Deleuze and Film*, Edinburgh: Edinburgh University Press, pp. 137–54.
Kaldaras, Apostolos (2017), 'Nychtose kai sto Yedi to skotadi einai vathy' [Night Falls and in Yedi the Dark is Deep], <https://www.imerodromos.gr/ap-kaldaras-nychtose-kai-sto-genti-to-skotadi-ine-vathy/> (last accessed 8 September 2021).
Karalis, Vrasidas (2012), *A History of Greek Cinema*, London: Continuum.
Karapostolis, Vasilis (1993), *Katanalotiki symperifora stin Elliniki koinonia, 1960–1975* [Consumerist Behaviour in Greek Society, 1960–1975], Athens: EKKE.
Kyriakidis, Achilleas (1994), *Tonia Marketaki*, Thessaloniki: 35th Thessaloniki International Film Festival.
Mermigka, Ioulia (2015), '*Ioannis o Viaios* kai I kinimatografiki michani tis Tonias Marketaki' [*John the Violent* and Tonia Marketaki's Cinematic Machine], in Maria Komninos and Myrto Rigou (eds), *Oi politikes tis eikonas* [Politics of the Image], Athens: Papazisis, pp. 109–26.
Neale, Stephen (2000), 'Questions of Genre', in Robert Stam and Toby Miller (eds), *Film and Theory. An Anthology*, Oxford: Blackwell, pp. 157–98.
Nikolaidou, Afroditi, and Poupou, Anna (eds) (2019), *I hameni leoforos tou ellinikou cinema* [The Lost Highway of Greek Cinema], Athens: Nefeli.
Ragkos, Yiannis (2018), 'Alithina egklimata ston elliniko kinimatografo: apo ta proto-selida sti skoteini aithousa' [Real Crimes in Greek Cinema: From News Headlines to the Dark Hall], *Polar*, 1, 93–7.

10. THE UNBEARABLE QUEERNESS OF *SINGAPORE SLING*: TOWARDS A QUEER ETHICS AND POLITICS OF IRONY

Marios Psaras

Introduction to an Obscene Homage

Nikos Nikolaidis's uncompromising *Singapore Sling* (1990) opens to the violent sounds of a thunderstorm. 'Marni Film' appears against a black background, before giving way to a black-and-white shot of torrential rain flooding some low-lit steps, among heavy vegetation. A version of the well-known musical theme from Otto Preminger's *Laura* (1944) slowly fades in. The film's title appears, followed by the production year, which is inscribed at the bottom left, next to the copyright credits, if only to remind us that what we are about to watch is not Preminger, but a rather perverted version of the Austrian-American director's classic noir. In the next shot – a beautiful close-up of a small stream pouring out of a brick wall in the rain – the subtitle of the film appears in Greek, reading: 'The Man Who Loved a Corpse'. In no more than two shots, Nikolaidis introduces his audience to his film's cynical, twisted yet visually sophisticated tone, mood and feel.

The rest of the title sequence is a series of similar, sharply contrasted, black-and-white shots of heavy rain falling on rich vegetation. The lyricism of the wet landscape is awkwardly disturbed by the spectacle of two women, Mother (Michelle Valley) and Daughter (Meredyth Herold), struggling to dig a pit in the ground, dressed in heavy raincoats over baroque lingerie that leaves little to the imagination, as their private parts are generously exposed. Before things get too parodic with the two semi-naked women digging in the mud, the orchestral strings of the *Laura* theme give way to a jazzier tune; the film crossfades to a shot of a man lying on the ground, dressed in a raincoat: the Detective (Panos Thanassoulis). Between close-ups of his bleeding hand, his exhausted face and the relentless rain falling heavily on bodies and surfaces, the man starts to narrate his fruitless endeavour to investigate the case of a missing girl named Laura, in a quasi-lyrical voiceover. With his shoulder wounded by a bullet, the Detective slowly crawls to reach an old-fashioned car parked nearby; he manages to pull his body into the back seat in an effort to hide himself from the odd women who, unruffled, pull the corpse of their chauffeur from behind the bushes – as the Daughter suggestively confesses to the camera – in order to bury it. The women's criminal action is infused with slapstick moments that verge on the parodic, culminating in the Mother being hit on the head by the shovel she was holding, and her falling into the chauffeur's makeshift grave.

The above opening sequence is only a mild introduction to a series of extraordinary visual assaults on the unsuspicious viewer who is unacquainted with Nikolaidis's oeuvre: Mother and Daughter capture the unnamed Detective and subject him to torture and extreme, kinky sex, including vomiting, urination and bondage. They also engage in incestuous intercourse and re-enactments of murderous acts, which they claim to have committed in the past. One of their victims was presumably Laura (a direct allusion to the film's eponymous primary intertext), the object of the Detective's affection and investigation. Daughter impersonates Laura to get closer to the Detective and conspires with him to kill Mother, thus escaping her asphyxiating authority. After the murder, the sexual games and re-enactments continue between Daughter and the Detective, with the latter being assigned the role of Mother. However, in one such re-enactment the Detective replaces a dildo (or penis) with a knife, thus killing Daughter and taking revenge for Laura's murder. Before she dies, Daughter manages to shoot the Detective, who makes his way to the garden and buries himself alive in a grave he had previously dug.

Nikos Nikolaidis's masterfully shot *Singapore Sling* pays a rather obscene, if not scandalous, homage to the American genre of film noir, voicing out, or better, over-visualising its unconscious or coded desires. Pairing an extensive use of noir techniques and style with outrageous characters and a plot filled with kinky sex, incest and torture, Nikolaidis makes palpable noir's queerness in the most irreverent and campy fashion. Most importantly, as I argue in this chapter, Nikolaidis's ironic deployment of filmic techniques and strategies from noir's opulent repository of excessive style to construct ultra-glamorised images of sexualised violence and disgust is ultimately an ethical enterprise. Stretching the limits of the socially acceptable and the representable on screen, *Singapore Sling* emerges as a violent exercise in queer textuality and cinematic irony that challenges the ethics and politics of mainstream representation and, most crucially, raises questions about spectatorial affect, voyeurism and ethics.

The Limited and Limiting Reception of *Singapore Sling*

Singapore Sling was the fifth feature film by the Greek cult auteur. He co-produced it with the Greek Film Centre, and it is considered his magnum opus, having received six major awards at the Thessaloniki Film Festival in 1990, a home-video release in North America and significant critical attention, both at home and abroad. Since its premiere and release the film has divided critics and audiences alike, with reactions ranging from awe to disgust. These reactions are due to the film's subversive content, unconventional form and excessive style, which conjure up exploitation sensations such as Curt McDowell's *Thundercrack!* (1975) and John Waters' *Pink Flamingos* (1972).

Although almost unanimously praising 'Aris Stavrou's pristine black-and-white noir-styled cinematography',[1] critics and reviewers describe the film variously as 'a near-masterpiece of art/trash cinema [. . .] a crazy, perverted, taboo-filled slice of bizarro, and at the same time a beautifully shot, perfectly acted gem of a movie',[2] 'a mix of classic noir and niche pornography',[3] which 'oozes style in equal proportion to perversion'.[4] The less generous talk about a film that is 'riotous and repellent in equal measure'.[5] Commenting on the text's mixed reception, Nikolaidis himself has confessed:

> When I was shooting *Singapore Sling*, I was under the impression that I was making a comedy with elements taken from Ancient Greek Tragedy . . . Later, when some European and American critics characterized it as 'one of the most disturbing films of all times' [*sic*], I started to feel that something was wrong with me. Then, when British censors banned its release in England, I finally realized that something is wrong with all of us.[6]

Though certainly filled with atrocious scenes and abject images that are challenging to watch, what is largely missed by most reviewers' accounts is the layered texture behind those images that bears witness to the film's self-conscious intertextuality and self-reflexive character (Figure 10.1). These latter elements, in my view, comfortably position Nikolaidis among a celebrated rank of radical auteurs of postmodernism, the likes of Pedro Almodóvar, David Lynch and Lars Von Trier. As Greek film scholar Mikela Fotiou notes,

> Nikos Nikolaidis is a postmodern *auteur* with a controversial body of work [. . .] influenced by popular culture and especially by the classic film noir of the 1940s and 1950s. A great cinephile, Nikolaidis creates pastiche films that are intertexts of a combination of genres, styles, modes and original films. (2017: 343)

Figure 10.1 Mother (Michelle Valley) and Daughter (Meredyth Herold) plotting over the unconscious body of the Detective (Panos Thanassoulis). Digital still from *Singapore Sling*.

Referring specifically to *Singapore Sling*'s intertextuality, film historian Vrasidas Karalis astutely observes that

> Nikolaidis created a palimpsest of cinematic references, from Gene Tierney to Sylvia Kristel, from Otto Preminger to Marco Ferreri, from Nagisa Oshima to Louis Buñuel, with underlying philosophical discourses on eroticism, necrophilia, perversion, and the 'divine filth' by Georges Bataille, and the sublime immorality of the Marquis de Sade. (2012: 228)

Singapore Sling's noir atmosphere is infused with elements from gothic horror, comedy and Greek drama, which make Fotiou identify the film as an exemplary case of pastiche cinema. However, Fotiou does not use the term here in the way Fredric Jameson conceptualises it, that is, as uncritical, ahistorical and apolitical, 'a random cannibalization of all the styles of the past' (Jameson 1991: 18), which, limited to a nostalgic recreation of the style and image of the original lived history, 'displaces "real" history', to use his own words (1991: 20). Instead, Fotiou proposes *Singapore Sling* as 'a pasticcio of pastiches', using a term formulated by Richard Dyer to describe films characterised by 'a combination of pastiches which comprise elements that might at first seem incompatible (elements from different genres, modes, etc.) and which are preserved separate and intact in the new piece of work' (Dyer 2007: 126). As Fotiou argues, Nikolaidis's film 'renders genres and styles "repositories of situations" from where he borrows, imitates and combines elements that express his narrative and his ideology' (2017: 347). According to Fotiou, 'combination and imitation are paramount in Nikolaidis's work', as he critically chooses elements from different genres and films to make 'a new film with a different meaning' (2017: 348). In this sense, on the one hand, *Singapore Sling*'s sustained focus on noir style reveals the director's nostalgia for the genre, while, on the other, the 'overall excessiveness, extravagance and extremity that the pasticcio of pastiches grants Nikolaidis' creates a space for two types of sociopolitical critique (Fotiou 2017: 355). As Fotiou explains, the first is an attack on the corrupt Greek upper class, achieved through the controversial representation of the two female protagonists whose perverse lust for control and power 'symbolize[s] the respective authoritative control over the citizens in modern societies' (2017: 355). The second is a meta-cinematic comment on the decline of cinema and filmgoing in Greece in the early 1990s, due to the domination of TV, implied through the director's refusal to produce a commercial film, but rather insisting on 'perpetuat[ing] his cinematic style' (Fotiou 2017: 355).

The Thin Veil of Nostalgia

Nikolaidis's nostalgia for classical noir is evident throughout the film at the levels of form, style and narrative. The references to narratives and characters from celebrated noir films, such as Preminger's *Laura* and Billy Wilder's *Sunset Boulevard* (1950), are aptly identified by Fotiou, as are the formal and stylistic allusions to the genre, including the flashback trope, the use of voiceover, and the black-and-white cinematography with extensive use of chiaroscuro. However, Nikolaidis's film is also a playful nod to the subversive iconography of the pre-Code era of the 1920s and 1930s that saw directors such as Stroheim and Sternberg experiment with genres such as horror and gothic, testing the limits of the representable on screen. Nikolaidis arguably draws from these early cinematic traditions of aesthetic, affective and sexual excess, pushing their boundaries to extreme ends, if only to suggest noir's own veiled campiness and, through it, its meticulously disguised queerness. Camp is understood here both in Sontag's (1964) original formulation of the term as the ironic excess that exposes cinematic artificiality, and in Cleto's (1999) queer reconfiguration of the particular style as deconstructive of gender and sexuality.[7]

In a characteristic scene halfway through the film, the three characters are in the mansion's dungeon, trying to put together the pieces of Laura's story. Mother starts to narrate the mysterious disappearance of Laura, which initiated the

Detective's involvement in the case. Dressed in black transparent lingerie, complete with a sumptuous headpiece with netting and a long, black veil, Mother narrates Laura's story with unparalleled solemnity; her excessive make-up highlights her piercing gaze, which is directed towards the camera. The carefully crafted frame is pointedly divided in half, with Mother occupying the left-hand side in medium shot, and Daughter in the background, in soft focus, dressed as Laura, and hanging on a saltire cross – a strong reference to BDSM practices. Elaborate medium shots of Daughter/Laura – who at times interrupts the narration – and of the frail, tortured Detective, complete the overly staged scene. As the voiceover narration continues, the film cuts to the bathroom, where Mother and Daughter – now dressed in white gowns with fetish leather details – put the passed-out Detective in the bathtub. Mother turns again to the camera, continuing the storytelling, before eventually giving way to Daughter, who takes over the narration with grace and delight, as if she were narrating the most joyous love story, while disregarding the awoken Detective's futile attempts to escape.

Clearly, the scene described above is only one example of how *Singapore Sling*'s nostalgic tone is compromised by the excessive baroque and gothic aesthetic of the props and costumes, the self-consciously overacted performances and repeated re-enactments, the self-reflexive direct camera address and, of course, the unapologetically obscene and gory imagery. Nikolaidis's nostalgic love for the genre is evident throughout the film; yet, rather than a cherry-picking process of combination and imitation towards the end-product of a new, different meaning, what we end up with is an all-encompassing exercise in irony and irreverence. The Greek auteur is, indeed, being both critical and political in his film; however, his politics are not contained within representation, but rather positioned against it. In effect, *Singapore Sling* is as much a celebration of noir as it is a trenchant queer critique of mainstream cinema's canonical mode of representation, and the spectatorial tradition it has engendered; the film essentially constitutes an ironic critique of a rather closeted voyeurism that has required its own responsibility for the production and reproduction of glamorised images of sex, gore and violence to remain covert.

Irony or Beyond Representation

Having buried the chauffeur, Daughter addresses the camera to narrate to the audience the first crime she and Mother committed together: namely, Laura's murder. Here we have yet another nod to a noir trademark, as Daughter is an unreliable (first-person) narrator. Framed in medium shot, and almost romantically lit, Daughter enjoys the comfort of the living room's armchair; unperturbed by the menacing sound of the wind blowing outside, she is rather focused on her storytelling, which she conducts in a calm, nostalgic tone, half naïve and half eerie, yet always impassive. While explaining how she and Mother re-enact the crime scenes in their so-called 'games', the film cuts to a flashback of such a re-enactment. A low-key long shot shows Daughter dressed as Laura, walking down a dark corridor, carrying a suitcase; on the right side of the frame, white curtains are being blown by the wind, in classic noir fashion. In the next shot, Daughter/Laura enters the living room and approaches the lady of the house, namely Mother, who is sitting in an armchair with her back turned to the camera, thus completing a supposedly suspenseful setup. As the voiceover gives way to a conversation between the two women, Mother is revealed in a flaunting medium shot that underscores her elaborate costume: yet another extravagant headpiece and matching jewellery, a fine silk dress underneath a robe with feathered trimmings, and leather gloves. The exchange between Mother and Daughter is often interrupted by Mother's unexplained spasms and French speaking, as well as by Daughter's pretended reticence, before Mother makes a signal to Daughter to come closer and all hell breaks loose. Daughter is made to kneel and perform fellatio on the strap-on dildo that Mother was hiding under her dress. The phallic Mother then turns the young woman around, pulls down her undergarments, and starts penetrating her from behind. Daughter recites the house's rules, while enjoying what must have been Laura's rape. Mother then gags Daughter, and forces her to the kitchen, where she assaults her with a large knife. The kitchen sink and worktop fill with what look like human organs, which the two women decorate with pearls and other pieces of expensive jewellery; all this to the accompaniment of Rachmaninov's Piano Concerto No. 3.

The film cuts back to the original armchair scene of the narration, as Daughter continues to recount her memories to the camera, this time reminiscing about the moment when her father took her virginity. Replete with chains, racks with candles, nets and white sheets hanging from the ceiling, the house's dungeon accommodates what could have been one of the film's most disconcerting moments: the re-enactment of child molestation. Yet the scene is filled with black humour, as Daughter narrates her experience to the camera, while indulging in being slammed from behind by a mummy, the strong wind blowing open the door and throwing leaves in their faces.

The above scenes gloriously serve as paradigms of how Nikolaidis skilfully deploys a consistently obscene content, an eclectically excessive style and a defiantly direct mode of address in the service of an unconditionally and unapologetically performative, non-representational logic; essentially, the matter of irony. The film defies realism at every turn, forestalling the canonical operations of characterisation, and blocking the long-established pleasures of identification and narrative immersion. Karalis accordingly observes:

> Throughout [his] career [Nikolaidis] shaped new forms of oppositional aesthetics that were to disrupt the post-Restoration optimism about what

constituted cinematic language and the role of cinema in contemporary societies. More importantly, [. . . he] 'problematised' the dominant narrative about reality by constructing 'non-logical' narrative idioms, permeated by the surrealist 'marvellous' and by a special concern for non-linear forms of representation. (2012: 174)

Clearly, *Singapore Sling* was not Nikolaidis's first or last attempt at experimenting with noir; one should mention here *Tha se do stin kolasi agapi mou/See You in Hell, My Darling* (1999), *O chamenos ta pairnei ola/The Loser Takes It All* (2002) or the more imaginative mix of sci-fi and noir *Proini peripolos/Morning Patrol* (1987). However, what makes *Singapore Sling* stand out is precisely the exorbitance and distortion of the noir space that corresponds to an ample narrative leakage, where filmic time is looped, loosened or intensified, at all times wasted and perished. As a result of such an idiosyncratic spatio-temporal construction, the possibility of reading the film as a sociopolitical commentary on corruption and authority becomes thinner; Nikolaidis's critical and political preoccupations can hardly be exhausted within representation when its means are severed and its rhetoric defied. The film's opulent 'excessiveness' and 'extravagance', to use Fotiou's words (2017: 354), more than a pasticcio of pastiches, envelop it with a queer sensibility that, as is evident in the above scenes, encompasses the camp and the parodic. Ultimately, irony emerges as the film's primary mode of address. And irony becomes the primary analytical lens for any exploration of Nikolaidis's film and filmic politics. In relation to irony, Paul de Man notes:

> [w]ords have a way of saying things which are not at all what you want them to say [. . .] There is a machine there, a text machine, an implacable determination and a total arbitrariness [. . .] which inhabits words on the level of the play of the signifier, which undoes any narrative consistency of lines, and which undoes the reflexive and dialectical model, both of which are, as you know, the basis of any narration. (1996: 181)

Departing from reflection and the dialectical unfolding of events, the effect of irony resembles the syntactical violence of anacoluthon, de Man explains (1996: 178). In this way, by breaking the narrative chain of events, the mindless violence of the machine that irony is exposes the meaningless machinery of the Signifier and severs the continuity that is essential to the very logic of making sense. In other words, the elaborated reflexive technique of irony attacks the very structure of representation – if not intelligibility itself – by compromising the linear and coherent construction of the consistent representational spatio-temporality on which narrativity relies to produce meaning.

Accordingly, if we were to replace 'words' with 'images' and 'lines' with 'sequences' in de Man's thought, we could draw a theory of film irony that would enable us to understand Nikolaidis's mode of address. As is evident in the scenes analysed above, *Singapore Sling* reveals itself as an exemplary case of ironic, non-representational cinema. This is achieved not only through the arbitrary narrative leaks engendered by episodic re-enactments and performative acts of sexual and physical abuse, which are repeated without recourse to meaning. Most importantly, the film's ironic mode is made manifest in the way conventional form is disturbed by an entire apparatus of self-reflexive film techniques evident in the excessive compositions, editing, performances, costumes and framing. As I explain below, this defiance of the mainstream narrative tradition of meaning-making, this deconstruction and, ultimately, thwarting of representation through irony, serves a broader meta-cinematic concern that turns the spotlight not on what is happening in front of the camera, but rather on what happens in front of the screen; it is an ethical inquiry into the unnamed and unchecked vices of spectatorship. Indeed, the film refuses to represent, or to produce (a new) meaning. It rather provokes and attacks.

The Queer Architecture of Noir

The defiance of representation that infuses the rhetoric of Nikolaidis's ironic take on noir interestingly mirrors the epistemological anxieties that enveloped the era from which noir emerged, and to which it responded. Critic Alain Silver identifies 'the loss of meaning, the end of representation [. . .] at the end of noir's corridor' (Silver and Ursini 1999: 127). A spatial framing of unintelligibility in relation to noir landscape is of great use to us here, as it throws light on the possibility of reading Nikolaidis's deployment of noir aesthetics in this film beyond the (reductive) scope of nostalgia and, rather, as an ideal formal and aesthetic landscape to accommodate a sinister reframing of the viewers' implication in traditions of onscreen violence and suffering.

Silver writes that 'in a very tangible way, [noir's] landscape and cityscape defy the spectator to anticipate them, draw emotional impact but resist systematic interpretation' (Silver and Ursini 1999: 127). As Kelly and Trigo explain, the confusion is caused not by 'a dearth of symbols to interpret, of signs to follow, but by its very opposite' (2003: 214). The excess of spatial symbols and allegories in noir produces a hyper-demarcation of filmic space that, according to Kelly and Trigo, alludes to Freud's eternal city in *Civilization and its Discontents*, this apt representation of the impossibility of mapping out the mind, of the failure of representation itself. As Kelly and Trigo put it, '[i]t is the plethora of walls in Freud's eternal city that makes it an absurd, unimaginable, unrepresentable image. There is a direct correlation between the superimposing walls, or the continuous stratification of the psychic apparatus, and loss of meaning' (2003: 214).

If nothing else, *Singapore Sling* is characterised by an excess of space, reflected in a cornucopia of signifiers spread over large rooms and corridors,

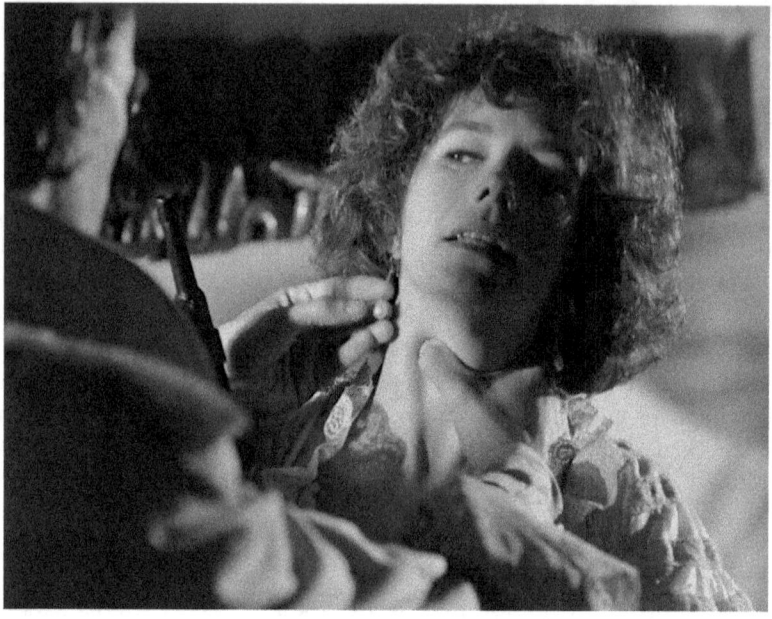

Figure 10.2 The Detective and Daughter. Digital still from *Singapore Sling*.

filled with baroque furniture, curtains, textiles, plants and random objects that appear and withdraw from the frame, without narrative significance or coherent links to characterisation; an opulent yet claustrophobic space, at times poorly lit, at others blinding to watch (Figure 10.2). The film's architecture constructs an utterly absurd space, resisting cartography, coherence or identity, and, indeed, meaning; it thus mirrors the depthlessness of characterisation that dominates the film, and the failure to map out or stratify the labyrinthine psyches and minds of the protagonists.

As Kelly and Trigo suggest, architecture and geography are yet another sign, alongside camerawork, sound and narrative structure, of the film noir's staging of the 'unstable and paradoxical process of identity formation' (2003: 212). As they argue, 'in film noir, identity is formed, consolidated, or fortified against unconscious threats' by 'mechanisms such as displacement, condensation, repression, matricide, and uncanny doubling' (2003: 211). Nevertheless, as the two scholars highlight, the very mechanisms that consolidate identity, and protect it from the threats posed by 'ambiguous borders', are the ones that at once empty identity of meaning, creating holes and gaps, and producing 'the anxiety that haunts film noir [. . . in] the form of vertigo, phobia, melancholia, abulia, or fatalism' (2003: 211). Similarly in *Singapore Sling* one is tempted to focus on the body of Daughter: trapped in an absurd universe of excessive signification that blurs borders and identities, and haunted by corpses, ghosts and perverse desires, this body soon emerges as the vessel for a fractured and fragmented subjectivity. Unable or unwilling to resist or manage the threats posed by what Kelly and Trigo describe as 'ambiguous borders', Daughter rather embraces them, surrendering to the unbearable queerness of her experience, and of the film that constructs it. And queerness is no stranger to noir.

As Richard Dyer argues (2004: 100), film noir was characterised by an unmatched (by the standards of the classical Hollywood era) un-American pessimism, which reflected the epistemological and sociopolitical ambivalences of the post-war era through confusing images, storytelling and characters. Such threatening, ambiguous borders invariably produce noir's primary affective mode: uncertainty. According to Dyer, queerness was one of the major tropes in the performance of uncertainty in film noir. A great number of queer characters paraded in the deceptive and disorienting universe of noir cinema, from Waldo Lydeker in *Laura* to Mrs Danvers in *Rebecca* (dir. Hitchcock, 1940). Clearly, under the infamous Production Code, sexual practices could not be named, let alone screened. Therefore, homosexuality could only be implied through visual indicators that the producers of noir films considered queer, and ones that, presumably, viewers would decode as queer. This practice thus relied on shameless stereotyping and the ignorant erasure of the distinction between gender and sexuality. 'Un-masculine' or 'un-feminine' – under heteronormative standards – gender expressions, achieved through dress, gesture and personality traits, were applied to suggest the homosexuality of characters who, nonetheless, more often than not also appeared as married. As Dyer explains, 'by referencing gender misfit rather than sexual practice [. . .] it's not surprising that these stereotypes generate uncertainty even as they attempt to produce certainty' in relation to the uncontested sexuality of the straight male protagonist (2004: 94). Implication and connotation, rather than explicitness, were not simply noir's way of avoiding censorship, but one of the central strategies underpinning its 'endemic epistemological uncertainty', as Dyer puts it (2004: 101). Queers served this strategy by constituting 'a disturbance in knowledge', that is, by unsettling 'the process of knowing that drives the narrative and contribut[ing] to the experience of not knowing that is such a characteristic flavour of noir' (2004: 101).

A Queer Noir *par excellence*

Singapore Sling does not simply allude to classical noir's ubiquitous yet closeted queerness. Nikolaidis's almost parodic take on sexuality, and his unrepentant emphasis on sexual aggression and perversion through narrative and visual explicitness, function in a somewhat homeopathic way to make palpable what had been previously repressed or suppressed. His narrative and characters' uninhibited and unchallenged embracing of queerness defies and surpasses the genre's structural affect, which is uncertainty. Nikolaidou and Alexiou observe that the modern world of lifestyle, mass media and consumerism in Preminger's *Laura* evolves here into 'a nightmarish, secluded, confining domestic space of incestuous relationships, scatological desires, repetitions and hypocritical swirls that move away from the absolute economy of emotion to a hysterical disarticulation of bodies' (2019: 154).[8] Indeed, Nikolaidis not only preserves the labyrinthine structure of Preminger's universe, but turns it upside down to expose and celebrate its previously latent queerness and, significantly, to expose and celebrate the failure of the established regimes of meaning-making, of representation itself, as per postmodernism's inductions.

Such embracing of the failure of representation and loss of meaning feature as characteristic elements of a queer textuality, according to Teresa de Lauretis. Queer, she writes, is 'a text of fiction – be it literary or audiovisual – that not only works against narrativity, the generic pressure of all narrative toward closure and the fulfilment of meaning, but also pointedly disrupts the referentiality of language and the referentiality of images' (2011: 244). As analysed above, *Singapore Sling* constitutes, indeed, a repository of ironic assaults on meaningful cinematic space and time. Nevertheless, one should be wary before rushing to assume that any noir film – or any film, for that matter, that raises meaninglessness as a possibility – is necessarily queer, based simply on the uncertainty produced at the level of either form or content, or the lack of referentiality. For, apart from the aesthetic challenges posed to intelligibility, de Lauretis adds another 'not sufficient but necessary specification' for queer textuality: 'a queer text carries the inscription of sexuality as something more than sex' (2011: 244).

In de Lauretis's terms, such a consideration of sexuality surpasses the representation of non-normative sexual desire or practices, and rather captures 'sexuality as an unmanageable excess of affect [. . .] an undomesticated, unsymbolizable force, not bound to objects and beyond the purview of the ego, a figure of sexuality as, precisely, drive' (2011: 245). De Lauretis calls queer a space in which Freud would imagine the drive to operate (2011: 246); a figural, but not referential, heterotopic space 'of a transit, a displacement, a passage and transformation', mastered not by conscious emotions, but by violent, self-shattering 'intensities of affect' that are 'outside representation' (2011: 246). These intensities dissociate sexuality from gender, sexual identity or even anatomy (2011: 248), and rather imbue 'the human's attraction to the abnormal, the perverse, the abject, the nonhuman in its contingent phenomenal appearance as disease, violence, and death' (2011: 247). As de Lauretis notes, being 'the most pervasive dimension of human life', sexuality for Freud ranges 'from perversion to neurosis to sublimation; it is compulsive, noncontingent, and incurable' (2011: 249–50).

Following de Lauretis, Nikolaidis's film appears as a queer space *par excellence* – if something like that could ever be possible: a figural, non-referential, heterotopic space accommodating bodies and images in various forms of constant transit, displacement and transformation, mastered by violent and self-shattering intensities of meaninglessness. Replete with intertextual references, yet ultimately devoid of referentiality, *Singapore Sling* foregrounds a view of sexuality beyond sex. In one scene Daughter is witnessed in salacious close-up, masturbating with a kiwi fruit, rubbing it against her breast and genitals, while in another she is chained and bound in the dungeon, emerging as an incarnation of untamed drive, as she indulges in an oscillation between pain and hedonism. In the permanently lascivious face of Daughter, desire is annihilated and rather replaced by the relentless force of the drive; a place beyond the pleasure principle. Sexuality becomes the centrifugal force that directs the film's narrative, only to, ultimately, spiral out of control in a vicious circle of violence, disgust, filth and perversion.

No Need for a Keyhole, or the Queer Ethics and Politics of Irony

Fotiou argues that

> Nikolaidis's use of noir is exemplary in Greek cinema, as he pastiches film noir together with other genres, and creates a body of work that is personal, political, and self-reflexive. Nikolaidis's greatest concern in all his films is the future of society and of cinema, a concern that takes the form of a nightmare that is imminent. (Fotiou and Fessas 2017: 118)

Reading *Singapore Sling* through de Lauretis's queer methodological approach, the above statement gains a whole new meaning. For, despite the emphatic political aspects of noir cinema's thematic preoccupations in both its classical and neo-noir versions, Nikolaidis's heavily noir-invested film operates in an entirely distinct sphere of politics, beyond content and towards form. Its ravaging, non-representational logic does not allow for critical engagement with its otherwise subversive thematics. Content is severed by, and over, the plundering force of ironic film form, which denies the film's rhetoric any power for political confrontation, let alone the setting out of a vision, other than perhaps one of endless negativity informed by sexual perversion and, indeed, meaninglessness.

Consequently, if the film's ironic mode amounts to something, it is more of a queer encounter with an ethical reflection on cinema, and indeed noir itself; or, to put it otherwise, it is more of a queer ethical critique of the politics of representation and, most importantly, an ethical engagement with the spectatorial phenomenon. Ironic, parodic, visually and formally radical, *Singapore Sling* is a queer text that, more than merely unearthing the queerness of the genre and exposing its well-hidden workings and desires, installs the ethical question at the heart of its subversive content and form: the involvement of the spectator in the proliferation of images of sex and violence. For behind the well-crafted façade of black-humour lightness, the blunt imagery can never be unseen. The viewer leaves the cinema haunted by what has been a relentless barrage of disconcerting imagery. The film, then, raises the question: how much of this was not really a product of/for their own pursuit?

Michele Aaron argues that film spectatorship is 'inherently contractual and hooked on the "real" or imagined suffering of others' (2007: 112). Drawing on the classic psychoanalytic paradigm, she explains that underwriting mainstream 'film's management of perverse desire (its socio-moral scale) and illusion (its fiction-status)', psychoanalytic theory has unearthed the disavowing strategies of mainstream illusionist cinema, which sought to maintain the 'safe distance between the spectator and the dangers suggested by and within the cinematic spectacle, be they emotional or psychological (or even ethical)', while simultaneously allowing him or her to indulge in (ostensibly 'authentic') fantasy (2007: 92). In this way, as she argues, spectatorship's 'contractual nature' (2007: 88–90) exposes its inextricable link to the issue of responsibility. Following ethical philosopher Emanuel Levinas's conceptualisation of responsibility (1989: 82–4), 'both as a kind of subjectivity-in-action ([responsibility as] a reflexive state of self-constitution) and [responsibility] as our obligation to the other', Aaron contends that, so long as film viewers are implicated not only as consumers, but also 'as consensual parties in the generation of characters' suffering for our entertainment', spectatorship emerges as 'intrinsically ethical', as it 'depends upon our intersubjective alignment with the prospective suffering of others' (Aaron 2007: 111–12).

Against mainstream cinema's inexorable proliferation of images of violence and suffering as spectacle for mass consumption, Aaron then posits a strand of postmodern cinema that might constitute a site of resistance. As she argues, practices and strategies such as self-reflexivity, intertextuality, stylistic excess and interpretational vacuity are only some examples of how cinema might deliberately break the spectatorial contract, 'aggravating the act of "artful forgetting"' (Aaron 2007: 92) and/or pushing the limits of the representable (2007: 112). As Aaron explains, self-reflexivity 'performs that radical Brechtian practice of distanciation, drawing attention to the myth of separation, of dissociation, and the necessary fiction of self-coherence' (2007: 98). In this respect, it is a device that exposes film spectatorship as 'intimately connected to the issue of responsibility', as it questions our 'mythic distance and safety, the irresponsibility or neutrality of looking on' (2007: 97). Indeed, as Aaron asserts, spectatorship is, ultimately, nothing less than 'a negotiation of personal pleasures and others' interests' and 'a marker of socio-political responsibility' (2007: 88). Discussing

Haneke's early films, as well as the films of *Dogme 95*, Aaron suggests that such examples of contemporary 'anti-moral cinema' are 'contra-disavowal', not only because of their self-reflexive nature, but 'also in their characters' banal enactment of extreme brutality which defamiliarises the spectators' experience, denying them any insulation from the most unconscionable of acts' (2007: 118–19).

Though largely distinct in terms of style and aesthetics from the aforementioned films, *Singapore Sling*'s affective impact runs along the same lines, both by way of its pervasive meta-cinematicism, as well as in its blatantly deadpan depiction of extreme violence and abuse. Nikolaidis's film is, indeed, a genre extravaganza, characterised by stylistic excess, multi-layered intertextuality, parodic appropriation and unapologetic indulgence in the production of uberglamorised scenes of sex, violence, filth and disgust. Identification is utterly obstructed by the impassive emotional expression or the lack thereof. Illusionism and narrative immersion are forestalled by the ubiquitous interpretational vacuity of the abject image, and the incessant dismantling of the fourth wall. The spectator is exposed, defenceless, prey to their own insatiable desire for visual excess. The utter collapse of a moral axis at the level of narrative and characterisation achieves next-to-nothing as a sociopolitical commentary, for the film's rhetorics cannot be consumed within (the politics of) representation.

Instead, through an ironic celebration of a noir queerness that foregrounds a meaningless, violent image, Nikolaidis's political investments in this film address the perverse cinematic experience of what Aaron calls 'the complex and alluring tension between witnessing violence and being somewhat entertained by it' (2007: 121). Oscillating between perverse desires and the socially problematic, *Singapore Sling*'s politics are not so much about the unconscionable, but rather about the boundaries of unconscionability, the boundaries (if any) of cinematic representation, indeed the limits of the representable and the acceptable on screen; essentially, about a renewed ontology and ethics of aesthetics itself. Stretching the limits of what is visually permissible, Nikolaidis's film ultimately becomes a litmus test for the affective relationship between film and spectator, poignantly and perversely exposing spectatorial complicity and responsibility in the proliferation of images of sex, violence and suffering, while questioning our position as viewers with respect to the moral, the immoral and the amoral *on* and *of* film. How much of that filmic filth isn't, indeed, a product of/for our own pursuit?

Notes

1. Available at <http://horror101withdrac.blogspot.com/2014/02/singapore-sling-1990-movie-review.html> (last accessed 15 January 2021).
2. Available at <http://horrornews.net/79912/film-review-singapore-sling-1990/> (last accessed 15 January 2021).

3. Available at <http://foritismansnumber.blogspot.com/2011/04/singapore-sling-1990.html> (last accessed 15 January 2021).
4. Available at <https://www.eyeforfilm.co.uk/review/singapore-sling-film-review-by-chris> (last accessed 15 January 2021).
5. Available at <http://gingernutsofhorror.com/film-gutter/film-gutter-singapore-sling#> (last accessed 15 January 2021).
6. Available at <http://nikosnikolaidis.com/singapore-sling/> (last accessed 15 January 2021).
7. Fabio Cleto (1999) departs from Susan Sontag's distinction between 'naïve' and 'deliberate' camp, arguing that camp can be perceived both as a 'failed seriousness', as well as an intentional acknowledgement of the unnatural, 'inessential' and contingent 'essence' of performance that privileges form and style over message or content. However, in his view, camp is always already queer, in the sense that it challenges such binary oppositions, exposing the artificial character of all social interaction, the theatricality of being, and doing as acting.
8. Translated by Marios Psaras.

References

Aaron, Michelle (2007), *Spectatorship: The Power of Looking On*, London: Wallflower.
Chris (2008), 'Singapore Sling', eyeforfilm.co.uk, 1 March, <https://www.eyeforfilm.co.uk/review/singapore-sling-film-review-by-chris> (last accessed 24 February 2019).
Cleto, Fabio (1999), 'Introduction: Queering the Camp', in Fabio Cleto (ed.), *Camp: Queer Aesthetics and the Performing Subject, A Reader*, Edinburgh: Edinburg University Press, pp. 1–42.
de Lauretis, Teresa (2011), 'Queer Texts, Bad Habits, and the Issue of a Future', *GlQ: A Journal of Lesbian and Gay Studies*, 17, pp. 243–63.
de Man, Paul (1996), *Aesthetic Ideology*, Minneapolis, MN: University of Minnesota Press.
Den Boer, Michael (2006), 'Singapore Sling', 10kbullets.com, 3 June, <https://10kbullets.com/reviews/singapore-sling/> (last accessed 24 February 2019).
Dr. AC (2014), 'Singapore Sling (1990) Movie Review', horror101withdrac.blogspot.com, 9 February, <http://horror101withdrac.blogspot.com/2014/02/singapore-sling-1990-movie-review.html> (last accessed 24 February 2019).
Dyer, Richard (2004), 'Queer Noir', in Harry M. Benshoff and Sean Griffith (eds), *Queer Cinema: The Film Reader*, Abingdon: Routledge, pp. 84–104.
Dyer, Richard (2007), *Pastiche*, Abingdon: Routledge.
Film Gutter Reviews (2016), 'Film Gutter: *Singapore Sling*', gingernutsofhorror.com, 8 September <http://gingernutsofhorror.com/film-gutter/film-gutter-singapore-sling#> (last accessed 24 February 2019).
Fotiou, Mikela (2017), 'Nikolaidis's Diptych *Those Who Loved a Corpse*: A "Pasticcio of Pastiches"', in Tonia Kazakopoulou and Mikela Fotiou (eds), *Contemporary Greek Film Cultures from 1990 to the Present*, Bern: Peter Lang, pp. 343–68.
Fotiou, Mikela, and Nikitas Fessas (2017), 'Greek Neo-Noir: Reflecting a Narrative of Crisis', *Filmicon: Journal of Greek Film Studies*, 4, pp. 110–37.

Jameson, Fredric (1991) *Postmodernism, or, the Cultural Logic of Late Capitalism*, Durham, NC: Duke University Press.

Karalis, Vrasidas (2012), *A History of Greek Cinema*, New York: Continuum.

Kelly, Oliver, and Trigo, Benigno (2003), *Noir Anxiety*, Minneapolis, MN: University of Minnesota Press.

Leonard, Sean (2013), 'Film Review: *Singapore Sling* (1990)', horrornews.net, 17 December, <http://horrornews.net/79912/film-review-singapore-sling-1990/> (last accessed 24 February 2019).

Levinas, Emanuel (1989), 'Ethics as First Philosophy', in Sean Hand (ed.), *The Levinas Reader*, Oxford: Basil Blackwell, pp. 75–87.

Nikolaidou, Afroditi, and Alexiou, Alexis (2019), '*Singapore Sling*', in Afroditi Nikolaidou and Anna Poupou (eds), *I Hameni Leoforos tou Ellinikou Cinema* [The Lost Highway of Greek Cinema], Athens: Nefeli, pp. 152–4.

Silver, Alain, and Ursini, James (1999), *The Noir Style*, Woodstock, NY: Overlook Press.

Sontag, Susan ([1964] 2018), *Notes on Camp*, London: Penguin.

Tylerandjack (2011) '*Singapore Sling* (1990)', foritismansnumber.blogspot.com, 15 April, <http://foritismansnumber.blogspot.com/2011/04/singapore-sling-1990.html> (last accessed 25 July 2021).

11. HONG KONG AND ATHENS: CONTESTED SPACES OF THE GLOBAL AND THE LOCAL IN THE NEO-NOIR OF JOHN WOO AND ALEXIS ALEXIOU

Yun-hua Chen

Noir as the Contested Intersection between the Global and the Local

Since its inception, the production of film noir in the US context has drawn thematic and aesthetic inspiration from European and other world cinemas; in return, the noir elements, established by US noir, have also had a significant impact on European and world cinemas. Like a chain reaction, these European and world cinemas, which once found inspiration in Anglo-American film noir, would invigorate Hollywood neo-noir later on. This is what Fay and Nieland (2009: 9, 68, 109) call 'global film noir', and what Desser (2003: 516) calls 'global noir'.

Through this lens, John Woo's *A Better Tomorrow* (1986) and Alexis Alexiou's *Tetarti 04:45/Wednesday 04:45* (2015) form an interesting pair of examples that can be used to look into the dynamics between the global and the local within the genre framework. An almost three-decade gap separates their creation, but there is a remarkable affinity between the two films. On the one hand, Alexiou pays tribute to John Woo. On the other, as I argue in this chapter, this affinity can be read as a strategy on Alexiou's part to connect with international neo-noir, and to relate the local concerns of Greek noir to global ones; this affiliation through noir demonstrates global interdependencies theorised by Sassen (2001: 267), Appadurai (1996: 32–5) and Featherstone (1996: 65) under the term 'the global', as well as Hardt and Negri's 'Empire' (2000: 39).

While reflecting on these two films' temporal-spatial intersection between the local and the global in the background, this chapter will discuss transcultural and local aspects of *A Better Tomorrow* and *Wednesday 04:45*, as well as the globalised noir space. I will first contextualise both films in their respective sociopolitical and economic conditions. I will also discuss the films' interaction with noir aesthetics and genre conventions, before moving on to examine the proliferation of non-places in Hong Kong and Athens, and the creation of globalised cities.

Film noir as a term as well as its scope have long been contested (Park 2011: 2; Schrader [1972] 2003: 230; Bordwell 1998: 77). The term was coined in the early post-war years by French critics Nino Frank (1946) and Jean-Pierre Chartier (1946); since then, films noirs and neo-noirs have constantly been reworked and reappropriated in different local contexts, and reinvented in self-reflexive manners, having influenced cinemas all around the world, while subsequently and simultaneously being influenced by them. Noir is, therefore, sensitive to the local consequences of globalisation and the threats posed to urban culture, while demonstrating heterogeneity and hybridity (Fay and Nieland 2009: 131–3; Neale 2000: 174; Thanouli 2006: 185–7).[1] Film noir has always been nurtured by global concerns and 'dramatize[s] the crises of local spaces' (Fay and Nieland 2009: ix); at the same time, there exists a transnational and intertextual genre of 'global noir' (Desser 2003: 516). In this chapter I aim to shed some light on how the Greek noir[2] *Wednesday 04:45*, through its affiliation with neo-noir and especially John Woo's *A Better Tomorrow*, is connected to the global film scene. While clearly stemming from very local sociopolitical problematics, noir can be used as a way to look towards the global.

Hong Kong Cinema and *A Better Tomorrow*

A Better Tomorrow and *Wednesday 04:45* were made under very different socio-economic and geopolitical conditions: pre-handover Hong Kong and post-crisis Athens. In the case of Hong Kong cinema, it was first brought to the attention of non-Chinese-speaking film buffs with the release of the Shaw Brothers' production *Five Fingers Death* in the United States in 1973 and the subsequent kung-fu craze of the 1970s. A decade later, the distribution of John Woo's *The Killer* (1989) in the US would direct the global audience's interest towards Hong Kong cinema once again (Fu and Desser 2000: 2–4). Alexiou was part of a large audience of young, and cinematically knowledgeable, global viewers who discovered Woo's films on video (Chalkou 2016).[3] What made Hong Kong cinema especially appealing at that time was its reflection of Hong Kong's complexity and hybridity. As the city straddled East and West, British rule (from 1841 to 1997) and Chinese ('one government, two systems' from 1997 onwards), and localised features and international appeal, Hong

Kong cinema reflected this inherent transnationality. As one of the most distinctive representatives of the Hong Kong filmmakers of his generation, Woo precisely celebrated this hybridity, while contemplating the city's search for an identity. Constantly crossing artistic, cultural and generic boundaries, his works are usually a pell-mell of action, slapstick comedy and sentimentalist drama. As Kenneth E. Hall points out ([1999] 2012: 7–8), Woo is inspired both by American genre films (for example John Ford) and European arthouse cinema (François Truffaut and Jean-Pierre Melville) and, at the same time, he subsumes the East Asian influence of *wuxia pian* (martial arts films), samurai and bushido (for example, Kurosawa Akira and King Hu). His oeuvre, thus, extends across West and East, as well as across Christianity and Confucianism, and foregrounds what Ng has described as the intertextual referencing of transcultural cinephilia (2005: 67).

In fact, *A Better Tomorrow*, the first film Woo made after a frustrating experience in Taiwan, denotes a turning point in the director's career: it integrates, but also departs from, his earlier comedy, drama and action films in a very self-conscious manner. In Hall's ([1999] 2012: 69) words, '*A Better Tomorrow* broke new ground, both for him [Woo] and for the Hong Kong film industry'. It is much more focused and serious, with more understated comical and kung-fu elements, more nuanced dramatic layers, and more emphasis on gunplay. Certain images and concepts in *A Better Tomorrow*, such as the well-known scene of Chow Yun-fat in a trenchcoat firing a pair of guns, or the dilemma between the underworld and the 'virtuous' way guided by moral doctrine, have gained emblematic status both in Woo's oeuvre and in wider Hong Kong cinema. The watershed film through which Woo rose to the status of a famed filmmaker in the action genre, *A Better Tomorrow* has thus been chosen as embodying the visual elements and topics that continued to be replicated and transformed throughout his career, and inspired other filmmakers such as Alexiou. It is through self-conscious reference to Woo, as well as to other filmmakers such as Takeshi Kitano (*Hana-bi/Fireworks*, 1997) and American neo-noir films of the 1960s and 1970s, such as *Straw Dogs* (dir. Peckinpah, 1971), that Alexiou opened up his own spaces of intertextuality in *Wednesday 04:45*.

A Better Tomorrow was conceptualised at a moment of transition and precariousness, between the time of the Sino-British Joint Declaration in 1984, which announced the transfer of sovereignty over Hong Kong, and 1997, when the handover was realised. Hong Kong was facing an imminent change from the colonial to the post-colonial era, and from economic liberalism and free-market capitalism under British rule to potentially increased constraints under 'socialism with Chinese characteristics'. Strong feelings of uncertainty and anxiety thus prevailed, and many of Hong Kong's wealthiest residents emigrated to the United States or Canada.

It was at this crossroads between the colonial period (during which Hong Kong's identity was not recognised) and the 'one China' discourse (in which the Hong Kong way of life was in danger) that Hong Kong films celebrated the city's local culture. According to Fay and Nieland (2009: 110), 'Hong Kong experienced a new kind of localism – a desire to define a specific cultural identity neither British nor Chinese, but specific to Hong Kong'. In Abbas's words ([1997] 2002: 7), '[t]he imminence of its disappearance [. . .] was what precipitated an intense and unprecedented interest in Hong Kong culture [. . .] We are witnessing [. . .] "some original and yet untheorized" form of culture, what I propose to describe as *a culture of disappearance*' (italics in original). One important way in which Hong Kong filmmakers chose to celebrate and advocate localist characteristics, those at risk of being effaced during the change, was through film noir, in the way 'Noir East' would reflect the anxieties of postmodern Asia after 1997 (Collier 2007: 138).

'Elsewhere' in Relation to Athens and Hong Kong

Before delving into my analysis, let me first briefly offer synopses of *A Better Tomorrow* and *Wednesday 04:45*. The first film focuses on the dynamics among three male characters, Ho (Ti Lung), Mark (Chow Yun-fat) and Kit (Leslie Cheung Kwok-wing). Kit is Ho's brother, and is about to graduate from the police academy. He is also aware of Ho's involvement with criminal activities. Ho and Mark, whose profound friendship is akin to blood brotherhood, are two key members of a Triad group, a Hong Kong-based underworld that specialises in counterfeiting US dollars. While Ho is imprisoned in Taiwan for three years, after being betrayed by Shing, profit-driven competition and exploitation intensifies in Hong Kong, as well as within the Triad. Meanwhile, Kit vows to support law enforcement in uprooting the Triad; Mark injures his leg while avenging Ho. He ends up working as a car cleaner for the traitor-turned-boss Shing at the parking garage of the Triad's skyscraper. As Kit works his way up the ladder at the police force's towering headquarters, Mark sinks downwards, both socially and spatially. Three years later, Ho is working as a taxi driver in Hong Kong's central commercial area, a place of glass-windowed skyscrapers and underground tunnels connecting the city to the port. It all ends in a mass shootout, during which Mark sacrifices himself to rescue Ho and Kit. Ho eventually kills Shing with a gun that Kit lends him.

Wednesday 04:45 was the second feature-length film by Alexis Alexiou, following his *Istoria 52/Tale 52* (2008). Co-produced by Greece, Germany and Israel, *Wednesday 04:45* was distributed following its participation in various international film festivals, including Jeonju International Film Festival, Karlovy Vary International Film Festival and Tribeca Film Festival. This reflects a 'marked transnationality' (Hjort 2010: 13–14) unavailable to Woo at the time of *A Better*

Tomorrow.⁴ Against the backdrop of the Greek financial crisis, *Wednesday 04:45* follows an Athenian jazz-club owner, Stelios (Stelios Mainas), who risks losing his club to the Romanian mafia loan shark Roumanos (Mimi Branescu) should he fail to pay his debt within a day. He spends the day trying to borrow money and is also assigned by Roumanos to collect a debt from a strip-club owner, the Albanian immigrant Omer (Giorgos Symeonidis). Before the day ends, Stelios agrees to meet Roumanos to hand over his ownership of the jazz club, and takes a gun with him in a metal briefcase. On the rooftop of an abandoned, half-complete building, he becomes involved in a gunfight with Roumanos's gang, during which he is wounded before managing to escape and returning home (Figure 11.1).

Figure 11.1   The final scene on the roof of a deserted building in the centre of Athens. Stelios (Stelios Mainas) shooting his enemies. Digital still from *Wednesday 04:45*.

As Barton Palmer has argued, 'the film noir juxtaposes the false promise of a future with the reality of a present that, instead, turns back to the past, trapping the protagonist "between times" and in a multiplicity of irreconcilable spaces' (2004: 63). Pre-handover neo-noirs in Hong Kong, and post-crisis neo-noirs in Athens, for very different reasons, both confront the collective feelings of angst, uncertainty and frustration of their respective time periods, while reflecting nostalgia for a more glorious past, all provoked by the continuing transformation of urban space. Since the Greek financial crisis erupted in 2009, Greece has been struggling with high levels of unemployment, a rapidly worsening social welfare system, dramatically lowered standards of living and climbing suicide rates. The crisis is not only financial, but also diplomatic, sociopolitical and humanitarian, having a devastating impact across the social spectrum. Alexiou is very overt about his intention to mirror the Greek crisis in *Wednesday 04:45*, and to use the noir genre to reflect the socio-economic situation in Greece (Fotiou and Fessas 2017: 124).

In both films examined here, urban spaces are intruded upon, and governed by, an 'elsewhere'. This 'elsewhere' embodies different forms of globalised presence, each with comparatively stronger or weaker political and economic power. While the globalised presence comes from beyond the original geographical and psychological boundaries, it represents different versions and degrees of neoliberalism, as well as the globally interconnected networks of ethnoscapes, mediascapes, technoscapes, financescapes and ideoscapes theorised in Appadurai's new configuration of the global cultural economy (1996: 32–5). Both Hong Kong and Athens are cities that keep being redefined in relation to others, and whose identity is subject to the approval of more powerful geopolitical forces. In this urban space, people from diverse places meet and work, information is exchanged, and money comes and goes. Hong Kong was handed over by a European coloniser to an 'outsider' regime out of touch with its historical path, development of civil society and sociocultural nuances, whereas Greece had no choice but to continuously negotiate with the European Union and the International Monetary Fund for relief of the country's debt. Hong Kong is a popular destination for domestic workers from Southeast Asia, while Greece attracts migrant workers from the countries of the former Eastern Bloc, such as Albania and Romania.

In the case of *A Better Tomorrow*, in the 1980s, the 'elsewhere' is not only Taiwan across the strait (the interconnected triangle area between Hong Kong, Taiwan and Macau where the gang in the film operates) but also the US as, simultaneously, a dream destination, safe haven and playground for further criminal activities (as is the case in the sequel, *A Better Tomorrow II*, dir. Woo, 1987). In fact, the plotline about Taiwan was scripted with reference to Woo's autobiography. After leaving the production company Golden Harvest Films – where he directed some low-budget kung-fu films, as well as *Dinü hua/Princess Cheung Ping* (1976) and *Fat chin hon/Money Crazy* (1977) – to join the newly formed Cinema City Enterprises (founded in 1979 and defunct by 1991), Woo was sent to Taiwan as a director, but ended up doing an administrative job. Two years later, Tsui Hark's Film Workshop offered him the opportunity to direct *A Better Tomorrow*, so Woo finally returned to Hong Kong (Hall [1999] 2012: 73–5). It is worth noting the absence of mainland China from *A Better Tomorrow*, since it was not yet a dominant 'elsewhere' in the 1980s, but would become the most important 'elsewhere' in Hong Kong cinema of the twenty-first century.

As for *Wednesday 04:45*, it is the relationship between Greece, the Balkans and other European countries (Albania, Romania, Bulgaria and Poland in particular) that is constantly under negotiation. After the collapse of the Soviet Union and the Eastern Bloc in the 1990s, for two decades Greece became a destination for immigrants from these countries, until the crisis shifted the power relationships. When Omer replaces his long-term employee, a 35-year-old

Polish stripper named Agnieszka, with a Congolese erotic dancer whose fees are much lower, the 'elsewhere' highlights the fierce competition for cheaper labour and lower costs in an era of globalised capitalism and neoliberalism that prioritises profit and turns human beings into commodities that can be easily substituted.

Filmic Worlds in *A Better Tomorrow* and *Wednesday 04:45*

Both filmic worlds are composed of convoluted and entangled webs of characters, narrative threads and meandering paths, and, in their respective manners, both are infused with societal corruption, fear and greed. Compared to what takes place in *Wednesday 04:45*, in *A Better Tomorrow* these webs are visibly a lot bloodier and more directly connected to the underworld. Seventeen minutes into *A Better Tomorrow*, there are already parallel gun fights happening in Ho's apartment in Hong Kong and at the countryside meeting point in Taiwan. The fights last eight minutes, and are followed by another sequence of four minutes, featuring Mark's revenge and the famous double-pistol jump. In *Wednesday 04:45* violence is more of a lurking presence than a direct confrontation, with the first gunfight occurring towards the very end of the film. After all, by the 1980s Hong Kong's film industry had already established its reputation in the production of globally consumed, commercial genre films, and its film production often features crafted fight choreography, whereas in Greece the crime genre is by no means dominant in the market.

In *A Better Tomorrow*, betrayal is driven by the desire to usurp the Triad mob boss's throne, whereas in *Wednesday 04:45* the characters are chased by financial troubles; the underworld is only brought into the picture because of the debts. In the filmic world, as well as in the daily reality of Greece, the real pressure comes not from actual gunshots, but rather from the stress of finding money. Money is thus a key theme in numerous interactions between the characters in Alexiou's film: the debt-ridden jazz-club owner is forced by the Romanian mafia loan shark to collect a debt from a strip-club owner; debt collectors kidnap the strip-club owner's child; the loan shark's employee bargains with an African street vendor for a pirated CD with a price tag of seven euros. It is also for the sake of money that a drug addict begs at the traffic lights, in the rain, through car windows, shouting 'If you touch me, you won't die', and that a Congolese dancer is hired to replace an Eastern European one. If the struggle in *A Better Tomorrow* is bloody, between life and death, between crooks and brothers, and between the two sides of law enforcement, the one in *Wednesday 04:45* comes mainly from a scarcity of money: in times of wider financial crisis, a character's plight is often connected to their country's plight. If *A Better Tomorrow* reflects the overall rise of criminal activities in Hong Kong between 1981 and 1986 (Broadhurst et al. 2008), *Wednesday 04:45* demonstrates the general misery caused by the financial crisis as a permanent and aggravated state of neoliberalism, one that affects the full social spectrum, including middle-class entrepreneurs, street vendors and beggars.

Both films focus on an upright, middle-aged, male character who, despite the corruption, deception and crime in his personal and professional environment, insists on a certain, though sometimes ambiguous, self-defined moral standard, and remains kind-hearted and morally upright. In this male-dominated world, and in sharp contrast to those compassionless neoliberals and bloodthirsty usurpers around them, the male leads understand family values and cherish friendship, brotherhood, loyalty, morality and honour. In *A Better Tomorrow*, Ho intends to retire from the underworld for the sake of his family and in response to his father's request, especially because his younger brother is graduating from the police academy. Mark is capable of killing without blinking, but also of making kind gestures: he hands a pile of cash over to his driver, who is heard coughing, so that the man can go to the hospital. In *A Better Tomorrow*, Ho and Mark are loyal and devoted brothers without blood ties, ready to sacrifice their lives for each other, just as Stelios's friend Vassos (Dimitris Tzoumakis) would do for Stelios in *Wednesday 04:45*. Stelios is also a good employer; despite the chaos around him, he keeps his promise to attend the christening of his employee's son, and lends money to employees in need without hesitation. While being unwillingly entangled in the kidnapping of Omer's young son, Stelios's priority is to protect the child, rather than to elude the mafia gangsters.

Hong Kong and Athens as Non-places

The emphasis on the anonymous and transient spaces of nightclubs, bars, dark alleys and hotel rooms, where characters negotiate, participate in gunfights, or flee from them, has been a trademark of post-war American film noir. These portrayals of space are rooted in film noir's ambience of detective story and crime thriller, the unfamiliar and the perverse, the dark and the non-familial. They are the noir 'non-places' that are globally recognisable across borders, and which we also see in *A Better Tomorrow* and *Wednesday 04:45*. According to Marc Augé's anthropological framework, 'supermodernity' refers to a time characterised by rapid and extensive exchanges of information, commodities, images and people, during which 'non-places' proliferate (1996: 177–8). Non-places are contrasted to anthropological places, which are relational and concerned with history and identity. They are transitory spaces, where people simply pass through, such as airport lounges, petrol stations and hotel rooms (Augé 1995: 77–8). In the context of film noir, these non-places are even more fleeting and unaffectionate, because they are tainted by violence, vengeance and the need to escape afterwards. They are not neutral spaces like Augé's examples, but rather transit points where drugs are purchased, beatings take place and criminals temporarily hide.

Both *A Better Tomorrow* and *Wednesday 04:45* share an iconic noir topology of non-places; the cityscapes are full of underground parking lots, dark alleys with limited visibility, gaudy neon light coming from shop and bar signs, and cars that meander along hectic streets. In *Wednesday 04:45*, a dimly lit tunnel is where Stelios buys cocaine from a young dealer on roller skates, and where he witnesses how the dealer is beaten up and possibly even killed by other dealers. In *A Better Tomorrow*, a nightclub's back alley is where Kit pushes Ho against the wall to interrogate him, and a dark port is where the final shootout takes place. At the beginning of *A Better Tomorrow*, when Ho and Mark are having drinks in a bar after a successful transaction, we see shades of orange-red neon light in the background. This is also the colour palette used in *Wednesday 04:45* for Omer's strip club and the night-time cityscape seen from the perspective of Stelios's speeding car, right before the final scene. These non-places seem to stem from a sense of insecurity and instability permeating the respective sociopolitical contexts. Like the characters in classic American noir who are faced with an estranged urban life, alienated interpersonal relationships and fierce economic competition in capitalist modernity, Woo's heroes deal with changing value systems, an endangered cultural identity, uncertain economic prospects, an existential identity crisis due to the imminent handover, and a fluctuating sociopolitical order. In their pressure-cooker society, Alexiou's heroes are confronted by financial strain at both national and personal levels and, consequently, they fall further into a downward spiral. Noir is Alexiou and Woo's 'answer' to these changes, the destroyed harmony and the shattered interpersonal connectedness; as the characters lose their bonds with people and places, as in the way Stelios is alienated from his family and on the brink of losing his club, they turn to non-places for solutions. Hence, we see Stelios's first meeting with Roumanos (where they talk about Stelios's debt) taking place in the latter's hotel room – a non-place by definition. Stelios then embarks on a hectic journey through a variety of other non-places, from an abandoned tunnel to a sombre bar and then to a parking lot. As for Ho, his downfall is caused from within his 'place' by the betrayal of a younger gang-member whom he trusts and brings to Taiwan for a business trip. Ho is later rejected by his blood brother Kit when their father dies as a result of the intrusion of a hitman. On his return to Hong Kong, Ho is beaten up by Kit in the rain and has no 'place' to go, no home to return to; with the transition going on in the sociopolitical context and on a personal level, 'places' become linked to an unreliable and cynical existence. Through camerawork, lighting and editing, *A Better Tomorrow* and *Wednesday 04:45* either deploy an abundance of non-places, or demonstrate the disappearance of places in order to affiliate themselves, as texts, with the genre of global noir in a spatial manner.

Non-places are where chance encounters happen. In *Wednesday 04:45*, for example, in the telling scene mentioned earlier involving the negotiation for a pirated CD, a tracking shot is used to follow a dreadlocked street vendor in flashy red trousers walking from left to right across the frame, first in slow motion and then back at a normal pace, in front of a row of Athenian flats. When he passes a gangster in front of an SUV, waiting with his cigarette in hand, the gangster stops him and the bargaining process for the pirated CD begins. The use of a tracking shot here mirrors the feelings of passing by a non-place. In *A Better Tomorrow*, as an indication of Mark's plight after Ho's imprisonment, he is shown eating takeaway food from its container while sitting on an abandoned black sofa in a parking lot, thus using a non-place as a substitute for a place. Typically in Woo's films, as well as in films that draw inspiration from him, non-places are where standoffs take place between multiple characters drawing guns. Whereas a Mexican standoff takes place on the warehouse floor in *Reservoir Dogs* (dir. Tarantino, 1992), Alexiou's multiple-character shootout sequence on the rooftop on a rainy night, like many scenes in Tarantino's films, is also a cinephilic reference to Woo. Stelios's gun drops from his briefcase to the floor in slow motion, after which the different parties (Roumanos, his bodyguards, and two Greek gangsters who collaborate with him), after a moment of silence that is stretched by slow motion, draw their guns. Stelios is wounded and falls down, and then the Greek gangsters and Roumanos's gang turn on each other. Close-ups of hands holding guns, and of raindrops falling on to the roof, mixed with blood slowly forming puddles, alternate with medium shots of the characters pointing their guns, firing and falling down, one after another. Between these shots and a long shot of the positioning of the characters on the rooftop, we also see the atmospheric shot of an umbrella being thrown away in slow motion, reminiscent of Woo's films. It is raining heavily as all this happens, and the yellow-green tone of a streetlight flickers in the background. Through the use of recognisable tropes from well-known neo-noir classics, and by situating the action in non-places, Alexiou pays homage to Woo, and intentionally aligns his films with the aesthetics of global noir, while demonstrating a case of what Hjort has described as '*milieu*-building' through affiliation to genre conventions and 'globalizing transnationalism' (2010: 16).[5]

Globalised Space in the Noir Genre

What *A Better Tomorrow* and *Wednesday 04:45* demonstrate spatially are the negotiations between places and non-places, and the reciprocal influence between the local and the global; they are deeply rooted in their respective, local subject matters, but also actively connected with the global through genre conventions and cinematic references. While both films use the globalised genre to transcend the local, they also enrich the global noir with their contribution from the local. The push-and-pull of globalism and localism from different perspectives creates an encounter and a tension, as both forces are situated within the global world-order of capitalism.

Local specificities of Hong Kong and Athens are certainly observable in *A Better Tomorrow* and *Wednesday 04:45*. Hong Kong's localness can be encountered in the policemen's uniforms, the police cars and the skyscrapers next to the highway at the beginning of *A Better Tomorrow*, seen through a car window. In *Wednesday 04:45* we see stereotypical Athenian flats built after the 1960s, with sunshades on the balconies. We also see images of clashes between demonstrators and policemen on TV sets in the background, anarchist graffiti on the walls, riots and protests on the streets, and a bar decorated with a plastic Greek flag and a half-torn poster advertising Greece as a tourist destination. Meanwhile, there is a sense of nostalgia for the places that have disappeared or are about to disappear, as we can see in Stelios's obsession with live jazz music in the bar. What triggers Stelios to initiate the shootout is the plan of Roumanos's son to revamp Stelios's place after the takeover into a discotheque playing hip hop and Greek pop music. The importance of jazz, for Stelios, reflects his nostalgia for 'an idealized past (and a pervasive melancholia for its irretrievable loss), when everything supposedly was more pure, innocent, and optimistic' (Fotiou and Fessas 2017: 131).

The localised characteristics, which are based on exchanges in 'places', are then intertwined with the proliferation of anonymous 'non-places' that reveal the globalised space (Featherstone 1996: 46–7; Appadurai 1996: 32–5). As the camera navigates through nameless corners, dark rooms, dingy bars, highways and subterranean passages, Hong Kong and Athens, despite the time gap between *A Better Tomorrow* and *Wednesday 04:45*, seem strikingly similar. Non-places prevail in the depictions of both cities. Their similarity is not only due to Alexiou's self-conscious tribute to Woo. More importantly, the two cities are connected through global noir aesthetics, 'the global', and the disorienting timelessness of the postmodern dystopian landscape that Jameson (1991: 160, 384) has described. The two cities appear to be, to a certain extent, interchangeable, and can be translocated elsewhere: the port that is packed with containers, boats and cars in the final shootout scene of *A Better Tomorrow* could have been shot in Greece; and the music hall where Jackie auditions could as well be located in Athens; young Lefteris's taekwondo classroom is indistinguishable from a taekwondo studio in Hong Kong; and those endless highway tunnels through which Stelios drives could pass for an expressway in Hong Kong. This depiction of Athens as a global noir city, in line with the western European and Asian metropolises, was intentionally designed by Alexiou, along with cinematographer Christos Karamanis and the art director Spyros Laoktario (Challtou 2016). It is an Athens that does not really exist, except as a simulacrum, to use

Baudrillard's famous term – a hyperreal, 'artificial resurrection', a double that shows all the signs of the real (Baudrillard 1994: 4–10). Alexiou's hyperreal and simulated Athens looks similar to what Hong Kong used to be in Woo's films and no longer is, while it is also the 'actual' Athens with its real-time crisis. For that reason, Hong Kong and Athens do not become Koolhaas's ([1995] 1998: 1249–50) centre-less, identity-less, history-less and logo-like 'generic city'. Their affinity connects them to the global cinema scene, but does not homogenise them into faceless spaces; their subject matters and modes of expression remain well grounded and locally relevant.

Despite not being a global city populated with multinational corporations like Hong Kong, but rather being a 'globalised city' (or a city that globalisation has happened to), in *Wednesday 04:45* Athens manages to achieve the status of a metropolitan city where money flows in and out, and where Romanians, Poles, Bulgarians, Albanians and Congolese arrive to look for work or business opportunities; both the old and the new Athenians suffer from the financial crisis together. As the Romanian mafia boss sends his son to run the jazz club in Athens, and the Albanian strip-club owner's son is being cared for by the Polish dancer, Athens is caught in the globalised networks of nameless transnational influxes. This image of Athens corresponds to Sassen's analysis of global cities (2001: 267) and Hardt and Negri's 'Empire' (2000: 247, 249). The 'Empire' largely takes over the role of nation-states and their function as nodal points where the processes of production are coordinated and modernised, technology flows are exchanged, global human resources converge and finances are centrally managed (Hardt and Negri 2000: 298, 308–9) – 'a new economic-industrial-communicative machine' with a discontinuous flow between centre and margins (2000: 39–40).

Meanwhile, while Athens and Hong Kong are interconnected through networks of information and goods, and through the prevalence of non-places, they suffer, in their own ways, from the consequences of the global. In Woo's film, Hong Kong's status as a global city is achieved, but comes at the price of stringent class division. When Ho returns to Hong Kong and looks for Mark outside the Triad's headquarters, he witnesses him dragging his lame leg with a rag tied to his trousers, and cleaning Shing's car window. Then Shing descends from the skyscraper in a perfectly white trenchcoat, wearing sunglasses, and is captured by a high-angle shot that highlights his grandiosity. In *A Better Tomorrow*, life as a working-class person, such as a car-window cleaner or a taxi driver, is in sharp contrast to the life of owning, or working for, a multinational enterprise in a skyscraper – even if it is a criminal organisation.

This class division between luxury-car owners and car-window cleaners in a highly competitive society run according to neoliberal ideas in Hong Kong becomes even harsher in the version of Athens portrayed in *Wednesday 04:45* three decades later. Here, middle-class entrepreneurs attempt to lead the lives of mansion owners, as if they belonged to the upper class, and appear to own numerous luxury items, even though they can actually lose their financial security and become bankrupt overnight. Compared to the Hong Kong of the 1980s represented in *A Better Tomorrow*, the support network in post-crisis Athens is more vulnerable, the stakes much higher, and the wealth discrepancy much wider.

Cinematically, *A Better Tomorrow* and *Wednesday 04:45* both portray a globalised noir space, using suspenseful music, fast cutting, close-ups from oblique angles and a sombre colour palette. The two films feature swift camera movements, scanning through space, and fast cutting between images, shots from multiple angles and with different tonalities to create a jarring sense of mismatch through numerous editing surprises. This gives us a quick, generic impression and sense of the noir city. Both films use an abundance of radically high and low angles; the underground parking lots in both films are usually shot with a wide-angle lens and with light coming from the ceiling to distort the spatial perception and increase the feeling of eeriness. Tight framing that uses door and window frames to 'entrap' the characters and reveal their spatial surroundings is used only partially, to create the feeling of claustrophobia. Many scenes are shot from inside a moving car. Tightly framed, half-obscured between doors and columns, cramped and nocturnal, and combined with close-ups, the car space is cluttered. The light usually comes from one side of the frame, and leaves the other side obscure and concealed in darkness, achieving chiaroscuro effects. Sometimes the light comes from an odd angle, partially distorting the characters' faces. The orange, green and blue hue of dim street lights in *Wednesday 04:45* resonates with the nightclub scene in *A Better Tomorrow*, when Ho and Mark bump into Shing, while the encounter is stealthily observed by Kit. These global noir elements can be read as externalisations of the male psyche and anxiety; the faces of male characters are observed through close-ups, and sometimes also through freeze-framing and stylised slow motion, especially during shootout sequences.

Conclusion

Through the proliferation of non-places and the use of global noir aesthetics, *Wednesday 04:45* connects itself with *A Better Tomorrow* and the global genre of noir – bringing the local to the global. In their globalised spaces, *A Better Tomorrow* and *Wednesday 04:45* address specific local themes, and use noir elements to reflect upon societies in turmoil and upheaval. They are not particularly preoccupied with the post-war crisis of male identity and authority that characterised the American film noir from its inception (Fay and Nieland 2009: 149), nor the post-Vietnam/post-Watergate America of the neo-noir period (Collier 2007: 154), but their noirness is symptomatic of the films' particular contexts. In both films, history, culture and power are at play, while the characters struggle to reorient themselves and to deal with their deep-rooted anxiety about their hybridity between a Hong-Kongese and a Chinese identity, or between a Greek and a European identity. The noir mood suits the general sense of despair and frustration in post-crisis Athens for Alexiou, as well as the feelings of anxiety and fatalism in Hong Kong of the mid-1980s for Woo. By reworking the forms of noir, both directors reassert their alliance and affiliation with transnational noir productions.

In this respect *A Better Tomorrow* and *Wednesday 04:45* demonstrate the fluid dynamics between the local and the global in noir; the universal and the particular, anonymous spaces and rooted places are juxtaposed in a non-linear way. Whereas in noir the local is used to dramatise and foreground a specific socio-economic situation, noir is also a tool that directors from various national backgrounds use in order to connect with the global discourse and the transnational flow in a self-reflexive way. This is even more evident in the case of neo-noir. While anonymous noir 'non-places' make globalised cities look blurred and analogous, the films examined in this chapter are also deeply rooted in local specificities, raise questions about local concerns, and indicate relative power relationships between here and 'elsewhere'; meanwhile, this globalised 'elsewhere' dynamically influences and impacts on the local. In their own versions of glocalism, and in their respective eras of filmmaking, Woo and Alexiou draw inspiration from, and also contribute to, the collective cultural past, as well as the potential future(s) of noir, while rendering Hong Kong and Athens cinematic cities through the use of visuals, thematics and tropes.

Notes

1. Some of these traits are theorised by Eleftheria Thanouli as 'post-classical narration' (2006: 185–7), which turns hybrid and multi-generic films into the norm, uses hypermediacy and high-dose subjective realism, explores the scope of parody and diversifies narrative goals through a plurality of characters and interactions.
2. For a history of Greek film noir, see Fotiou and Fessas (2017).
3. In the interview with Chalkou (2016), Alexiou mentioned that he explored Hong Kong's New Wave, as well as American genre films and European arthouse films when he was growing up in the 1980s.
4. In Hjort's definition, '[a] film might be said to count as an instance of marked transnationality if the agents who are collectively its author (typically directors, cinematographers, editors, actors, and producers) intentionally direct the attention of viewers towards various transnational properties that encourage thinking about transnationality' (2010: 13–14).
5. Hjort's *milieu*-building transnationalism is rule-governed and collaborative, while, on the other hand, globalising transnationalism is a conscious attempt to seek global appeal in international co-productions, in order to recuperate production costs (2010: 18, 21–2).

References

Abbas, Ackbar ([1997] 2002), *Hong Kong: Culture and the Politics of Disappearance*, Minneapolis, MN: University of Minnesota Press.

Appadurai, Arjun (1996), *Modernity at Large: Cultural Dimensions of Globalization*, Minneapolis, MN: University of Minnesota Press.

Augé, Marc (1995), *Non-Places: Introduction to an Anthropology of Supermodernity*, London: Verso.

Augé, Marc (1996), 'Paris and the Ethnography of the Contemporary World', in Michael Sheringham (ed.), *Parisian Fields*, London: Reaktion, pp. 175–9.

Baudrillard, Jean (1994), *Simulacra and Simulation*, Ann Arbor, MI: University of Michigan Press.

Berry, Chris (2010), 'Imaging the Globalized City: Rem Koolhaas, U-thèque, and the Pearl River Delta', in Yomi Braester and James Tweedie (eds), *Cinema at the City's Edge: Film and Urban Networks in East Asia*, Hong Kong: Hong Kong University Press, pp. 155–70.

Bordwell, David (1998), 'The Case of Film Noir', in David Bordwell, Janet Staiger and Kristin Thompson (eds), *The Classical Hollywood Cinema: Film Style & Mode of Production to 1960*, London: Routledge, pp. 77–80.

Broadhurst, Roderic, King Wa, Lee, and Ching Yee, Chan (2008), 'Crime Trends in Hong Kong, China', in Wing Hong Chui and T. Wing Lo (eds), *Understanding Criminal Justice in Hong Kong*, London: Willan, <https://papers.ssrn.com/sol3/papers.cfm?abstract_id=2171539> (last accessed 18 December 2021).

Chalkou, Maria (2016), 'I nychta, i poli kai i ptosi: Synentefksi me ton Alexi Alexiou' [The Night, the City and the Downfall: Interview with Alexis Alexiou], *Filmicon Blog*, <https://filmiconjournal.com/blog/post/49/h-nyxta-h-poli-kai-h-ptosi> (last accessed 24 August 2021).

Chartier, Jean-Pierre (1946), 'Les Américains aussi font des films noirs', *La Revue du cinéma*, 2, pp. 67–70.

Collier, Joelle (2007), 'The Noir East: Hong Kong Filmmakers' Transmutation of a Hollywood Genre?', in Gina Marchetti and Tam See Kam (eds), *Hong Kong Film, Hollywood and New Global Cinema: No Film is an Island*, Abingdon: Routledge, pp. 137–58.

Desser, David (2003), 'Global Noir: Genre Film in the Age of Transnationalism', in Barry Keith Grant (ed.), *Film Genre Reader III*, Austin, TX: University of Texas Press, pp. 516–36.

Fay, Jennifer, and Nieland, Justus (2009), *Film Noir: Hard-Boiled Modernity and the Cultures of Globalization*, Abingdon: Routledge.

Featherstone, Mike (1996), 'Localism, Globalism and Cultural Identity', in Rob Wilson and Wimal Dissanayake (eds), *Global/Local: Cultural Production and the Transnational Imaginary*, Durham, NC: Duke University Press, pp. 46–77.

Fotiou, Mikela, and Fessas, Nikitas (2017), 'Greek Neo-Noir: Reflecting a Narrative of Crisis', *Filmicon: Journal of Greek Film Studies*, 4, pp. 110–37.

Frank, Nino (1946), 'Un nouveau genre policier: l'aventure criminelle', *L'Écran français*, 61, 28 August, pp. 8–9, 14.

Fu, Poshek, and Desser, David (2000), 'Introduction', in Poshek Fu and David Desser (eds), *The Cinema of Hong Kong: History, Arts, Identity*, Cambridge: Cambridge University Press, pp. 1–12.

Hall, Kenneth E. ([1999] 2012), *John Woo: The Films*, Jefferson, NC: McFarland.

Hardt, Michael, and Negri, Antonio (2000), *Empire*, Cambridge, MA: Harvard University Press.

Hjort, Mette (2010), 'On the Plurality of Cinematic Transnationalism', in Nataša Durovicová and Kathleen E. Newman (eds), *World Cinemas, Transnational Perspectives*, Abingdon: Routledge, pp. 12–33.

Jameson, Fredric (1991), *Postmodernism, or, the Cultural Logic of Late Capitalism*, Durham, NC: Duke University Press.

Koolhaas, Rem ([1995] 1998), 'The Generic City', in Rem Koolhaas and Bruce Mau (eds), *S, M, L, XL*, New York: The Monacelli Press, pp. 1248–64.

Neale, Steve (2000), *Genre and Hollywood*, Abingdon: Routledge.

Ng, Jenna (2005), 'Love in the Time of Transcultural Fusion: Cinephilia, Homage and *Kill Bill*', in Marijke de Valck and Malte Hagener (eds), *Cinephilia: Movies, Love and Memory*, Amsterdam: Amsterdam University Press, pp. 65–79.

Palmer, R. Barton (2004), '"Lounge Time" Reconsidered: Spatial Discontinuity and Temporal Contingency in Out of the Past', in Alain Silver and James Ursini (eds), *Film Noir Reader 4*, New York: Limelight, pp. 53–65.

Park, William (2011), *What is Film Noir*, Lewisburg, PA: Bucknell University Press.

Sassen, Saskia (2001), 'Spatialities and Temporalities of the Global: Elements for a Theorization', in Arjun Appadurai (ed.), *Globalization*, Durham, NC: Duke University Press, pp. 260–78.

Schrader, Paul ([1972] 2003), 'Notes on Film Noir', in Barry Keith Grant (ed.), *Film Genre Reader III*, Austin, TX: University of Texas Press, pp. 229–42.

Sheringham, Michael (1996), 'Introduction', in Michael Sheringham (ed.), *Parisian Fields*, London: Reaktion, pp. 1–7.

Thanouli, Eleftheria (2006), 'Post-Classical Narration: A New Paradigm in Contemporary Cinema', *New Review of Film and Television Studies*, 4:3, pp. 183–96.

12. DARKER WORLDS COME IN SMALL PACKAGES: NEO-NOIR SENSIBILITY IN GREEK CYPRIOT SHORT FILMS

Costas Constandinides

The dominant paradigm of full-length Cypriot films, dubbed 'the cinema of the Cyprus Problem', has been described as suffering 'from an excess of politics often to the detriment of compelling narrative dramaturgy' (Constandinides and Papadakis 2014: 147). Films placed under this broad category go to great lengths to explain the twentieth-century conflicts and ongoing division of Cyprus, mostly through scenes, supporting/minor characters and symbolism that are surplus to narrative development. A group of recently produced Greek-Cypriot full-length films departs from the above conventions, as they focus on patriarchal violence and the dehumanisation of those suffering from it.[1] *Rosemarie* (dir. Florides, 2018) stands out from this group as possibly the first Cypriot-produced (funded only by local sources) feature[2] that consciously applies neo-noir elements.[3] Nonetheless, a film language akin to noir can already be found in works belonging to the realm of Cypriot live-action fiction shorts. Such works focus on the adventures of criminal characters, or characters beaten by the system; their fortune or fall is prescribed by the dark cloak looming over the worlds they inhabit. Thus, the main aim of this chapter is to examine how elements traditionally associated with noir and neo-noir films make their way into Greek-Cypriot shorts produced during the last decade. Furthermore, I will argue that the ominous themes and imagery of the specific Greek-Cypriot shorts can be read as an alternative to 'the cinema of the Cyprus Problem' and other stereotypical, usually idyllic, treatments of the Cypriot landscape. Despite the general understanding of the short film as a transitional form of cinema, the shorts in question display a substantial level of innovation, since they explore a genre-oriented cinema as opposed to the majority of full-length Cypriot films, which have focused on 'offering analysis, comments, and interpretations of the traumatic past and its outcomes related to the Cyprus Problem' (Constandinides and Papadakis 2014: 21).

More specifically, this chapter discusses four Greek-Cypriot live-action fiction shorts that employ noir characteristics to explore the complexities, as well as the limits, of familiar and simultaneously disconcerting circumstances: Ioakim Mylonas's *Oedipus* (2010), funded by the Ministry of Education, Culture, Sport and Youth (MECSY) of the Republic of Cyprus, and his no-budget short *Greenhouse* (2013); the independently made *I metamesonyktia grammi/The Midnight Shift* (2015) by Andreas Kyriacou (aka *Splash*); and *Quidnunc* (2018) by Harry Ayiotis, also funded by MECSY.

Oedipus is a modernised, much darker retelling of Sophocles' *Oedipus Tyrannus* (also known as *Oedipus Rex*) that situates the action in a setting reminiscent of the comic-book art qualities and noirish atmosphere of *Sin City* (dir. Miller and Rodriguez, 2005). A private eye (portrayed by Greek actor Yiannis Stankoglou) is persuaded by the seductive wife (Greek actress Katerina Didaskalou) of a ruthless mafia boss to investigate her son's disappearance. The woman has never seen her child, alive or dead, since she gave birth to him. In *Greenhouse*, a film crew documents the everyday activities and rants of a greenhouse employee (Marios Ioannou). The main character has lost his previous job due to the 2013 financial crisis, leading to more problems, including divorce. Beaten down by the system, he decides to take matters into his own hands. *The Midnight Shift* is a modern take on the myth of Charon, the boatman of Hades, whose duty was to transport the souls of the dead from the world of the living to the underworld, receiving a coin placed in the mouth of the deceased as a form of payment. The role of the modern-day boatman, reimagined as a taxi driver, is assumed by a bank robber (Christodoulos Martas) who cannot escape the eyes of a higher law (Figure 12.1). Lastly, *Quidnunc* is a one-shot psychological thriller depicting the attempt of a young woman, Melanie (Niovi Charalambous), to end her life. Instead she ends up trying to save the life of another woman who seems to suffer at the hands of her partner (Marios Mettis), who exhibits violent sexual behaviour.

The visual narratives of *Oedipus*, *Greenhouse*, *The Midnight Shift* and *Quidnunc* do not celebrate any of the charming or historically important topographies usually associated with representations of Cyprus, which Stylianou and Philippou refer to as 'official visual narratives' (2019: 103). On the contrary, the films challenge such imaginings by using unheroic and disillusioned characters out on the streets of a darker Cyprus; this marks a clear departure from the picturesque locations or conflict-ridden areas previously experienced in Cypriot cinema. Even though the films examined in this chapter appear at first

Figure 12.1   Digital still from *The Midnight Shift*.

glance to engage in intertextual play, they also share a political undertone or commentary, which addresses societal ills and stark economic realities usually overshadowed by two things: the dominant position that the Cyprus Problem holds in local political life, as well as the foregrounding of sun-and-sea stereotypes that aim to promote the island as a tourist destination. Thus, I argue that in the films analysed in this chapter, social commentary is often expressed through the representation of the locales where the action is situated. On the one hand, the films echo conventional noir settings. On the other, they redirect the gaze of the viewer from a stereotypical onscreen representation of Cyprus – wondrous Nature scarred by war atrocities, or an island in the sun, blessed by Aphrodite, the goddess of love – to its cynical and sinister twin, fraught with power-thirsty mafia bosses and criminals lurking unpunished in the night, as well as socially alienated characters prone to flawed decision-making.

A Brief Note on the State of Shorts in Cyprus

Aside from 'how to' guides, there has been little academic-oriented book-length discussion published on the live-action short fiction film (Raskin 2002; Felando 2015). Interestingly, Felando observes that 'for short film cinephiles this is an enormously exciting time as shorts are more visible and easier to access than ever before' (2015: 1), due to online availability. Indeed, the short film titles discussed in this chapter are free-to-view online. In general, locally produced live-action shorts enjoy increased visibility because of the various short film festivals or events with live screenings, organised annually in Cyprus and abroad, which promote Cypriot productions. Some examples include the Cyprus Comic Con, the International Motion Festival Cyprus, Paphos International Film Festival and the London-based Cyprus Short Film Day, organised by the Cultural Section of the Cyprus High Commission United Kingdom. The state-funded International Short Film Festival of Cyprus (ISFFC) is the major annual event for shorts and is a European Film Academy partner that plays a central role in the circulation of short films through island-wide special screenings and the Short Film Day initiative, as well as through collaboration with the Cyprus Broadcasting Corporation, the public service broadcaster of the Republic of Cyprus.

Felando writes that 'the live-action fiction short is generally characterized as a transitional form – as a useful practice medium for students or aspiring filmmakers' (2015: 6). The existing regulations for the funding of short fiction films by MECSY describe the short film in a similar vein: 'The main purpose of the program is to serve as a springboard for the emergence of new film scriptwriters, film directors and technicians' (Cultural Services 2017: 35). For the funding of feature-length films, the regulations require that the designated director must have directed at least one feature-length film, or at least two short films. Several state-funded or independently produced Greek-Cypriot shorts of the last decade or so can be considered instrumental in the development of Cypriot cinema, as well as in the success of recent full-length fiction films.[4] For example, *Oedipus* together with Mylonas's 2006 short *Pharmakon*, both Drama International Film Festival award-winners, are included in a DVD collection funded by MECSY with the aim of promoting Cypriot cinema abroad through special screenings organised by embassies of the Republic of Cyprus. *Pharmakon* was the first ever Cypriot short selected to compete at the Venice Film Festival in its 2006 edition.

Contrary to the dominant understanding of the short film as a transitional stage, recent scholarship (Martin 2015; Felando 2015) treats it as an art form in its own right. Likewise, the shorts by Mylonas, Ayiotis and Kyriacou are treated here as works that belong to the film culture of Cyprus, and as works that have managed to create uncanny worlds that hold the attention of the viewer in a convincing way, regardless of their small-scale logistics. The following sections of this chapter avoid placing the films under the categories proposed by Felando (2015), as their content and style vary. Still, *Oedipus*, *Greenhouse*, *The Midnight Shift* and *Quidnunc* combine the characteristics and strengths of what Felando broadly describes as the 'well-made short' and the 'genre short'. The 'well-made short' refers to a longer version of a short film that affords narrative unity and reasonable character development, while the 'genre short' describes films that partly use the generic conventions of their feature-length equivalents. In other words, imagery remains in the service of a 'coherent and intelligible story' (Raskin 2002: 3), without the development of the story itself being limited to the rules of sequential structure.

Mylonas, Kyriacou and Ayiotis are currently working on their debut features. Furthermore, all three participated in the making of *Rosemarie*:

Mylonas was a cast member, Kyriacou assumed second unit director duties and Ayiotis was credited as the digital image technician. *The Midnight Shift* was later developed into an idea for a TV series, which participated in the MIDPOINT programme. It was pitched during the final session of the programme at Sarajevo Film Festival in 2017, and won the HBO Europe Award. Ayiotis joined Kyriakou as a member of the writing team for *The Midnight Shift* series. Ayiotis's *Quidnunc* won Best Cinematography in the ISFFC's Cypriot films competition section, with actress Niovi Charalambous (who also starred in Florides' *Rosemarie* as a daughter who is raped by her father) receiving a special mention for her performance in the Greek films' competitive category of the International Short Film Festival in Drama, Greece.

Miniature Landscapes and Film Noir in Recent Cypriot Visual Culture

Stylianou and Philippou's recently published analysis of the latter's *Sharki*, a collection of twenty-seven polaroid photographs, proves particularly useful in pointing out the ways the shorts in question disturb existing lens-based representations and documentations of Cyprus.[5] The authors write that Philippou's work replaces the Greek-Cypriot iconography that focuses on idyllic scenery and 'the ever-present sunshine' (2019: 102). They add that the photographer challenges the 'giant' narratives of 'an archetypal Mediterranean topos, offering an alternative reading to overused, mainstream national and cultural understandings' (2019: 102). Stylianou and Philippou refer to an 'official visual narrative' (2019: 103) that has been influenced by the local government's overreliance on aspects of Greek and Byzantine tradition to brand Cyprus. The authors observe the following recurrent elements in photographic representations of the local landscape produced by the Press and Information Office and the Cyprus Tourism Organisation, the main aim being the depiction of Cyprus as a paradisal destination: 'bright sun, crystal-clear waters, green mountains, blooming almond and olive trees, Hellenistic ruins, Byzantine churches, donkeys, stone-built houses' (2019: 103–4). The recent video produced by the Press and Information Office, in collaboration with the Cyprus Tourism Organisation, to promote Cyprus as a filming destination for the purposes of the official presentation of the local government's incentives scheme during the Cyprus Film Summit in 2018 reaffirms Stylianou and Philippou's understanding of the official visual narrative, as well as their claim that such approaches continue in the present.[6]

Interestingly, Wells notes that Philippou's polaroids 'connote a mood familiar from film noir' (2019). She hints at American noirs where the action takes place in under-populated places, motels and gas stations, while she maintains that, even though there is no storyline or plot, the 'haze of the surface of the film' adds to the grimness of Philippou's landscapes and the objects that mark them. Philippou's images are indeed reminiscent of the locales in the Coen brothers' *No Country for Old Men* (2007). Even though the locales in which the stories of Mylonas, Kyriacou and Ayiotis are set do not echo *No Country*, the way they treat their characters is suggestive of the Coens' invitation to watch characters with a detached curiosity. As Snee (2009) has argued, this allows viewers to appreciate the Coens' unique directorial approach, which is defined by attributes such as allusions to film styles and transgressions of convention. For example, *No Country* has been described as a hybrid in the way it mixes the Western and gangster genres, the latter being the twentieth-century 'urban equivalent of the Western', according to Cant (2009: 56). Unlike Philippou's choice of overlooked spaces, Mylonas and Kyriacou use urban locations not only to project the uncertainty of their worlds, but also to convey a sense of omnipresent surveillance. Ayiotis sets the action in what feels like an isolated and quiet hotel, but also expresses a sense of surveillance by using a male voiceover not as a narrator, but as an unseen character who haunts the female protagonist. Similarly to the small-scale polaroids in *Sharki*, the shorts discussed here challenge existing 'official' visual narratives by focusing on locales that come into sharp contrast with established imaginings of Cyprus.

Oedipus and Greenhouse

Shot in black and white, *Oedipus* (running time 24 minutes) tells the story of a young and power-thirsty private eye who is hired by the attractive wife of a mafia boss to investigate the loss of a baby boy who was taken from her right after she gave birth to him, twenty-nine years earlier. She later receives news that the boy died, even though she never witnessed this herself. The mafia boss learns of his wife's intentions and subsequent sexual affair with the detective, and pays the latter a visit at his office in order to silence the investigation. Undaunted by the mafia boss's tactics, the detective lethally retaliates, thus fulfilling a prophecy that he would kill his own father. In an act of defiance, the protagonist knowingly marries his mother, fully satisfying his transgressive desires and greed for power by claiming everything previously 'owned' by his father.

The film opens with an extreme close-up framing a female breast, soon approached by the lustfully thirsty mouth of the protagonist, who massages the aroused nipple with his lips and tongue. The shot fades to black, followed by an extreme close-up of a mature woman's fiery eyes; she is later revealed to be the protagonist's mother. Her back is shown in the next shot while on top during sexual intercourse. The viewer listens to the protagonist's voiceover saying 'Ever since I can remember myself . . . I always wanted to kill my father. . .', right before the director cuts to the film's title.

The protagonist's wife-mother is reintroduced as an archetypal *femme fatale*: 'a woman whose attractiveness masks a predatory ambition', and who will compel the existentially vulnerable male protagonist to 'cheat and murder someone to whom she is attached' (Shillock 2016: 136). Elegantly dressed, the woman seen having sex with the protagonist in the opening flash-forward visits his not-so-fancy office to hire his services, and also to warn him about the dangers of this investigation, should he choose to accept the case. Her entrance is reminiscent of Faye Dunaway's striking first appearance in Polanski's *Chinatown* (1974), in which her sophisticated posture and stylish costume upset the routine of Jack Nicholson's private-eye practice. The actress portraying the wife-mother in *Oedipus* shows only subtle expressions of emotion, retaining an enigmatic, and to a certain extent *blasé*, look throughout the film. The early encounters between the protagonist and his wife-mother seem opportunistic, as both essentially desire, for their own reasons, the demise of the mafia-king father: the mother believes that he is the one responsible for the disappearance of their child; the son sees this case as an opportunity to bring him down and make a name for himself as the one who stood up to the mafia boss, but in the process he realises that he can, instead, claim what was 'rightfully' his.

The following scene takes place in a bar, where the protagonist talks about the dangers of the case with his assistant. Mylonas creatively provides a sense of ever-present surveillance when the bartender disappears into the darkness, right after the two investigators begin to discuss the case. He reappears when the assistant ends the conversation by saying: 'I am going to have to protect you from her too' – referring to the enigmatic nature of the *femme fatale*. The bartender deviously listens to the exchange while disappearing and reappearing in the scene. Unsurprisingly, the mafia boss visits the private eye shortly after the investigation begins.

Grindstaff notes that '[m]any scholars have interpreted *noir* films as remakes of *Oedipus Rex*, a myth of destiny in which the son learns to know and accept his place under the law' (2002: 291). In Mylonas's film, when the son learns the truth about his past, he does not gouge out his eyes in horror at his actions but goes on a killing spree, and assumes power while knowing that he is the killer of his father and that he is marrying his mother. Mylonas uses elements that became characteristic of the look and feel of the first cycle of American film noir, which, for many scholars, began in 1941 with *The Maltese Falcon* (dir. Huston) and ended with *Touch of Evil* (dir. Welles) in 1958. Mylonas's shots are populated by chiaroscuro interiors and exteriors, cigarette smoke, claustrophobic spaces, gunfights and atypical framing. These visual elements are interweaved with backgrounds that combine the qualities of German Expressionist set design and those of a comic book-like metropolitan cityscape that can be seen through a large window behind the private eye's desk. The sets and special effects (rear projection when the protagonist is driving through the night) allude to the visuals of *Sin City* which, of course, in turn allude to the studio-created noirs of the first cycle.

Mylonas briefly uses voiceover narration, which is another cinematic device of the noir style. As previously noted, during the opening shots the protagonist expresses his desire to kill his father. This is a line that does not inspire character likeability; hence Mylonas arguably abandons one of the goals of narrative engagement, that is, character–viewer identification, which usually implies that a character's desires are justified based on principles or values upheld by the audience. Despite this initial voiceover, we do not see the main character's face until the ninth shot, and the director chooses often to have the character's face half-covered by shadow or cigarette smoke. This could be seen as an attempt to playfully deny predictability, or as a way to engage the viewers; for example, with an alarmed curiosity about how the protagonist's desire will progress, as the titular character's act of killing his father is all-too familiar. This approach could be read alongside Snee's reading of the Coen brothers' treatment of direct address. Snee argues that the use of direct address devices, such as 'voice-over narration, flashbacks, dream sequences and point-of-view shots' in the films noirs of the 1940s and 1950s (2009: 221), fails to visually translate the first-person narration of their literary sources. He concludes that the Coens have replaced the attempt to offer the illusion of direct address with the element of intertextual play that renders their cinematic universe inviting – encouraging the viewers to establish a relationship with the Coens' distinct way of telling a story.

Mylonas does call attention to his *own* way of telling the story through a multi-dimensional engagement with the classic text. Moreover, I would add that the final shot, in which the main character cheekily looks directly at the camera, could be seen as the director's way of telling us that he has met the challenge of revamping an ancient classic, or that we might as well enjoy the film without having to test the character's morality. *Oedipus* might be also read as Mylonas's attempt, consciously or otherwise, to enter a dialogue with another noirish and violent reimagining of the Oedipus myth, namely *Oldboy* (dir. Park, 2003). *Oldboy* begins with the main character's wish to tell his story. Contrary to Mylonas's *Oedipus*, we are positioned to care about the emotionally desperate protagonist, Oh Dae-su. Furthermore, unlike Oh Dae-su's acts of self-punishment and his effort to 'unbury his own sins' (Hee-seung 2016: 6), Mylonas's protagonist buries his sins and rewards himself with 'forbidden pleasures'.

Mylonas explores direct address by employing a documentary-like technique in his next short, *Greenhouse*, whereby the protagonist speaks directly to the camera of a film crew present in the narrative world of the film. Mylonas invites the viewers to sympathise with the struggles of the protagonist, but abruptly interrupts the established connection when the character becomes increasingly nervous. For this zero-budget short, also shot in black and white,

Mylonas drew inspiration from the Belgian mockumentary *Man Bites Dog* (dir. Belvaux, Bonzel and Poelvoorde, 1992). Mylonas's protagonist has been severely affected by the 2013 financial crisis in Cyprus, but his plan to punish those responsible for his suffering goes wrong. A film crew follows his *flâneur*-like, day-to-day protest against things such as the mushrooming of churches and monuments during a period of crisis.[7] In one scene he is filmed walking towards a monument which appears (as the crew films the action from a distance) to commemorate acts of heroism related to a national struggle. The character's negative reaction works as a political critique that may not be intended to undermine the heroic act associated with the monument, but certainly implies that local power structures are sweeping their mismanagement of the crisis under the carpet by foregrounding past glories.

Later in the film, the protagonist drives the crew through the streets of an urban environment, and asks them whether they can see anything aesthetically rich or pleasing around them, in order to claim that, even when Cyprus was financially stable, the population chose to enter a hibernation-like state instead of investing in education and the arts. It is later revealed that the protagonist was, from the outset, preparing a large-scale violent act to 'shock' those responsible. His position becomes even gloomier as he realises that his ex-wife and their child are visiting the part of the city where a deadly explosive device, engineered and placed by him, is about to go off.

Greenhouse may not offer the pleasures of a playful noir aesthetic, but the director's choice to use black-and-white photography establishes a sinister atmosphere that is, at times, highly evocative of German Expressionist style, especially during the scene when the protagonist lights a fire to keep himself warm in the dilapidated house where he lives. The resulting chiaroscuro effect creates menacing shadows that swallow the protagonist and, along with him, any sign of pulling back from his thoroughly planned act of violence.

Macek lists some of the key characteristics associated with neo-noir through his analysis of *8mm* (dir. Schumacher, 1999) and *Strange Days* (dir. Bigelow, 1995), stressing the readiness of the films to 'indulge in ever more graphic, ever more shocking depictions of the violence and perverse sexuality that have long been central ingredients of the genre' (Macek 2002: 375). Furthermore, he notes that the neo-noir films of the 1990s 'cultivate a distinctly apocalyptic mood and are set in foreboding, cesspool cities, overrun by crime and torn by deep social divisions, which function as potent icons of vice and evil' (2002: 375). More so than *Oedipus*, *Greenhouse* meets the above description, as Mylonas places his protagonist in a real, rather than a highly stylised and studio-created, urban environment. Even though *Greenhouse*'s story is not driven by a complex investigation incited by a *femme fatale*, it nevertheless presents a nightmarish world against the backdrop of the banking crisis in Cyprus. In his article on neo-noir films of the 1970s, Willis argues that 'an anchoring of the term

[noir] as a descriptor of films that have at least part of their narrative organization, representational strategies or visual style rooted in a response to the society that produced it is vital' (2013: 31). Hence, Mylonas's *Greenhouse* is a neo-noir response to a society experiencing the consequences of a financial crisis; a no-budget film which offers a pessimistic interpretation of the conditions that produced it.

Mylonas does not shy away from critiquing the urban environments of Cyprus; he does so by showing that the urban setting does not provide any sense of comfort to the protagonist, and by offering a fitting analogy in naming his film *Greenhouse*. The city enhances the limitations felt by the character, and forms an aesthetic alternative to visual narratives that depict Cyprus as an exotic and unspoiled place. Both *Oedipus* and *Greenhouse* mirror a morally bankrupt world, but *Greenhouse*'s documentary-like style helps provide a starker reading of a society struggling with high levels of unemployment and austerity measures, including severe budgetary cuts to the annual funding allocated for the development of film works. Notably, for the period 2013–14 no state funding for films was granted due to the financial crisis. Mylonas's no-budget short can, thus, be seen as a protest film, and his lone protagonist possibly mirrors the director's effort to react to a dire sociopolitical condition. *Greenhouse* can be read as a comment on society's mild reaction to the mismanagement of the crisis, since no significant mass social movement emerged, and no public protest took place, unlike what happened elsewhere.

THE MIDNIGHT SHIFT AND QUIDNUNC

The Midnight Shift (running time 14 minutes) opens with a quote from Dante's *Divine Comedy*, ending with the phrase 'All hope abandon, ye who enter here.' The quote is followed by a mobile, aerial, night-time shot of an urban setting, the silence of which is interrupted by the sound of an emergency vehicle, complemented by an ominous musical score. In the suspense-filled opening, the camera gradually reveals a building in flames, while it slowly ascends to frame the fast-moving vehicle. A news announcement is simultaneously introduced, informing the viewer that 'a major bank branch in the city centre is on fire', and further reporting that one of the security guards is still in the building, and that the police are investigating a suspected arson attack aimed at robbing the bank. The following series of shots introduce the main character, who jumps out of a rubbish skip where he has been hiding. He then walks towards a taxi service office located across the street, carrying a duffel bag. A handwritten note, taped to the window on the front façade of the office, informs the main character that a taxi driver is needed for the midnight shift. We view the main character framed from various angles, while he waits for someone to appear, until a mysterious voice on the radio starts giving instructions. The newly hired driver takes the keys located among photos pinned on a notice board. The photos seem to have been taken in a not-so-distant past, and at different locations, with one man inexplicably appearing in all of them. The driver walks to the basement garage of the building, guarded by three dobermans (an allusion to Cerberus, the three-headed hound that guards the gates of the underworld), to locate the old taxi that he will be driving during his shift. It is later revealed that the driver is one of the criminals on the run from the bank heist, which apparently went wrong, forcing him to take cover as a taxi driver. His first passenger is the dead security guard caught in the fire; guilt-ridden, the driver gives the duffel bag containing the stolen money to the guard's family as a form of recompense for his acts, before resuming his duties.

Kyriacou and his team described the film as 'Med-noir', when they presented it as part of their pitch during the MIDPOINT TV launch at the 2017 Sarajevo Film Festival (Economou 2017). 'Med-noir' hints at the intention of Kyriacou and his team to offer an alternative reading to commonplace representations of Mediterranean topographies, in a manner that brings to the surface the bleak underbelly of Cypriot society, since the protagonist journeys through the streets of nocturnal Cyprus to drive the dead to their final destination. Unlike the other shorts examined in this chapter, in *The Midnight Shift* the protagonist is given the opportunity to redeem himself, as well as to act as a positive narrative agent, bringing a sense of closure to those affected by his actions.

Ayiotis's 27-minute *Quidnunc* is a Cypriot addition to the one-shot short film trend. The film's main character is a seemingly mentally ill woman, Melanie, who checks in at a hotel in the mountainous region of Cyprus to end her life. She makes a last phone call to her mother, in order to listen to her baby boy's voice. Ominous music prepares the viewer for the introduction of a male voice, which interrupts her plan. Apparently the voice has been haunting her for some time, as she carries a voice recorder with her in the hope of capturing it on tape. Her unsuccessful effort ends with the odd reintroduction of a character she met earlier in the hotel lift who, dressed as a cowboy (a possible reference to David Lynch's habit of bringing together sinister and seemingly mundane elements), performs a ritualistic cowboy dance on an area extending outside Melanie's room's balcony. The camera follows the man, who enters his hotel room through an open balcony door, revealing a female character handcuffed and gagged in his bathroom. The camera moves outside the bathroom, showing Melanie standing on the balcony, holding a gun and a recording device, while listening to the screams of the woman in the bathroom. That is when she decides to 'investigate' (hence the title of the film)[8] what is happening in the room next to hers. The man's perverse behaviour escalates, forcing the main character to act more decisively, which leads to Melanie shooting him. In a sudden twist of events, when the bound woman is freed by Melanie, she runs to the dead body, which turns out to be that of her husband, screaming that the whole thing was part of a sexual roleplay. The male voice celebrates Melanie's unsuccessful heroism, yet the film ends with the wife pointing the gun at Melanie, as the latter walks towards the gun to aggravate the situation.

Melanie does not invite a typical *femme fatale* reading, as she is not introduced in a sexually provocative manner and does not carefully plan her actions. She is not a dispassionate character, nor does she seem able to control her demeanour. However, she does not hesitate to use a gun, which might suggest that the man whose voice haunts her met an end similar to that of the pervy hotel guest. The film builds the story in a manner that encourages viewers to experience it as a female revenge movie, but Ayiotis offers a different development that succeeds in further detaching viewers from the world of the film, since he does not reveal much about Melanie's past to begin with. Still, the director establishes his film's connection to noir sensibility by offering a noir type of alienation from the perspective of a female character, who is drawn into a dangerous situation by the masculine theatrics of one of the hotel guests.

On the one hand, Ayiotis's choice to include a scene in which Melanie wants to listen to the voice of her baby boy on the phone deepens the mistrust and uncertainty permeating the film's narrative world, as the mother sees herself as a threat to the potentially healthier world on the other end of the phone. On the other hand, the presence of a child works to humanise Melanie, who goes to great lengths to protect the woman in the room next to hers. Unlike *Oedipus*'s nihilism, *Greenhouse*, *The Midnight Shift* and *Quidnunc* seek to negotiate the forces that lead to violence by foregrounding families and children as a means of humanising their protagonists. However, *Greenhouse*, *The Midnight Shift* and *Quidnunc* do not represent children as victims of abuse, but as characters that the protagonists, in their role as parents or bearers of bad news, care about.

Conclusion

This chapter began with a brief description of the dominant paradigm of full-length Cypriot films, as well as of recent trends, to illustrate that a genre-oriented cinema, and in effect a noir style, can be predominantly found in Greek-Cypriot shorts made from 2010 onwards. I have argued that the treatment of locales in the specific shorts, as well as the anti-heroic portrayal or the unsuccessful heroism of the protagonists, form an alternative aesthetic, and a reading that challenges the political aspirations of the cinema of the Cyprus Problem, as well as 'official' visual narratives depicting Cyprus as an idyllic place. I examined the use of noir elements in four Greek-Cypriot live-action fiction shorts. *Oedipus* playfully uses noir iconography to stylise a modern and darker retelling of Sophocles' *Oedipus Rex*, in which Oedipus is imagined as a private eye who violently reclaims his fate and rises to power. *Greenhouse* traps its protagonist in a suffocating urban environment, against the backdrop of the 2013 financial crisis in Cyprus. The black-and-white cinematography helps to establish a world in despair, and a society deeply affected by financial stagnation. *The Midnight Shift* creates a mysterious universe that blurs the boundaries between fantasy and reality which in essence reflects the growth of supernatural noir in film and television. The short features a protagonist who is hired by a higher power in order to transport the dead to their resting place, as a form of punishment for his criminal activities. *Quidnunc* negotiates the struggle of its female protagonist to escape a past about which the audience does not learn much. However, the film does this in such a way that the slice of her life that the viewers get to experience is enough to convince them of the strange world she is placed in, and the uncanny nature of her relationship with a haunting male voice.

All these films reject the use of locales associated with sun-and-sea stereotypes and the ongoing division of Cyprus, while they illustrate a desire to explore, and simultaneously contest, generic conventions. By doing so, they offer a social commentary that does not focus on the past, but on feelings of alienation, loss, stagnation and inconceivable criminal acts characterising less visible aspects of Cypriot society. Finally, this chapter aimed to put the shorts discussed here at the centre of Cypriot cinema's treatment of neo-noir qualities, in the hope of contributing to the growth of a subfield, namely short-film studies, which currently receives minimal scholarly attention.

Notes

1. *Boy on the Bridge* (dir. Charalambous, 2017), *Rosemarie* (dir. Florides, 2018) and *Pause* (dir. Mishiali, 2018) focus on the character of the tyrannical father, who subdues family members through rape or domestic violence.
2. Cypriot-born director Yannis Economides's works such as *Knifer* (2010) and *Stratos* (2014) can be discussed along the lines of neo-noir sensibility. However, Cyprus participates as a minor co-producing country, and the films' themes, characters and locations are explored through a Greek-oriented lens.
3. *Rosemarie*'s main character is a TV soap-opera writer, who draws inspiration from the dysfunctional family living next to the apartment he has recently moved into. Inspiration gradually becomes an obsession that entangles the main character into a sort of *Rear Window* meets *Chinatown* (the title *Rosemarie* also works as a reference to Polanski's cinema) web of mystery. Eventually the main character uncovers the monstrous nature of the patriarch of the family, who has raped and impregnated his daughter.
4. For example, the recent Greek–Cypriot debut features *Smuggling Hendrix* (dir. Piperides, 2018) and *Pause* received international critical acclaim. The former won the 'best international narrative feature' award at Tribeca Film Festival, while the latter secured official selection status at Karlovy Vary International Film Festival. It should be noted, however, that the shorts directed by Piperides (*The Immortalizer*

[2013] – available online) and Mishiali (*Dead End* [2013] – also available online) already provided a sense of cinematic complexity and intelligence, establishing the two as powerhouse artists within local culture.
5. See the images included in a review of Philippou's *Sharki* by Liz Wells, available at <https://medium.com/exposure-magazine/nicos-philippous-sharqi-4ba4e6cb6f9b> (last accessed 9 July 2021).
6. The video is available on YouTube: <https://www.youtube.com/watch?v=Vs0OleIMVEg> (last accessed 9 July 2021).
7. The location is not named, but a local viewer would recognise parts of the city of Limassol.
8. According to the Cambridge Dictionary Online, a quidnunc is 'someone who enjoys knowing and talking about other people's private lives'. Available at <https://dictionary.cambridge.org/dictionary/english/quidnunc> (last accessed 9 July 2021).

References

Cant, John (2009), 'Oedipus Rests: Mimesis and Allegory in *No Country for Old Men*', in Lynnea Chapman King, Rick Wallach and James Welsh (eds), *No Country for Old Men: From Novel to Film*, Lanham, MD: Scarecrow Press, pp. 46–59.

Constandinides, Costas, and Papadakis, Yiannis (eds) (2014), *Cypriot Cinemas: Memory, Conflict, and Identity in the Margins of Europe*, London: Bloomsbury Academic.

Cultural Services – Ministry of Education and Culture (2017), *Funding Programmes regulation for the Support of Cinematographic Films*, Lefkosia, <http://filmingincyprus.gov.cy/wp-content/uploads/2018/02/NEW-PROGRAMMES-REGULATION-2017-2020-pdf.pdf > (last accessed 30 September 2020).

Economou, Vassilis (2017), '"Med-noir" Series *The Midnight Shift* wins at MIDPOINT TV Launch in Sarajevo', *Cineuropa*, 21 August, <https://cineuropa.org/en/newsdetail/333250/> (last accessed 30 August 2021).

Felando, Cynthia (2015), *Discovering Short Films: The History and Style of Live-Action Fiction Shorts*, New York: Palgrave Macmillan.

Grindstaff, Laura (2002), 'Pretty Woman with a Gun: *La Femme Nikita* and the Textual Politics of "The Remake"', in Jennifer Forrest and Leonard R. Koos (eds), *Dead Ringers: The Remake in Theory and Practice*, Albany, NY: SUNY Press, pp. 273–308.

Hee-seung, Irene Lee (2016): '"My name is Oh Dae-su": A Mirrored Image of Oedipus in Park Chan-wook's *Oldboy*', *Journal of Japanese and Korean Cinema*, 8:2, pp. 1–13.

King, Lynnea Chapman, Wallach, Rick, and Welsh, James (eds) (2009), *No Country for Old Men: From Novel to Film*, Lanham, MD: Scarecrow Press.

Macek, Steve (2002), 'The Political Uses of the Neo-Noir City: Ideology, Genre, and the Urban Landscape in *8mm* and *Strange Days*', *The Journal of American Culture*, 25:3–4, pp. 375–83.

Martin, Adrian Paul (2015), 'Jumping from the Feature-length Bridge', *Empedocles: European Journal for the Philosophy of Communication*, 5:1–2, pp. 19–24.

Raskin, Richard (2002), *The Art of the Short Fiction Film: A Shot by Shot Study of Nine Modern Classics*, Jefferson, NC: McFarland.

Scott, A. O. (2011), 'An Oscar Film Festival, All in One Screening', *The New York Times*, 10 February, <https://www.nytimes.com/2011/02/11/movies/11oscar.html> (last accessed 30 August 2021).

Shillock, Larry (2016), '*Black Widow*, Gender Criticism, and the Narrative Agency of the *Femme Fatale*', *Interdisciplinary Humanities*, 33:1: pp. 136–49.

Snee, Brian J. (2009), 'Soft-Boiled Cinema: Joel and Ethan Coens' Neo-Classical Neo-Noirs', *Literature Film Quarterly*, 37:3, pp. 212–23.

Stylianou, Elena, and Philippou, Nicos (2019), 'Miniature Landscapes', *Photographies*, 12:1, pp. 99–116.

Wells, Liz (2019), [Review of *Sharqi* by Nicos Philippou], *Exposure Magazine*, 15 June, <https://medium.com/exposure-magazine/nicos-philippous-sharqi-4ba4e6cb6f9b> (last accessed 9 July 2021).

Willis, Andy (2013), 'Neo-Noir: The Cultural Significance (and Insignificance) of a Film Style', *Film International*, 11:5, pp. 31–7.

13. GREEK SLEUTHS AND TOUGH COPS: NOIR MASCULINITIES IN TELEVISION CRIME SHOWS (1992–2020)

Georgia Aitaki and Spyridon Chairetis

This chapter engages with noir scholarship to investigate how three Greek television crime shows, produced during different chronological periods and broadcast by different channels, have contributed to varied and complex constructions of noir masculinities. The empirical focus is placed on *Tmima ithon/Vice Squad* (ANT1, 1992–95), which centres around the adventures of a gender-mixed group of police officers dealing with cases of marginalised delinquents and organised criminal networks; *Oi istories tou astynomou Beka/The Stories of Officer Bekas* (ALPHA, 2006–08), a television adaptation of Yannis Maris's popular eponymous book series; and *Eteros ego: Hamenes psyches/ The Other Me: Lost Souls* (COSMOTE, 2019–20), a recent show aired by a pay TV network featuring a male-dominated cast and a thematic structure borrowing from both local and foreign detective models.[1] Drawing from discussions around the cinematic legacies of noir and its international expressions on the small screen, the primary aim of this chapter is to shed light on yet another neglected area of the Greek noir universe, that of the noirness of television fiction.

While the above television shows are largely labelled as crime shows, they employ aesthetics, narrative structures and conventions that accommodate the expression of noir influences and/or ambitions. More specifically, the selected texts do more than simply allowing the viewer to follow the detectives' journey through the investigation of the crime to its final resolution. Ever since the 1940s, noir's 'baggage' has been linked with 'specific cultural preoccupations and ways of speaking about men' (Studlar 2013: 372). Thus, noir is as much about diagnosing masculinities as it is about detecting crime. In nominating noir masculinity as the key analytical lens of this chapter, we examine representations of male detectives woven into the main narrative of the texts they 'inhabit', as well as the actors who embody these roles, their star personas and career trajectories (Gates 2006: 6). To do so, we conduct a character and performance study, registering the ways that character and performance signs (Butler 2012; Cantrell and Hogg 2018; Dyer 1998a), including appearance, style, tone, rhythm, objective correlatives – that is, individual objects linked to characters (Butler 2012: 62) – as well as the actors' image and performances in other roles, inform and allow for a more thorough understanding of noir masculinities in the context of Greek television fiction.

Noir Masculinities on Television

Noir constitutes a term which is easier to trace than to define (Auerbach 2011; Conard 2007; Krutnik 1991). The plurality of components characterising film noir has been summarised as a specific cycle of films beginning in the early 1940s and lasting until nearly the end of the 1950s, with a distinctive visual style drawing from German Expressionist cinema and French Surrealism, a highly fatalistic sensibility, and point of view reflecting American hard-boiled fiction (Sanders 2008: 2). By extension, neo-noir emerged as a term to describe post-classic noir period texts, containing noir themes and sensibilities (Conard 2007: 2). Today, more than ever, noir has arguably become 'a distended, indistinct term that can describe almost any object, text, or cultural phenomenon that projects a mood of unhappiness or moral confusion' (Steenberg 2017: 62).

Although the exact terms and conditions of noirness are continuously under negotiation, diverse academic voices converge around the fact that, as a cultural category, noir provides fertile ground for examining ambiguities and complexities relating to gender. Ever since its establishment as 'a retrospectively constructed category' (Sonnet 2010: 10), noir has been addressed as a vehicle for understanding masculinity (Short 2019). Traditionally, in noir texts, male protagonists, typically cast as private detectives, police officers or criminals, exert varying degrees of violence and machismo, embodying 'a certain anxiety over the existence and definition of masculinity and normality' (Dyer 1998b: 115). Such preoccupations regarding the quest for, and the maintenance of, a 'proper' masculinity have led scholars to envision noir as a 'male-dominated form' (Spicer 2002: 85). Thus, noir proffers possibilities to problematise how men are represented on screen, as well as the ways they experience emotions, selfhood and their relationships with other male, as well as female, characters (Cohan 1997; Martin 1999). The male protagonists of film noir are frequently tied to the image of the 'hard-boiled' hero that is endemic in classic crime fictions of the

1920s and 1930s. This supposedly unassailable image, however, is characterised by inconsistencies and even failures. More often than not, noir protagonists are prone to mistakes or flaws that sabotage their attempts to retain their power (Paretsky 2007) and separate themselves from a 'chaotic, variable, shifting' societal system and the violence it holds (Day 1993: 127).

TV noir bears a long genealogy in the history of the medium, and a strong resemblance to film noir. From the mid-1950s to the late 1960s, shows broadcast on US television featured both upcoming (young) and more established (older) male actors in leading roles. From the famous Jack Webb starring as Sergeant Joe Friday in *Dragnet* (NBC, 1951–58) to James Franciscus and John McIntire as Detective Jimmy Halloran and Lieutenant Dan Muldoon respectively in *Naked City* (ABC 1958–59, 1960–63), men serving in working-class environments constitute prominent figures in the TV noir universe. Such detectives and detective groups are characterised by teamwork and professionalism; they employ investigative technology, while exuding a type of masculinity that appears to be 'organized, methodical, and driven by duty' (Gates 2006: 90). Whereas the 1970s signified a partial eclipse of noir from television (Sanders 2008: 4), the following decade witnessed a resurgence of noir. Notably, productions such as *Miami Vice* (NBC, 1984–89) and *Crime Story* (NBC, 1986–88) proposed images of detectives whose hypermasculine physique, 'wise-cracking defiance and a lot of firepower' (King 1999: 2) highlighted their difference from earlier portrayals of their colleagues, and reflected an attempt to dissociate themselves from women and society, thus reducing the perceived risk of 'feminisation'.

More recently, new interpretations of noirness on the small screen bring to light male protagonists who defy the tradition of physical toughness, and are eager to endorse more 'feminine' aspects of masculinity and 'intellectual' personality traits. Such permutations are noticeable in the recent cycle of Nordic noir; shows such as *Wallander* (TV4, 2005–13), *Forbrydelsen/The Killing* (DR1, 2007–12) and *Bron/Broen/The Bridge* (SVT1/DR1, 2011–18) are replete with socially and emotionally challenged, even melancholic, characters (Waade 2017), and thus reiterate the common noir trope of utilising bleak locations and landscapes as symbols of the psychological state of the detective (Creeber 2015).

An interest in gender, with a particular focus on the construction and reception of noir masculinities, has also been picked up by Greek academia in studies of both older and more recent cinematic texts that discuss Greek film noir, its characters and their ways of relating to one another (Fessas and Kosma 2017; Fotiou and Fessas 2017; Kyriakos 2017), studies of masculinities informing and defining the police thriller of the 1950s and 1960s (Poupou 2019), as well as attempts to address disability, sexuality and desire as components of the construction of noir characters in 1960s films (Fessas 2020). This chapter contributes to the above tradition, taking the first step towards the study of televisual manifestations of noir on Greek television by means of dissecting the male leads of three popular crime shows. We adopt a diachronic analytical lens that zooms in on texts from different historical periods of Greek television and society, in an attempt to capture the defining characteristics of the Greek TV male detective, as well as their development across time. An analysis of this kind, synthesising textual, intertextual and extratextual elements, approaches noirness from a multi-directional perspective, uncovering a nexus of threads that inform our understandings of noir texts, but also (noir) men and masculinities.

VICE SQUAD: POLICE VETERANS AND HUNKY HARD-BOILED COPS

Director Manousos Manousakis is known for a number of sentimental/social television dramas that utilise the 'difficult romance' trope to address societal issues that beset and polarise Greek society (Aitaki 2020). Yet long before his name became synonymous with this narrative and thematic formula, Manousakis experimented with police/crime drama, creating *Vice Squad* (Figure 13.1).[2] Chronicling for three seasons the adventures of a team of police officers working for the Vice Department of Athens, the show attracted hundreds of thousands of viewers, and has cemented its status as one of 'the most compelling hardcore

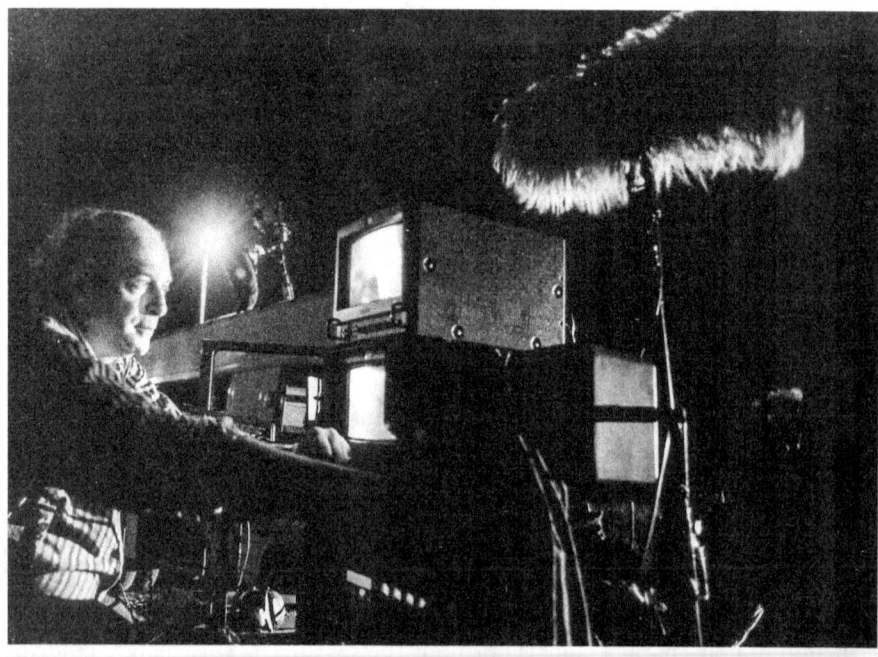

Figure 13.1   The director of *Vice Squad*, Manousos Manousakis, on set.

crime dramas' in the history of Greek television (Anon. 2020).³ The show's raw iconography, vulgar language and scopophilic elements broke many boundaries back in the 1990s, and continue to do so.⁴

According to Kassaveti and Papoulis (2019: 42), three main traditions shaped the way that crime series came about on Greek television: nineteenth-century European paraliterature, 1960–70s Greek crime literature – especially as popularised by Yannis Maris – and US radio and television genres (under formation in the late 1940s). Already in the 1970s, 'Maris's branded' television adaptations were appearing on Greek state-run television, while the author himself wrote the scripts for some of these (Kassaveti and Papoulis 2019: 42–3), such as *Astynomikes istories/Police Stories* (YENED, 1973) and *Ypopsies/Suspicions* (ERT, 1977). *Vice Squad* constitutes both a continuation and a disruption of this tradition. In fact, *Vice Squad* inherited many of the genre's thematic and structural ingredients; Athens is consistently presented as a dark and dangerous space, in which the police emerge as the only available institution to tackle violence, disorder and social unrest by any possible means. Unlike its predecessors, however, *Vice Squad* integrated a rather flexible use of the 'whodunit' formula and gave place to a constellation of characters in the roles of police officers/detectives.

From a close examination of *Vice Squad*'s main characters, it is possible to identify groupings and common elements among some of the male protagonists of the show. For example, Lieutenant Michalis Kessanlis (Christos Tsagkas) and Sub-Lieutenant Apostolos Velios (Timos Perlegas)⁵ – the senior and relatively older officers – are old-school detectives whose experience, wisdom and authority position them at the top of the hierarchy of the squad, and assign them a type of paternal function. Both men embody the archetypal loner detective, prioritising work over their private lives and, thus, existing outside the 'socioeconomic order of family, friends, and home' (Scaggs 2005: 59). Both of these figures also correspond to the archetype of the veteran cop: wise and reliable in work settings, but troubled, hurt and even failed in the private sphere – reminiscent of characters such as *Law & Order*'s (NBC, 1990–2010) Lennie Briscoe. In several episodes, viewers witness the two male detectives describing the condition of their personal lives: stern but melancholic Kessanlis is divorced because his wife could not tolerate his busy professional schedule, while congenial Velios remains single by choice, and reluctant to invest in relationships outside his professional network.

The other end of the spectrum of this professionally hierarchical and symbolically parent–child relationship is occupied by younger officers. Generally, male officers tend to endorse facets of macho masculinity, often engaging in dismissive and patronising comments directed towards female suspects and members of the police force. By concentrating on the perceived (and even 'innate') differences between women and men, *Vice Squad* makes clear that this is primarily a show about the latter, with the women playing secondary roles. In most cases, this aspect of the show is fully illustrated through the young officers' hypermasculine performances, as they compete to attain the alpha male position (under the watchful eye of Kessanlis) within the team. One such tension is triggered early on by the arrival of Stavros Karras (Apostolos Gletsos), a newly appointed officer who is asked to collaborate with the more experienced Pavlos Kampanis (Theofilos Vandoros). Eventually, the two of them evolve as supplementary forces, often embodying the good cop/bad cop trope in their encounters with suspects and criminals. Karras (a role that propelled Gletsos to fame and to the status of one Greece's most recognisable macho sex symbols)[6] is depicted as the newbie, sensitive, clean-cut, book-smart police officer, whose credentials are primarily associated with excellent grades in the police academy; however, he has to toughen up in order to be able to cope with the exigencies of his role in the team. In this way, he contributes to another common trope that works both in terms of antithesis and complement to the 'veteran' figures; young and inexperienced police officers, such as Steve Keller in *The Streets of San Francisco* (ABC, 1972–77) or, more recently, Sebastian Drummer in *La Trêve/The Break* (Netflix, 2016–), intensify the tension between youth/quixotism and experience/cynicism. On the other hand, Kampanis is the street-smart cop, familiar with the 'code of the night'. His sly manner and sleazy way of approaching women, combined with his casual clothing and brutal interrogation methods, can camouflage him as comfortably belonging to the world of the margins. What further renders Kampanis a unique figure in *Vice Squad* and, rightfully, one of the most iconic characters of 1990s Greek television (this was surely the most recognisable role of Vandoros's career – he died in 2021) is the character's long pony-tail; the symbolic dimension of Kampanis's hair is particularly important, since long hair was decoded as a deviant corporeal appearance associated with crime (Avdela 2008), before eventually turning into a fashionable hairstyle for men.

A further reshuffling of masculine dynamics takes place with the arrival of Angelos Rokos, a tough and intimidating, as well as slightly arrogant, cop with several years of experience under his belt, and a black leather jacket as his trademark style. Played by Panos Michalopoulos, an actor who has left a deep imprint in Greek popular culture through roles in 'videomovies' (*videotainies*) of the 1980s,[7] Rokos, more than any other character in *Vice Squad*, makes the show's noir undertones visible, not only by embodying a version of the archetypal hard-boiled cop who finds it difficult to separate his professional and private life, but also by exemplifying the 'detective on the edge' model (Turnbull 2014: 126). Encoded as a man of few words, Rokos appears lost in his own world; he consumes alcohol while on duty, and becomes emotionally involved in the cases he undertakes, adhering to a genealogy of detectives who cannot escape aspects of their past. According to popular criticism, such mavericks, that is, 'screwed-up sleuths whose inner demons command almost as much attention as the stomach-churning crimes they solve, using methods invariably described as "unorthodox"' (Chu 2010), constitute exemplifications of a European crime/noir TV drama (and literary) tradition that turns the spotlight on tormented cops, including characters such as the Scottish Inspector John Rebus, the Swedish Inspector Kurt Wallander and the English Detective Chief Inspector John Luther, whereas roles with similar characteristics are mainly reserved for private investigators in examples from across the Atlantic (Ibid.).

Officer Bekas: The (Fatherly) Detective Next Door

Officer Bekas is an iconic popular culture figure created by pulp detective fiction writer Yannis Maris in the early 1950s. Bekas was introduced by Maris in his first novel (from a serialised story) *Eglima sto Kolonaki/Murder in Kolonaki* in 1953, 'obviously influenced by the work of prolific Belgian novelist Georges Simenon' (Agathos 2018: 105) and his legendary *commissaire* Jules Maigret. The significance of Bekas, especially regarding Maris's sociopolitical surroundings, has been elaborated in valuable self-standing treatises (Apostolidis 2012; Leontaritis 2013), but also in the form of explanatory supplements integrated in reissues of the novels.[8] Through this type of contextualisation, Bekas has become established as a product of specific historical and political conditions related to social transformations in the urban society of the 1960s, but also as a character of recognisable personality and iconography, described as an 'angry fat tomcat', resembling a neighbourhood grocer rather than a member of the police force (Apostolidis 2012: 35).

While the literary and cinematic versions of Bekas have been placed under the scholarly microscope and found their place within broad discussions regarding noir representations and debates, less attention has been directed towards the televisual Bekas. Officer Bekas, just like Maigret and many other fictional detectives who span media forms and historical periods, has been incarnated by various actors on the small screen, the most memorable interpretation of the role being that of Stavros Xenidis in both public and private television productions.[9] In *The Stories of Officer Bekas*, Bekas returns in the guise of Ieroklis Michailidis. Consistent with Xenidis's performance, Michailidis's Bekas is genial and approachable, asking questions with a certain degree of naivety, without appearing threatening to his interlocutors. Encompassing the model of the cerebral detective, Bekas's toolbox for solving riddles (primarily murders) draws heavily from psychological interpretations of people and situations, resonating with Maigret's observant style (Davis 2017), and infusing it with the confidence of age and the wisdom of experience; professional and dedicated to his job, he derives pleasure from putting together the pieces of the puzzle, while he is driven by a sense of duty. One could argue that this an important point of convergence between Michailidis's Bekas and Minas Chatzisavvas's Kostas Charitos in *Nychterino deltio/Late News* (ET1, 1998–99) and *Amyna zonis/ Zone Defence* (ET1, 2007–08), as both characters contribute to the televisual mosaic of middle-class and middle-aged police officers, who are not necessarily characterised by exceptional intellectual abilities, but rather by an aptitude for understanding human relationships and, mainly, motives (Chartoulari 1998).[10]

Michailidis's Bekas radiates familiarity, ordinariness, old-fashionedness and fatherhood, blended together in the character's construction and performance. First, Michailidis is a recognisable performer to many generations of Greek audiences, and a 'friendly' vehicle for the reintroduction of Bekas to younger viewers who are not necessarily familiar either with the character's literary background or with the previous TV appearances.[11] Furthermore, Michailidis's stocky body type and realistic age casting (he was between 46 and 48 years old during the time he was playing the part) make him a good fit for a character who is meant to appear as ordinary as a man next door. Much like Bekas in Maris's stories, Michailidis's Bekas is interested in a traditional way of life, and stays away from anything modern(ist); he wears old-fashioned suits, has his hair combed back, and always keeps a handkerchief in his pocket. He refuses to give up on his old Ford Taurus TC (a model produced between 1970 and 1975), does not watch television and despises the A/C. We also often see him having his meals either at home, cooked by his wife, or at a *taverna*, with a preference for traditional cuisine such as *gemista* (stuffed tomatoes or peppers) with feta cheese, and smoking 'heavy' cigarettes using a cigarette holder. He only drinks 'Greek' coffee and, on the rare occasion that he is obliged or invited to have a drink, he prefers cognac to the trendy 'mosquito', as he – jokingly or not – mispronounces the popular cocktail mojito. Of particular importance is the character's rhythm and movements; Michailidis plays Bekas at a characteristic slow pace (albeit avoiding the drowsy version of the character described by Maris). Even the way that he walks, holding his hands behind his back (sometimes also 'playing' with his keys), as if wandering, rather than walking, towards a particular destination, are reminiscent of a kinesiology attached to an older generation.

Fatherhood enters the equation through the hierarchical and generational distance between Bekas and his subordinates, Petros Athanasiou (Pygmalion Dadakaridis), Angeliki Christoforou (Pinelopi Anastasopoulou in the first season) and Eleni Sotiroglou (Lilly Tsesmatzoglou in the second season), as well as the fact that Bekas's daughter is close to their age. Resonating with Krutnik's model of 'masculine potency' (1991: 93), Bekas is a workplace father figure who knows best, a role that he embraces frequently; he uses the diminutive 'Angelikoula' to address Christoforou, scolds both Athanasiou and Christoforou for ordering unhealthy takeaways, and orders soft drinks for them when they are out together. Apart from providing continuity with the paternal aura that often characterises the cinematic Bekas (Poupou 2019: 365–7), the televisual Bekas aligns with a masculinity *not* in crisis, maintaining the privileged male position in the patriarchal order, and sustaining control and authority over the world. Moreover, Bekas tends to bring up this paternal association when he interacts with witnesses and suspects, perpetrators and victims, specifically with younger women, thus erasing any romantic potential. As a faithful, happily married family man, Bekas embodies a sexuality that has a 'retired' tone.[12]

The Other Me: The Special(ist) Male Lead

Sotiris Tsafoulias's crime thriller *The Other Me* (2016),[13] the precursor of *Lost Souls*, introduced audiences to the figure of Dimitris Lainis (played by Pygmalion Dadakaridis), a professor of criminology helping the police in their investigation of a series of murders by decoding the mathematical clues left at the crime scenes. In the mini-series that succeeded the film, Lainis takes on a similar task, investigating yet another series of murders with strong symbolic elements. What differentiates *Lost Souls* from the previous two texts examined in this chapter is that Lainis is not an official member of the police force, but rather fits the trope of the '"specialist" who may bring to the case in question a particular gift or knowledge set that equips him or her with the necessary powers to solve the crime' (Turnbull 2014: 125).

Described by his colleagues as 'eccentric but genius', suggesting an alignment with the 'detective on the edge' model (Ibid.: 126), Lainis is not only dealing with profoundly violent murders, but also with his own 'demons': a feeling of sorrow following the loss of his father and his break-up with his girlfriend. Simultaneously, Lainis is a character on the autistic spectrum; as such, the feelings of loneliness and abandonment are intensified by a generalised discomfort related to issues of social interaction and communication, informing a psychosocial background potentially already familiar to viewers through both male (Sherlock Holmes and Adrian Monk) and female (Saga Norén) 'ASD' (McHugh 2018) and 'neuro noir detectives' internationally (Sweeney 2017).[14] Embodying a case of high-functioning autism, Lainis's neurodiverse status is represented not as a 'deficit' but as a defining factor in the successful detection of crimes (Ziogas 2019).

Having been 'promoted' from playing Officer Bekas's sidekick to a more central role,[15] Dadakaridis delivers a subtly powerful performance infused with the logic behind a cerebral, rather than a physically expressive, character. His delivery of Lainis is somewhat mannered: the tone of voice and the way he walks are obviously adjusted to connote a character on the spectrum and, as such, difference and loneliness. Lainis's quirkiness and disconnection are also signified by object correlations that include old-fashioned pyjamas and wristwatch, as well as a vintage car (an Alfa Romeo Giulia, a model produced between 1962 and 1977). However, Lainis does not entirely fit the iconography of the noir loner, since he (selectively) seeks to connect with people, in the contexts of friendship, romance or mentorship; nor does he share the same level of discomfort that other neuroatypical characters, such as Adrian Monk, experience in even mildly sexually charged situations (Pickens 2013). Especially when it comes to romance, Lainis embodies a model of dormant sexuality: he is not actively looking to form romantic relationships, but he appears open to them, and is represented as attractive and desirable to other people. One could argue that this is in line with Dadakaridis's subtle sex appeal.

The range of noir masculinities present in *Lost Souls* is complemented by other central characters, mainly Officer Apostolis Barasopoulos (Manos Vakousis) and Lieutenant Pantelis Sklavis (Petros Lagoutis) (Figure 13.2). The latter constitutes a continuation of the hard-boiled detective, often called to play the role of the 'bad cop', displaying physical and explosive masculinity in tandem with a secret trauma: the loss of his brother. The former could be read as a continuation of the older authority figure featured, for example, in *Vice Squad*.[16] Barasopoulos is a senior officer, responsible for the team

Figure 13.2 From left to right: the criminologist Lainis (Pygmalion Dadakaridis) and officers Barasopoulos (Manos Vakousis) and Sklavis (Petros Lagoutis) investigating a crime. Still from the TV show *Eteros ego*.

investigating the crimes of a serial killer. In line with other older detectives, he shows a significant devotion to his job, which often gets in the way of his private life. However, unlike the examples of older detectives from previous decades, namely Kessanlis with his resigned sexuality and Bekas with his retired sexuality, Barasopoulos is a sexually interested and active, yet rather inexperienced man, eventually acquiring a love interest in the person of forensics specialist Eleni Marouda (Katerina Didaskalou) and engaging in sexual intercourse. Even though close to professional retirement, Barasopoulos embodies an age-positive masculinity that is not only physically/sexually active, but also emotionally available.

Conclusion

According to Sanders, 'TV has become indispensable for transmitting the legacy of film noir and producing new forms of noir' (2008: 1). The case studies examined in this chapter point to this statement and reflect the evolution of well-established noir tropes, as well as the prominence of diverse conceptions of masculinity during different chronological periods in Greek television history. As such, this chapter follows an understanding of noir as 'a kind of mythology' (Naremore 1998: 2), more expansive in its scope than just a genre. Greek television continues to be discussed as a fertile site for the re-examination of otherwise neglected texts of the past, as well as for the reconsideration of themes, content and cultural knowledge emerging from them (Aitaki and Chairetis 2019). Thus, noirness can be explored as a cultural category, rejuvenating itself and pushing the boundaries of what is available in crime shows produced and received across different moments in Greek television history. As we have attempted to show here, noir might also be envisioned as a useful lens for understanding the dialectic of Greek (noir) television within the realms of gender and ideology, as well as reflecting upon the role of foreign television influences on the making of Greek noir masculinities, as they have been narrativised on screen.

Notes

1. This chapter only focuses on the first season of *The Other Me: Lost Souls*. A second season, subtitled *Catharsis*, was broadcast between December 2020 and February 2021. A third season, subtitled *Nemesis*, was in the works while this chapter was being written.
2. The spin-offish *Dromoi tis polis/City Streets* (ANT1, 1995–96), directed by Manousakis, was anchored in similar logics, but delivered in a slightly lighter tone.
3. According to Nielsen TV ratings, *Vice Squad* consistently ranked among the top three most-watched shows in 1994, and attracted about a million viewers every time it was broadcast.

4. According to the creators, the show was made during a time when television productions enjoyed a high degree of creative freedom over what could be broadcast on screen. In interviews with Georgia Aitaki in July 2016, both director Manousakis and his executive producer (and wife) Maria Manousaki expressed their surprise that they were actually able to make this show in the way they wanted to, addressing provocative and difficult topics.
5. Perlegas died unexpectedly on 19 April 1993. The character's last appearance was in the episode 'Plasta dolaria'/'Counterfeit Dollars' (season 1, episode 27).
6. After his participation in *Vice Squad*, Gletsos redeemed much of his fame and following by consolidating the role of 'the ultimate male'. In the 1990s he starred in a number of television dramas and romantic comedies including *Psythiroi kardias/ Whispers of the Heart* (MEGA, 1997–98) and *Sofia orthi/Wisdom Arose* (ANT1, 1996–98), while in 2008 he played an aggressive Stanley Kowalski in a stage adaptation of *A Streetcar Named Desire*. The image of the macho, short-tempered man accompanied Gletsos in the later years of his career. Even when he turned to politics, Gletsos found himself involved in loud, physical disputes, including fistfights, with other men, thus blurring the boundaries between his fictional and public personas. Yet in 2017, while serving as mayor of Stylida, Gletsos appeared on a late-night show hosted by Petros Kostopoulos, and informed an unprepared television audience of his past sexual experiences with men through the use of a line that has since become famous in Greece: 'The fish can be grilled from both sides.' Although the evolution of Gletsos's star persona could well constitute the object of separate research, it is still worth noting here how the personal, fictional and public aspects intersect to produce identities that either support or dismantle stereotypical star images.
7. Some of Michalopoulos's most iconic performances include parts in Yannis Dalianidis's social dramas *Ta tsakalia/The Jackals* (1981), *I strofi/The Turn* (1982) and *Oi epikindynoi/The Dangerous* (1983), as well as in comedies such as *Vasika kalispera sas/Basically Good Afternoon* (1982), all of which contributed to, and foreshadowed, the rebellious and tough Rokos in *Vice Squad*. Compared to the qualities of his 1980s co-stars, including Stamatis Gardelis's boyish charm, Stathis Psaltis's goofy, unforced charisma, and Nikos Papadopoulos's elegant appeal, Michalopoulos exuded a manly magnetism and a more 'mature' version of young masculinity. His physique differentiated him from the other actors, as his muscular body and hairy chest stood out from the seemingly still-forming body types of his contemporaries. Furthermore, his acting style, bringing together both dramatic and comedic elements, as well as his stage performance training and experience, allowed him to deliver powerful performances in many different genres later on in his career.
8. See, for example, Kostas Kalfopoulos's addendum in *Iliggos/Vertigo* (Maris [1961] 2013).
9. In the 1970s an early version of the fabled officer, initially named Lekkas and played by Giorgos Siskos, made its TV debut in *Leschi mystiriou/Mystery Club* (ERT, 1976) and *Ypopsies/Suspicions* (ERT, 1977–78). A decade later, Stavros Xenidis revived the character, this time bearing the name of Giorgos Bekas, in *O thanatos tou Timotheou Konsta/The Death of Timotheos Konstas* (ERT2, 1987). In his first

interpretation of Bekas, Xenidis delivered a performance characterised by discreet dominance, without mannerisms or exaggerations; his presence defines the overall tone of the show, without overshadowing the suspenseful plot and the strong (theatrical) performances of his co-stars (including Nikos Galanos, Mimi Ntenisi, Tryfon Karatzas and Takis Chrysikakos among many others). Xenidis reappeared as Bekas in later adaptations of Maris's novels, broadcast by private channels: *To mystiko tou Ari Bonsalenti/The Secret of Aris Bonsalentis* (MEGA, 1990–91) and *Mia gynaika apo to parelthon/A Woman from the Past* (ANT1, 1992).

10. 'Consciously modelled' on Maris's Bekas (Agapitos 2016: 94), Inspector Kostas Charitos, a creation of Petros Markaris, constitutes an additional important pillar of Greek crime fiction and noirish masculinity. Although the differences between the literary characters have been addressed by Agapitos, a detailed comparative perspective on the televisual renditions has yet to appear.
11. With an active career in television since 1997, alongside multiple theatrical and cinematic performances including his role as Savvas Iakovidis in Tasos Boulmetis's *Politiki kouzina/A Touch of Spice* (2003), Michailidis is also well known as a key member (writer, director, performer, singer) of the satirical musical/comedy troupe *Agamoi Thytai/Single Victimizers* since 1990.
12. Michailidis reappeared as a member of law enforcement, playing the role of family man Prokopis in the comedy *L.A.P.D: Lekanopedio Attikis Police Department/ L.A.P.D: Athenian Basin Police Department* (MEGA, 2008–10), a TV series that, interestingly, offers a form of deconstruction, through parody, of generic, tough-cop, phallic masculinities such as those analysed in this chapter.
13. The film had a theatrical release in January 2017; however, Tsafoulias withdrew it a few weeks later, after suspicions that the murder of a taxi driver in Kifisia might have been inspired by it. A few months later, the director uploaded the film on YouTube.
14. The term, according to Sweeney, is used to address 'mysterious detectives whose neurological condition affects their thinking, influences their relationships, and both hinders and facilitates investigations' (2017: 231).
15. In between these two occasions, Dadakaridis also played the role of incorruptible cop Dimitris Glaros in the noir comedy series *Mavra mesanychta/Pitch-Black Midnight* (MEGA, 2008–09).
16. Some Greek viewers might also remember him as Officer Skaloubas in Nikos Foskolos's iconic soap opera *I lampsi/The Shining* (ANT1, 1991–2005). There, Vakousis delivered a performance characterised by nervousness and creepiness which, supported by physical traits such as greasy hair and watery paranoid eyes, led to him being considered a suspect for the crimes committed by Evlogitos, one of the most vicious fictional serial killers ever to appear on Greek television. Vakousis has also participated in four episodes of *Vice Squad*.

References

Agapitos, Panagiotis (2016), 'Bloody Metalanguage? Crime Fiction in Greece, 1991–2011', in Börte Sagaster, Martin Strohmeier and Stephan Guth (eds), *Crime Fiction in and around the Eastern Mediterranean*, Wiesbaden: Harrassowitz, pp. 93–102.

Agathos, Thanassis (2018), 'Eglima sto Kolonaki: To "athinaiko astynomiko mythistorima" tou Yanni Mari stis ellinikes othones tou 1960' [Murder in Kolonaki: An 'Athenian Detective Story' by Yannis Maris on the Greek Screens of 1960], *A Journal for Greek Letters*, 19, pp. 105–20.

Aitaki, Georgia (2020), 'In Search of the Greek Television Author: The Social Dramas of Manousos Manousakis', *Screen*, 61:3, pp. 403–22.

Aitaki, Georgia, and Chairetis, Spyridon (2019), 'Introduction to Greek Television Studies: (Re)Reading Greek Television Fiction since 1989', *Filmicon: Journal of Greek Film Studies*, 6, pp. 1–16.

Anon. (2020), 'Itan to *Tmima Ithon* i pio hardcore elliniki astynomiki seira?' [Was *Vice Squad* the Most Hardcore Crime Series in Greece?], *Ratpack*, 11 March, <https://www.ratpack.gr/buzz/story/18332/itan-to-tmima-hthon-i-pio-hardcore-elliniki-astynomiki-seira> (last accessed 29 July 2021).

Apostolidis, Andreas (2012), *O Kosmos tou Yanni Mari* [The World of Yannis Maris], Athens: Agra.

Auerbach, Jonathan (2011), *Dark Borders: Film Noir and American Citizenship*, Durham, NC: Duke University Press.

Avdela, Efi (2008), 'Corrupting and Uncontrollable Activities: Moral Panic about Youth in Post-Civil War Greece', *Journal of Contemporary History*, 43:1, pp. 25–44.

Butler, Jeremy G. (2012), *Television: Critical Methods and Applications*, Abingdon: Routledge.

Cantrell, Tom, and Hogg, Christopher (2018), 'Introduction', in Tom Cantrell and Christopher Hogg (eds), *Exploring Television Acting*, London: Methuen Drama, pp. 1–12.

Chartoulari, Mikela (1998), 'Oute Poirot oute Marlowe. Aplos Ellinas' [Neither Poirot nor Marlowe. Just Greek], *Ta Nea*, 24 June.

Chu, Henry (2010), 'British Cops are a Tormented Lot', *Los Angeles Times*, 14 November, <https://www.latimes.com/archives/la-xpm-2010-nov-14-la-ca-british-crime-shows-20101114-story.html> (last accessed 29 July 2021).

Cohan, Steven (1997), *Masked Men: Masculinity and the Movies in the Fifties*, Bloomington, IN: Indiana University Press.

Conard, Mark T. (2007), *The Philosophy of Neo-Noir*, Lexington, KY: University of Kentucky Press.

Creeber, Glen (2015), 'Killing Us Softly: Investigating the Aesthetics, Philosophy and Influence of Nordic Noir Television', *The Journal of Popular Television*, 3:1, pp. 21–35.

Davis, J. Madison (2017), 'The Faces of Maigret', *World Literature Today*, 91:1, pp. 24–6.

Day, Marele (1993), 'Bitch City', in Delys Bird (ed.), *Killing Women: Rewriting Detective Fiction*, Sydney: Angus and Robertson, pp. 125–35.

Dyer, Richard (1998a), *Stars*, London: BFI.

Dyer, Richard (1998b), 'Resistance through Charisma: Rita Hayworth and *Gilda*', in E. Ann Kaplan (ed.), *Women in Film Noir*, London: BFI, pp. 115–22.

Fessas, Nikitas (2020), 'Representations of Disability in 1960s Greek Film Noirs: *The Secret of the Red Mantle* and *The Fear*', *Journal of Literary & Cultural Disability Studies*, 14:3, pp. 281–99.

Fessas, Nikitas, and Kosma, Yvonne (2017), 'The Crisis of Gender Identity in the Greek Film Noir: Sexuality, Paranoia and the Unconscious in *Efialtis/Nightmare* (1961) and *O Ergenis/The Bachelor* (1997)', *Filmicon: Journal of Greek Film Studies*, 4, pp. 83–109.

Fotiou, Mikela, and Fessas, Nikitas (2017), 'Greek Neo-Noir: Reflecting a Narrative of Crisis', *Filmicon: Journal of Greek Film Studies*, 4, pp. 110–37.

Gates, Philippa (2006), *Detecting Men: Masculinity and the Hollywood Detective Film*, Albany, NY: SUNY Press.

Kassaveti, Ursula-Helen, and Papoulis, Athanasios (2019), 'Outside of Society: The Representation of Athenian Outcasts in *Tmima Ithon/Vice Squad*', *Filmicon: Journal of Greek Film Studies*, 6, pp. 40–68.

King, Neal (1999), *Heroes in Hard Times: Cop Action Movies in the U.S.*, Philadelphia, PA: Temple University Press.

Krutnik, Frank (1991), *In a Lonely Street: Film Noir, Genre, Masculinity*, New York: Routledge.

Kyriakos, Konstantinos (2017), *Epithymies kai Politiki: I Queer Istoria tou Ellinikou Kinimatografou (1924–2016)* [Politics and Desire: The Queer History of the Greek Cinema (1924–2016)], Athens: Aigokeros.

Leontaritis, Giorgos (2013), *O Yannis Maris kai i Epochi tou* [Yannis Maris and his Times], Athens: Agra.

Maris, Yannis ([1961] 2013), *Iliggos/Vertigo*, Athens: Agra.

Martin, Richard (1999), *Mean Streets and Raging Bulls: The Legacy of Film Noir in Contemporary American Cinema*, Lanham, MD: Scarecrow Press.

McHugh, Kathleen (2018), 'The Female Detective, Neurodiversity, and Felt Knowledge in *Engrenages* and *Bron/Broen*', *Television & New Media*, 19:6, pp. 535–52.

Naremore, James (1998), *More than Night: Film Noir in its Contexts*, Berkeley, CA: University of California Press.

Paretsky, Sara (2007), *Writing in an Age of Silence*, London: Verso.

Pickens, Therí A. (2013), '"It's a Jungle Out There": Blackness and Disability in *Monk*', *Disability Studies Quarterly*, 33:3, <https://dsq-sds.org/article/view/3391> (last accessed 18 December 2021).

Poupou, Anna (2019), 'Monachikoi likoi, exipna lagonika, thumomenoi gatoi: Andrismoi sto elliniko kinomatografiko astynomiko thriler ton dekaetion 1950 kai 1960' [Lonely Wolves, Smart Sleuths, Angry Cats: Masculinities in the Greek Cinematic Police Thriller of the 1950s and 1960s], in Dimitra Vasileiadou, Yannis Yannitsiotis and Androniki Dialeti (eds), *Andrismoi: Anaparastaseis, ypokeimena kai praktikes apo ti mesaioniki mehri ti sinchroni periodo* [Masculinities: Representations, Subjects and Practices from the Medieval to the Contemporary Period], Athens: Gutenberg, pp. 356–78.

Sanders, M. Steven (2008), 'An Introduction to the Philosophy of TV Noir', in Steven M. Sanders and Aeon J. Skoble (eds), *The Philosophy of TV Noir*, Lexington, KY: University Press of Kentucky, pp. 1–29.

Scaggs, John (2005), *Crime Fiction*, Abingdon: Routledge.

Short, Sue (2019), *Darkness Calls: A Critical Investigation of Neo-Noir*, Basingstoke: Palgrave Macmillan.

Sonnet, Esther (2010), 'Why Film Noir? Hollywood, Adaptation, and Women's Writing in the 1940s and 1950s', *Adaptation*, 4:1, pp. 1–13.
Spicer, Andrew (2002), *Film Noir,* Abingdon: Routledge.
Steenberg, Lindsay (2017), 'The Fall and Television Noir', *Television & New Media*, 18:1, pp. 58–75.
Studlar, Gaylyn (2013), 'The Corpse on Reprieve: Film Noir's Cautionary Tales of "Tough Guy" Masculinity', in Andrew Spicer and Helen Hanson (eds), *A Companion to Film Noir*, Chichester: Wiley-Blackwell, pp. 369–86.
Sweeney, Susan Elizabeth (2017), 'Unusual Suspects: American Crimes, Metaphysical Detectives, Postmodernist Genres', in Chris Raczkowski (ed.), *A History of American Crime Fiction*, Cambridge: Cambridge University Press, pp. 221–35.
Turnbull, Sue (2014), *The TV Crime Drama*, Edinburgh: Edinburgh University Press.
Waade, Anne Marit (2017), 'Melancholy in Nordic Noir: Characters, Landscapes, Light and Music', *Critical Studies in Television: The International Journal of Television Studies*, 12:4, pp. 380–94.
Ziogas, Georgios (2019), 'Eteros Ego: Hamenes Psyches' [The Other Me: Lost Souls], *Filmicon: Journal of Greek Film Studies*, 6, pp. 184–9.

14. MEDITERRANEAN FILM NOIR: TWILIGHT FALLS ON *MARE NOSTRUM*

Dennis Broe

The noir style was established in France in the 1930s as the more bitter current of what was termed Poetic Realism in the wake of the defeat of the Popular Front. It then emerged full-blown in the US during and after the Second World War as the dark style was utilised to mourn the beating back of the energy of organised labour and the emergence of the repressive forces of McCarthyism. At the same time the style spread across the world in indigenous moments in England, Italy and Japan where, in league with labour unrest, it was employed to lodge a critique of the corporate reshaping of the post-war world.

The most dominant and dynamic formations of the movement at the moment centre not around Hollywood productions but around three regional noir sites: Asia, Scandinavia and, the oldest of these, the Mediterranean. Asian noir, especially in its Chinese variant, has been employed to highlight the gap between official optimism about development and resentment over who is most clearly benefiting from that development in such films as *Tian zhu ding/A Touch of Sin* (dir. Zhangke, 2013), *Ren shan ren hai/People Mountain, People Sea* (dir. Shangjun, 2011), *Bai ri yan huo/Black Coal, Thin Ice* (dir. Yinan, 2014) and *Da xiang xidi erzuo/An Elephant Sitting Still* (dir. Bo, 2018). Scandinavian noir has often employed the dark style to expose the fissures in societies that have attempted to reconcile an egalitarian lifestyle with the capitalist imperative of profit (*Smilla's Sense of Snow*, August 1997; *The Millennium Series*, 2011–18; *The Killing*, DR1 2007–12). Mediterranean noir unearths and plays upon tensions resulting from longstanding inequality in the region. To explore these class tensions it is useful to employ Fernand Braudel's (1972) concept of how Mediterranean geography, centred around mountains and sea, influenced uneven development, but also provided the space for persistent pockets of resistance to entrenched power.

In the post-classical neo-noir period, which in its later phase is coterminous with the rise and dominance of neoliberalism, Mediterranean noir has often traced the history of this unsettling imposition of a more avaricious mode of capitalism on the region. Here the style captures the breakdown of long-existing communal patterns and their replacement by increasingly individualistic and desperate modes of relating. Thus western Mediterranean noir traces the roots of contemporary crisis to Francoist exploitation in Spain's *La Isla Minima/Marshland* (dir. Rodríguez, 2014), registers the impact of the Berlusconi era in the film version of *Arrivederci amore, ciao/The Goodbye Kiss* (dir. Soavi, 2006) and the hierarchisation of subordinate groups in Italian society in *A Ciambra* (dir. Carpignano, 2017), as well as exploring uneven racial and ethnic relations in Marseilles in adaptations of the French novelist Jean-Claude Izzo. Eastern Mediterranean noir employs the style in Algeria to describe the carrying of the Algerian war to the French homefront in *Hors la loi/Outside the Law* (dir. Bouchareb, 2010), in Turkey to describe a gradual criminalisation of the economy in *Çakal/The Jackal* (dir. Kozan, 2010), in Egypt to unearth the rampant corruption in the post-Tahrir Square Sisi dictatorship in *The Nile Hilton Incident* (dir. Saleh, 2017), and in Greece to lay out the structure of feeling of the debt crisis in *Tetarti 04:45/Wednesday 04:45* (dir. Alexiou, 2015).

Films in these regional formations decentre film noir from its persistent critical lodging as simply a widespread American ethos and illustrate how, in the contemporary period, noir filmmakers have continued the critical thrust of the classical period, which was always global, rather than simply American. Greek noir illustrates directly how Mediterranean filmmakers have enlarged the critical scope of the style by fitting it to crises engendered throughout the region by the coming of neoliberalism and austerity.

The Emergence of a Style

Noir itself, far from being a Hollywood construct, began not in Los Angeles in the 1940s but rather in France in the late 1930s, at a moment when the dismantling of the workers' gains from the Popular Front was expressed in an aesthetic formation that may be termed late Poetic Realism or early film noir. The form includes such films as Marcel Carné's *Quai des brumes/Port of Shadows* (1938), *Le Jour se lève/Daybreak* (1939) and Jean Renoir's *La Bête Humaine/The Human Beast* (1938). These dark tracts centred around Jean Gabin's doomed working-class male outsider – and the equally doomed women who accompanied him – and featured a character whose ultimate exile through death was emblematic of the expunging of working-class ideals in the light of capital's offensive to regain its hold; a change that ultimately led to the fall of the Republic and the victory of fascism.

With the failure of a hoped-for change after the Second World War and a global corporate rollback and repression largely instituted under the rubric of the Cold War, directors retreated to dark stories of outsiders who bravely battled the forces of order to clear their names of crimes they often did not commit. These characters figured the left itself which, in the wake of the global US-led communist purge, was being hounded and pursued for its 'unlawful' actions in prompting labour and people's campaigns for a more equal world. Film noir expressed this global lament for a lost opportunity, and a critique of the return of the old order. This sentiment was on display in the US in such films as *Out of the Past* (dir. Tourneur, 1949) and *The Big Clock* (dir. Farrow, 1948); in Italy in 'neorealismo nero' in Guiseppe De Santis's *Caccia tragica/Tragic Pursuit* (1947) and *Riso amaro/Bitter Rice* (1949), and Alberto Lattuada's *Il bandito/The Bandit* (1946) and *Senza pieta/Without Pity* (1948); in the UK in 'spiv' and 'criminal-on-the-lam' films such as *It Always Rains on Sunday* (dir. Hamer, 1947) and *They Made Me a Fugitive* (dir. Cavalcanti, 1947); and in Japan in Akira Kurosawa's warning about the return of the imperial fascist order in questioning the precepts of the crime film in *Yoidore tenshi/Drunken Angel* (1948) and *Nora inu/Stray Dog* (1949).[1]

The noir style lay dormant through the later part of what was termed in France *Les trente glorieuses*, the thirty Glorious Years (1945–75) of relative economic peace and a semblance of equality in the Western world. However, with the breaking of the business–labour pact signalled by the ascent in the US of Ronald Reagan and in Britain of Margaret Thatcher, and the imposition of more draconian measures that exacerbated inequality and went under the term 'neoliberalism', the dark style reappeared in what came to be known as 'neo-noir'. Neo-noir, which flourished during the Reagan–Bush years (1980–92), employed its black palette and violent themes to highlight distortions in Reagan's America in places such as the Sunbelt, 'Reagan's spiritual home', in *After Dark, My Sweet* (dir. Foley, 1990), and in a heartland ravaged by de-industrialisation and a global wage race to the bottom in *At Close Range* (dir. Foley, 1986). Noir delineated the corruption that lurked behind the 'can do' spirit of Reagan-era optimism, and located this critique at the heart of the law enforcement agencies waging Bush's 'war on drugs' in *Bad Lieutenant* (dir. Ferrara, 1992), *Internal Affairs* (dir. Figgis, 1990), *Unlawful Entry* (dir. Kaplan, 1992) and *Q&A* (dir. Lumet, 1990).

This reimagining of the classic style then spread across the globe, where it was inflected with regional concerns and crossed with indigenous genres in somewhat the same way that rap and hip hop culture became a language appropriated by peoples struggling under a global corporate tyranny. The dark style has emerged as a site of critique in at least three prominent regions: Asia, including Japan and Korea, but now most strongly in China; Scandinavia as Nordic noir; and the Mediterranean, in both its European (Italy, France, Spain) and Afro-Middle-Eastern (Algeria, Egypt, Turkey) variants, with Greek neo-noir occupying a crossroads position between these formations.

Nordic noir, perhaps closest in themes to its Mediterranean variant, is often concerned with the excesses and corruption of the Scandinavian social democracies, and with how the rhetoric of those democracies regarding equality and shared possibilities does not match the contemporary picture of lethal corruption in a decaying infrastructure that makes a mockery of platitudes about social equality.

A Sea Not Like all the Others: Noir and the Mediterranean Imaginary

To evoke a Mediterranean imaginary suggests a sort of politico-geographical linking of the land and sea formations of the Mediterranean basin with a model of an entrenched power structure that features a high level of wealth concentrated in a few hands. The 'deep state' of the hidden power structure is often represented in the noir world not as a corporate-government complex that overrides democracy or the people's will, but rather as the machinations of gangsters who exert control over their underlings and those around them in a land where, as Braudel says, mountain people's codes of conduct, including the vendetta, were often 'in revolt against the establishment of the modern state and its *carabinieri*' (1972: 39).

Noir, as an aesthetic formation, is adept at exposing these formations because the form itself embeds its critique within a kind of 'deep style' that uses oblique angles and shadows to describe murky spaces hidden from the ordinary, everyday world of daylight; a style that is very much in evidence in Italian noir, which constantly hints at the shadowy interconnections of a world where power, wealth and force converge. Noir is also uniquely capable of using the crime metaphor as a way of suggesting that the daily use and abuse of power in the region is constructed not around democratic processes, but around back-room arrangements involving coercion, as illustrated by the repeated scenes in the office of the gangster bosses in the Turkish noir *The Jackal*.

Braudel cites two currents, both relevant to the history of noir in general, as central to the Mediterranean. He attributes the region's 'traditionalism and rigidity' (1972: 77) to the fact that newly cleared plains remained in the control of rich and powerful landowners who dominated the area in the sixteenth century, the time in which his study of the Mediterranean takes place. This history is opposed to, say, America where the land belonged, despite its Indigenous occupants, to those who cleared it. Thus, in Sicily, Andalucía, the Balkans and Turkey, 'the rich are very rich and the poor very poor' (1972: 76).

Mediterranean neo-noir might be further distinguished from its northern cousin, just as Braudel distinguishes the region from the rest of Europe, by a salient common characteristic, that is, the colour,[2] of the sea, of the sky, of the landscape; its 'almost gaudy yellows, reds, ochres, and above all blues' versus the 'blacks and browns of Northern Europe' (Reynolds 2006: 4).[3] Increasingly this colour scheme is becoming saturated and appears infinitely less natural, as in the neon green that bathes the world of *Wednesday 04:45* and the lush landscapes of *To mikro psari/Stratos* (dir. Economides, 2014), represented not as paradise, but as desolate liminal spaces at the edge of the world.

Western Mediterranean neo-noir is strongly founded in literature, in detective and crime fiction. This is especially true of Spain, where the *novela negra* is the most prominent purveyor of noir. The best-known Spanish crime author is Manuel Vázquez Montalbán, whose Pepe Carvalho series describes the mean streets, rapidly being gentrified, of his native Barcelona just after the break with fascism in the mid-1970s. Carvalho is relatively poor but 'the pleasures of sex, eating and friendship are important to him [. . .] When he pulls the thread leading to a criminal', as in the best-known of the series *Southern Seas* that focuses on the destruction of a poor neighbourhood, 'he often finds that a leading capitalist is behind the crime. How else could it be in a criminal capitalist society?' (Mike Eaude, quoted in Lloyd 2012).

Recently Spanish cinema has been catching up with its literature, and the ultimate Spanish neo-noir may be *Marshland*, a film which, in recalling *Chinatown* (dir. Polanski, 1974), attempts to peel away the fascist layers underlying a society on the brink of either throwing off those vestiges or embedding them more deeply. The action, which involves two cops, is centred in the south, seat of Franco's power, and involves a murderous landlord/agri-business owner who hides his crimes under a veneer of wealth and respectability, resembling the incestuous developer Noah Cross in the American film.

The Spanish noir most directly linked to the Greek noir is the television series *Casa de Papel* (dir. Pina, 2017) or *House of Paper*, retitled for Anglo audiences *Money Heist*. The two titles together indicate what is radically different about the series, a great success in Europe in the wake of the twin responses to the debt crisis: the printing of money for the rich and the defunding of social programmes and increase in debt for everyone else. The series, about a team of professional thieves who break into the Spanish government mint, defines 'quantitative easing' as, to quote John Huston's phrase about crime in an earlier heist film *The Asphalt Jungle* (1950), 'a left-handed form of human endeavour', that is, illegitimate. The thieves in this new twist break into the bank not to steal but to create money using the national banknote press. Their action calls attention to the way market capital and the European Central Bank have adopted a policy of pumping phoney money into the economy to cover the bloated speculation of the rich, while the rest of society, in this case represented by the mostly down-and-out thieves who gather for the break-in, are fed a lean diet of austerity and debt. To paraphrase Brecht's 'What is the crime of robbing a bank, compared to the crime of opening one', *House of Paper* asks of the European financial institutions in the post-crisis austerity era: 'What is the crime of laundering money, compared to the crime of printing it?'[4]

French Mediterranean neo-noir often centres around Marseilles, and is driven by a trilogy of novels by Jean-Claude Izzo (*Total Chaos*, 1995; *Chourmo*, 1996; *Solea*, 1998), tracking the long-embedded power structure of the city in its central description of police corruption. Marseilles is viewed through the eyes of the criminal-turned-cop Fabio Montale who, in the course of the trilogy, becomes disgusted with corruption on the force and quits. The opening novel *Total Chaos* unwinds Montale's history as a street hoodlum, whose one boyhood friend dies at the hands of the police while avenging another friend as part of a mafia-police cabal that Montale eventually exposes. The novel is much better than the French-Italian television series *Fabio Montale* (2001), with Alain Delon, which, though co-scripted by Izzo, is more an extended tribute to an ageing Delon than a critical perspective on Marseilles.

It is in Italy, with Massimo Carlotto and *The Goodbye Kiss* (2001), that this form both reaches its novelistic peak and, at the same time, is finally surpassed in its 2006 screen version. In Carlotto's novel, the protagonist is not an innocent fugitive, but rather a representative of the ultimate corruption that both the novel and, to a greater extent, the film attribute to the Berlusconi era in Italy, an era when, in the words of the novel, 'the legal and illegal economies were merged in a single system, offering the opportunity to grow rich and build a discreet position of power' (Carlotto 2006: 108). In both novel and film, 'business, crime and politics' (2006: 108) are mixed to such an extent as to seem inseparable. Both describe a more blatant grab for wealth by this new power elite. 'I represent a group of businessmen and professionals who have long been marginalized in the political life of this city. But now the wind has changed and we intend to count more and more' (2006: 102), is how the Italian senator in the book expresses this change under Berlusconi.

The film, directed by Dario Argento protégé Michele Soavi, has a gaudy, tarnished quality that is reminiscent of the *gialli*, the yellow novels and films from the 1970s that traded both in soft-core porn and garish horror. This tacky effect, though, is appropriate to express the seamy quality of the corruption under Berlusconi; the sex scandals and the mixing of private and public finances. The protagonist Giorgio brutally murders both the corrupt cop, who is his partner, and his young bourgeois wife who discovers his violent past. The coda has Giorgio, now pardoned for his past actions, at his wife's funeral in dark, torrential rain. He says he is now, having been pardoned, 'a man like all the others', a perfect echo of Berlusconi's oft-repeated defence of his criminal acts as being simply like everyone else: 'Why must I be chased from parliamentary life for tax evasion, when many other Italians cheat on their taxes?' (Ridet and Fressoz 2013: 17).[5] That the film continues to have resonance in Italy can be seen in a later Netflix update (or rip-off) titled *The Ruthless* (dir. de Maria, 2019), a more blood-soaked and less politically aware version of the earlier film again set in Berlusconi's *città* of Milan, detailing the rise of the Calabrian mafia, the 'Ndrangheta, in northern Italy over the three decades of Berlusconi's rule and influence.

Jonas Carpignano's *A Ciambra* (2017), in its sombre palette, charts the strata of the social structure in post-Berlusconi Italy, as the 14-year-old Roma boy Pio must betray his Senegalese friend in order to gain access to the Italian crime boss who lords it over the neighbourhood. The film was produced by Martin Scorsese and harkens back to Scorsese's own mapping of Italo-American struggles to escape the rigidity of the neighbourhood in *Mean Streets* (1973) and *Who's That Knocking at My Door* (1967).

Eastern Mediterranean Noir: Sunlight Gleaming off a Battered. 38

Neo-noir in the eastern part of the sea, in its Algerian, Egyptian and Turkish variants, has similar characteristics to the west, especially in its critique of a deeply embedded power structure and either the continuation of an outright dark palette or the adoption of paler tones that mask the bright light of the region.

Rachid Bouchareb's *Outside the Law* (2010) is an Algerian-French co-production that attempts to combine the neorealist and the noir traditions. The film presents the eruption of the Algerian War in France in its quoting of both *The Battle of Algiers* (dir. Pontecorvo, 1966) and the stylistic gangster tropes of Coppola, De Palma and Scorsese, as they have been simplified and absorbed by films such as *American Gangster* (dir. Scott, 2007). The film shifts from its opening neorealist moments depicting the slaughter of Algerians by the French in Setif just after the war, to a noir battle of cops and gangsters in France. The style after this shift is a duplication of the contemporary American gangster film, complete with dark palette, glistening low-angle shots of the machine-gun battles of the FLN (National Liberation Front) and the police terrorist squad the Red Hand, and a sadistic undercurrent of violence. *Outside the Law*, though, critiques both the ruthlessness of one of a trio of brothers' revolutionary tactics, and of another's violence in becoming a killer for the revolution, while validating the third brother's following of his, more peaceful, passion of having a boxer beat the French in the ring. These character paths imply, as embedded in the liberation moment itself, a critique of the future trajectory of a rigid, corrupt, post-revolutionary state, now perhaps in the process of being overthrown, which continues to this day to utilise the memory of the revolution to sustain its power.

In Egypt, *Cairo Confidential* – US title *The Nile Hilton Incident* – traces the path of a hardened Cairo cop who seems oblivious to politics but slowly wakes to the deadly force of those in power around the US-backed El-Sisi dictatorship who treat the rest of the country with impunity. His dogged tracking of the murderer of a popular club singer to the upper echelons of society in a noir tale indicates that the open truth-telling of the Arab Spring must now be submerged in more obscure forms.

Erhan Kozan's *The Jackal* depicts the fatalism of Akin, a young man who lives in one of the poorest sections of Istanbul, where the unemployed gather in the shadows of a castle, the remnant of an entrenched feudal power structure. His almost preordained fall into the Turkish gangster world is often expressed through his voiceover ('Whatcha gonna do? Some die, some go on living'). Akin's gangster bosses, who he eventually rebels against ('I'm also a dog . . . [but] without an owner'), stress their control over the world ('We Live. They die. Life, it's damn cruel'), and chortle while doing a line of coke and celebrating what they think is the execution of both a rival and Akin. But Akin's friend kills both gangsters and the boy escapes, at least in his mind, to the aquarium he urged his gangster boss to buy. For the young man, the aquarium is a utopia in a bottle, a miniature world that recapitulates the world of the sea that is everywhere present in Istanbul, but that in the present reality is confining, while in the miniature world presents the hope of escape.

There is yet another variant of noir which has similarities to eastern Mediterranean noir, especially in its dealing with coloniser/colonised, and that is Indigenous noir. This variant exists beyond the borders of any region – from the Native American-themed *Wind River* (dir. Sheridan, 2017) to the French-Swedish television series *Midnight Sun* (dir. Mårlind and Stein, 2016) about the original inhabitants of Scandinavia, the Sami or Laplanders – and is most prominently exhibited in an Australian film and television trilogy about an aboriginal cop, two of whose iterations are titled *Mystery Road*. The setting for all three (*Mystery Road*, dir. Sen, 2013; *Goldstone*, dir. Sen, 2016; *Mystery Road*, TV series 2018–) is the desert area of northern Australia. The recurring character in each is an Aboriginal cop, Jay Swan (Aaron Pedersen). The predominant theme of the series is the continual exploitation of Indigenous land by the white settlers, and the persistent disempowering of those who live on it, most strongly evoked in *Goldstone*'s depiction of the ruthlessness of the town mayor and mining head colluding over a gold mine. There is a strong similarity to *Wind River*, in which the thuggery of the energy company and its henchmen results in a massacre on the reservation the company is exploiting. Indigenous noir gives a voice to disparate peoples scattered across the globe, with a similarity being the common enemy that is oppressing them in the pursuit of the land and resources they inconveniently possess.

Greek Film Noir: Austerity, Neoliberalism and the Dark Style

Contemporary Greek noir, most prominently *Stratos* and *Wednesday 04:45*, follows hard upon the American version established under the neoliberalism of Reagan and Bush in responding to the imposition of austerity and the neoliberal order on Greece, after the sub-prime crisis and Great Recession of 2008. Pre-crisis films in the earlier part of the decade such as *O vasilias/The King* (dir. Grammatikos) and *O hamenos ta pairnei ola/Loser Takes All* (dir. Nikolaidis), both released in 2002, confirm that the destitution and marginality that marked the country post-crisis already existed before austerity was imposed from outside. *Stratos* and *Wednesday 04:45* feature a regional and international interplay with other genres (Figure 14.1). The languorous quality of the pacing of *Stratos*, the lingering on desolate, isolated but stunning landscapes, and the long fades to black all recall the European art film in both its Greek (Theo Angelopoulos) and Turkish variants, most prominently in the art noir of Nuri Bilge Ceylon's *Once Upon a Time in Anatolia* (2011). *Wednesday 04:45* more directly utilises Tarantino-style violence, transforming a final killing sequence into a slow-motion musical number, but also recalls, in its stressing throughout the film of a debtor's deadline that will end in a shootout, similarly structured and similarly titled Westerns such as *3:10 to Yuma* (dir. Daves, 1957; dir. Mangold, 2007) and the original deadline film *High Noon* (dir. Zinnemann, 1952).

The Greek debt crisis, which arrived full-blown in 2010, a period both films recount, was used by European financial forces (the European Commission, European Central Bank and the International Monetary Fund – collectively termed 'the Troika') to install in Greece a particularly wrenching form of monetarism and neoliberalism. This framework, patented by the IMF, had previously

Figure 14.1 The owner of the strip club announces to Agnieszka (Nikol Drizi) that she will be fired because of the recession, while a TV programme in the background comments on austerity measures. Digital still from *Wednesday 04:45*.

figured only in the developing countries of Latin America and Africa. It focused on debt repayment as an excuse for wholesale cutting of social services. The monetarist aspect of this imposition, in line with the Chicago School of Milton Friedman which had triumphed in Chile in the wake of the Pinochet dictatorship and ultimately left the country destitute, argued that state spending to stimulate the economy was useless. All that was really needed was a healthier export structure that would allow the 'free market' to pump more money into the economy, the profits from which would then be dedicated to repaying the debt.

The neoliberal aspect of the formula featured 'freeing' workers to work more hours generally for lower wages, limiting the power of trade unions and collective bargaining, deregulating financial institutions, and a degrading of the image of the state that then promoted privatisation and the selling off of state assets at bargain prices.[6] The onslaught featured, at one point, Troika members going through government offices and literally counting each position to see which to remove, as merger and acquisitions teams did in the corporate realm, as well as a massive attack on the healthcare system that saw expenditures cut by 30 per cent (Roufos 2018: 93–4). We see the terrorising effects of these measures on labour in a scene in *Stratos*, where a female labourer at the bakery, where the lead character works, is assaulted and then fired by the boss for working too slowly, with no one in the plant defending her.

To justify these measures the European financial institutions, led by the German and French banks that had loaned heavily to Greece, concocted a 'moralistic fairy tale' (Roufos 2018: 114). This narrative identified lazy southerners, and the Greeks in particular, for their lack of fiscal discipline, as the key element in promoting the crisis in an insolvent Greece that was dragging the EU down with it.[7] In fact, the entire EU banking structure was taxed, primarily due to its involvement in the unsafe and unsavoury debt accrued in the US housing crisis which had brought on the global recession. Later moments of the crisis confirmed that it was not just Greece but other countries as well that were affected, as Cyprus threated to cancel its debt, and as Italy faced a 400 billion dollar readjustment by 2013 (Roufos 2018: 115).

The actual motivation for the austerity measures was confirmed by the German Bundesbank president who said that the goal was to save foreign banks and their money in Greece (Roufos 2018: 91). Likewise, another outside financial representative maintained that the end result and motive for cutting wages and government support was that 'the soundness of the banking sector will be restored' (Roufos 2018: 91). *Wednesday 04:45* and *Stratos*, both set in the bloody aftermath of the financial collapse, feature lead characters who are either burdened with debt or working to pay off the construction of a project. The question of who is responsible for the debt is a key question in Greek society, though in the two films both characters themselves 'take responsibility' for their own lives, with only a dim awareness that the source of the problem might spring from outside them and might be a structural and not a personal failure.

Two films made prior to the crisis, *The King* and *Loser Takes All*, each present a form of a more ancient Greek hero updated to add noir elements. *The King* is Christ-like not only in his long flowing hair and his communal ways, but also as someone who attempts to outwit or escape the drive for profit and merchandising of society. Homer praised pirates over merchants as the Aegean was being opened to traders, valuing warriors who exchanged gifts over a Phoenician merchant whom he labelled 'a man of deceitful mind, a weasel, who had done a lot of harm to people' and part of a 'very devious' nation of 'petty criminals' (quoted in Abulafia 2011: 88). In *The King*, Vangelis – as in evangelist, a bearer of the gospel – is released from prison and attempts to right his life and escape his old gang by returning to the country, where, as a prophet dishonoured in his own land, he is persecuted by the locals for his communal or socialist ways, and finally hangs or crucifies himself. The plot recalls Michael Caine's killer, homeward bound to the English industrialised north in *Get Carter* (dir. Hodges, 1971), and is unusual in noir for its heavy religious overlay. The film anticipates two moments of the crisis: the (forced) retreat to the land by youth who have been impoverished in the city by the austerity measures, and the emergence of a primitive fascist force, in the film the villagers, and in the country as a whole Golden Dawn.

Loser Takes All features a broken-down Athens as viewed by a petty criminal, a 19-year-old singer/addict and an African strip-club performer, all trying to make a score in outwitting both the cops and the drug dealers, who in the film are practically indistinguishable. The film forecasts both the digital age and the coming crisis, as the lead petty thief proclaims his dislike of technology ('With the cops, you fight them. What can you say to a computer, you're shit as far as it's concerned'), and is told in an eerie forecasting of the future to 'Wake up while there's still time to defend the things we have, before they all go straight to hell.' In the end, the petty thief and the young singer he befriends die in a hail of gunfire, but that is not shown. Instead, the two sing a duet as they await their fate, knowing there is no possibility of escaping a world where money and the hope of a future only exist as a fantasy. The ending is an eerie echo of Jean Gabin's failure to escape his world on a South American freighter in *Port of Shadows*, as he is instead gunned down in the street, in a film made at the onset of the fascist period.

Greek Austerity Noir: Bailing Out the Banksters

There are a number of similarities between *Stratos* and *Wednesday 04:45*, released respectively in 2014 and 2015. The action in both takes place around the height of the crisis in 2010, with *Wednesday 04:45* being specific about this dateline through frequent television newscasts showing a country in flames. Both lead characters, the hangdog hitman in *Stratos* and the jazz-club owner referred to as The Artist in *Wednesday 04:45*, are engulfed in a world where money rules all relationships. Both endeavour, instead, to maintain human values in the face of the profit motive, as they are confronted either with their own debt or the consequences of what those around them do to get out of debt.

The hitman Stratos attempts to spring his friend from jail, and Stelios the nightclub owner attempts to maintain his jazz club in the face of money he has borrowed coming due. Both act ethically to save children, here symbolising the future, with the actions of both, rather than righting the situation, leaving them alone and either dead or dying. It must be remarked also that both exist in utterly misogynist worlds, where women are relegated to the roles of wife, mistress, sex-worker or stripper, with only the Polish club dancer Agni/Agniezska in the Albanian club, the obverse of Stelios's jazz club, displaying the consciousness to call out the club owner for his hiring of an African dancer who will work for less money after Agni has built up the club.

The hitman Stratos is called a 'legend' for his former gutting of his victims, a term which conjures up, as with Greece, his once glorious past. As the film opens, he continues to execute petty debtors, but has no joy in it as he also works in a bakery in an attempt to legitimise his earnings. His haggard, world-weary look, emphasised by his puffed-up cheeks, is a precursor of Marcello Fonte's canine-groomer-turned-slaughterer in the Italian film *Dogman* (dir. Garrone, 2018), which also describes a no-man's land in the suburbs of Rome in the wake of Italian austerity (Figure 14.2). Stratos's goal in continuing to murder is to spring his friend and mentor Leonidas from jail by raising money for what amounts in this world to a public works project, a tunnel that another

Figure 14.2   Stratos (Vangelis Mourikis), just before his first murder. Digital still from *Stratos*.

gangster, Yorgos, and the mentor's wife are digging under the prison. The effort goes awry, however, when Stratos is finally told that Yorgos was simply using this excuse to extract money from him, so he could leave with Leonidas's wife. Stratos trudges alone through the now deserted tunnel, a dead space reminiscent of the endemic corruption that ended in unfinished projects after the economic contraction.

The second half of the film focuses on debt, as Stratos's neighbour Makis struggles to escape the borrowings that placed him under the thumb of another gangster, Petropoulos, who wants to employ Stratos. To get out of debt, Makis is pimping his sister Vicki, while also selling her first to the gangster and then to the gangster's son. Stratos observes Vicki humiliated by Petropoulos, but then balks when the disabled Makis wants to sell Vicki's young daughter to the gangster to pay off the rest of the debt. He lures Vicki and Makis to the tunnel by claiming it is a gold mine, and then murders both and leaves their bodies in this null space. He has, meanwhile, failed to do a job for his employer, who calls himself 'the Painter', in a perverted sense of artistry in this world. Stratos takes the money for the job, and ends by being shot by the Painter's henchmen.

If the first part of the film is about the corruption around collective projects, the second part concerns the utter abandonment of values in the wake of debt. The business executive who Stratos finally refuses to execute describes this world by saying it is one where 'Big fish eat the little fish.'[8] Throughout, Stratos is tossed and turned by those higher than him who take advantage of his loyalty and fellow feeling or by those around him who are utterly corrupted by their own overspending. The film, which does have an arthouse pallor, was featured at the Berlin Film Festival, where the critic for *The Hollywood Reporter* chided it for not having more fun as Greece burns, noting that it 'could have been a Tarantino-esque riff on classic pulp fiction tropes' (Dalton 2014). Instead the film is a grim reckoning and recounting of a world where all relations are subsumed by money, or the lack of it. As such, *Stratos* escapes more superficial Hollywood flattening and commercialising of the noir impulse.

Stratos defines the post-crisis landscape as a series of bleak locations on the edge of the world. *Wednesday 04:45* is all urban spaces in the heart of Athens at the height of the crisis, in its tale of a middle-class jazz-club owner living heavily in debt. The film has been called 'apocalyptic' and compared to *Blade Runner* (dir. Scott, 1982) (Fotiou and Fessas 2017) in its otherworldly spaces that feature, in one scene, an eerie elevator which seems to descend from nowhere. The predominant visual element is a green gauze that bathes everything in its highly artificial light, although this is the colour of nature. Here, green is the colour of money which saturates the landscape and the characters in an artificial, neon glow they cannot escape, and which is as much their present condition trapped in the currents of money and monetarism as it is a glimpse into a decayed future.

Wednesday 04:45 is a middle-class noir whose protagonist, the club owner Stelios, is waking up to the fact that his debt, in this case to a Romanian gangster, has placed him in a perilous situation. The film takes place as union leaders, lawyers, prosecutors and judges were beginning to realise that they too were being harmed by budget cuts that they expected to affect only workers (Roufos 2018: 95). The film is a detailing of the process not only of this awakening, but also of the pressure that the debt exerts on the character.

In the opening, in voiceover Stelios says 'The time you are given is not enough.' He is then confronted by the loan shark with a deadline, the title of the film, which keeps marking in titles the time ticking away as the beleaguered club owner tries to come up with the money. The gooey green haze that envelops the film is amplified by the main character's inability to sleep, as the pressure mounts over the two days of the deadline, echoing the American neo-noir *Insomnia* (dir. Nolan, 2002), featuring an increasingly restless Al Pacino. Stelios at first wants to pay back the loan with a post-dated cheque, that is, to delay payment by using fictional accounting, but is told by his translator that the Romanian will not take cheques. This outside force which now has power over him is echoed in a conversation, nominally about football, overheard in a bar, which concerns an Italian coach who is imposing his will on the Greeks, and which could be a reference to Mario Draghi, the head of the European Central Bank, one wing of the Troika.

The management of the jazz club is compared to the economic history of Greece itself, when Stelios recounts its story in front of an audience. He had bought a top-of-the-line sound system in 1993, before the introduction of the euro, when the economy looked rosier. He then changed the console in 2004 during the Olympics, at a time when that event seemed to signal Greece's emergence as an economic power. Finally, though, he had to tear out the sockets as 'something went wrong in 2006', at the beginning of the global downturn instigated by the sub-prime crisis.

Later Stelios wonders in front of his hired muscle Vassos, 'what this world is coming to?' Vassos, who will later betray him to the Romanian, answers in trying to open his eyes. 'It's not "coming to" my boy. It's been there all along.' Finally, when Stelios cannot pay, he is informed by the Romanian that the latter will take over his club, with Stelios merely as a co-manager along with the Romanian's son, who 'has a lot of ideas for remaking the club' that include featuring what for Stelios are the degraded musical genres of disco, house and Greek pop. Stelios's fate echoes that of the Greeks themselves who, through foreign intervention including the privatisation of much of their patrimony, were becoming mere functionaries in their own country, as it was taken over lock, stock and barrel by those who helped manipulate the country into debt. A bloodbath ensues in which Stelios kills the Romanian, his son and the two henchmen who betrayed him, and then, in frustration, also murders two Greek cops and, much like the two characters in *Loser Takes All*, awaits his fate alone on his verandah.

Greek film noir, in line with its Mediterranean cousins, employs the dark style not only to describe generalised modes of power in the region but, in these cases, also to chart the inner feelings and emotions engendered by the specific moment of the debt crisis. In doing so, this variant of a globalised and regionalised form connects to an originary moment in classic noir both in the US and across the world of a frontal attack on workers and equality. Greek austerity noir illustrates how the dark style can be utilised as an effective tool for mapping this latest, most destructive phase of neoliberal capitalism.

Notes

1. For a full account of this moment, see Broe (2014).
2. An early cinematic manifestation of Mediterranean noir was classic period director René Clément's *Plein Soleil/Purple Noon* (1959) which, as a critic in *Le Monde* noted on the occasion of the 2013 re-release of the film, was the *première* injection of the colour aesthetic as part of European film noir (Blumenfeld 2013: 13).
3. This similar spectrum follows also from a 'homogeneous' climate, occasioning, as Braudel puts it, 'the same seasonal rhythm, the same vegetation, the same colours [. . .] the same landscapes, identical to the point of obsession; in short, the same ways of life' (1972: 235).
4. A disturbing trend in Spanish-language cinema as a whole is films that employ a hyper-version of the noir style (pulse-pounding music, 'choker' close-ups, mysterious rendezvous at night) to give the appearance of exposing corruption, but shed little light on the nature of that corruption; that is, there is a hollowed-out content, so that corruption simply becomes a McGuffin that propels the plot forward. This is true of both Spain's *El Reino/The Candidate* (dir. Sarogoyen, 2018) and Peru's *Caiga quien Caiga/Let Fall What May* (dir. Guillot Meave, 2018).
5. Unless otherwise stated, all translations are by the author.
6. The wholescale plundering of state assets has now moved from Greece, at the periphery of the Eurozone, to the centre, as the ultimate neoliberal Macron is now selling off, or leasing for seventy years, the Paris airports and their concessions, a profitable well-run enterprise that private capital wants to pluck (Werly 2019: 8).
7. Much as in the US, working-class borrowers hoping to have a home were blamed for the financial crisis and were not bailed out, while the banks were rewarded with huge payoffs.
8. The Greek title of the film was *To mikro psari*, meaning 'The Small Fish'.

References

Abulafia, David (2011), *The Great Sea: A Human History of the Mediterranean*, Oxford; Oxford University Press, Kindle Edition.
Blumenfeld, Samuel (2013), '"Plein soleil", film impur et métissé, *Le Monde*, 12 July, p. 13.

Braudel, Fernand (1972), *The Mediterranean and the Mediterranean World in the Age of Philip II*, vol. 1, New York: Harper and Row.

Broe, Dennis (2014), *Class, Crime and International Film Noir: Globalizing America's Dark Art*, Basingstoke: Palgrave Macmillan.

Broe, Dennis (2009), *Film Noir, American Workers, and Postwar Hollywood*, Gainesville, FL: University of Florida Press.

Carlotto, Massimo (2006), *The Goodbye Kiss*, Rome: Europa Editions.

Dalton, Stephen (2014), 'Stratos (*To micro psari*): Berlin Review', *The Hollywood Reporter*, 11 February, <https://www.hollywoodreporter.com/review/stratos-mikro-psari-berlin-review-679241> (last accessed 31 July 2021).

Ferri, Sandro (2018), 'Towards a History of Mediterranean Noir: 3,000 Years of Sunbaked Noir, from Cain to Camus to Khadra', CrimeReads, 20 April, <https://crimereads.com/towards-a-history-of-mediterranean-noir/> (last accessed 18 December 2021).

Fotiou, Mikela, and Fessas, Nikitas (2017), 'Greek Neo-Noir: Reflecting a Narrative of Crisis', *Filmicon: Journal of Greek Film Studies*, 4, pp. 110–37.

Lloyd, Nick (2012), 'Man of the People – Manuel Vásquez Montalbán', *Metropolitan Barcelona*, 30 March, <https://www.barcelona-metropolitan.com/features/man-of-the-people-manuel-v%C3%A1zquez-montalb%C3%A1n/> (last accessed 31 July 2021).

Reynolds, Michael (ed.) (2006), *Black and Blue: An Introduction to Mediterranean Noir*, Rome: Europa Editions.

Ridet, Philippe, and Fressoz, Françoise (2013), 'La Berlusconisation de Nicolas Sarkozy', *Le Monde*, 12 July, p. 17.

Roufos, Pavlos (2018), *A Happy Future is a Thing of the Past: The Greek Crisis and Other Disasters*, London: Reaktion.

Werly, Richard (2019), 'La privatisation d'ADP, un imbroglio politique', *Le Temps*, 17 March, p. 8.

APPENDIX: GREEK FILMS AND TELEVISION SERIES/SHOWS FEATURING DOMINANT NOIR OR NEO-NOIR TROPES

Nikitas Fessas

FILMS

Aftoptis martys/Eye Witness, dir. Markos Holevas (GFC, ERT, 1993).
Agria triandafylla/Wild Roses, dir. Angelos Provelengios (Giorgos Karapanagiotis, Giorgos Kaltsas, Angelos Provelengios, 1993).
Agrypnia/The Wake, dir. Nikos Grammatikos (Graal S.A., ERT, 2005).
Akoma mia fora . . . prin xepsyhiso/Gynaikes polyteleias/One More Time Before I Die/Luxury Women, dir. Giorgos Papakostas (Klak Films, 1970).
Akros aporriton: Ypothesis Ermis/Top Secret: The Hermes Case, dir. Dimitris Zannidis (Hatz Film, 1967).
Aliosha, dir. Thanassis Scroubelos (GFC, ERT, 1999).
Alyti/Entwined, dir. Minos Nikolakakis (Greece/UK, Inkas Films, 2019).
Amfivolies/Doubts, dir. Grigoris Grigoriou (Roussopoulos Bros, G. Lazaridis, D. Sarris, K. Psarras, 1964).
An eheis tyhi. . ./If you Are Lucky. . ., dir. Giorgos Petridis (Savas Films, 1964).
Anaparastasi/Reconstruction, dir. Theodoros Angelopoulos (Giorgis Samiotis, 1970).
Aoratos/Invisible, dir. Dimitris Athanitis (DNA Films, 2015).
Apagogi/Abduction, dir. Kostas Karagiannis (Karagiannis, 1964).
Athina: I klopi tis odou Stadiou/Athens: Robbery on Stadiou St., dir. Nasos Bibelas (Grigoris Dimitropoulos, 1968).
Avrio tha nai arga/Too Late Tomorrow, dir. Laya Yourgou (Laya Yourgou, 2001).
Big Hit, dir. Karolos Zonaras (Veronique Leclerc, 2012).
Ble vasilissa/Blue Queen, dir. Alexandros Sipsidis (Alexandros Sipsidis, 2017).
Dakrya gia tin Ilektra/Tears for Elektra, dir. Giannis Dalianidis (Finos Film, 1966).

Dama spathi/Queen of Clubs/Love Cycles, dir. George Skalenakis (Damaskinos – Michaelides, 1966).
Digger, dir. Georgis Grigorakis (Greece/France, Haos Film, 2020).
Do It Yourself, dir. Dimitris Tsilifonis (View Master Films, 2017).
Efialtis/Nightmare, dir. Erricos Andreou (Erricos Andreou, 1961).
Eglima sto Kavouri/Death Kiss/The Rape Killer/He Murdered His Wife, dir. Kostas Karagiannis (Karagiannis–Karatzopoulos, 1974).
Eglima sto Kolonaki/ Murder in Kolonaki, dir. Tzanis Aliferis (Tzal Film, 1959).
Eglima stin Omonoia/Crime in Omonoia, dir. Christos Lathouropoulos (Lafis Films, 1962).
Eglima sta Paraskinia/Murder Backstage, dir. Dinos Katsouridis (Damaskinos–Michaelides, Techni S.A., 1960).
Eleftheri katadysi/Love Knot, dir. Giorgos Panousopoulos (GFC, Stefi Film, Filmiki Etaireia, 1995).
Eno sfyrize to treno/While the Train Was Whistling, dir. Iason Charalambous, Nikos Hatzithanasis (Kalia Film, 1961).
Epikindyno paihnidi (a.k.a. Anametrisi)/Dangerous Game, dir. Giorgos Karypidis (GFC, 1982).
Erastes sti mihani tou hronou/Lovers Beyond Time, dir. Dimitris Panayiotatos (ERT, GFC, Prooptiki, 1990).
Erotas stin kafti ammo/O drapetis/Love on the Scorching Sand/The Fugitive, dir. Stelios Zografakis (Anervos, 1966).
Eteros ego/The Other Me, dir. Sotiris Tsafoulias (Green Dragon & Blonde, 2016).
Exodos kindynou/Emergency Exit, dir. Nikos Foskolos (Greka Film, 1980).
Frenitis/Frenzy, dir. Giannis Hristodoulou (as Jan Christian) (Makedonia Film, 1971).
Gavriela i amartoli tis Athinas/Gavriela the Sinful of Athens, dir. Giorgos Papakostas (Faros Film, 1966).
Halvai 5-0, dir. Manos Kampitis (Comedy Factory, Smile, 2020).
Hamenoi angeloi/Fallen Angels, dir. Nikos Tsiforos (Finos Film, Tzella Film, 1948).
Hamenos paradeisos/Stream, dir. Thanasis Antoniou (Marathon Films, 2000).
Horis martyres/Without Witnesses, dir. Nikos Papamalis (Greka Film, Mouviola Film, 1983).
Horis taftotita/Without Identity, dir. Giannis Dalianidis (Finos Film, 1963).
Humphrey, dir. Steven Gekas (Steven Gekas, 2017).
Idiotiki mou zoi/Her Private Life, dir Omiros Efstratiadis (Ora Films, 1971).
I agnostos/Madame X, dir. Orestis Laskos (Finos Film, 1956).
I balada tis trypias kardias/Ballad for a Pierced Heart, dir. Yannis Economides (Argonauts, Faliro House Productions, EZ Films, 2020).
I epohi ton dolofonon/A Time to Kill, dir. Nikos Grammatikos (Panos Papahadzis, GFC, 1993).
I leoforos tis prodosias/Treason Highway, dir. Hristos Kyriakopoulos (Kyriakopouloi Bros, 1969).
I leoforos tou misous/The Avenue of Hatred, dir. Nikos Foskolos (Finos Film, 1968).
I Lola tis Troumbas/Lola, dir. Dinos Dimopoulos (Finos Film, 1964).
I megali apofasis/The Big Decision, dir. Dimis Dadiras (Greka Film, 1977).

I nyhta me ti Silena/The Night with Silena, dir. Dimitris Panayiotatos (GFC, Dimitris Panayiotatos, 1986).
I ora tis alitheias/The Hour of Truth, dir. Byron Pallis (Byron Pallis, 1969).
I parexigisi/Misunderstanding, dir. Dimitris Stavrakas (GFC, ERT, 1983).
I psyhi sto stoma/Soul Kicking, dir. Yannis Economides (Argonauts, 2006).
I Stefania/Stefania, dir. Giannis Dalianidis (Finos Film, 1966).
I teliki apopliromi/The Final Payoff, dir. Alexander Leontaritis (Desmida Visual Creations, 2013).
I triti nyhta/The Third Night, dir. Dimitris Panayiotatos (GFC, ERT, Arcadia, 2003).
I zougla ton poleon/The City Jungle, dir. Stavros Tsiolis (Finos Film, 1970).
I valitsa me to ptoma/The Suitcase with the Dead Body, dir. Giorgos Lois (Foutros Film, 1963).
Iligos/Vertigo, dir. Giannis Dalianidis (Finos Film, 1963).
Ioannis o viaios/John the Violent, dir. Tonia Marketaki (Tonia Marketaki, 1973).
Istoria 52/Tale 52, dir. Alexis Alexiou (Alexis Alexiou, Tugo Tugo Productions, 2008).
J.A.C.E., dir. Menelaos Karamaghiolis (Greece/Portugal/Turkey/Netherlands/FYROM, Menelaos Karamaghiolis, Fenia Cossovitsa, 2011).
Tzo o tromeros/ Joe the Terrible, dir. Dinos Dimopoulos (Anzervos, 1955).
Kamia sympatheia gia ton diavolo/No Sympathy for the Devil, dir. Dimitris Athanitis (GFC, DNA Films, 1997).
Katahrisis exousias/Abuse of Power, dir. Stavros Tsiolis (Finos Film, 1971).
Kataskopoi sto Saroniko/Assignment Skybolt, dir Gregg G. Tallas (Stamatis Prentoulis, 1968).
Katharsi/Cleansing, dir. Fokion Bogris (Ground Floor Films, 2009).
Katigoro to kormi mou/I listeia/I Blame my Body, dir. Erricos Andreou (Art Films, James Paris, 1969).
Katigoro tous anthropous/I Blame the People, dir. Dinos Dimopoulos (Finos Film, 1966).
Kierion, dir. Dimos Theos (Giorgos Papalios, Dimos Theos, 1968).
Kleisti strofi/U-Turn, dir. Nikos Grammatikos (Panos Papahadzis, Nikos Grammatikos, 1991).
Koinonia ora miden/Society Zero O'Clock, dir. Dinos Dimopoulos (Finos Film, 1966).
Kourastika na skotono tous agapitikous sou/I'm Tired of Killing Your Lovers, dir. Nikos Panayotopoulos (GFC, ERT, Filmnet, Marianna Film, Cinegram, 2002).
Kravgi. . ./Cry. . ., dir. Kostas Andritsos (Marvik Film, 1964).
Ligo prin ximerosei/Just Before the Crack of Dawn, dir. Odysseas Kosteletos (Pan Film, 1963).
Listeia stin Athina/Robbery in Athens, dir. Vangelis Serdaris (Kostas Pitsios, Vangelis Serdaris, 1969).
Lolites tis Athinas/Lolitas of Athens/Satan in Blond, dir. Giorgos Papakostas (Faros Film, 1965).
Magiki polis/The Magic City, dir. Nikos Koundouros (Athinaiki Kinimatografiki Etaireia, 1954).
Mahairovgaltis/Knifer, dir. Yannis Economides (Greece/Cyprus. Panos Papahadzis, 2010).
Marionetes/Puppets, dir. Pantelis Kalatzis (Showtime Productions, 2015).

Me fovo kai pathos/With Fear and Passion, dir. Nikos Foskolos (Finos Film, 1972).
Mia gynaika katigoreitai/A Woman is Accused, dir. Grigoris Grigoriou (Spiliotis Film, 1966).
Moiraia shesi/Fatal Relationship, dir. Erricos Andreou (G.K. Production, 2009).
Monemvasia: I zoi mou einai diki sou/Monemvasia: My Life is Yours, dir. Yiorgos Sarris (Athina Film, 1964).
Netrino, dir. Yannis Paraskevopoulos (Yannis Paraskevopoulos, Apostolos Gletsos, Dimitris Galanopoulos, Vasilis Alatas, 1999).
Noir Project, The, dir. Gregory Vardarinos (ERT, OTE TV, 2014).
Neiata sto pezodromio[/Youth on the Sidewalk, dir. Ilias (Liakos) Mylonakos (Myli Film, 1964).
O anthropos tou trenou/The Man on the Train, dir. Dinos Dimopoulos (Olympos Film, 1958).
O dolofonos agapouse poly/The Killer Loved a Lot, dir. Ion Daifas (Giannis Drimaropoulos, 1960).
O drakos/The Orge of Athens, dir. Nikos Koundouros (Athinaiki Kinimatografiki Etaireia, 1956).
O ergenis/The Bachelor, dir. Nikos Panayotopoulos (GFC, ERT, Marianna Film, 1997).
O fakelos Polk ston aera/The Polk File On Air, dir. Dionysis Grigoratos (ERT, GFC, Cine Group, 1988).
O fovos/The Fear, dir. Kostas Manoussakis (Damaskinos–Michailides, 1966).
O gios tou Tsarly/Charlie's Son, dir. Karolos Zonaras (Troon Films, Metavision, 2008).
O hamenos ta pairnei ola/The Loser Takes All, dir. Nikos Nikolaidis (Marni Film, GFC, ERT 2002).
O katiforos/The Downfall, dir. Giannis Dalianidis (Finos Film, 1961).
O kipos tou Theou/The Garden of God, dir. Takis Spyridakis (Afaia Film Production, 1994).
O krachtis/The Decoy, dir. Kostas Andritsos (Phoenix Film, 1964).
O lagopodaros/Rabbitfoot, dir. Odysseas Kosteletos (Andreas Haliotis, 1964).
O Labiris enantion ton paranomon/Labiris versus the Outlaws, dir. Giannis Gazis (Foivos Film, 1967).
O metoikos/The Resident/Koritsia me vromika heria/Girls with Dirty Hands, dir. Kostas Karagiannis (Art Film, 1977).
O reporter/The Reporter, dir. Andreas Thomopoulos (1982).
O stohos/O epanastatis prepei na pethanei/The Target/The Rebel Must Die, dir. Nikos Foskolos (Festival Film, 1983).
O thanatos tha xanarthi/Death Will Return, dir. Errikos Thalassinos (Finos Film, 1961).
O vasilias/The King, dir. Nikos Grammatikos (Inkas Film Productions, 2002).
O valtos/The Swamp, dir. Dinos Dimopoulos (Finos Film, 1973).
O zestos minas Augoustos/The Hot Month of August, dir. Sokrates Kapsaskis (Victoria Kapsaski, 1966).
Oi adistaktoi/The Ruthless, dir. Dinos Katsouridis (Savas Film, 1965).
Oi aisthimaties/The Sentimentalists, dir. Nikos Triantafyllidis (Marina Danezi, 2011).

Oi apanthropoi/Ransom Baby/The Sick Killers, dir. Pavlos Filippou (Pavlos Filippou, 1972).
Oi arithmimenoi/Numbered, dir. Tasos Psarras (ERT, GFC, 1998).
Oi ehthroi/The Enemies, dir. Dinos Dimopoulos (Finos Film, 1965).
Oi ekviastai/The Abductors, dir. Pavlos Filippou (P.F. Productions, Karagiannis-Karatzopoulos, 1972).
Oi ftohodiavoloi/The Poor Devils, dir. Giannis Christodoulou (John Christian) (Spentzos Film, 1964).
Oi satanades tis nyhtas/Devils of the Night, dir. Marios Retsilas (Art Film, 1972).
Oi stigmatismenoi/The Stigma of Corruption, dir. Kostas Andritsos (Ioannidis Film, Foinix Film, 1966).
Oratotis miden/Visibility Zero, dir. Nikos Foskolos (Finos Film, 1970).
Orgia se timi efkairias/The Greek Connection, dir. Kostas Karagiannis (Karagiannis–Karatzopoulos, 1974).
Otan i polis pethainei/When the City Dies, dir. Giannis Dalianidis (Finos Film, 1969).
Pandora, dir. Yiorgos Stamboulopoulos (Metavision S.A., 2006).
Panikos/Panic, dir. Stavros Tsiolis (Finos Film, 1969).
Parangelia!, dir. Pavlos Tasios (Greka Film, 1980).
Pedro Noula, dir. Karolos Zonaras (Zonaras Productions, GFC, ERT, A&G Films, 2016).
Plateia Amerikis/Amerika Square, dir. Yannis Sakaridis (Greece/UK/Germany, Ilioupolis Films, 2016).
Poreia/On the Road, dir. Stavros Parharidis, (Alfa Productions, GFC, 2004).
Pothoi ston kataramenο valto/Lust in the Swamps, dir. Grigoris Grigoriou (Spiliotis Film, 1966).
Proini peripolos/Morning Patrol, dir. Nikos Nikolaidis (GFC, 1987).
Prosopa lismonimena/Forgotten Faces, dir. Yorgos Th. Tzavellas (Finos Film, Orion Film: 1946).
Prostimo/Amercement, dir. Fokion Bogris (Chase the Cut, 2020).
Pyretos stin asfalto/The Asphalt Fever, dir. Dinos Dimopoulos (Finos Film, 1967).
Randevou me mia agnosti/One Night For Love/Appointment with an Unknown Woman, dir. Vasilis Georgiadis (Damaskinos–Michaelides, 1968).
Republic, The, dir. Dimitris Tzetzas (ABC Production, Point Blanc Pictures, NOVA Cinema, 2015).
Short Fuse, dir. Andreas Lampropoulos and Kostas Skiftas (USA/Greece, Konstantinos Moutsinas, 2015).
Singapore Sling: O anthropos pou agapise ena ptoma/Singapore Sling: The Man Who Loved a Corpse, dir. Nikos Nikolaidis (Marni Film, Cinekip, GFC, 1990).
Sti skia tou fovou/In the Shadow of Fear, dir. Giorgos Karypidis (Giorgos Karypidis, ERT 1, GFC, 1988).
Sti skia tou Lemmy Kosion/In the Shadow of Lemmy Caution, dir. Nikos Zervos (Media Team S.A., GFC, 2002).
Sti thanasimi dini tou hronou/Deep End, dir. Thanasis Antoniou (Yvonne Roman Films, 2008).
Syntrimmia tis zois/Casablan, dir. Larry Frisch (Greece/Israel/USA, Anzervos, Natas Film, 1963).

Ta skylia gleifoun tin kardia mou/Dogs Licking My Heart, dir. Nikos Triantafyllidis (Astra Theama & Akroama, 1993).
Tetarti 04:45/Wednesday 04:45, dir. Alexis Alexiou (Twenty Twenty Vision, CL Productions, Pie Films, 2015).
Tha se do stin kolasi, agapi mou/See You in Hell, My Darling, dir. Nikos Nikolaidis (Nikos Nikolaidis, GFC, ET 1, 1999).
Thema syneidiseos/A Matter of Conscience, dir. Petros Lykas (Finos Film, 1973).
Thyella sto spiti ton anemon/Storm in the Windy House, dir. Byron Pallis (Foivos Film, 1968).
To hamogelo tis Pythias/To kolpo tou tounel/Intrigue in Delphi, dir. Sergio Bergonzelli, Soulis Georgiadis (Telecolor S.A., 1979).
To katharma/I markissia tou limaniou/The Scum, dir. Kostas Andritsos (Foinix Film, 1963).
To kynigi tou lagou/The Hunt of the Hare, dir. Nikos P. Vezyrgiannis (Upstate Movies, 1999).
To koritsi tou 17/The Girl of Number 17, dir. Petros Lykas (Petros Lykas, 1969).
To mikro psari/Stratos, dir. Yannis Economides (Faliro House Productions, Argonauts Productions S.A., Match Factory Productions, Y.E. Films, 2014).
To mystiko tou kokkinou mandya/O kokkinos mandyas/To megalo mystiko/The Secret of the Red Mantle, dir. Kostas Fotinos (Anotati Scholi Kinimatografou, 1960).
To mystiko tou Noemvri/Secret November, dir. Takis Papagiannidis (GFC, ERT, Telefilm, 2002).
To Pontikaki/The Little Mouse, dir. Giorgos Asimakopoulos and Nikos Tsiforos (Anzervos, 1954).
To remali tis Fokionos Negri/The Bum of Fokionos Negri, dir. Kostas Karagiannis (Kikos Film, 1965).
To thavma tis thalassas ton Sargasson/The Miracle of the Sargasso Sea, dir. Syllas Tzoumerkas (Greece/Germany/Netherlands/Sweden, Homemade Films, 2019).
Trikymia mias kardias/A Heart's Storm, dir. Filippos Fylaktos (Kostas Tsoukalas, 1969).
Trouba'67, dir. Grigoris Grigoriou (A.K. Films, 1967).
Vromiki polis/Dirty City, dir. Kostas Andritsos (Tele Cine, Foinix Film, 1965).
Waiter, The, dir. Steve Krikris (Filmiki Productions, 2018).
Wild Duck, dir. Yannis Sakaridis (Yannis Sakaridis, 2013).
Ypogeia diadromi/Underground Passage, dir. Apostolos Doxiadis (Kinimatografiki Etaireia Athinon, GFC, 1983).
Ypothesi Polk/The Polk Case, dir. Angelos Malliaris (Telecolor, 1978).
Zitima zois kai thanatou/A Matter of Life and Death, dir. Vangelis Serdaris (Geniki Kinimatografikon Epiheiriseon, 1973).

Television

10i entoli/10th Commandment, dir. Panos Kokkinopoulos et al. (Frenzy Films, Alpha TV, 2004–15).
13o anakritiko grafeio/Interrogator's Office Number 13, dir. Manolis Mavromatis, Alexis Triantafyllou (Eklogi, EIRT, 1971).

APPENDIX

38o astynomiko tmima/38th Precinct, dir. Jimmy Corinis (Victory, Astynomia Poleon, YENED, 1972-3).
42°C, dir Jorgo Papavassiliou (Cosmote TV, Tanweer Productions, 2021-).
Aftoptis martys/Eye Witness, dir. Markos Holevas (GFC, ERT, ET1, 1996).
Amyna zonis/Zone Defence, dir. Filippos Tsitos, Lefteris Charitos (Bad Movies S.A., ERT, NET, 2007-8).
Anatomia enos eglimatos/Anatomy of a Crime, dir. Panos Kokkinopoulos (Frenzy Films, ANT1, 1992-5).
Apodrasi/The Escape, dir. Costas Ferris (Pantas TV, ERT, 1987).
Aporitos fakelos 27/Classified File Number 27, dir. Giorgos Arion (Astynomia Poleon, YENED, 1972).
Astynomikes istories/Police Stories, dir. Giorgos Papakostas, Petros Pantazis (Organismos Pissanos, YENED, 1973-4).
Athoos i enohos/Innocent or Guilty, dir. Dimitris Arvanitis (Dimitris Arvanitis, ET1, 1989).
Athoos i enohos/Innocent or Guilty, dir. Manousos Manousakis, Grigoris Karantinakis (Tilekinisi, ANT1, 2000–01).
Belades gia dyo/Trouble for Two, dir. Dimitris Arvanitis, Vassilis Tselemengos (Mega Channel, 1992).
Defteri pnoi/Second Breath, dir. Vangelis Serdaris (Vangelis Serdaris, ET2, 1988).
Dioxi eglimatos/Crime Squad, Dimitris Noris (Kanali 5, 1996).
Dipli alitheia/Double Truth, dir. Panos Kokkinopoulos (Frenzy Films, ET1, 1997–98).
Dromoi tis polis/City Streets, dir. Manousos Manousakis, Kostas Kostopoulos (Tilekinisi, ANT1, 1995).
Efialtis/Nightmare, dir. Mitsos Ligizos, Giorgos Dabasis (Astir TV, EIRT, 1973–75).
Eglima kai pathos/Crime and Passion, dir. Dimitris Arvanitis (D-Port Productions, ANT1, 2018).
Eis thanaton/Sentenced to Death, dir. Yannis Vasileiadis (ANT1, 1997).
Ellinikes Istories Mystiriou kai Fantasias/Greek Tales of Mystery and Imagination/Tales of Love and Terror, dir. Dimitris Panayiotatos (ET2, 1989).
Epagelma reporter/Profession: Reporter (SKAI, 1994–95).
Epifaneia/Surface, dir. Vasilis Tselemengos (Studio ATA, Mega, 2001).
Epikindyni lipsi/Dangerous Shot, dir. Grigoris Petriniotis (Machi TV, Mega, 1990).
Epikindynes sheseis/Dangerous Relations, dir. Giorgos Mylonas (VCA ET2, 1992).
Eteros ego: Hamenes psyches/The Other Me: Lost Souls, dir. Sotiris Tsafoulias (Cosmote TV, 2019).
Eteros ego: Catharsis/The Other Me: Catharsis, dir. Sotiris Tsafoulias (Cosmote TV, 2020).
Exapsi/Heat, dir. Vassilis Tselemengos (Pedio Productions, Mega, 2021).
Exodos kindynou/Emergency Exit, dir. Kostas Lyhnaras (Epsilon TV, ERT, 1978).
Fakelos 38/File Number 38, dir. Kostas Karagiannis (ERT, Christos Negas, 1978).
Filippos Marlis, o detectiv/Philippos Marlis, the Detective, dir. Aris Fotiadis (ET2, 1990).
Fonos horis taftotita/Murder Without Identity, dir. Kostas Lyhnaras (Mega, 1990).
Fos sto tounel/Light in the Tunnel (Skai, Alter, Alpha, Mega, 1995–)

Fovos kai pathos/Fear and Passion, dir. Yiannis Hartomatzidis (Antonis Maniatis, ANT1, 1990–91).
Froutopia/Fruitopia, dir. Faidon Sofianos, Ivi Sofianou, Petros Dedegiannis, Ninos Elmatzioglou (ERT, 1985–89).
Gova stileto/Stiletto Heels, dir. Reina Eskenazy (Greece, ANT1, 1993).
Hara agnoeitai/Hara is Missing, dir. Alexandros Pantazoudis (Studio ATA, Mega Channel, 2009).
Haravgi/Crack of Dawn, dir. Takis Papagiannidis, Thodoris Konstadopoulos (On Productions, Mega, 1994–95).
Heimerini exodos/Winter Exit, dir. Makis Moraitis (Lidra S.A., ET1, 1993).
Horis anasa/Breathless, dir. Kostas Koutsomytis, Giannis Genitsariotis (Nikos Nikolareas, EIRT, 1973).
I agapi tis gatas/A Cat's Love, dir. Andreas Thomopoulos (Stratos Markidis, Mega Channel, 1991–92).
I dikaiosyni milise/Justice Has Spoken, dir. Grigoris Grigoriou (ERT, 1976).
I diki/The Trial, dir. Antonis Tempos (Linos TV, ET2, 1991).
I ekdromi/The Excursion, dir. Alexandros Pantazoudis (ANT1, 2014–15).
I ekti entoli/The Sixth Commandment, dir. Kostas Lyhnaras (Linos TV, ET2, 1989).
I etymigoria/The Verdict, dir. Thanos Sandas and Paul Sklavos (YENED, Dyas TV, 1978–80).
I exafanisi tou Tzon Avlakioti/The Disappearance of John Avlakiotis, dir. Erricos Andreou (Andreas Lapas, Giorgos Michaelides, ERT, 1985).
I koursa tou thanatou/The Death Race, dir. Kostas Andritsos (Aris Hatzopoulos, ERT, 1982).
I orgi ton theon/The Wrath of Gods, Kostas Lyhnaras (Orasis, SKAI, 1994–95).
I pagida/The Trap, dir. Giorgos Mihailidis (Pantas TV, ERT, 1986).
I vendeta/Ekdikisi/Vendetta/Revenge, dir. Dimitris Pontikas (TV Group, ERT 2, 1986–87).
Ihni/Traces, dir. Vassilis Tselemengos (TV Epsilon, Mega, 2007).
Istories apo tin apenanti ohthi/Stories from the Other Side, dir. Aris Bafaloukas, George Kordellas, Nikos Grammatikos, Panagiotis Fafoutis (Cut Productions, ANT1, 2007).
Istories me aproopto telos/Stories with an Unexpected Ending, dir. Jimmy Corinis (ET2, Jimmy Corinis, 1992).
Istories Mystiriou/Mystery Stories, dir. Aris Bafaloukas, Panagiotis Fafoutis, George Kordellas, Yorgos Gkikapeppas (Cut Productions, ANT1, 2007).
Kalimera zoi/Good Morning Life, dir. Nikos Foskolos et al. (ANT1, 1993–2006).
Katadioxi/Chase, dir. Michalis Papanikolaou et al. (YENED, Set TV, 1977–79).
Kleista parathyra/Closed windows, dir. Giorgos Lazaridis (Papandreou, ET1, 1992–93).
Kokkinos kyklos/Red Circle, dir. Panos Kokkinopoulos et al. (Frenzy Films, Alpha, 2000–02).
L.A.P.D.: Lekanopedio Attikis Police Department/L.A.P.D.: Attica Basin Police Department, dir. Stefanos Blatsos (Studio ATA, Mega, 2008–10).
Leshi mystiriou/Mystery Club, dir. Soulis Georgiadis (ERT, 1976–77).
Magiki nyhta/Magic Night, dir. Dimitris Panayiotatos (ET1, 1995).
Me thea sto pelago/With a View to the Sea, dir. Giannis Vasileiadis (TV Epsilon, Stefi Productions, Mega, 2003-4).

Mia gynaika apo to parelthon/A Woman from the Past, dir. Erricos Andreou (Andreas Lapas, ANT1, 1992).
Mystikes diadromes/Secret Routes, dir. Antonis Kokkinos, Stella Manola (Mythos, Point Pictures, Alpha, 2001).
Nyhterino deltio/Evening News, dir. Panos Kokkinopoulos (Frenzy Films, ERT, 1998–99).
O 3os nomos/The 3rd Law, dir. Panos Kokkinopoulos et al. (Frenzy Films, Mega, 2010).
O anthropos dihos prosopo/The Man Without a Face, dir. Mitsos Ligizos, Vasilis Vlahodimitropoulos (Astir TV, EIRT, 1972–73).
O defteros anthropos/The Second Man, dir. Nikos Antonakos (ET1, 1993).
O dikos mas anthropos/Our Man, dir. Erricos Andreou (Lakis Komninos, ERT, 1984).
O dolofonos pou eklaige/The Murderer Who Cried, dir. Jimmy Corinis (Victory, YENED, 1973).
O episkeptis tis omihlis/The Visitor in the Fog, dir. Antonis Tempos (Mega, 1991).
O fovos/The Fear, dir. Giorgos Mylonas and Pavlos Philippou (Block S.A., ET2, 1991–92).
O kitrinos fakelos/The Yellow File, Kostas Koutsomytis (Elite TV Production, ANT1, 1990–92).
O pyrgos ton Moskof/The Moscow Tower, dir. Tom Sears (Studio ATA, ET1, 1991–92).
O thanatos tou Timotheou Konsta/The Death of Timotheos Konstas, dir. Erricos Andreou (Hellas TV Productions, ERT2, 1987).
O Vagiannis xanahtypa/Vagiannis Strikes Again, dir. Nikos Zervos (ERT2, 1987).
Oi axiopistoi/The Trustworthy, dir. Erricos Andreou (TV Kosmos, YENED, 1982).
Oi dikaioi/The Just, dir. Antonis Tempos (Dyas TV, YENED 1974–76).
Oi enohoi/The Guilty, dir. Kostas Koutsomytis (Aronis-Efthymiadis, 1977).
Oi epagelmaties/The Professionals, dir. Yiorgos Konstantinopoulos, Dimitris Pantelias, Panos Thomaidis (TV Epsilon, Mega, 1996).
Oi ierosyloi/The Sacrilegious, dir. Kostas Lyhnaras (Dimitris Pontikas, ERT2, 1983–84).
Oi istories tou astynomou Beka/The Stories of Officer Bekas, dir. Grigoris Karantinakis et al. (PLD Productions, Alpha, 2006).
Oi prostates tou nomou/The Protectors of the Law, dir. Pavlos Parashakis (Denis Petropoulos, YENED, 1973).
Ou fonefseis/Thou Shall Not Kill, dir. Panos Kokkinopoulos (Frenzy Films, Open, 2018–19).
Pagides tou kalokairiou/Summer Traps, dir. Nikos Zapatinas (Lakis Komninos, ET2, 1989).
Pano apo to nomo/Over the Law, dir. Nikos Kritikos (ANT1, 2007).
Paraxeno spiti/Strange House, dir. Kostas Arzoglou (Risos Kyriakidis, ET1, 1991).
Paraxenos taxidiotis/Strange Traveller, dir. Kostas Koutsomytis (Eklogi, EIRT, 1972–73).
Peirasmos/Temptation, dir. Giannis Diamantopoulos (Anosi S.A., Mega, 1995–96).
Plektani/Plot, dir. Kostas Vakkas (ET2, 1990).
Poios einai o enohos/Who is the Guilty One?, dir. Ion Daifas (YENED, 1973–74).
Poios skotose ton Avel?/Who Killed Abel?, dir. Dimitris Pontikas (Dimitris Pontikas, ET2, 1988).

Reportaz stin omihli/Reportage in the Mist, dir. Thoedoros Konstadopoulos et al. (Mega, Star, 1993–99).
Siopilos dromos/Silent Road, dir. Vardis Marinakis (Filmiki Productions, Mega, 2021).
Skies pano apo tin poli/Shadows Over the City, dir. Antonis Tempos (Liana Patera, Mega, 1994).
Skorpios/Scorpion, dir Antonis Kafetzopoulos, Antonis Kioukas (On Productions, Pirate Productions, Mega, 1995–96).
Skoteines dynameis/Dark Forces, dir. Kostas Lyhnaras (Epsilon TV, ERT, 1976–77).
Skoteini thalassa/Dark Sea, dir. Grigoris Karantinakis (Alter Ego Mass Media S.A., Mega, 2022).
Sta dihtya tis arahnis/In the spider's web, dir. Marios Retsilas (EIRT, Art Film, 1972–73).
Tavros me toxoti/Taurus with Sagittarius, dir. Manousos Manousakis, Vassilis Tselemengos (Tilekinisi, ANT1, 1994–95).
Thriller loipon/Thriller, Then, dir. Michalis Papanikolaou (ET2, 1988).
To 13o kivotio/The 13th Box, dir. Tasos Psarras (Georgiadis Films TV Productions, 1992–93).
To asimenio dinario/The Silver Dinar, dir. Dimitris Arvanitis (Dimitris Arvanitis, ANT1, 1994).
To avrio mas anikei/Tomorrow Belongs to Us, dir. Vasilis Douros (Pedio Productions, Mega, 2021–).
To fterougisma tou glarou/The Fluttering of the Seagull, dir. George Kordellas (ET1, 1998).
To galazio diamanti/The Blue Diamond, dir. Takis Papagiannidis, Hristos Paligiannopoulos (TPS, ANT1, 1992–93).
To kanali ton paranomon/The Outlaws' Channel, dir. Georgis Agathonikiadis (Dimitris Tsebelis, ET2, 1989).
To mati tou fidiou/The Eye of the Snake, dir. Antonis Tempos (Telerama, Skai, 1994).
To mavro kleidi/The Black Key, dir. Jimmy Corinis (Pavlos Pissanos, YENED, 1973).
To mystiko tou Ari Bonsalenti/The Secret of Aris Bonsalentis, dir. Vangelis Serdaris (Hellas TV productions, Mega, 1990–91).
To mystiko tou Asprou Vrahou/The Secret of the White Rock, dir. Michalis Papanikolaou (Faros-Film, YENED, 1982).
To paihnidi/The Game, dir. Kostas Koutsomytis (ERT, 1979).
To tatouaz/The Tattoo, dir. Andreas Georgiou, Stamos Tsamis, and Kostas Anagnostopoulos (Greece/Cyprus, Make It Productions, Alpha, 2017–19).
To trast/The Trust, dir. Vangelis Fournistakis (Antonis Maniatis, ANT1, 1990)
Tmima ithon/Vice Squad, dir. Manousos Manousakis (Tilekinisi, ANT1, 1992–95).
Ypopsies/Suspicions, dir. Pavlos Filippou, Dimis Dadiras, Yannis Smaragdis, Kostas Papanikolopoulos, Errikos Thalassinos (Soulis Georgiadis, EPT, 1977–78).

In compiling these lists I have aimed for width, comprehensiveness, (reasonable) diversity and eclecticism. However, the final product should by no means be considered definitive, exhaustive or written in stone. The lists' imaginary borders are not static but remain flexible, porous and constantly expanding.

Similarly, the generic boundaries of each film listed are fluid, with numerous texts falling under multiple, non-exclusionary or composite (sub-)categories, such as mystery/noir, noir thriller, fantasy noir, sci-fi noir, noir Western, horror noir, reality TV noir, noir comedy, gothic noir, soap opera with noir elements, spy noir, exploitation noir, Weird noir, eco-noir, and so on. For the list of films, the following were consulted: Athanassatou (1999), Chalkou (2008), Dermentzoglou (2005; 2007), Kampanakis (2003), Karalis (2012), Komninou (2011), Kosyfologou (2013), Newsroom HuffPost Greece (2016), Poupou (2019; her 2011–12 and 2017–18 Greek cinema course curricula), Taskou (2017) and Valoukos (2001; 2008). Titles were also found in a 2011 blog entry by a user under the name JOHNPIT (the blog has since been taken down). The following were also consulted: the websites retrodb.gr, cine.gr, myfilm.gr, tainiothiki.gr, flix.gr, filmfestival.gr, cineuropa.org, hellenica.de, science.fandom.com, the fora on retromaniax.gr, Jimmy Corinis's Wikipedia page, Zevgiti (2018), Rangos (2018) and Kassaveti (2019). I would also like to thank Georgia Aitaki and Spyridon Chairetis. The list does not include any titles released straight to video.

References

Athanassatou, Gianna (1999), 'Ellinikos kinimatografos (1950–1967): Laiki mnimi kai ideologia' [Greek Cinema (1950–1967): Popular Memory and Ideology], PhD dissertation, National and Kapodistrian University of Athens, <https://thesis.ekt.gr/thesisBookReader/id/12629#page/1/mode/2up> (last accessed 7 November 2021).

Chalkou, Maria (2008), 'Towards the Creation of "Quality" Greek National Cinema in the 1960s', PhD dissertation, University of Glasgow.

Dermentzoglou, Alexis (2005), *To petagma tou anaptira: Sygritiki matia sto evropaiko kai sto amerikaniko noir* [The Throwing of the Lighter: A Comparative Look at European and American Noir], Thessaloniki: Erodios.

Dermentzoglou, Alexis (ed.) (2007), *In a Dark Passage: Film Noir in Greek Cinema*, Thessaloniki: Erodios.

Johnpit (2011), 'To xehasmeno elliniko astynomiko film noir tou '60' [The Forgotten Greek Crime Film Noir of the 1960s], Cinefil.pblogs.gr, <http://cinefil.pblogs.gr/2011/03/to- xehasmeno-ellhniko-astynomiko-film noir toy-1960-meros-1o.html>, <http://cinefil.pblogs.gr/2011/03/to-xehasmeno-ellhniko-astynomiko-film-noir-toy-1960-meros-2o.html> (last accessed 27 March 2012).

Kampanakis, Iosif (2003), 'O astynomikos ston palaio elliniko kinimatografo' [The Policeman in the Old Greek Cinema], *Astynomiki Anaskopisi*, 20:218, pp. 178–81, <https://crimefictionclubgr.wordpress.com/criminology-cinema/> (last accessed 9 August 2021).

Karalis, Vrasidas (2012), *A History of Greek Cinema*, New York: Continuum.

Kassaveti, Ursula-Helen (2019), 'Apo ton Astynomo Beka ston Lekka: Oi tileoptikes anamniseis enos astynomou meta ti Metapolitefsi' [From Officer Bekas to Lekkas: The TV Memories of a Policeman after Metapolitefsi], *Polar*, August, pp. 97–9.

Komninou, Maria (2011), *Apo tin agora sto theama: Meleti gia ti sygrotisi tis dimosias sfairas kai tou kinimatografou sti synchroni Ellada 1950–2000* [From the Market to the Spectacle: A Study on the Composition of the Public Sphere and Cinema in Contemporary Greece, 1950–2000], Athens: Papazisis.

Kosyfologou, Aliki (2013), 'I ideologia tis gynaikeias sexualikotitas: Anaparastaseis kai sygrotisi protypon ston elliniko erotiko kinimatografo tis dekaetias tou '60' [The Ideology of Female Sexuality: Representations and the Construction of Role Models in Erotic Greek Cinema of the 1960s], PhD dissertation, National and Kapodistrian University of Athens.

Newsroom HuffPost Greece (2016), 'Nostalgia gia to parelthon: 3 ellinika film noir pou den prepei na hasete' [Nostalgia for the Past: 3 Greek Film Noirs that You Should Not Miss'), Huffington Post Greece, 10 May, <https://www.huffingtonpost.gr/2016/05/10/ote-ellinika-film-noir-_n_9868244.html> (last accessed 9 August 2021).

Poupou, Anna (2019), 'Monachikoi likoi, exipna lagonika, thumomenoi gatoi: Andrismoi sto elliniko kinomatografiko astynomiko thriler ton dekaetion 1950 kai 1960' [Lonely Wolves, Smart Sleuths, Angry Cats: Masculinities in the Greek Cinematic Police Thriller of the 1950s and 1960s], in Dimitra Vasileiadou, Yannis Yannitsiotis and Androniki Dialeti (eds), *Andrismoi: Anaparastaseis, ypokeimena kai praktikes apo ti mesaioniki mehri ti sinchroni periodo* [Masculinities: Representations, Subjects and Practices from the Medieval to the Contemporary Period], Athens: Gutenberg, pp. 356–78.

Rangos, Yannis (2018), 'Alithina eglimata ston elliniko kinimatografo: Apo ta protoselida sti skoteini aithousa' [Real Crimes in Greek Cinema: From the Front Page to the Dark Movie Theatre], *Polar*, July, pp. 93–7.

Taskou, Ilias (2017), 'Eglimata pathous kai paranoias sto elliniko cinema!!!' [Crimes of Passion and Paranoia in Greek Cinema!!!], *Myselvi.gr*, 24 May, <https://myselvi.gr/egklimata-pathous-ke-paranias-sto-elliniko-sinema/> (last accessed 9 August 2021).

Valoukos, Stathis (2001), *Filmografia ellinikou kinimatografou (1914–2007)* [Filmography of Greek Cinema (1914–2007)], Athens: Aigokeros.

Valoukos, Stathis (2008), *Istoria tis ellinikis tileorasis* [History of Greek Television], Athens: Aigokeros.

Zevgiti, Maria (2018), 'O mitos tis Ariadnis: theoria kai praxi sto senario mias astynomikis tiletainias' [Ariadne's Thread: Theory and Praxis in the Script of a Crime TV Movie], MA thesis, Hellenic Open University.

INDEX

Note: page references in *italics* indicate figures; 'n' indicates chapter notes.

20th Century-Fox, 62, 64
38th Precinct (television series, 1972–73), 8
100 Hours of May/Ekato ores tou Mai (dir. Lambrinos and Theos, 1963–64), 164

Aaron, Michele, 212–13
Abbott, Megan E., 144
Acropolis (newspaper), 84, 130
actors
  in early films of Nikos Koundouros, 32
  female and *femme fatales*, 127, 128, 130
  in *Kierion* (dir. Theos, 1967–74), 164–5
  in post-war noir and *The Little Mouse/To Pontikaki* (dir. Asimakopoulos and Tsiforos, 1954), 49, 50, 55
  queer typecasting, 142
  in runaway productions and *The Angry Hills* (dir. Aldrich, 1959), 63, 65, 68, 76
  in television crime series, 248, 249, 252, 258nn5–7
  in the works of Yannis Maris, 84, 94
aesthetics, 10, 266
  of Cypriot short films, 240
  of early films of Nikos Koundouros, 27, 29, 31, 32, 33, 37, 38, 41, 43
  of *Kierion* (dir. Theos, 1967–74), 164, 169
  of post-war noir, 48
  of *Reconstruction* (dir. Angelopoulos, 1970), 178
  of runaway productions and *The Angry Hills* (dir. Aldrich, 1959), 63, 69
  of *Singapore Sling* (dir. Nikolaidis, 1990), 203, 204, 207, 213
Agnes of the Port/I Agni tou limaniou (dir. Tzavellas, 1952), 49, 51, 52, 57n4
Akin, Fatih, *In the Fade* (2017), 14
Aldrich, Robert, 63–6, 68, 70, 73, 75–6, 77
  The Angry Hills (1959), 4, 62–75, *72*, *74*, 78n8, 78n10, 78nn1–5

INDEX

Aldrich, Robert (*cont.*)
   Kiss Me Deadly (1955), 63, 65
   Ten Seconds to Hell (1959), 65
Alexander, Paris, 139
Alexandrakis, Alekos, 89, 94, 94–5
Alexiou, Alexis, 210, 217, 229n3
   Wednesday 04:45/Tetarti 04:45 (2015), 216–29, 220, 267, 271, 271–6
Algerian noir, 264, 266, 269
alienation, 35, 175, 191, 224
Aliferis, Tzanis, *Murder in Kolonaki/ Eglima sto Kolonaki* (1959), 5–6, 49, 68, 76, 82, 83, 90, 93, 95, 114, 127, 128
allegory, 63, 67, 73–5, 135
Altman, Rick, 12
Alton, John, 29
Amercement/Prostimo (dir. Bogris, 2020), 9
American film noir, xix–xxi, 8, 14, 47, 63, 117n6
   and *A Better Tomorrow* (dir. Woo, 1986), 224
   and contemporary Mediterranean noir, 263, 265
   and Cypriot short films, 236, 238
   and the early films of Nikos Koundouros, 35, 40, 43
   female characters, 122–3
   reception in Greece of, 122, 123–4, 129
   and *Singapore Sling* (dir. Nikolaidis, 1990), 200
   and the work of Yannis Maris, 82, 91, 92, 93
   see also Hollywood cinema
Ancient Greece, 2–3, 177, 273
   theatre, 122, 130
   see also mythology
Andreou, Erricos, 77, 78n12
   Nightmare/Efialtis (1961), 2, 6, 7, 76, 77, 103, 114, 149, 157n44
Andrew, Dudley, xxi, 85
Andritsos, Kostas
   Cry. . ./Kravgi. . . (1964), 114
   The Scum/To katharma (1963), 155n19
Angelopoulos, Theo, 1, 8, 165, 172, 174
   Reconstruction/Anaparastasi (1970), 2, 33, 163, 172–9, 191
   The Travelling Players/O thiasos (1975), 36
The Angry Hills (dir. Aldrich, 1959), 4, 62–75, 72, 74, 78n8, 78n10, 78nn1–5
Anna Roditi (dir. Filippou and Gaziadis, 1948), 52
Anzervos (production company) 29–30, 46, 50–1, 52, 53, 55
Apogevmatini (newspaper), 84
Apostolidis, Andreas, 18n13, 88, 126
Appadurai, Arjun, 216, 221
Applause/Heirokrotimata (dir. Tzavellas, 1944), 30
Arab Spring, 14, 270
Aravantinou, Marilena, 84, 130, 132, 133
arthouse/art cinema, 8, 9, 12, 30, 49, 185, 218, 271, 275
Arvanitis, Giorgos, 189
Asian noir, xxi, 263, 265–6
Asimakopoulos, Giorgos, 52–3, 58n5
   The Little Mouse/To Pontikaki (1954), 4, 46, 48–9, 52–7, 55, 57n1, 126
   The Tower of Knights/O pyrgos ton ippoton (1952), 52, 53
   Wind of Hate/O anemos tou misous (1954), 52, 53–4, 58n6
The Asphalt Fever/Pyretos stin asfalto (dir. Dimopoulos, 1967), 7, 103–4, 114
Athenian Cinematic Company, 31
Athens, xxii, 3, 4–6, 9, 12, 13, 126
   in contemporary Mediterranean noir, 273
   in early films of Nikos Koundouros, 30, 31, 32, 33, 34
   film production in, 64, 65, 67, 72, 75, 76
   in *John the Violent* (dir. Marketaki, 1973), 182, 183, 189, 191, 192
   in *Kierion* (dir. Theos, 1967–74), 164, 169, 171, 177
   and the music of Mimis Plessas, 108, 110

in queer noir and *The Bum of Fokionos Negri* (dir. Karagiannis, 1965), 147, *147*, *148*, 156nn26–7, 157n40
in runaway productions and *The Angry Hills* (dir. Aldrich, 1959), 69–73, *72*, 75
in television crime shows, 251
in *Wednesday 04:45* (dir. Alexiou, 2015), 220, *220*–5, 226
in the work of Yannis Maris, 81, 82, 84, 87, 89–90, 93
Athinaia (magazine), 146–53, *147*, *148*, 155n25, 156n26
audience, 39, 47, 49, 52, 54, 75, 107, 125; *see also* spectatorship
audio *see* sound effects and design
Augé, Marc, 223
austerity, 241, 264, 267–8, 271–3, 274, 277nn6–7; *see also* debt; Greek financial crisis; money
austerity noir, 273–7
Australia, emigration to, 48, 54, 56, 57
Australian noir, 270
auteurism, 10, 12, 47, 163, 183, 184–7, 201
authoritarianism, 4, 41, 163, 168, 169, 173
Avdela, Efi, 190–1
Avgeris, Nikos, 114–15
I Avgi (newspaper), 36, 85
Ayiotis, Harry, 235–6
 Quidnunc (2018), 233–4, *235*, *236*, *237*, 241–3

Bakatakis, Thimios, 12
Bakoyiannopoulos, Yannis, 177, 193
Ballad for a Pierced Heart/I balada tis trypias kardias (dir. Economides, 2020), 9
Barkoulis, Andreas, 128
bars and nightclubs, 91, 93, 149, 238, 274, 276
 and the music of Mimis Plessas, 106, *109*, 109–10, 115
 see also dance and striptease scenes; tavernas

Barthesian indices, 91, 97n11
Battle Cry (dir. Walsh, 1955), 64
Becker, Jacques, *Honour Among Thieves/Touchez pas au grisbi* (1954), 95
becoming-murderer and becoming-other, 182, 183, 187, 191, 193–7
Bekas, Officer/Inspector, 18n17, 84–6, 89–92, 94, *94*, 98n27, 105, 108–9, 127, *131*
 The Stories of Officer Bekas/Oi istories tou astynomou Beka (ALPHA, 2006–08), 247, 253–5, 258–9nn8–12
Belantis, Dimitris, 189
Bennett, Richard, 78n10
Benshoff, Harry M., 154n5
Berlin, 65
Berlinale Film Festival, 1, 275
A Better Tomorrow (dir. Woo, 1986), 216–29
Bezzerides, Albert Isaac, 63–4, 66–7, 68, 73, 75–6, 77
Biesen, Sheri Chinen, 121, 125
Bitter Bread/Pikro psomi (dir. Grigoriou, 1951), 30
B-movies, 50, 139
Bogris, Fokion, *Amercement/Prostimo* (2020), 9
Borde, Raymond, xx, 123
Bordwell, David, 173, 177
Bouchareb, Rachid, *Outside the Law* (2010), 269
Bould, Mark, 28
Bourdji island, 133, *134*
box office revenue, 7, 47, 49, 51, 64, 67, 78n4, 85
Boy on a Dolphin (dir. Negulesco, 1957), 62, 64
Bracher, Mark, 153
Bradshaw, Peter, 36
Braudel, Fernand, 264, 266, 267
British cinema, 62, 65, 67, 78n2, 92, 265
Broe, Dennis, xxi, 157nn38–9
Broken Hearts/Ragismenes kardies (dir. Laskos, 1945), 53
Buhler, James, 105, 117n15

293

INDEX

The Bum of Fokionos Negri/To remali tis Fokionos Negri (dir. Karagiannis, 1965), 7, 139–46, 150, 153, 155n16, 155nn22–3, 157n44
Butler, David, 104, 115

cabaret *see* bars and nightclubs; dance and striptease scenes
Cacoyannis, Michael, 4, 31, 33
   A Girl in Black/To koritsi me ta mavra (1956), 43n3
   Stella (1955), 33
Cairo Confidential/The Nile Hilton Incident (dir. Saleh, 2017), 270
camerawork and angles, 10, 29, 39, 85, 88, 94, 132, 170, 177
   close-ups, 38, 39, 132
   point-of-view (POV) shots, 88, 129, 132
   see also cinematography; framing
Cannes Film Festival, 106
Cant, John, 237
capitalism, 14, 33, 34, 43n1, 166, 189, 222, 224, 226, 277; *see also* austerity; debt; neoliberalism
cardinal functions, 86, 96n5
Carlotto, Massimo, 268
Carné, Marcel, 52, 264
   Port of Shadows/Le Quai des brumes (1938), 29, 51, 52, 273
Carpignano, Jonas, *A Ciambra* (2017), 269
Carreras, Michael, 65
Casanova Club, London, 71
censorship, xxii, 3, 6–7, 48, 70, 89, 91, 95, 164, 189; *see also* Production Code Administration (PCA)
Chalkou, Maria, 85, 229n3
Chandler, Raymond, 139
Chaplin, Charlie, 37
characters
   in contemporary Mediterranean noir, 265, 272–3
   in Cypriot short films, 239
   in early films of Nikos Koundouros, 28, 33, 38, 39
   and the music of Mimis Plessas, 100

   in post-war noir and *The Little Mouse/To Pontikaki* (dir. Asimakopoulos and Tsiforos, 1954), 49, 50, 52, 55
   queerness and gay male, 142
   in runaway productions and *The Angry Hills* (dir. Aldrich, 1959), 62, 66, 68–9, 71
   in *Wednesday 04:45* (dir. Alexiou, 2015) and *A Better Tomorrow* (dir. Woo, 1986), 222
   in the work of Yannis Maris, 82–4, 85–6, 87, 89, 92, 95
   see also female characters; male characters
Charalambous, Niovi, 236
Chartier, Jean-Pierre, 123
Chatzisavvas, Minas, *184*, 254
Chaumeton, Étienne, xx, 123
Chekhov, Anton, *The Story of a Nobody*, 38
chiaroscuro see lighting and light contrasts/*chiaroscuro*
Chinatown (dir. Polanski, 1974), 238
Chinese noir, 266
Chronopoulou, Mary, 127
A Ciambra (dir. Carpignano, 2017), 269
Cinema City Enterprises, 221
cinemas, 30, 49, 54, 70, 129, 149, 156n33
cinematography
   in early films of Nikos Koundouros, 29, 32, 35, 38, 39
   in *John the Violent* (dir. Marketaki, 1973), 189, 192, 196
   in *Kierion* (dir. Theos, 1967–74), 164
   in post-war noir and *The Little Mouse/To Pontikaki* (dir. Asimakopoulos and Tsiforos, 1954), 51
   in *Wednesday 04:45* (dir. Alexiou, 2015) and *A Better Tomorrow* (dir. Woo, 1986), 226
   and the work of Yannis Maris, 84, 93–4
   see also camerawork and angles
cities *see* Athens; urban settings
Citizen Kane (dir. Welles, 1941), 191

Civil War *see* Greek Civil War (1944–49)
class, social, 5, 6
  in contemporary Mediterranean noir, 264–5
  in early films of Nikos Koundouros, 34
  female characters and *femme fatales*, 127–8, 131, 134, 135
  in *John the Violent* (dir. Marketaki, 1973), 183
  in *Kierion* (dir. Theos, 1967–74), 169
  male characters and *The Bum of Fokionos Negri* (dir. Karagiannis, 1965), 141, 144, 149, 151
  in *Singapore Sling* (dir. Nikolaidis, 1990), 203
  in television crime shows, 254
  in *Wednesday 04:45* (dir. Alexiou, 2015) and *A Better Tomorrow* (dir. Woo, 1986), 227–8
  in the work of Yannis Maris, 82, 87
claustrophobia, 38, 43, 92, 94, 134, 170, 176, 177, 208, 228
Clément, René, *Purple Noon/Plein Soleil* (1959), 277n2
Cleto, Fabio, 203, 214n7
CLM (*Crime and Letters*), 10
codes, 3, 9, 30, 31, 39, 122, 142
Coen brothers, *No Country for Old Men* (2007), 237, 239
Cold War, 48, 265
comedy/comedies, 13, 53, 54–5, 56, 142, 150
  black humour, 205, 212
  dark comedy, 37, 38
  musical comedy, 51
comic strips, 82
communism, 4, 54, 56, 73, 74, 188, 189, 265
Constantinou, Marita, 65, 71
Corinis, Jimmy, 5
corruption, 7, 166–8, 171, 192, 203, 206, 222, 265, 266, 268, 275, 277n4
The Counterfeit Coin/I kalpiki lira (dir. Tzavellas, 1955), 35

Covid-19 pandemic, 2
crime and criminality
  in contemporary Mediterranean noir, 267, 273
  in early films of Nikos Koundouros, 34, 37
  in *John the Violent* (dir. Marketaki, 1973), 190–1
  and the music of Mimis Plessas, 105
  in post-war noir and *The Little Mouse/To Pontikaki* (dir. Asimakopoulos and Tsiforos, 1954), 47, 50, 54–7, 55
  in *Wednesday 04:45* (dir. Alexiou, 2015) and *A Better Tomorrow* (dir. Woo, 1986), 222–3
  in the work of Yannis Maris, 82
  see also violence
Crime at Omonoia/Eglima stin Omonoia (dir. Lathouropoulos, 1962), 128
crime fiction, xxi, 2, 4, 5, *5*, 18n13, 104, 156n29, 248–9, 251, 267; *see also* Maris, Yannis; pulp fiction
crime films, 3, 4, 6–7, 9, 10, 14, 49, 84–5, 92, 126, 129–30
crime shows *see* television crime shows
Cry. . ./Kravgi. . . (dir. Andritsos, 1964), 114
Crystal Nights/Krystallines nychtes (dir. Marketaki, 1992), 185
Cypriot short films, 232–44, *234*, 244n2
  context, 234–6
Cyprus and Cypriot visual culture, 50, 168, 236–7, 272
  'cinema of the Cyprus problem', 232–4, 243, 244nn1–4
Cyprus Ministry of Education, Culture, Sport and Youth (MECSY), 233, 235

Dadakaridis, Pygmalion, 255–6, *256*, 259n15
Daifas, Ion, *The Murderer Who Loved a Lot/O dolofonos agapouse poly* (1960), 95, 114

Damaskinos-Michaelidis (production and distribution company), 84, 85
dance and striptease scenes, 38, 41, 67, 70, 93, *109*, 109–10, 111, 115, 222; *see also* nudity
Dante Alighieri, *Divine Comedy*, 241
dark comedy, 37, 38
Dassin, Jules, 4
   Phaedra (1962), 121, 128–9
De Lauretis, Teresa, 210–11
De Man, Paul, 206
De Maria, Renato, *The Ruthless* (2019), 269
Death Strikes Again/O thanatos tha xanarthei (dir. Thalassinos, 1961), 50, 128
debt, 220, 222, 267–8, 271–7; *see also* Greek financial crisis; money
Deemer, Rob, 105, 117n15
Deleuze, Gilles, movement-images and time-images, 182–8, 191–7
Delveroudi, Eliza-Anna, 142
demonstrations and protest, 170–1
Dermentzoglou, Alexis, 37, 82, 117n4
dialogue, 55, 56, 66, 67, 73, 133
Dialyna, Rika (Mara Lanyie), 57n1
Dickos, Andrew, 68, 71
Dimokratiki Allagi (newspaper), 172
Dimopoulos, Dinos, 7, 47–8, 50, *50*, 82
   The Asphalt Fever/Pyretos stin asfalto (1967), 7, 103–4, 114
   Horse and Carriage/To amaxaki (1957), 43n1
   Joe the Terrible/Tzo o tromeros (1955), 4, 49, *50*
   The Man on the Train/O anthropos tou trenou (1958), 4, 30, 46, 49, 76, 82, 84, 130
   female gaze and subjectivity in, 122, 129–35, *134*
The Disappearance of John Avlakiotis/I exafanisi tou John Avlakioti (dir. Andreou; ERT television series), 78n12
Doane, Mary Ann, 122
documentary form/style

in Cypriot short films, 239–40, 241
and the early films of Nikos Koundouros, 34, 35, 37
in *John the Violent* (dir. Marketaki, 1973), 189–90, 196
in *Kierion* (dir. Theos, 1967–74), 164, 169, 171
in *Reconstruction* (dir. Angelopoulos, 1970), 172–3, 178
in the work of Yannis Maris, 93
Dogman (dir. Garrone, 2018), 274
Dostoevsky, Fyodor, *Notes from Underground*, 38
Doubts/Amfivolies (dir. Grigoriou, 1964), 128, 139
Doxiadis, Kyrkos, 154n3
The Drunkard/O methistakas (dir. Tzavellas, 1950), 35
Dyer, Richard, 142, 144, 145, 146, 149, 202–3, 209

Economides, Yannis, 244n2
   Ballad for a Pierced Heart/I balada tis trypias kardias (2020), 9
   Knifer/Machairovgaltis (2010), 9
   Stratos/To mikro psari (2014), 9, 267, 271, 272, 273–5, *274*
EDA (Eniaia Dimokratiki Aristera/ United Democratic Left), 5, 164
Edeson, Arthur, 29
editing, 30, 90, 94, 132, 187, 192, 194, 228
Edwards, Jason, 152
Egyptian noir, 264, 266, 269, 270
Eleftheria (newspaper), 85
Empros (newspaper), 123–4
Epidaurus theatre, 134
Epirus (region), 172, 176
escapism, 2, 35, 47, 169, 176
ethics, 200–1, 207, 211–13
Ethnikos Kyrix (newspaper), 84
European cinema, 8, 164, 173, 218, 264, 266
European noir, xx–xxi, 14, 47–8
Eva (dir. Plyta, 1953), 121, 129
expressionism, 29, 37, 38, 39, 55, 93, 170, *see also* German Expressionism

Fallen Angels/Hamenoi angeloi (dir. Tsiforos, 1948), 3, 49–50, 53, 55, 121, 126
falsehood/falsification, 186
　powers of the false, 182, 186, 187, 192–7
family relationships, 91, 129, 150, 243
　family values, 3, 6, 7, 18n8, 223
　fatherhood/father figures, 254–5
　marriage and marital norms, 189, 195
Farber, Stephen, 136n4
fascism, 3, 14, 171, 265, 267, 273
Fay, Jennifer, xxi, 219
fear, 33, 37, 105, 142, 170, 192, 222
Featherstone, Mike, 216
Felando, Cynthia, 234, 235
female body, 122, 175, 208–9, 237
female characters, 125–9, 135–6
　in contemporary Mediterranean noir, 274
　in Cypriot short films, 233, 237–8, 242–3
　ingénues, 46, 84, 91, 126
　in *John the Violent* (dir. Marketaki, 1973), 182–3, 185, 189–90
　'luxurious woman', 126–8, *131*, 133
　from operas, 122
　in post-war noir and *The Little Mouse/To Pontikaki* (dir. Asimakopoulos and Tsiforos, 1954), 49, 56, 57
　in *Reconstruction* (dir. Angelopoulos, 1970), 174–8
　in runaway productions and *The Angry Hills* (dir. Aldrich, 1959), 68, 70, 72–3
　in *Singapore Sling* (dir. Nikolaidis, 1990), 199–200, 204–5, 208–9, 211
　stereotypes and archetypes, 121–6, 128, 136n1
　in the work of Yannis Maris, 85–6, 87, 90–1, 95
female empowerment, 124, 129
female gaze, 122, 129–35, 144
female homosexuality, 133, 146, 155n11
female sexuality, 121–2, 127, 189–91, 195
female subjectivity, 129–35

female *see also* women
femininities, 36, 124, 126, 128, 144
feminism and feminist film theory, 124
femme fatales, xxii, 10, 12, 121–5, 128–9, 135, 136nn2–5
　absence of, 125–9, 135–6
　in *The Bum of Fokionos Negri* (dir. Karagiannis, 1965), 143, 144, 148
　in Cypriot short films, 238, 243
　in early films of Nikos Koundouros, 28, 40
　in *Reconstruction* (dir. Angelopoulos, 1970), 174–6
　in the work of Yannis Maris, 93, 95, 98n28
Fessas, Nikitas, 30, 79, 98n28, 98n30
Festival of Epidaurus, 134
fetishism, 39, 141, 147, 151, 152, 192
Fileleftheros (newspaper), 52
Filippou, Yannis, and Michalis Gaziadis, *Anna Roditi* (1948), 52
filles fatales, 122
film noir genre, xx, 29, 41, 43, 52, 66, 67, 68, 264–6
　classic period, xx, 63, 90, 91, 104, 125, 143
　classification of, xix, 27–8, 42, 47, 104, 117n5, 122, 124, 187
　term, 14, 84
financial crisis *see* Greek financial crisis
Finos Film/Filopoimin Finos (production company/producer), 3, 29–30, 47, 49–50, 50–1, 84, 113
First Week of Greek Cinema (1960), 85, 106
flashbacks
　female subjectivity in *The Man on the Train* (dir. Dimopoulos, 1958), 129, 132
　in *John the Violent* (dir. Marketaki, 1973), 183, 187–91, 193, 195, 197n3
　in *Kierion* (dir. Theos, 1967–74), 168
　in post-war noir and *The Little Mouse/To Pontikaki* (dir. Asimakopoulos and Tsiforos, 1954), 54

297

flashbacks (*cont.*)
  in *Reconstruction* (dir. Angelopoulos, 1970), 174
  in *Singapore Sling* (dir. Nikolaidis, 1990), 205
  in the work of Yannis Maris, 88, 90, 93
Flery, Yannis, 108
Florides, Adonis, *Rosemarie* (2018), 232, 235–6, 244n1, 244n3
Ford Foundation grants, 185, 197n1
Forgotten Faces/Prosopa lismonimena (dir. Tzavelas, 1946), 3, 30, 46, 49, 52
Foskolos, Nikos, 7, 50, 124
Fotiou, Mikela, 98n30, 201–3, 206, 211
Fotopoulos, Mimis, 55
Foucault, Michel, 151, 152, 154n3, 196
framing, 39, 132, 175, 177–8, 192
France, 47, 78n8, 91, 265, 277n6
Frank, Nino, 122–3
Franklin, Stuart, 34
French cinema, xx, 4, 29, 49, 52, 82, 126
  polar, 10, 82
French film noir, 8, 48, 51, 52, 88, 91, 95, 122–4, 126, 136n3, 263, 264, 268
French New Wave, 8, 84
French Surrealism, 248
Freud, Sigmund, 207, 210
Frith, Simon, 115

Gabin, Jean, 94, 98n26
gangs and gangsters, 32, 34, 38, 54, 55, 56, 72, 266, 270, 274–6
gangster films, xx, 4, 34, 37, 48, 51, 126
Garçon, François, 48
The Garment Jungle (dir. Sherman, 1957), 63, 65
Garrone, Matteo, *Dogman* (2018), 274
Gavras, Costa, *Z* (1969), 167, 168
Gaziadis, Dimitris, 49
Gaziadis, Michalis, 48–9
gender, xxii, 1, 3, 6, 12
  anxieties, 6, 9, 122, 124, 129
  binaries, 147, 148
  gender-segregated audiences, 125

identities, 14, 41, 144–7
  in *John the Violent* (dir. Marketaki, 1973), 183, 189, 191
  and queerness and *The Bum of Fokionos Negri* (dir. Karagiannis, 1965), 139, 141, 143, 147, 154n9
  in *Singapore Sling* (dir. Nikolaidis, 1990), 203, 209, 210
  and television crime shows, 248, 249, 251–2, 257
genre, 4, 6, 10, 13, 18n6, 30, 37, 38, 41, 47, 48, 187
genre cinema, 2, 5, 12, 13, 49, 65, 142, 143
Georgiadis, Vasilis, *The Red Lanterns/Ta kokkina fanaria* (1963), 9, 17n1
German Expressionism, xx, 29, 32, 48–9, 104, 238, 240, 248
German Occupation, xix, 4, 31, 46, 47, 49, 52–3, 56, 62, 82, 86, 88–9, 91, 105, 132, 166
  collaboration, 88, 91
  Nazi narrative elements, 70–5, 78n12, 82, 88, 91
  Resistance movement, 4, 62, 72–3, 88, 134–5, 165
Germanos, Freddy, 67, 77
A Girl in Black/To koritsi me ta mavra (dir. Cacoyannis, 1956), 43n3
The Girl with the Flowers/To koritsi me ta louloudia see *The Little Mouse/To Pontikaki* (dir. Tsiforos, 1954)
Gletsos, Apostolos, 252, 258n6
global and local intersectionality, 216–17, 221, 225–9
  'elsewhere', 221–2, 229
global/international noir, xxi, 14, 47, 52, 217, 225, 226–8
Gogol, Nikolai, 'The Overcoat', 38, 39
Golden Harvest Films, 221
Goldstone (dir. Sen, 2016), 270
The Goodbye Kiss/Arrivederci amore, ciao (dir. Soavi, 2006), 264, 268–9
Gorbman, Claudia, 115
gothic literature/style, 88, 203, 204
gothic thrillers, 125, 129–30, 133
Gousgounis, Kostas, 65

Grammatikos, Nikos, *The King/O vasilias* (2002), 271, 273
graphic novels, 10, *11*, 17n6
Greek cinema, 1–8, 10, 28–31, 33, 37, 41–2, 47, 48, 51, 53, 54, 58n5, 67, 185, 203
  commercial/Old Greek Cinema, 6–8, 12, 84, 103, 108, 113–16, 116n2, 126, 130, 144, 163
  'Golden Age', 30, 42, 77
  'Greekness' of, 51–2, 74, 74–5
  Weird Wave, 1, 9, 12
Greek Civil War (1944–49), 3–4, 12, 31, 47, 56, 63, 73–5, 82, 88, 107, 123, 134–5, 164, 188–91
Greek Film Centre, 201
Greek film noir, xxi–xxii, 1–17, 47–51, 54, 63–8, 75–7, 117n6, 266
  classic period, 122, 136n2
  contemporary, *271*, 271–3
  early forms/style, 27–33, *32*
  periodisation of, 3–9, *5*, *8*
  pragmatic approach to, 9–15, *11*, *13*
Greek film production, 3, 4, 6–7, 12, 27, 30–2, 41–2, 47–51, 63–4, 66
  distribution system, 28, 29, 49
  studio system, 3, 4, 7–8, 12, 28, 29–30
  women professionals in, 122, 125, 129, 130, 136
Greek financial crisis, 1–2, 3, 9, 15
  austerity following, 241, 264, 267–8, 271–3, 274, 277nn6–7
  in contemporary Mediterranean noir, 264, 271–2
  in Cypriot short films, 233, 240–1
  in *Wednesday 04:45* (dir. Alexiou, 2015) and *A Better Tomorrow* (dir. Woo, 1986), 220, 221, 223, 227–8
  see also austerity noir; debt; money
Greek junta (1967–74), 7–8, 156n29, 163, 164, 166, 168, 173, 182, 184, 188, 192, 197
Greek society *see* society and sociopolitical contexts
Greek Union of Film Critics, 51
Greek-Cypriot short films *see* Cypriot short films

Greene, Max, 29
Greenhouse (dir. Mylonas, 2013), 233–4, 235, 237–41, 243–4, 245n7
Grierson, John, 34
Griffin, Gabriele, 154n3
Grigoriou, Grigoris, 7
  Bitter Bread/Pikro psomi (1951), 30
  Doubts/Amfivolies (1964), 128, 139
  Red Cliff/O kokkinos vrahos (1949), 30
Grindstaff, Laura, 238

Hadjikyriacou, Achilleas, 142
hairstyles, 252
Hall, Kenneth E., 218
Hanson, Helen, 121, 125, 133
Hardt, Michael, 216, 227
Hatzidakis, Manos, 35, 41
heterogeneity, 217, 229n1
Hirsch, Foster, 43
Hitchcock, Alfred, 105, 139
Hjort, Mette, 225, 229n5
Hollywood cinema, xx, 3, 4, 8, 29, 32–4, 48, 51, 62–5, 74, 104, 124–5, 128, 129, 173, 263
  runaway productions in Greece, 4, 62, 64–8, 76, 77
  see also American film noir
homage, 9, 37, 199–201, 225
homme fatale, 139
homoeroticism, 41, 139
homosexuality, 139–46, 154n5, 209
  discourses, 146–53, *147*, *148*, 157n44, 157nn39–40
  female, 133, 146, 155n11
  see also queerness
Hong Kong, 218–19, 221, 223–5, 226
  cinema, 217–19, 221, 222
Honour Among Thieves/Touchez pas au grisbi (dir. Becker, 1954), 95
honour codes, 145, 155n16, 189, 190–1
horror/*giallo* films, 8, 203
Horse and Carriage/To amaxaki (dir. Dimopoulos, 1957), 43n1
Horton, Andrew, 173
The Hot Month of August/O zestos minas Avgoustos (dir. Kapsaskis, 1966), 7

House of Paper/Casa de Papel/Money Heist (dir. Pina, 2017), 267–8
Hungary, 56
Huston, John, 267
   In This Our Life (1942), 123
hybridity, 2, 8, 9, 10–12, 33, 34, 41, 42, 125, 131, 217–18, 229, 229n1, 237
Hydra (island), film production on, 64

iconography, 63, 69, 71, 72, 135, 164, 177, 203, 236, 256
   Byzantine, 37, 43n2
identity and impersonation motif, 88–9, 135, 177
identity/ies, 4, 5, 14–15, 40–1, 104, 141, 144, 146–7, 178, 208–9
   cultural, 104, 166, 219, 221, 224, 229
   sexual, 5, 140–7, 153, 210
ideology/ies, 4, 6, 7, 30, 32, 48, 184, 257
Iliopoulos, Dinos, 39, *50*
imaginary
   cinematic, 28, 29, 31, 36
   Mediterranean, 266–9
   social, 104
immigration/immigrants *see* migration/migrants
In the Fade (dir. Akin, 2017), 14
In This Our Life (dir. Huston, 1942), 123
Indigenous noir, xxi, 270
individuality/individuals, 29, 35, 39, 48, 175
industrialisation *see* modernisation
ingénues, 46, 84, 91, 126
Ingster, Boris, *Stranger on the Third Floor* (1940), 29
international *see* global noir; transnationality
International Short Film Festival of Cyprus (ISFFC), 235
intertextuality, 136n2, 201–2, 211–13, 217, 218, 234, 239
irony, 200, 203, 204–7, 211–13
Italian neorealism, 29, 33, 186, 265
Italian noir, 264, 266, 268–9, 274
Italy, 272, 274
Izzo, Jean-Claude, 268

The Jackal/Çakal (dir. Kozan, 2010), 270
Jameson, Fredric, 202, 226
Japanese cinema, 265, 266
jazz, 103–16, 171, 179n6, 200, 226
Jeancolas, Jean-Pierre, 47
Jews, 53, 82, 165
Joe the Terrible/Tzo o tromeros (dir. Dimopoulos, 1955), 4, 49, *50*
John and the Road/O Yannis kai o dromos (dir. Marketaki, 1967), 184
John the Violent/Ioannis o viaios (dir. Marketaki, 1973), 2, 36, 182–97, *184*, *190*, 197nn1–2
journalism and journalists, 148–50, 194
   in *Kierion* (dir. Theos, 1967–74), 164–6, 168
   in *Reconstruction* (dir. Angelopoulos, 1970), 174, 178
   and the work of Yannis Maris, 81, 82, 87, 89, 94, 95
   see also press
junta *see* Greek junta (1967–74)
Just Before the Crack of Dawn/Ligo prin ximerosi (dir. Kosteletos, 1963), 114

Kalinak, Kathryn, 105, 116
Kalogeras, Yiorgos D., 66, 75
Kambanellis, Iakovos, 37, 38
Kanellopoulos, Takis, 4
Kaplan, E. Ann, 124
Kapnisis, Kostas, 114
Kapsaskis, Socrates, *The Hot Month of August/O zestos minas Avgoustos* (1966), 7
Karagiannis, Kostas, *The Bum of Fokionos Negri/To remali tis Fokionos Negri* (1965), 7, 139–46, 150, 153, 155n16, 155nn22–3, 157n44
Karalis, Vrasidas, 77, 85, 117n4, 202, 205–6
Karamanis, Christos, 226
Karapostolis, Vasilis, 189
Kartalou, Athena, 10
Karydis-Fuchs, Aristeidis, 29, 84, 93, 96, 132, 133

Kassabian, Anahid, 107, 113
Kassaveti, Ursula-Helen, 251
Katrakis, Manos, 32
Katsaros, Yorgos, 114
Katsouridis, Dinos, 7, 76, 78n11, 84
  Murder Backstage/Eglima sta paraskinia (1960), 6, 49, 68, 76, 77, 81, 84–96, *94*, 96n4, 98n27, *131*
  music by Mimis Plessas, 103–16, *109*, *112*, 117n4, 117n14
  The Ruthless Ones/Oi adistaktoi (1965), 90
Kelly, Oliver, 207, 208–9
Kierion (dir. Theos, 1967–74), 163–72, *167*, 178–9
The King/O vasilias (dir. Grammatikos, 2002), 271, 273
Kiss Me Deadly (dir. Aldrich, 1955), 63, 65
Klavvas, Kostas, 113
Klein, Michael, 85
Knifer/Machairovgaltis (dir. Economides, 2010), 9
Kokkalenios, Panos, 37
Kontou, Maro, 95, 98n30, 127, *131*
Koolhaas, Rem, 227
Korean noir, 266
Korras, Giorgos, 194
Kosma, Yvonne-Alexia, 154n3
Kosteletos, Odysseas, *Just Before the Crack of Dawn/Ligo prin ximerosi* (1963), 114
Kosyfologou, Aliki, 154n3
Kounadis, Argyris, 55
Koundouros, Nikos, 4, 27–43
  early films of, 30–5, 43n2
  interviews with, 38, 42
  memoirs, 35, 36–7, 39–40, 42
  The Magic City/Magiki polis (1954), 31–6, *32*, 37, 38, 126
  The Ogre of Athens/O drakos (1956), 2, 4, 10, 31, 32, 33, 36–43, *39*, 126
  The Outlaws/Oi paranomoi (1958), 31, 43
  The River/To potami (1960), 31, 43
Kourtis, Nikolas, *Berlin: Protos Thanatos* (graphic novel), 10, *11*

Koutsogiannopoulos, Thodoris, 116
Kovács, András Bálint, 163, 179
Kozan, Erhan, *The Jackal/Çakal* (2010), 270
Kurosawa, Akira, 265
  Stray Dog/Norainu (1949), 29
Kyriacou, Andreas, 235–6, 242
  The Midnight Shift/I metamesonyktia grammi/Splash (2015), 233–4, *234*, 235, 236, 237, 241–3, 244
Kyriakos, Konstantinos, 139

Lambrinos, Fotos, *100 Hours of May/Ekato ores tou Mai* (1963–64), 164
landscapes *see* Mediterranean landscapes
Lang, Fritz, 29
Lanthimos, Yorgos, 1
Laskaris, Spyros, 226
Laskos, Orestis, *Broken Hearts/Ragismenes kardies* (1945), 53
Lassaly, Walter, 29
Late News/Nychterino deltio (ET1, 1998–99), 254, 259n10
Lathouropoulos, Christos, *Crime at Omonoia/Eglima stin Omonoia* (1962), 128
Latin American cinema, xxi
Laura (dir. Preminger, 1944), 3, 124, 199, 210
left-wing politics, 36, 73–4, 88, 163–72, 173, 184, 265
Levinas, Emanuel, 212
Liappa, Frieda, 9
lighting and light contrasts/*chiaroscuro*
  in Cypriot short films, 238, 240
  in early films of Nikos Koundouros, 29, 30, 33, 38, 39
  in *John the Violent* (dir. Marketaki, 1973), 189, 196–7
  in *Kierion* (dir. Theos, 1967–74), 166, *167*, 170
  in *Murder Backstage* (dir. Katsouridis, 1960), 132
  and the music of Mimis Plessas, 109
  in post-war noir and *The Little Mouse/To Pontikaki* (dir. Asimakopoulos and Tsiforos, 1954), 51

INDEX

lighting and light contrasts/ *chiaroscuro (cont.)*
   queer noir, 147, *147*, *148*
   in runaway productions and *The Angry Hills* (dir. Aldrich, 1959), 69, 71–2, 72
   in *Singapore Sling* (dir. Nikolaidis, 1990), 208
   in *Wednesday 04:45* (dir. Alexiou, 2015) and *A Better Tomorrow* (dir. Woo, 1986), 228
   in the work of Yannis Maris, 87, 88, 90, 94
The Little Mouse/To Pontikaki (dir. Asimakopoulos and Tsiforos, 1954), 4, 46, 48–9, 52–7, *55*, 57n1, 126
location shooting, 130, 132, 133–4, *134*, 164, 170
The Loser Takes All/O hamenos ta pairnei ola (dir. Nikolaidis, 2002), 271, 273
low- and no-budget productions, xxii, 31–2, 164, 233, 241
Lymberaki, Margarita, 35, 129, 136

Macek, Steve, 240
I Machi (newspaper), 81
machismo, 248, 251, 258n6
magazines, 4, 5, 13, 139–40; see also press
The Magic City/Magiki polis (dir. Koundouros, 1954), 31–6, *32*, 37, 38, 126
Makridis, Babis, 12
Makronisos (Greek island), 88
   Koundouros's imprisonment on, 32, 33
male body, 143, 144, 147, 151–2
male characters, 49, 95, 124, 126, 129, 136, 175, 219, 223, 228
   fatherhood/father figures, 254–5
   queens, 139
   see also queerness; masculinities
male gaze, 127, 144
Manousakis, Manousos, 250, *250*
The Man on the Train/O anthropos tou trenou (dir. Dimopoulos, 1958), 4, 30, 46, 49, 76, 82, 84, 130

female gaze and subjectivity in, 122, 129–35, *134*
marginalisation, 14, 33, 56, 142–3
Maris, Yannis, 4, 5, 13–14, 17n6, 18n13, 46, 49, 78n12, 81–4, *83*, 93–6, 126, 130–1, 148, 251, 253
   The Death of Timotheos Konstas, 155n10
   The Lady of the Night, 128
   The Man in the Grey Suit, 82, 130, 132–3
   Murder Backstage, 82, 84, 85–93, 95
   Murder in Kolonaki, 126, 127
   script for *Murder Backstage* (dir. Katsouridis, 1960), 81, 84–5, 86, 95, 96n4
   see also Bekas, Officer/Inspector
Markaris, Petros, 2
Marketaki, Tonia, 8
   Crystal Nights/Krystallines nychtes (1992), 185
   John and the Road/O Yannis kai o dromos (1967), 184
   John the Violent/Ioannis o viaios (1973), 2, 36, 182–97, *184*, *190*, 197nn1–2
   The Price of Love/I timi tis agapis (1984), 185
Mårlind, Måns, and Bjoern Stein, *Midnight Sun* (2016), 270
masculinities, 29, 40, 41, 71, 136n4, 139–41, 143–6, 149, 153
   machismo, 248, 251, 258n6
   in television crime shows, 247–57, *250*, *256*
   see also male characters; patriarchy; queerness; misogyny
Maska (Mask), pulp magazine, 4, 5
Matsas, Nestoras, 84, 96n4
Mavropoulou, Gelly, 128
media see journalism and journalists; press
Mediterranean landscapes, 38, 133, 236, 242, 264, 267, 271, 277n3; see also location shooting; rural settings
Mediterranean neo-noir, 266–7
Mediterranean noir/Med-noir, 14, 242, 263–77, 271, 274, 277n2

Meeker, David, 104
Meet the Father-in-Law/Na Petheros, Na Malama (dir. Nousias, 1959), 76–7
Melas, Pete, 49
melodrama/s, 3, 6, 9, 10, 30, 47, 49, 52, 68, 78n5, 114, 121, 125, 128–30
Melville, Jean-Pierre, 82
meta-cinematicism, 203, 207, 213
metaphor, 177, 266
MGM, 62, 65, 70, 78n2, 78n4
Michailidis, Ieroklis, 253–4, 259nn11–12
Michalopoulos, Panos, 252, 258n7
Midnight Sun (dir. Mårlind and Stein, 2016), 270
The Midnight Shift/I metamesonyktia grammi/Splash (dir. Kyriacou, 2015), 233–4, 234, 235, 236, 237, 241–3, 244
migration/migrants, 5, 9, 12, 14, 46, 56, 174, 176, 178, 191, 221
  to Australia, 48, 54, 56, 57
  see also refugees
Mikelides, Ninos Fenek, 85
Milas Film, 52, 58n6
Milonas, Ioakim, 12
The Miracle of the Sargasso Sea/To thavma tis thalassas ton Sargasson (dir. Tzoumerkas, 2019), 1–2, 9
mise en scène, 28, 33, 38, 132
misogyny, 122–4, 141, 143
Mitchum, Robert, 63, 65, 67, 72, 77
Mitropoulou, Aglaia, 37, 96n4
modernisation, 30, 33, 34–5, 43n1, 146, 169, 189; *see also* urbanisation
modernism, 5, 8, 12–13, 18n13, 66, 90, 95, 114, 116, 163, 171; *see also* postmodernism
modernist film movements *see* New Greek Cinema
modernity, xxi, 3, 5, 6, 7, 12–13, 28, 92, 122, 169, 170, 174, 254
  imported/corrupting, 145–6, 152, 153
  supermodernity, 223
money, 53, 140, 220, 222, 274, 275; *see also* austerity; debt

montage, 30, 32, 38, 56, 194
morality and moral ambiguity, 7, 13, 27, 123, 141, 190, 223, 241; *see also* social and moral panics
Morgan, Janice, xx–xxi
Mulvey, Laura, 124, 136n5
Murder Backstage/Eglima sta paraskinia (dir. Katsouridis, 1960), 6, 49, 68, 76, 77, 81, 84–96, 94, 96n4, 98n27, *131*
  music by Mimis Plessas, 103–16, *109*, *112*, 117n4, 117n14
Murder in Kolonaki/Eglima sto Kolonaki (dir. Aliferis, 1959), 5–6, 49, 68, 76, 82, 83, 90, 93, 95, 114, 127, 128
The Murderer Who Loved a Lot/O dolofonos agapouse poly (dir. Daifas, 1960), 95, 114
music
  in *The Bum of Fokionos Negri* (dir. Karagiannis, 1965), 141
  in early films of Nikos Koundouros, 35, 41
  jazz, 103–16, 171, 179n6, 200, 226
  in *John the Violent* (dir. Marketaki, 1973), 189
  in *Kierion* (dir. Theos, 1967–74), 169, 171
  'Matia Stratigoi' song, 76, 78n10
  musical comedy, 51
  in Old Greek Cinema, 103–4, 108, 113, 115, 116, 116n2
  popular music, 103, 107, 114, 116, 276
  in post-war noir, 55
  in *Singapore Sling* (dir. Nikolaidis, 1990), 199
  videos, 12
  in the work of Yannis Maris, 84, 88, 94, 96n4
  see also Plessas, Mimis; sound effects and design
Musuraca, Nicholas, 29
Mylonas, Ioakim, 235–6
  Greenhouse (2013), 233–4, 235, 237–41, 243–4, 245n7

Mylonas, Ioakim (*cont.*)
  Oedipus (2010), 233–4, 235, 237–41, 243
  Pharmakon (2006), 235
Mystery Road (dir. Sen, 2013), 270
Mystery Road (TV series 2018–), 270
mythology, Greek and Roman, 122, 128
  Dionysian rituals, 41
  Oedipal themes, 3, 12, 18n7, 141, 239

Nafplion, 131, 134, *134*
Naremore, James, xxii, 18n13, 28, 42, 117n5
narration, 93, 132, 165, 174, 183, 188, 239
  first-person, 93, 165, 168, 171–2, 204, 205
  see also voiceover
narrative cinema, 185–6
nationalism, 1, 4, 7, 9, 10, 188, 189, 196
Native-American noir, 270
Nazi Germany *see* German Occupation
Neale, Steve, 121
Negri, Antonio, 216, 227
Negulesco, Jean, *Boy on a Dolphin* (1957), 62, 64
neoliberalism, 1, 14, 221, 222–3, 227–8, 264, 265, 271–3, 277, 277n6;
  see also capitalism
neo-noir, xx, 1–2, 9, 10–12, 14, 30, 124
  contemporary Mediterranean, 264, 265, 267, 269
  international, 216
  and *John the Violent* (dir. Marketaki, 1973), 182, 183, 184–9, 191, 193–7
  and the music of Mimis Plessas, 103, 104–5
  sensibilities in Greek Cypriot short films, 232–44, *234*
neo-realism, 34, 46, 90, 132, 169, 178, 269
  Italian, 29, 33, 186, 265
Ness, Richard R., 115
Neumeyer, David, 105, 117n15
New Greek Cinema, 7–8, 47, 163, 164, 182, 184, 185
New Hollywood, 124

newspapers *see* press
Ng, Jenna, 218
Nieland, Justus, xxi, 219
Night Wanderings/Nyhtoperpatimata (dir. Zervoulakos, 1964), 154n9
nightclubs *see* bars and nightclubs
Nightmare/Efialtis (dir. Andreou, 1961), 2, 6, 7, 76, 77, 103, 114, 149, 157n44
Nikolaidis, Dimitris, 65, 74, 76
Nikolaidis, Nikos, 9, 30, 201
  The Loser Takes All/O hamenos ta pairnei ola (2002), 271, 273
  Singapore Sling (1990), 199–213, *202*, *208*
Nikolaidou, Afroditi, 210
Nikolinakos, Michalis, 76
Nikoloudis, Manolis, 77
No Country for Old Men (dir. Coen brothers, 2007), 237, 239
noir *see* film noir
Noirsville (blog), 9, 17n1
Nordic noir, xxi, 9, 249, 263, 266, 270
nostalgia, 9, 203–4, 220, 226
Nousias, Marios, *Meet the Father-in-Law/ Na Petheros, Na Malama* (1959), 76–7
Novak, Jason, 29
nudity, 67, 70, 78n8, 91, 127; *see also* dance and striptease scenes

Odets, Clifford, 72
Oedipal themes, 3, 12, 18n7, 141, 239
Oedipus (dir. Mylonas, 2010), 233–4, 235, 237–41, 243
The Ogre of Athens/O drakos (dir. Koundouros, 1956), 2, 4, 10, 31, 32, 33, 36–43, *39*, 126
Oldboy (dir. Park, 2003), 239
Olympic Games (2004), 9, 276
Olympos Film (production company), 49
oppression, 28, 33, 41
Other/Otherness, 104, 105, 113–16, 197
The Other Me: Lost Souls/Eteros ego: Hamenes psyches (COSMOTE, 2019–20), 247, 255–7, *256*, 257n1, 259nn13–16

The Other Me/Eteros ego (dir. Tsafoulias, 2016), 9
The Outlaws/Oi paranomoi (dir. Koundouros, 1958), 31, 43
Outside the Law (dir. Bouchareb, 2010), 269

Palmer, Barton, 220
Panayotopoulos, Nikos, 9
Panousopoulos, Giorgos, 170, 189
Papadoukas, Panagiotis, 52–3
Papagiannopoulos, Dionysis, 49, 55
Papamichalis, Vion, 84
Papanikolaou, Dimitris, 146, 155n25, 156n27, 156n29, 157n40
Papas, Irene, 121, 126
Papastathis, Lakis, 38
Papoulis, Athanasios, 251
Pappas, Giorgos, 49, 55, 130, 131
Paraskinio (television programme), 38
Park Chan-wook, *Oldboy* (2003), 239
Parker, Gillian, 85
Parker, Ian, 152
parody, 9, 37, 49, 53, 154n9, 206, 209; *see also* satire
pastiche, 202–3, 206
pastoral genre, 48, 50
patriarchy, 3, 12, 37, 40, 143, 175, 176, 189, 232, 244n1, 244n3, 255
Pavlidi, Elena, 108
PCA (Production Code Administration), 70, 203, 209
perception, 186, 194
Pergantis Films, 50–1
perspectives, 33, 48
Petropoulos, Elias, 156n29
Phaedra (dir. Dassin, 1962), 121, 128–9
Phantom Lady (dir. Siodmak, 1944), 125
Pharmakon (dir. Mylonas, 2006), 235
Philippou, Nicos, *Sharki* (photography), 236–7
Philippou, Philippos, 88
Picasso, Pablo, *Guernica*, 171
Pillard, Thomas, 47, 49
Pina, Álex, *House of Paper/Casa de Papel/Money Heist* (2017), 267–8
Piperides, Marios, *Smuggling Hendrix* (2018), 244n4
Piraeus, 6, 46, 51, 54, 55–6, 75, 147
Place, Janey, 124–5
places and non-places, 223–8
Plessas, Mimis, 76, 77, 78nn10–11, 84, 88, 94, 94n4, 113
 early career and jazz music, 105–7, 117n8, 117n10, 117n14
 music to *Murder Backstage* (dir. Katsouridis, 1960), 103–16, *109*, *112*, 117n4
Ploritis, Marios, 33, 34, 51–2, 57n4, 85
Plyta, Maria, 7, 30
 Eva (1953), 121, 129
Polanski, Roman, *Chinatown* (1974), 238
police and policing
 chase scenes, 34, 56, 90
 in early films of Nikos Koundouros, 38
 in *John the Violent* (dir. Marketaki, 1973), 183, 189, *190*, 192
 in *Kierion* (dir. Theos, 1967–74), 166–8, *167*, 171
 in post-war noir and *The Little Mouse/To Pontikaki* (dir. Asimakopoulos and Tsiforos, 1954), 54, 55, 56, 57
 in *Reconstruction* (dir. Angelopoulos, 1970), 173, 175, 177
 see also Bekas, Officer/Inspector
police dramas *see* television crime series
political thrillers, 37, 167
politics, 3–5, 7, 8, 12, 47, 240
 and early films of Nikos Koundouros, 27, 36, 38
 in *John the Violent* (dir. Marketaki, 1973), 182, 188
 in *Kierion* (dir. Theos, 1967–74), 165–71
 left-wing, 36, 73–4, 88, 163–72, 173, 184, 265
 in *The Man on the Train* (dir. Dimopoulos, 1958), 135
 in post-war noir and *The Little Mouse* (dir. Asimakopoulos and Tsiforos, 1954), 54, 56
 right-wing, 36, 188

305

politics (*cont.*)
  in *Reconstruction* (dir. Angelopoulos, 1970), 177–9
  in runaway productions and *The Angry Hills* (dir. Aldrich, 1959), 63, 67, 75
  in *Singapore Sling* (dir. Nikolaidis, 1990), 204, 206, 211, 213
  see also communism; corruption; fascism; socialism; sociopolitical contexts
Polk, George, 164
pop culture, 81, 91
popularity of films, 3–4, 7, 13, 95, 129
Port of Shadows/Le Quai des brumes (dir. Carné, 1938), 29, 51, 52, 273
post-colonialism, 14, 185, 218
posters, 78n8
postmodernism, 9, 201, 210, 212, 226
Poupou, Anna, 76, 82, 114, 117n4, 117n6
poverty, 46, 54, 169, 178
  shantytowns, 33–4, 35
power and power structures, 41, 42, 167
  in contemporary Mediterranean noir, 264, 266, 268, 269, 270
  women representing, 121–2, 127, 136
Preminger, Otto, *Laura* (1944), 3, 124, 199, 210
press, 51, 54, 56, 146, 172, 190–1, 195
  serialisation in, 82, 84, 127, 130
  see also magazines
The Price of Love/I timi tis agapis (dir. Marketaki, 1984), 185
Production Code Administration (PCA), 70, 203, 209
prostitution and prostitutes, 70, 126, 129, 147, 151, 166, 189
Psarras, Tasos, *The Reason Why/Di'asimanton aformin* (1974), 197n3
psychoanalysis, 12–13, 39, 122, 124, 136n5, 150–1, 156nn35–6, 185, 212
psychological thrillers, 4, 14, 129–30
psychology, 27–8, 40, 132, 183, 192–3, 196, 255

pulp fiction, 4, 5, 13, 18n13, 66, 81, 95, 104, 126
Purple Noon/Plein Soleil (dir. Clément, 1959), 277n2

queerness, 139–54, 154n3, 154n9, 155n10
  camp, 200, 203, 206, 214n7
  discourses, 146–53, *147*, 147nn39–40, *148*, 157n44
  effeminacy, 142, 143, 145, 146, 149, 151
  'fterou', 154n9
  queer gaze, 144
  and *Singapore Sling* (dir. Nikolaidis, 1990), 199, 200, 203, 204, 206, 207–13
  transvestites and transsexuals, 148–9, 152
  see also homosexuality
Quidnunc (dir. Ayiotis, 2018), 233–4, 235, 236, 237, 241–3

Reagan, Ronald, 265
realism, 9, 46, 49, 51, 57, 66, 132, 169, 172, 185–6, 188, 189, 205
  Italian neorealism, 29, 33, 186, 265
  neo-realism, 34, 46, 90, 132, 169, 178, 269
The Reason Why/Di'asimanton aformin (dir. Psarras, 1974), 197n3
Reconstruction/Anaparastasi (dir. Angelopoulos, 1970), 2, 33, 163, 172–9, 191
Red Cliff/O kokkinos vrahos (dir. Grigoriou, 1949), 30
The Red Lanterns/Ta kokkina fanaria (dir. Georgiadis, 1963), 9, 17n1
refugees, 33, 34, 35, 56, 169; *see also* migration/migrants
relationships, 90, 91, 97n12, 140–1, 251–2, 274; *see also* family relationships
religion, 273
representation and non-representation, 204–7, 210, 211, 213
repression, 3, 7, 28, 38, 39, 43, 63, 135, 142, 178, 183, 189, 209, 265

Reservoir Dogs (dir. Tarantino, 1992), 225
revenue *see* box office revenue
Richardson, Michael, 105
right-wing politics, 36, 188
Río, Elena del, 187
The River/To potami (dir. Koundouros, 1960), 31, 43
Rizos, Nikos, 49
Robbery in Athens/Listeia stin Athina (dir. Serdaris, 1969), 7
Rosemarie (dir. Florides, 2018), 232, 235–6, 244n1, 244n3
Rosi, Francesco, *Salvatore Giuliano* (1962), 171, 178
runaway film production in Greece, 4, 62, 64–8, 76, 77
rural settings, 43, 48, 51, 68, 72–5, 89, 172, 174, 176, 178, 189; *see also* location shooting; Mediterranean landscapes
The Ruthless Ones/Oi adistaktoi (dir. Katsouridis, 1965), 90
The Ruthless (dir. de Maria, 2019), 269

Sakellarios, Alekos, 30, 52
Saleh, Tarik, *Cairo Confidential/The Nile Hilton Incident* (2017), 270
Salvatore Giuliano (dir. Rosi, 1962), 171, 178
Sanders, M. Steven, 257
Sarajevo Film Festival, 242
Sari, Georges, 95, 132
Sartzetakis, Christos, 167–8
Sassen, Saskia, 216, 227
satire, 4, 10, 37, 38, 49, 53; *see also* parody
Savvidis, Giorgos, 84
Scandinavian film noir *see* Nordic noir
Schatz, Thomas, 27
Schrader, Paul, xx, 41, 124
The Scum/To katharma (dir. Andritsos, 1963), 155n19
Second World War
noirs produced during, 123–5
Shoah, 53
see also German Occupation
Second World War, post-, 3, 4, 5, 12

and contemporary Mediterranean noir, 263, 265
and the early films of Nikos Koundouros, 27, 28, 29–30, 31
female representation and *femme fatales*, 124, 129, 135
and the music of Mimis Plessas, 105
noir productions and *The Little Mouse/To Pontikaki* (dir. Asimakopoulos and Tsiforos, 1954), 46, 47, 48, 49, 51, 52, 53–4, 56
runaway productions and *The Angry Hills* (dir. Aldrich, 1959), 62, 64, 73
see also traumas
Sedgwick, Eve Kosofsky, 152, 156n37
self-reflexivity, 92, 201, 204, 207, 212–13, 217, 229
semiotics, 42, 115, 183, 185
Sen, Ivan, 270
Serdaris, Vangelis, *Robbery in Athens/Listeia stin Athina* (1969), 7
set design, 84, 130, 238–9
sex, 140–1, 189–90, 200, 203, 204, 209, 237
sexual identities, 5, 140–7, 153, 210
sexuality, 12, 13
  in Cypriot short films, 240, 242–3
  in the early films of Nikos Koundouros, 39
  female, 121–2, 127, 189–91, 196
  and *John the Violent* (dir. Marketaki, 1973), 183, 189–90, 191, 192
  queerness and *The Bum of Fokionos Negri* (dir. Karagiannis, 1965), 139, 141, 143, 146, 148, 155n16, 155n22
  in *Reconstruction* (dir. Angelopoulos, 1970), 174–5
  in runaway productions and *The Angry Hills* (dir. Aldrich, 1959), 70, 73
  in *Singapore Sling* (dir. Nikolaidis, 1990), 203, 209, 210–11
  in television crime shows, 249, 255, 256, 257
Sfikas, Kostas, 167–8
Sheridan, Taylor, *Wind River* (2017), 270

Sherman, Vincent, *The Garment Jungle* (1957), 63, 65
short films *see* Cypriot short films
Silver, Alain, xx, 207
Simenon, Georges, Inspector Maigret (character), 89, 253
Singapore Sling (dir. Nikolaidis, 1990), 199–213, 202, 208
Siodmak, Robert
  Phantom Lady (1944), 125
  The Spiral Staircase (1946), 88
Stratos/To mikro psari (dir. Economides, 2014), 9, 267, 271, 272, 273–5, 274
Smuggling Hendrix (dir. Piperides, 2018), 244n4
Snee, Brian J., 237, 239
Soavi, Michelle, *The Goodbye Kiss/ Arrivederci amore, ciao* (2006), 264, 268–9
social and moral panics, 9, 27, 124, 183, 191, 195
social class *see* class, social
social control, 34, 189, 191; *see also* surveillance
Social Decay/Koinoniki sapila (dir. Tatasopoulos, 1932), 48
social inequality, 263–4, 266, 267–8
  marginalisation, 14, 33, 56, 142–3
  see also poverty
socialism, 88, 184, 273
society and sociopolitical contexts, xx, 3, 4, 9, 10, 12, 14–15, 18n8
  and contemporary Mediterranean noir, 272
  in Cypriot short films, 241
  and the early films of Nikos Koundouros, 27, 28, 33, 35, 36, 37, 41, 42, 43
  and femininities and *femme fatales*, 130, 135
  and *John the Violent* (dir. Marketaki, 1973), 183, 187, 196–7
  in *Kierion* (dir. Theos, 1967–74), 163, 164, 165, 167, 169–71
  in post-war noir and *The Little Mouse/To Pontikaki* (dir. Asimakopoulos and Tsiforos, 1954), 46, 47, 48, 52–4, 57
  queerness/homosexuality in, 150–1
  in *Reconstruction* (dir. Angelopoulos, 1970), 176, 179
  and television crime shows, 250, 254
  in *Wednesday 04:45* (dir. Alexiou, 2015) and *A Better Tomorrow* (dir. Woo, 1986), 217–22, 224, 229
  see also Greek financial crisis; modernisation; modernity; politics
Society of Greek Theatre Writers, 53
Soldatos, Yannis, 85
solidarity, 35, 36, 41, 89
Sontag, Susan, 203, 214n7
sound effects and design, 51, 110, 170, 178, 188–9, 192; *see also* music
Soviet cinema, 29, 32
space, 133, 237
  in early films of Nikos Koundouros, 29, 30, 31, 32, 34, 37, 38, 39, 41
  in *Kierion* (dir. Theos, 1967–74), 166, 170
  in *Reconstruction* (dir. Angelopoulos, 1970), 177–8
  in *Singapore Sling* (dir. Nikolaidis, 1990), 206, 207–8
Spanish noir, 264, 266, 267, 277n4
special effects, 238–9
spectatorship, 42, 207, 212; *see also* voyeurism
Spentzos Films (production company), 29–30
The Spiral Staircase (dir. Siodmak, 1946), 88
Spyropoulos, Vasilis, 52
Stamatiou, Kostas, 85
Stella (dir. Cacoyannis, 1955), 33
stereotypes, 121, 142, 183, 191, 209, 234
  female characters, 121–5, 126, 136n1
Stilwell, Robynn J., 115
The Stories of Officer Bekas/Oi istories tou astynomou Beka (ALPHA, 2006–08), 247, 253–5, 258–9nn8–12
Stranger on the Third Floor (dir. Ingster, 1940), 29

Stray Dog/Norainu (dir. Kurosawa, 1949), 29
striptease *see* dance and striptease scenes
Stross, Raymond/Raymond Stross Productions, 62, 64–5, 66, 71
Studio Alpha, 4, 67, 76–7, 78n10
studio system, 3, 4, 7–8, 12, 28, 29–30
Stylianou, Elena, 236
suburban settings, 6, 14, 32, 33, 147, 169, 274
subversion, 143, 153, 201, 203, 211, 212
surveillance (state), 4, 6, 38, 170, 189, 191, 237, 238
surveillance scenes, 94, 110, 111, 170
suspense and tension
  in Cypriot short films, 241
  female characters and *The Man on the Train* (dir. Dimopoulos, 1958), 127, 130–1, 134, 135
  and the music of Mimis Plessas, 108, 110–11, 112
  in post-war noir and *The Little Mouse/ To Pontikaki* (dir. Asimakopoulos and Tsiforos, 1954), 49
  in *Singapore Sling* (dir. Nikolaidis, 1990), 205
  in the work of Yannis Maris, 84, 92
symbolism, 31, 32, 90, 93, 136n2, 170, 177, 232, 251, 252, 255, 274
Synodinou, Anna, 130, 131

Taiwan, 221
Tarantino, Quentin, *Reservoir Dogs* (1992), 225
Tatasopoulos, Stelios, 30, 48
  Social Decay/Koinoniki sapila (1932), 48
taverna scenes, 67, 70–1, 76, 78n8, 90–1, 93, 95; *see also* bars and nightclubs
television crime shows, xxi, 7, 8, 9, 78n12, 247–57, 250, 256, 267
Ten Seconds to Hell (dir. Aldrich, 1959), 65
tension *see* suspense and tension
Thalassinos, Errikos, 50
  Death Strikes Again/O thanatos tha xanarthei (1961), 50, 128

Thatcher, Margaret, 265
theatre, 10, 17n6, 53, 76, 78n11, 91–2, 95
  ancient Greek, 122, 130
  shadow, 37
Theodoridis, Kostas, 29, 32, 35, 38, 39, 55
Theos, Dimos, 8, 164
  100 Hours of May/Ekato ores tou Mai (1963–64), 164
  Kierion (1967–74), 163–72, 167, 178–9
Thessaloniki, 164
Thessaloniki Film Festival, 185, 197n2, 201
thrillers, 9, 10, 122–3, 249
  gothic, 125, 129–30, 133
  political, 37, 167
  psychological, 4, 14, 129–30
Toland, Gregg, 29
torture, 56, 124, 166, 167, 192, 200
Toulas, Giorgos, 85
The Tower of Knights/O pyrgos ton ippoton (dir. Asimakopoulos and Tsiforos, 1952), 52, 53
tragedy, 9, 37, 43, 98n25
transgression, 69, 142, 145, 237
transnationality, 1, 4, 10, 47, 52, 217–19, 227, 229, 229n4, 229n5; *see also* global noir
trapdoor motif, 88, 172
traumas, 3, 4, 5, 6, 27, 28, 31, 47, 57, 88, 130, 133, 135, 168, 171
The Travelling Players/O thiasos (dir. Angelopoulos, 1975), 36
Trigo, Benigno, 207, 208–9
Troussas, Phontas, 107
truth, 164, 165, 167–9, 178, 186, 188, 191
  regimes of truth, 183, 193–7
Tsafoulias, Sotiris, 255, 259n13
  The Other Me/Eteros ego (2016), 9
Tsaganeas, Christos, 95, 98n30
Tsarouchis, Yannis, *Neon Café (Night)* (1965–66) (artwork), 13, *13*
Tsiforos, Nikos, 50, 52–3
  Fallen Angels/Hamenoi angeloi (1948), 3, 49–50, 53, 55, 121, 126

Tsiforos, Nikos (*cont.*)
  The Little Mouse/To Pontikaki (1954), 4, 46, 48–9, 52–7, 55, 57n1, 126
  The Tower of Knights/O pyrgos ton ippoton (1952), 52, 53
  Wind of Hate/O anemos tou misous (1954), 52, 53–4, 58n6
Tsiolis, Stavros, 7
Tsitsanis, Vassilis, 41
Turkish noir, 264, 266, 269, 270, 271
Tzal Films, 50–1
Tzanaki, Dimitra, 156n36
Tzavelas, Yorgos
  Agnes of the Port/I Agni tou limaniou (1952), 49, 51, 52, 57n4
  Applause/Heirokrotimata (1944), 30
  The Counterfeit Coin/I kalpiki lira (1955), 35
  The Drunkard/O methistakas (1950), 35
  Forgotten Faces/Prosopa lismonimena (1946), 3, 30, 46, 49, 52
Tzoumerkas, Syllas, *The Miracle of the Sargasso Sea/To thavma tis thalassas ton Sargasson* (2019), 1–2, 9

uncertainty motif, 132, 144, 183, 188, 209–10, 218, 220, 237, 243
United States of America (US), 3, 7, 27, 28, 62
  McCarthyism, 32, 157n39, 173, 263
  popular culture and music, 91, 113, 116
  Reagan-Bush era, 265, 271
  see also American film noir; Hollywood cinema
urban settings
  in Cypriot short films, 237, 238, 240, 241
  in early films of Nikos Koundouros, 34, 38, 41, 43
  in *Kierion* (dir. Theos, 1967–74), 168–9
  and the music of Mimis Plessas, 105
  in post-war noir and *The Little Mouse/To Pontikaki* (dir. Asimakopoulos and Tsiforos, 1954), 50, 51, 56
  in *Reconstruction* (dir. Angelopoulos, 1970), 177
  in runaway productions and *The Angry Hills* (dir. Aldrich, 1959), 66, 71
  in *Wednesday 04:45* (dir. Alexiou, 2015) and *A Better Tomorrow* (dir. Woo, 1986), 220–1, 224
  in the work of Yannis Maris, 87, 89–92
  see also Athens; rural settings; suburban settings
urbanisation, 12, 30, 33, 35, 189, 191; *see also* modernisation
urbanism, 5, 6, 27, 28, 31, 41, 48, 217
Uris, Leon, 64, 66, 67, 75, 78n3

Vahlioti, Deni, 128
Vakousis, Manos, 256, 256, 259n16
Vandis, Titos, 85, 94, *94*, *131*
Vengos, Thanassis, 32
Vice Squad/Tmima ithon (ANT1, 1992–95), 247, 250, 250–3, 257–8nn2–5
To Vima (newspaper), 84
violence, 3, 7, 18n8
  in contemporary Mediterranean noir, 269, 271
  in Cypriot cinema, 232, 233, 240, 243, 244n1, 244n3
  in early films of Nikos Koundouros, 34, 35, 41
  executions, 38, 73, 74, 74–5
  against female characters, 124
  and the Greek male queer, 142
  in *John the Violent* (dir. Marketaki, 1973), 190–1
  in *Kierion* (dir. Theos, 1967–74), 166–7, *167*
  in post-war noir and *The Little Mouse/To Pontikaki* (dir. Asimakopoulos and Tsiforos, 1954), 48
  in *Singapore Sling* (dir. Nikolaidis, 1990), 199–200, 204, 206, 207, 212, 213
  in television crime shows, 248

torture, 56, 124, 166, *167*, 192, 200
  in *Wednesday 04:45* (dir. Alexiou, 2015) and *A Better Tomorrow* (dir. Woo, 1986), 222, 223
  in the work of Yannis Maris, 84
Vlachou, Eleni, 96n4, 123
Vlahos, Anestis, 164, *167*
voiceovers
  in contemporary Mediterranean noir, 270, 276
  in Cypriot short films, 237, 239
  in *John the Violent* (dir. Marketaki, 1973), 183, 187, 188–9
  in *Kierion* (dir. Theos, 1967–74), 165, 168, 171–2
  in *The Man on the Train* (dir. Dimopoulos, 1958), 129, 132
  in *Reconstruction* (dir. Angelopoulos, 1970), 178
  in *Singapore Sling* (dir. Nikolaidis, 1990), 200
  in the work of Yannis Maris, 93
  see also narration: first-person
Vougiouklaki, Aliki, 46, 57
Voutsadaki, Antonia, 40
voyeurism, 133, 136n5, 141, 144, 148, 201, 204; *see also* spectatorship

Wagner, Geoffrey, 85
Walker, Michael, 68
Walsh, Raoul
  Battle Cry (1955), 64
  White Heat (1949), 90
Ward, Elizabeth, xx
Weber, Max, 41
Wednesday 04:45/Tetarti 04:45 (dir. Alexiou, 2015), 216–29, 220, 267, 271, 271–6

Weeks, Jeffrey, 154n3
Weird Wave, 1, 9, 12
Wells, Liz, 236
Wells, Orson, *Citizen Kane* (1941), 191
White Heat (dir. Walsh, 1949), 90
Willis, Andy, 240–1
Wind of Hate/O anemos tou misous (dir. Asimakopoulos and Tsiforos, 1954), 52, 53–4, 58n6
Wind River (dir. Sheridan, 2017), 270
window motif, 87, 169, 170, 177–8
women, 12, 129, 146
  directors/filmmakers, 30, 129, 184–5
  professionals in Greek film production, 122, 125, 129, 130, 136
  representations of, 40, 135, 141, 143
  see also female; femininities; feminism; *femme fatales*
Woo, John, 221
  A Better Tomorrow (1986), 216–29
Woolfolk, Alan, 40

Xanthopoulos, Lefteris, 40
Xenidis, Stavros, 253, 258n9

youth, 252
  ingénues, 46, 84, 91, 126
  juvenile delinquency, 46, 54, 56, 57

Z (dir. Gavras, 1969), 167, 168
Zervoulakos, George
  Night Wanderings/Nyhtoperpatimata (dir. Zervoulakos, 1964), 154n9
Zone Defence/Amyna zonis (ET1, 2007–08), 254, 259n10

EU representative:
Easy Access System Europe
Mustamäe tee 50, 10621 Tallinn, Estonia
Gpsr.requests@easproject.com

www.ingramcontent.com/pod-product-compliance
Lightning Source LLC
Chambersburg PA
CBHW050837230426
43667CB00012B/2033